SO-AUO-215

ON THIS VESSEL, to obtain a GPS position or report an emergency, follow this sequence:

Step 1: Turn **main battery** switch on (or): _____

Step 2: Push GPS unit **power** button on (or): _____

Step 3: Read display or push GPS **position** button then read the position.

In an emergency or imminent danger:

To summon help call "**MAYDAY, MAYDAY, MAYDAY**" on VHF Channel 16; **say the name of the vessel and its GPS position** to the coast guard or to nearby vessels. Give the vessel's call sign and description; describe the emergency and the help you need.

This **vessel's name** is: _____

This **vessel's call sign** is: _____

Repeat call several times as required to make contact.

TO RETURN to a Man Overboard, push the MOB button on the vessel's GPS and steer the course displayed on the GPS screen. **Do this immediately** upon learning of a man overboard.

To activate the **GOTO** function on this GPS push GOTO and follow screen prompts (or): _____

_____

To display the **Steering Diagram** on this GPS push **NAV** (or): _____

_____

Positions frequently used for this vessel:

Home berth: Lat: _____Long: _____

Harbour Entrance: Lat: _____Long: _____

Marina Entrance: Lat: _____Long: _____

GPS
Instant Navigation

From Basic Techniques
to Electronic Charting

SECOND EDITION

By Kevin Monahan
& Don Douglass

FineEdge.com

Important Legal Disclaimer

This book is designed to acquaint mariners with techniques and methods of using the Global Positioning System (GPS) in coastal and offshore navigation. It is not for navigation per se. A prudent navigator does not rely on any single technique or piece of equipment for navigation in critical situations. The user of this book must accept full responsibility for all consequences arising from its use. There may well be mistakes, both in typography and in content; therefore this book should be used only as a general guide, not as an ultimate source of information. No warranty, expressed or implied is made by Fine Edge Productions LLC as to the accuracy of the diagrams and related material, nor shall the fact of publication or personal use constitute any such warranty. No responsibility is assumed by Fine Edge Productions LLC or the authors in connection therewith. The authors, publisher and any governmental authorities mentioned herein assume no liability for errors or omissions, or for any loss or damages incurred from using this information.

The views expressed in this book are those of the authors, alone, and, except where quoted directly from Canadian Coast Guard publications do not reflect any policy, written or unwritten, of the Canadian Coast Guard.

Book design by Melanie Haage
Illustrations by Kevin Monahan
Computer Graphics by Sue Irwin, Faith Rumm, Chandler White
Front cover photograph courtesy of Nordhavn
Back cover photograph by Maria Steernberg, SeaSnaps

Library of Congress Cataloging-in-Publication Data

Monahan, Kevin, 1951–
    GPS instant navigation : a practical guide from basics to advanced techniques
/ by Kevin Monahan & Don Douglass.--2nd ed.
        p.   cm.
    Includes index.
    ISBN 0-938665-76-6 (pbk.)
    1. Global Positioning System.   I. Douglass, Don, 1932– .   II. Title.
VK562.M66   2000
623.89'33--dc21   00-035333

ISBN 0-938665-76-6

Address requests for permission to:
Fine Edge.com, 13589 Clayton Lane, Anacortes, WA 98221
Website: www.FineEdge.com

Printed in Canada

To my wife Nancy, without whom I would be neither
who I am nor where I am today.
—*KM*

To Réanne Hemingway-Douglass, my companion explorer
from 60° North to 56° South who knows the great Southern Ocean
like few others and who has always held the course when the seas
were confused, visibility was nil and our position doubtful.
—*DCD*

Mr. Rat: Believe me, my young friend, there is
nothing—absolutely nothing—half so much worth
doing as simply messing around in boats.

—*The Wind in the Willows* by Kenneth Grahame

Contents

Acknowledgements

Putting together a technical book of this magnitude would not have been possible without the support and help of many people. For furnishing information, technical assistance, and photographs, we wish to thank the following: Peter Bennett, Vancouver Power Squadron; Ian Gillis, Canadian Coast Guard; Doran Donovan, Maptech Corporation; Ruth Adams, A.R. Johnson, Nick Webb, the U.K. Hydrographic Office; Captain Nathan Reed; Jay Phillips, John Grady, Tim Whelan, Jeff Hummel and Matt Taylor, Nobeltec Corporation; Jim Brantingham, Electronic Charts Co. Inc.; QM1 Chip Hoynes, United States Coast Guard Navigation Center (NAVCEN); Captain M. Leonard-Williams, United Kingdom Marine Safety Agency; J.F. Cannon, Trinity House Lighthouse Service; Douglas T. Wilson, Scorpio Navigation Services; Rob Hare, Canadian Hydrographic Service; Commander L.P. Fenner, R.D., R.N.R., former Trinity House Pilot; Roy Thompson, Furuno USA; Helmut Lanziner, CANStar Navigation Inc.; Don Meyer, Angela Linsey-Jackson, Magellan Systems Corporation; Peter Jacobsen, Ocean PC Ltd.; Aimee Murray, Northstar Technologies; Lisa Thimas, Navionics Inc.; D.M. Kennedy, writing in *Navigation News*, the Magazine of the Royal Institute of Navigation; Neil P. Riggs, Scott Strong, Nautical Data International, Inc.; Duart Snow, *Pacific Yachting* Magazine; Dennis Mills and Anja Van Soest, Nautical Technologies; Paul N. Williams Advertising Agency; Koden/Si-Tex; Roderick Frazer Nash; Jeff Douthwaite; Brigadier General T.L. Hemingway, USAF Ret.; Captain Alan Donohue and the crew of "The Spirit of Vancouver Island."

We also wish to extend our appreciation to those reviewers, mariners, and friends who made suggestions for improving this book. As much as possible we have tried to include their suggestions. Thanks go to those who took time to read parts or all of the original manuscript and provide their critical comments: Chris Carver, Maris Group; Geza Dienes, Andrew Corporation; Joe Kawaky, Captn. Jacks Software Source; Jay Phillips, Nobeltec Corporation.

And not the least, our thanks go to chief editor, Réanne Hemingway-Douglass, assistant editor Elayne Wallis, and to our book designer, Melanie Haage.

Preface to the Second Edition

Since the publication of *GPS—Instant Navigation*, there have been numerous technological changes in the Global Positioning System, but the most significant in its impact on the recreational boater, was the removal of Selective Availability at midnight, Greenwich Mean Time, May 1, 2000. At that time, Selective Availability of the Global Positioning system was set to zero, bringing to a close a time when civilian GPS was less accurate than military GPS. Now, most of the time, GPS is accurate to about the length of an average boat. [See discussion of GPS errors in Chapter 3.]

Selective Availability, an intentional "dithering" of the satellite clocks, was originally introduced to degrade the accuracy of civilian receivers in order to ensure that in times of national emergency, only the United States military and its allies would have access to the highly accurate Precise Positioning Service.

Now, in recognition of the enormous importance of GPS to the international economy, the United States Department of Defense (DOD) has developed the ability to deny GPS signals to non-NATO users on a regional basis, instead of degrading GPS accuracy world-wide. The method by which this has been achieved is unclear, because the technology is classified. The end result of this new approach to national security is that civilian GPS receivers should now be able to provide positioning *accurate to within 20 meters* (instead of the 100-meter accuracy available prior to May 1, 2000).

This is similar to the length of a medium sized boat. Consequently, the location of the GPS antenna in relation to the bow of the boat is now a significant part of the navigational error equation. If your antenna is located at the stern of a 60-foot vessel, you will have to allow for the distance from the antenna to the bow of the boat (and a certain margin for error).

The accuracy of GPS now far exceeds the theoretical repeatable accuracy of Loran C, and is approaching that of the Precise Positioning Service (PPS) available only to NATO military forces. At this time, in the development of the Global Positioning System, small inaccuracies in the charts you are using will take on a greater significance than the error of your GPS.

It's not often you get something for nothing, but in this case, the incredible improvement in the accuracy of the satellite system comes at no extra cost to the user. As of midnight May 1, 2000 every GPS receiver in the world suddenly became more accurate and more useful to the boating community.

Unassisted GPS can now compete with the accuracy of Differential GPS (DGPS) but, despite its phenomenal new accuracy, the differential GPS service still offers valuable enhancements where accuracy and reliability are critical.

Clearly GPS is an emerging technology. With the introduction of a second civilian frequency in 2003, which will all but eliminate atmospheric propagation errors in the next generation of consumer GPS receivers, and with further improvements in the system beyond that, boaters can look forward to unparalleled navigational security.

As with all navigation, however, we must add a note of caution: don't be seduced into becoming overly reliant on your GPS Navigator. You should still exercise caution when you navigate in close proximity to land and other hazards. The new levels of GPS accuracy should not be cause to reduce your navigational vigilance or your margin of safety.

Kevin Monahan, Sidney, British Columbia
Don Douglass, *Baidarka,* Juneau, Alaska

Preface to the First Edition

At the dawn of the 21st century there is no question that marine navigation is undergoing a major revolution. Much of the traditional equipment and techniques of the 20th century will soon seem as ancient as taffrail logs and slide rules. For now, with a GPS receiver, it is possible to find your position *accurately and instantly* at any time of day or night wherever you are in the world. And when a GPS receiver is interfaced with other navigational equipment or electronic charts, the drudgery of day-to-day navigation essentially disappears.

For the foreseeable future GPS technology will continue to improve and mature. Already there is a huge choice of equipment and software available, much of which initially appears to be overly complex. But this book should take some of the fear out of dealing with these marvelous machines. Whether you are a weekend sailor or a serious offshore navigator you will be able to learn simple techniques to enhance your navigation skills. The navigator who knows how to use GPS to his best advantage will gain more pleasure from cruising and will sleep more soundly as a result.

Be aware, though, that GPS does not eliminate the need to know traditional navigation skills such as chart-reading and plotting; nor does it eliminate the requirement to cross-check GPS data with other instruments or to keep a sharp lookout. The strength of GPS lies in its ability to provide instantaneous, worldwide positioning and steering information without resorting to pelorus, sextants, almanacs, reduction tables, calculators, and other arcane devices.

The authors have witnessed the steady increase in capability of GPS technology and, after years of excellent performance, our initial frustrations have given way to feelings of awe at its simplicity and accuracy.

In describing the techniques which allow a navigator to achieve high performance from GPS, we have tried to maintain a tie with traditional navigation methods, yet capture the simplicity and responsiveness of GPS navigation. We have both considered it a challenge and a privilege to be able to develop some of the techniques described herein, and to share them with each other when our blue-water paths crossed, as well as now, with you the reader.

Kevin Monahan, Sidney, British Columbia
Don Douglass, *Baidarka*, Juneau, Alaska

CHAPTER 1

GPS Navigation Works!

What GPS Navigation Can Do for You

The NAVSTAR Global Positioning System, commonly called GPS, is a revolutionary navigation system that provides position information with accuracy to within the length of a medium-sized boat, 24 hours a day, anywhere in the world.

The new generation of GPS units display not only position, speed and course over the ground, but a number of other navigational variables, such as course and distance to a waypoint, that allow you to monitor your vessel's progress instantly and continuously without leaving the helm or distracting your attention.

GPS derives its universal coverage and reliability from coded microwave signals that are broadcast from a constellation of sophisticated satellites. The satellites' precise indications of latitude, longitude, velocity, and time information, are unaffected by darkness, fog or cloud cover and they suffer less from atmospheric and ionospheric effects than do high frequency radio waves.

The GPS satellites provide service to an unlimited number of receivers with no degradation to the system and without charge to the user. GPS is operated and maintained by the U.S. Air Force for the U.S. Department of Transportation and is rapidly becoming the dominant navigation system on land and in the air, as well as at sea.

The goal of this book is to help you feel comfortable with your GPS equipment, and to demonstrate to you that it is capable of doing far more than you initially anticipated. To learn to use the equipment in new and innovative ways, you will need to learn a little about the capabilities and limitations of the system. After that, you should be able to devise innovative ways to use the equipment yourself. If you, as a navigator, apply the techniques described in this book, you can enhance the safety and operation of your vessel and, with practice, harness the full potential of this remarkable system.

The GPS Receiver

Although the term "receiver" is often used in a generic sense to indicate any type of GPS equipment, the word itself implies that the equipment is capable of showing only the fundamental data of position, course, and speed; it will neither compute nor display information related to waypoints.

In this book, however, we use the term *receiver* to refer to that portion of a GPS Navigator that both *receives* the signal and *calculates* the fundamental functions. A GPS receiver monitors several satellites simultaneously, either by multiplexing a single channel receiver (to sample several channels sequentially) or, in most modern units, by using up to twelve discrete receiving channels.

The GPS Navigator

When coupled with the appropriate internal microprocessor and software, a GPS receiver is known as a GPS (waypoint) Navigator. In addition to its basic functions, a GPS Navigator performs sophisticated navigation functions by manipulating waypoints and routes. These functions, derived over time from the changes in position of the receiver, are displayed on user-friendly screens. A GPS Navigator can provide vital steering information to any pre-selected destination as well as information relating to a vessel's track history. Virtually all GPS equipment sold today includes these functions.

Though various types of Loran and SatNav waypoint navigators have been available since the early 1980s, none of these early systems combined the advantages of waypoint navigation with the accuracy, processing speed, and universal coverage of GPS.

It is the *instantaneous* nature of the GPS Navigator that has had a major effect on boating. With precise latitude and longitude displayed numerically on a screen at all times, anyone can plot co-ordinates on a paper chart to monitor progress or quickly summon help by radio. In addition, a skipper can instantly see and measure the effects of currents and wind on an intended course and calculate an updated estimated time of arrival (ETA) based on actual course over the ground.

In recent years, the number of functions available in GPS Navigators has increased while cost has decreased. Many of these additional functions are useful in situations requiring high performance (such as in racing). However, you may not need this level of complexity—a simple-to-operate unit may fill your needs.

Startup: Initializing Your Receiver

Before using your GPS receiver for the first time, initialize it by verifying the correct date and time and by entering your approximate latitude and longitude. You need only enter the nearest whole degree since these approximate numbers do not affect the accuracy of your displayed position. Some newer GPS receivers simplify the initialization process by allowing you to input geographic locations by state, country or regions. If you fail to enter an initial position and/or date and time, the GPS eventually figures it out, but the process, known as a "cold start," may take up to fifteen minutes while the receiver searches all possible combinations of satellite signals.

Once you initialize your receiver, it stores an almanac of basic satellite information so that when you next power it up, it will "warm start" with a delay of just a minute or so. *Note:* Every time you move a GPS receiver more than 300 miles from where it was last powered up, you must re-initialize it or it will default to a cold start. If the receiver is left off for more than 14 days, the almanac message broadcast by the satellites will have been updated, which may also cause a "cold start."

After your receiver loads an almanac, it decides which satellites to use for computing a position. The orbital information contained in the almanac signal is not precise enough to generate a position, so each satellite broadcasts precision data in an ephemeris message. When the GPS receiver decodes these messages, it "knows" the exact position of each satellite in view and can determine its own present position to within 20 meters (65 feet). Once it has acquired several satellite signals, the receiver continues to re-compute its position at intervals of approximately one second until you shut off its power.

Once it has accessed the almanac and ephemeris messages, the GPS receiver stores the data so that when powered up again, it has the information necessary to quickly "warm start" and begin generating position fixes.

Determining Where You Are

When you power up your initialized GPS receiver, it will display your present latitude and longitude. Some receivers default to the position display, others do not. Once your position is displayed you can begin navigating. As your vessel moves, latitude and longitude are updated every second of your trip. It's as simple as that!

As part of the start-up procedure before you leave your moorage, verify that your GPS is up and running. Record the latitude and longitude (co-ordinates) of your home berth on the Quick Reference page; you can then refer to these co-ordinates to verify that your unit is working correctly.

The Other Fellow

GPS can tell you where you are with great accuracy. But it can't tell you where the other fellow is. One of the most frightening sights at sea is a small boat suddenly emerging out of the fog at high speed, without radar or any apparent means to determine if another vessel is in the way. Your GPS will give you your exact position and nautical charts will pinpoint the permanent features of the landscape (such as shoals and reefs), but you cannot determine whether other vessels are in your path except with your eyes and (perhaps) radar. Don't let the GPS give you a false sense of security; you must always proceed with caution in poor visibility.

Most GPS units display latitude and longitude in degrees and minutes to three significant decimal places: 49°16.580' N. By definition, a minute of latitude (but not longitude) is equal to one nautical mile (6,076 feet); therefore, a tenth of a minute of latitude is equal to 607 feet; a hundredth of a minute about 60 feet; a thousandth of a minute 6 feet.

Notice that the last one or two digits of your display change in a slow random fashion. This apparent drift of position caused by normal GPS errors (up to 20 meters)—does not indicate a defective unit. Primary among GPS errors is atmospheric and ionospheric interference with the propagation of the signal. (The magnitude of the various sources of GPS error is discussed in Chapter 3; Differential GPS [DGPS] which eliminates the significant errors of GPS is discussed in Chapter 9.)

Summoning Help

In an emergency, you or your crew can refer to the instructions on the Quick Reference page to find the keystrokes necessary to power up and obtain your latitude/longitude. This position information can be relayed over a radiotelephone to summon help quickly. When you communicate position information, the standard protocol is to read latitude first and longitude second. For example, if you were alongside the Vancouver Harbour approach buoy west of Point Grey, a GPS screen would display: 49°16.58' N, 123°19.23' W.

Read your position over a radio as "latitude four nine degrees one six decimal five eight minutes north; longitude one two three degrees one nine decimal two three minutes west."

Although it is common usage to use the word "point," decimal is less likely to be confused under poor radio conditions or in non-English-speaking countries.

New automatic life-saving equipment fitted with tiny GPS chipsets is now available for mariners and the land-bound alike. Cellular phones will soon be required to transmit accurate location information in case of emergency. Now that GPS is capable of 20-meter accuracy, it is likely that this requirement will be achieved using GPS. The new E-911 service will allow highway emergency crews to be dispatched to the appropriate side of the highway, and coast guard rescue boats will be able to find distressed vessels in heavy fog, even if the caller is unable to provide a position. Marine Emergency Position Indicating Radio Beacons (EPIRBs) with GPS capability are available that alert Search and Rescue Satellites (SARSAT) to the exact location of a vessel in trouble; they also transmit a description of the vessel, its owner's name and address and the number of persons likely to be on board.

Inevitably some people will see the hand of "Big Brother" in these developments. But others see the technology as a life-saver, resulting in faster response to highway and marine accidents.

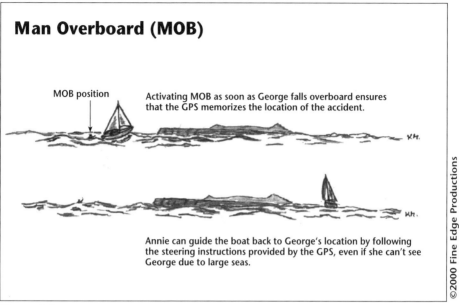

Man Overboard (MOB)

MOB position

Activating MOB as soon as George falls overboard ensures that the GPS memorizes the location of the accident.

Annie can guide the boat back to George's location by following the steering instructions provided by the GPS, even if she can't see George due to large seas.

©2000 Fine Edge Productions

Figure 1.1

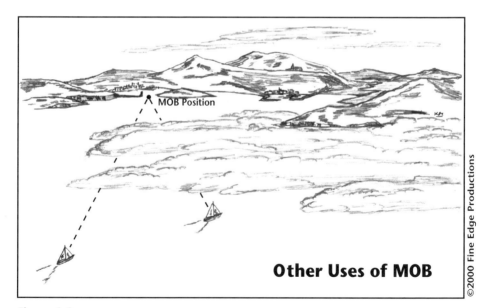

MOB Position

Other Uses of MOB

©2000 Fine Edge Productions

Figure 1.2

If you activate MOB just outside the harbour entrance, at any future time the GPS will indicate the precise direction and distance of the harbour entrance (the MOB position). Since this capability is unaffected by weather, the MOB position acts as a beacon, helping guide you to the harbour entrance through the dense fog.

How GPS Can Help You Return to a Man OverBoard (MOB)

Most GPS Navigators have a **MOB** (Man OverBoard) key that gives instant steering directions for returning to a man overboard. By initiating MOB, you override any other GPS functions [Figure 1.1]. The GPS Navigator instantly saves your present position and begins to calculate and display the steering directions to direct you back to that MOB position. The GPS screen displays corrected bearing and distance information and the shortest distance to the position at which you activated MOB, even if you followed a zigzag course after activating the key. (This information is particularly critical in large running seas where it's difficult to see the person who fell overboard.)

The GPS Navigator indicates the shortest straight-line course to return to a MOB position, but it cannot ascertain whether or not there is intervening land mass or an obstruction, so be aware of your course at all times.

After you have recovered your man overboard, de-activate the MOB function to continue normal navigational functions.

Note: A key part of any helmsman's instructions should be: "Push the **MOB key** the instant anyone yells 'man overboard' or whenever you see such an event."

Other Uses of the MOB Function

The MOB function can also be used to direct you back to a known point if, for example, visibility should worsen.

Suppose that upon leaving your harbour you notice a heavy offshore fogbank. If you press the MOB key as you leave the harbour, your GPS Navigator will continue to give you steering information to return to that point. If the fog rolls inshore before your return, your GPS display will show you how to return to the harbour entrance [Figure 1.2].

How GPS Helps You GOTO Your Dock

GOTO is a powerful function that creates simple route and steering information. Although most GPS Navigators have a keyboard with a GOTO key, some may offer the choice in a menu. You will use this GOTO function often, so it's a good idea to record the correct keystrokes for this feature on the Quick Reference page.

As a confidence builder, experiment using the following procedure (shown in Figure 1.3):

1. When you leave your marina, take your boat to a mid-channel position in the harbour entrance fairway. Write the position displayed on the GPS Navigator screen on your Quick Reference page. This position should be clear of dangers by 100 meters (or yards) in all directions. (Even though your GPS is accurate to within 20 meters, you must allow a margin for error). If your GPS set has a "Save" or "Quick Waypoint" feature, save the position to GPS memory. (Check your GPS manual to learn the procedure for saving your present position as a Waypoint.)

GOTO

When Pat and Cathie left their harbour this morning, they recorded the latitude and longitude of their position at ①. When they arrived near the lighthouse, they again recorded their position at ②.

As the sun sets, Pat activates the GOTO feature of his GPS. He enters the co-ordinates of position ②. Immediately, the GPS provides him with steering instructions that will take him to position ②. Once there, he will engage the GOTO again, this time entering the co-ordinates of position ①. He and Cathie will arrive at the harbour entrance well after dark, having had both a safe and enjoyable trip.

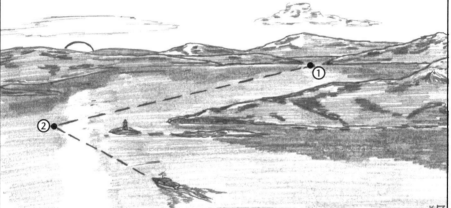

©2000 Fine Edge Productions

Figure 1.3

2. When you are ready to return to the harbour entrance fairway, activate the GOTO function. Then, when prompted to do so, enter the latitude and longitude of the center of the harbour entrance or pull up the Saved Waypoint from GPS memory. When you have entered the position you wish to "go to," your GPS displays distance and course to that destination.

3. As you approach the harbour entrance, the display indicates the decreasing distance. Check your position against the harbour chart to verify that your route is safe.

After reaching the harbour entrance, you can again initiate GOTO, this time keying in the mooring position you wrote on the Quick Reference page. The GPS will give you the direction and distance to your moorage.

If there are intermediate turning points between the harbour entrance and your moorage, you can repeat the GOTO sequence as many times as needed. *Remember:* even though your GPS is a superbly accurate instrument, the harbour entrance may be crowded with other vessels entering and exiting; therefore you must not navigate exclusively with GPS in small, crowded harbours. It is clearly up to the skipper to ascertain that the course ahead is clear and safe.

To use GPS in tight quarters, critical situations, and limited visibility, to get the highest possible performance (as in boat racing) or to optimize fuel consumption, a thorough knowledge of GPS limitations is essential. Chapter 8 deals with "Enhancing Your Understanding of GPS Accuracy."

The GOTO function creates a route with a single leg, in which your present position is the Departure Waypoint and what you keyed in is your Destination Waypoint. (Waypoint navigation, discussed in detail in Chapters 4 and 5, is the basis of much of GPS navigation.)

You can use GOTO when conditions change quickly and you have little time to program a full route. As demonstrated above, GOTO can be used sequentially with a series of intermediate positions to complete a complex route. If a skipper becomes incapacitated, the instructions above can be followed easily by any crew member.

Congratulations! You are already getting some fundamental results with your GPS Navigator—a taste of its possibilities. You will achieve significantly more precise and complex results as you learn the techniques described in this book.

GPS Setup Menus

A **GPS Setup Menu** usually includes choices for customizing your GPS displays. To get started, you can use the default options. To improve results or ease of operation, you may want to select your own parameters or measurement units. Customizing your display helps to minimize mistakes and gives you better results. The following setup options are typical of most GPS units, although your model may not include all of these options. (Refer to Appendix I for help in comparing equipment.)

Language: English; Espanol; Français; Deutsch; Italiano (English is the usual default.)

Velocity Average: Smoothing (Zero is the usual default, although we prefer 20 seconds.)

Magnetic Variation: Auto-Magnetic; True; User Set (Auto-Mag is the usual default; however, if you use a gyro compass, set Variation = zero.)

Measurement Units: Meter; Fathom; Feet

Distance/Speed Units: Statute mile; Nautical Mile (Nm); Kilometer (km); Knot (kn); and Kilometers Per Hour (kph); (Nautical mile and knots are the usual defaults.)

Co-ordinates: Lat/Long with decimal minutes; Lat/Long in degrees, minutes and seconds; OSGB; Universal Transverse Mercator (UTM); Loran C Time Differentials (TD)

Route Mode: Auto Switching; Manual Switching (Auto Switching is the usual default.)

Alarm Sounds: On; Off (Off is the usual default.)

Mode: 2D; 3D; Auto (Auto is the usual default.)

Date and Time: Universal Co-ordinated Time; Local with a.m./p.m.; Local with 24 hour (Default is usually set to local time a.m./p.m. or 24-hour time.)

Map or Horizontal Datum: WGS 84; WGS 72; NAD 27; GBR 36; AUSTR 84; EUROP 50; ALASK; MAUI; OAHU; KAUAI; TOKYO; some units have a long list of Horizontal Datums (WGS 84 is the standard default.)

Units with customizable screen displays let you select the information of most value to you. Some choices are COG; SOG; BRG; DTG; DMG; VMG; ETA; XTE; TTG; SOA; STD, etc. (See explanations in Chapter 4, as well as the Glossary.)

Hand-held GPS

The most basic GPS equipment available today is the hand-held model, capable of running for extended periods on batteries and small enough to fit in a shirt pocket [Figure 1.4].

In the past, hand-held equipment was bulky and capable of displaying only position, course, speed, and possibly time. This is certainly no longer true. Modern hand-held GPS Navigators are both complex and adaptable; some come equipped with interfacing ports which allow them to provide a data feed to other equipment such as radar, autopilots, plotters, or electronic charting systems. Many hand-held GPS sets are waterproof, making them ideal for use in open boats, and many are differential ready. Generally hand-held GPS equipment has limitations due to the size of the individual set and the restricted amount of software it can handle.

Photograph Courtesy of Magellan Systems Corporation

Figure 1.4   Small Hand-held GPS Navigator

A low-cost hand-held GPS Navigator with the antenna mounted internally in the upper portion of the set.

Antennas

The high frequency of the satellite signal (1575.42 MHz), means that the wavelength is very short (0.19 meter); thus, GPS antennas can be built small enough to fit into a hand-held receiver.

Most hand-held models utilize what is known as a patch antenna, which is nothing more than a small circuit board mounted in the top of the unit. Many manufacturers claim that the patch antennas included in their hand-held sets are just as sensitive as any fixed antenna. However, the weakness of the patch antenna is that, being a flat object, it is most sensitive to signals that come from a direction that is perpendicular to the flat surface. Thus, when you hold a hand-held set with a patch antenna, in order to receive signals from satellites overhead, you should ensure that the antenna is parallel to the horizon. You will find that hand-held receivers with this type of antenna fit comfortably in your hand with the antenna at the correct angle. When mounting one of these units, fix the bracket so that it duplicates this orientation.

On the other hand, some hand-held GPS sets utilize the same technology as a fixed antenna; the quad-helix or loopstick antenna. This antenna is constructed of tight spirals of wire wound on a cylindrical core. Quad-helix antennas are far more sensitive to low angle satellites than patch antennas, their only flaw being that the sensitivity is least along the axis (which generally points directly overhead). Each type of antenna has its advantages and disadvantages, the overall sensitivity depending on the quality of manufacture and the installed location on a vessel.

Even the most sensitive antenna is worthless if it is not placed in the path of the incoming signals. When taking a position in an open boat, hold the GPS in front of you at a height that allows it to see the satellites; don't block the signals with your body.

In an enclosed wheelhouse, especially one constructed of metal, the degraded signals you receive may render the hand-held GPS unreliable, thus increasing the time required to obtain a first fix (Time To First Fix—TTFF) unless it is connected to an externally mounted antenna. If you must, take it out on deck. *Remember*: For navigation information to be valid when steering toward a destination waypoint, the GPS must be in constant contact with the satellites. Otherwise, it will display only the information calculated the last time it was able to take a fix.

If possible, you should connect your hand-held GPS Navigator to an external antenna that is located for best reception [refer to Chapter 8], especially if you normally use the unit in the same location on the same vessel. Whenever you wish to take your hand-held in a small boat, it is easy to remove the antenna connection and use the portable antenna that came with the set.

Memory

With limited size comes limited memory. If you are navigating a route consisting of numerous waypoints and have many more waypoints stored in memory, a hand-held GPS Navigator may be slow to display steering information because its memory is nearly full.

In time you will learn the characteristics of your own set, but be aware of the potential for memory problems and keep just a limited number of waypoints in memory at one time. If the memory becomes overloaded, your hand-held GPS Navigator may freeze up entirely. The solution is to clear the memory and once you have done so you must re-enter all the waypoints and routes. In the case of a complete lock-up, you may have to re-initialize the receiver. Some hand-held units with limited memory may even require initialization each time you power them up.

Power

Unlike fixed equipment which is connected to a 12- or 24-volt power source, a hand-held GPS must be powered by batteries—either internal rechargeable Ni-Cad batteries or replaceable alkaline cells. While modern hand-held GPS equipment may be capable of operating for up to 24 hours on one set of batteries or on one charge, older sets will probably last just a few hours.

When battery life is limited, you should limit the time your GPS is powered up by taking occasional fixes then turning off the power until you need another fix. Although this limits the usefulness of the equipment, it is a small price to pay for convenience and portability.

When battery power is getting low, a warning of some sort appears. When you see or hear this warning, shut off the power or you will lose all the waypoints and routes stored in memory. Be sure you are familiar with the warning symbol or sound. If you fail to shut off the power and allow the batteries to discharge completely, you may lose *everything* in memory and have to re-initialize the set—a tedious chore!

How GPS Works

GPS uses a system of 26 to 30 earth-orbiting satellites in six different orbits. Within a 12-hour period each satellite circles 10,900 nautical miles above the earth in an orbit inclined at an angle of 55 degrees to the equator. Each satellite transmits precise timing signals (derived from two onboard atomic clocks) on its own specific channel. For a GPS satellite to be "visible" at a given location, the satellite must be above your horizon and in view of your antenna. Most receivers use a "mask angle" of 7.5 degrees. Below that the ionospheric model used in low-cost receivers causes considerable error. There will generally be six satellites in view greater than 15 degrees, eight greater than 10 degrees, and 12 satellites greater than 5 degrees above the horizon. A minimum of three visible satellites are required to determine a 2-dimensional position (latitude and longitude). A 3-dimensional position which includes altitude requires four visible satellites.

With a GPS receiver, you can choose an option to monitor the geometry and operational status—signal strength and other qualities—of the various satellites.

Each satellite broadcasts on two frequencies, L1 and L2. The L2 frequency is encrypted and can be decrypted by special receivers available only to the U.S. military and its allies. Known as the Precise Positioning Service (PPS), this provides position accuracy to less than 20 meters.

The L1 frequency, available to civilian users, provides the Standard Positioning Service (SPS). Prior to May 1, 2000, the timing signal on the L1 fre-

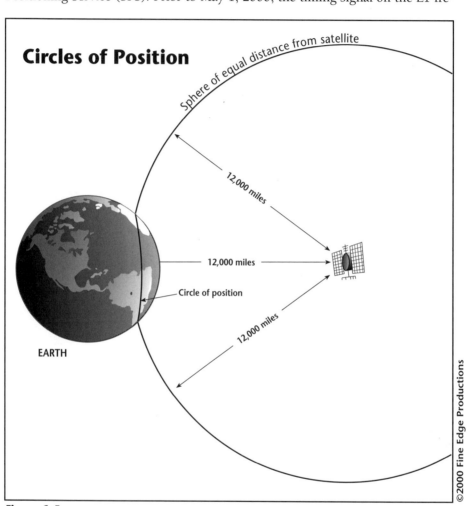

Figure 1.5

By timing the arrival of the GPS signal from a satellite, your GPS receiver calculates the distance to that satellite. If your receiver determines that you are 12,000 miles from the satellite, then you must be somewhere on the surface of a sphere of 12,000 mile-radius centered on the satellite. When this sphere intersects another, such as the surface of the planet Earth, a circle is formed on the surfaces of both spheres. This is a circle of position (COP) on the surface of the Earth. You must be located somewhere on that circle. However, this works only if you are at sea level, calculating a 2-dimensional fix. If you are at an unknown altitude (on land or in the air) your GPS receiver must utilize a second satellite's sphere of equal distance in order to obtain a COP. This is why more satellites are required for 3-D navigation than 2-D.

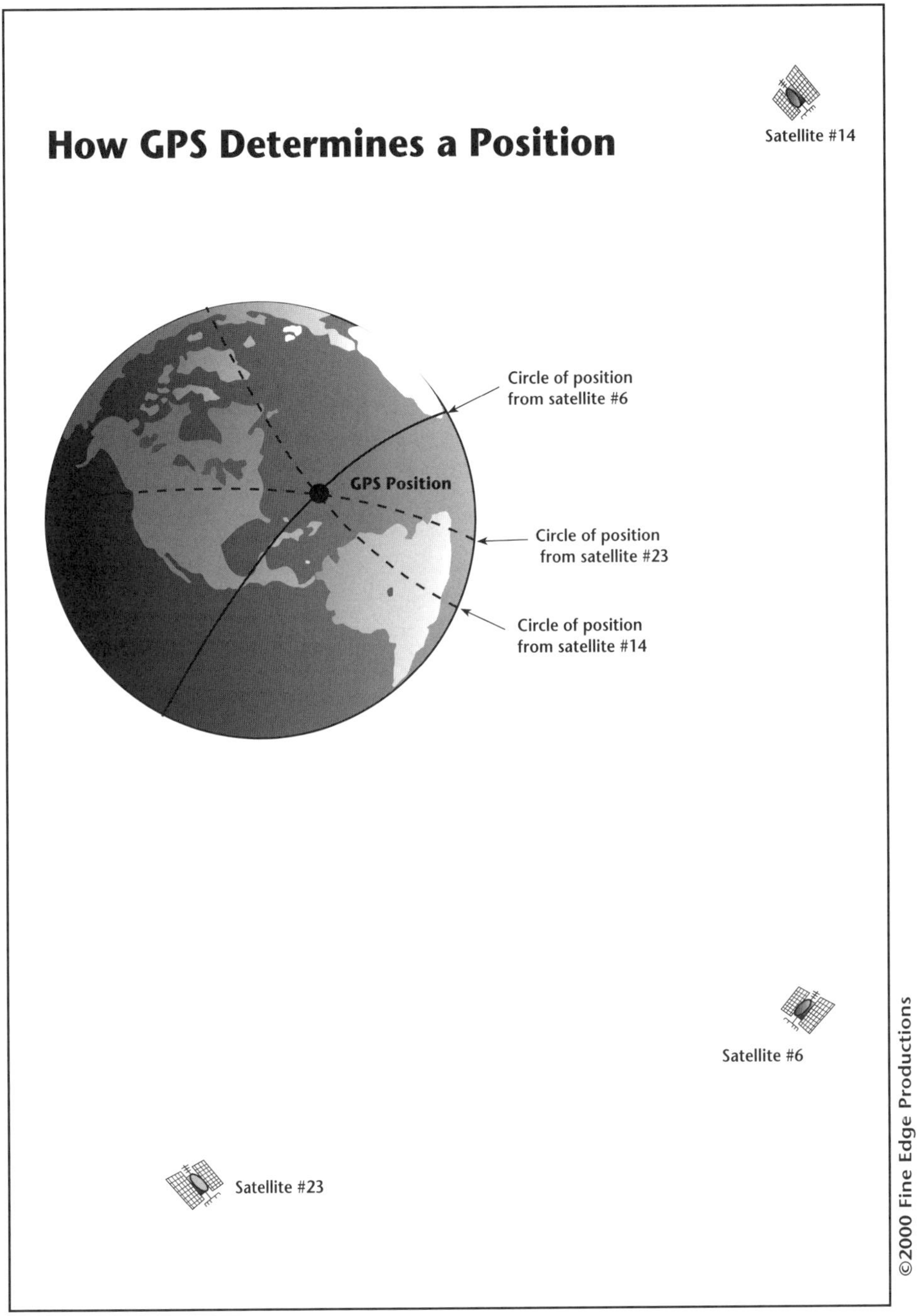

How GPS Determines a Position

Satellite #14

Circle of position
from satellite #6

GPS Position

Circle of position
from satellite #23

Circle of position
from satellite #14

Satellite #6

Satellite #23

Figure 1.6

By measuring the distance to three satellites, your GPS receiver knows it must be somewhere on all three circles of position. Just one position meets that requirement: the position where the three circles intersect. (For 3-D positioning, four satellites are required.)

quency was intentionally "dithered" by the introduction of random errors that degraded the accuracy of any position by up to 100 meters. This intentional degrading, known as Selective Availability (SA), constituted over half the total GPS error. Now that Selective Availability has been removed, the sources of remaining errors are due to atmospheric and ionospheric interference with the GPS signal and/or electronic interference from shipboard and other local sources.

Your earthbound GPS receiver uses a stored almanac to determine where to look for and locate satellites needed to determine a position. Using the ephemeris messages broadcast by these particular satellites, it determines the exact position of the satellites it has locked onto. By computing the amount of time it takes for the coded signal to travel from the satellite to your antenna, the receiver determines the *actual distance* between the satellite and your GPS antenna. [See Figure 1.5.]

If you know the distance to one satellite, you know *only* that you are somewhere on the circumference of a circle. By calculating the distance to three satellites, three circles of position are developed; the unique intersection of these three circles yields your exact latitude and longitude. [See Figure 1.6.] Since GPS receivers are passive devices, and do not interact directly with any satellites, the satellites can serve an unlimited number of earthbound receivers.

Satellite timing signals are subject to small errors, so each orbiting satellite is closely monitored from five sites around the world. The main control facility at Colorado Springs, Colorado, makes minor adjustments to keep the system within its prescribed limits of accuracy.

Once your GPS receives the satellite signals and you determine your position, additional navigation functions depend upon the internal computing power and software of your particular unit. A GPS Navigator continuously monitors changes in your position and derives navigational parameters regarding waypoints and routes.

A Brief History of GPS

In the early 1970s, the U.S. military predicted that it would soon need a highly accurate, world-wide, all-weather navigation system. The answer was NAVSTAR, now known as the Global Positioning System (GPS). Initial testing of the concept was carried out throughout the 1970s and, on January 6, 1980, the GPS atomic clocks onboard each satellite were activated. Over the next few years, the rest of the first group (Block I) of satellites was launched.

In 1983, after Korean Air Lines flight 007 was shot down by Soviet fighters over the Kurile Islands, President Ronald Reagan declassified the GPS project. Thus began public involvement in what had originally been a purely military project. In 1986, the Challenger shuttle disaster put the launching of more satellites on hold, delaying completion of the initial GPS constellation.

During the first testing period—with only 11 satellites in place—it was found that the Standard Positioning Service (SPS) provided greater accuracy to civilian users than the military wanted; consequently, in March 1990, it was deemed necessary to implement Selective Availability (SA)—an intentional "dithering" of the satellite clocks that reduced civilian accuracy to 100 meters, more or less.

Ironically, when the Persian Gulf War broke out in August of that year, the U.S. military did not have enough Precise Positioning Service (PPS) receivers for all its combat units. It turned off SA and equipped its soldiers with civilian GPS equipment!

During this same period, GPS caught the imagination of the general public. Although SA was reinstated in June 1991, commercial uses of GPS proliferated to a degree unanticipated a decade earlier.

By July 1995, the full constellation of 24 GPS satellites was finally in orbit and the system declared fully operational. Since that time, the U.S. Government has provided status and maintenance schedules to the public, greatly increasing the boating community's confidence in using the system for navigation.

By executive order, in February 1996, President Clinton dedicated GPS to worldwide peaceful uses, authorizing its operations to be supported by U.S. taxpayers in perpetuity. Billions of U.S. tax dollars have been spent to develop this technology. With the U.S. Government's pledge to maintain and upgrade the system, GPS should continue to perform its needed functions well into the 21st century. In his proclamation regarding Selective Availability, President Clinton stated that the deliberate degrading of the timing signals would be phased out no later than the year 2006 and possibly in 2002 or 2003 when a second civilian frequency is added. The President of the U.S. reserved the right to degrade GPS signals in times of dire national emergency but, by an agreement with the United Nations, he could not switch the system off!

On May 1, 2000, with only six hours warning, President Clinton announced that the United States Department of Defense had perfected a method of denying GPS signals on a regional basis, and that as a result, SA was no longer required to assure United States security and that it would be turned off forever. The removal of SA immediately increased the accuracy of existing civilian receivers by five to ten-fold.

In the meantime, several countries including Canada and the U.S. have set up a network of Differential GPS stations using low-frequency radio transmitters that compensate for the effects of atmospheric and ionospheric propagation errors.

Russia also has a space-based **GLO**bal **NA**vigation Satellite System (**GLONASS**). However, to date, technical and maintenance information regarding GLONASS has been limited. Although it appears to be less accurate than GPS, GLONASS receivers are starting to appear in European markets. The navigational techniques and procedures outlined in this book apply equally to GPS or GLONASS receivers. [For further information on GLONASS, see Chapter 3.]

Since the inception of GPS, a new generation of GPS satellites has been put in orbit and the frequent loss of signals experienced during the early years is now largely a thing of the past. New enhancements for civil use are being discussed on an ongoing basis—a survey of the literature available on the internet indicates the feverish pace of these new design ideas and applications. *Remember:* You do not need expertise in space theory, mathematics, or computer science to practice and achieve precise navigation with GPS.

Where to Find Current Information on GPS

The U.S. Coast Guard is responsible for broadcasting current status reports on the GPS system, including maintenance schedules, to all mariners. This information can be obtained on selected U.S. weather channels, from *Notices to Mariners, Notices to Shipping,* or from daily broadcasts by coast radio stations in many parts of the world. Further information on this service is available by writing or phoning:

> Commanding Officer
> USCG Navigation Center
> 7323 Telegraph Road
> Alexandria, Virginia 22315
> USA
> Tel: 703-313-5900; Fax: 703-313-5920
> GPS website:
> www.navcen.uscg.mil

[For the technically inclined, we list a number of GPS related internet sites in Appendix B.]

Getting More Out of Your GPS: the Next Step

Congratulations! You are now capable of simple GPS navigation at a level of accuracy that would have been considered magical by navigators of past generations. However, in order to increase the usefulness of your GPS unit, you need additional skills.

The ability to use geographic data from charts, take a position from a chart, and plot a position on a chart are skills fundamental to any form of navigation. Chapter 2 provides an introduction to latitude and longitude, nautical charts, and dead reckoning. Chapter 3 introduces you to GPS accuracy and its limitations. Chapters 4 and 5 describe waypoints and routes—powerful elements in making navigation simple and safe. With these skills you will be ready to learn the advanced techniques described in subsequent chapters.

Basic GPS Navigation

In this chapter we begin with basic navigational concepts. Subjects such as horizontal datum and the differences between precision and accuracy are essential to understanding GPS, as well as to guaranteeing safe and enjoyable cruises, so please be sure that you understand this chapter completely before you move on.

Why Use a Nautical Chart?

Your GPS tells you where you are located with an amazing degree of precision and accuracy, but unless you have it connected to a chart plotter or a computer with Electronic Charting capability, the display gives you only numbers representing position, course, speed, and other derived information. Without a chart to which you can reference them, these numbers (co-ordinates) will have little meaning for you.

You must first understand *how* information is presented on a marine chart [Figure 2.1]. When you look at a nautical chart, you will see that it is crammed with symbols and abbreviations. Some of the symbols are easy to decipher, but many are not. In addition, there are numerous abbreviations scattered about the chart, each with a specific meaning but without a legend. To help decipher the mass of symbols and abbreviations on their charts, **hydrographic** (chart making) **agencies** publish a manual available directly from them or from the dealer where you normally purchase your charts. Be sure to purchase this manual and use it!

For United States Charts:
Chart No. 1: "Nautical Chart Symbols and Abbreviations"
For British Admiralty Charts:
Number 5011: "Symbols and Abbreviations as used on Admiralty Charts"
For Canadian Charts:
Chart No. 1: "Symbols and Abbreviations used on Canadian Nautical Charts"

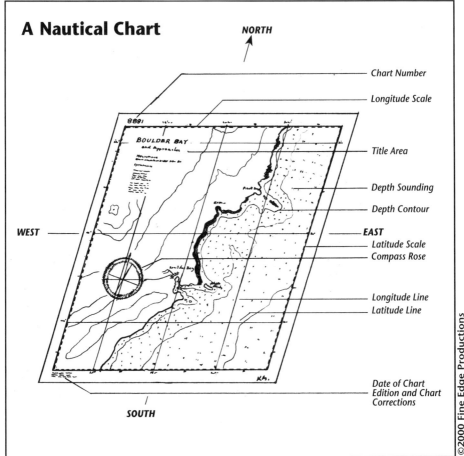

Figure 2.1

Major hydrographic agencies have agreed to use common symbols, so just one publication should satisfy your needs. When you use charts from non-English speaking countries, you should obtain a copy of relevant publications from that country's hydrographic agency.

Reading a Nautical Chart

Each chart has a title area where you find the name of the chart, its scale, the units used for depths and elevations (fathoms, feet, or meters), Horizontal Datum and, in some cases, the dates of the surveys on which the chart is based, as well as other information. In the lower margin there is a note indicating the dates of publication, printing, and the date of any corrections made to the chart.

The numbers scattered over the sea surface are soundings that indicate the depth of water at that location. Shallow areas are usually shown in blue; areas above water at extreme low tides are shown in green or brown. Unless you know the height of the tide, and the draft of your boat, you must assume that the tide is low and that you cannot pass over these drying rocks and shoals.

Nautical charts are similar to maps in two ways: 1) Landforms and other charted features are shown in their correct shapes as well as in proper angular relationship. This means that when you read a direction from one location to another on the chart, it will be the correct direction. On all nautical charts, you will find a compass rose to help you find these directions. 2) Virtually all nautical charts are printed with true north at the top, south at the bottom, and west and east to left and right respectively.

If you know how to read a chart, you can make rough approximations of direction and distance by eye alone; but for more precise navigation, you must be able to read latitude, longitude, and magnetic direction.

Scale

Any map, chart or drawing has a property known as **scale**. A chart with a scale of 1:500,000 (one to five hundred thousand) covers a large area—one inch on the chart represents a distance of 500,000 inches or 6.86 Nm. This is considered a **small-scale chart**, since the ratio 1:500,000 represents a small fraction.

A chart with a scale of 1:5000 (one to five thousand) covers a much smaller area. One inch on the chart represents 0.07 Nm and is considered a very **large-scale chart**.

Important note: A large-scale chart covers a small area; a small-scale chart covers a large area. (People often misunderstand these terms and thus misuse them.)

Latitude and Longitude

Any place on the surface of the earth can be identified by a unique "address" consisting of **latitude** and **longitude** co-ordinates. These are basically units of angular measure defined in terms of **degrees, minutes** and **seconds**, a system devised by the Babylonians over 3,000 years ago. From their perspective, the earth stood still and the sun moved across the stationary stars to return to the same location in 360 days. Any circle can be divided into 360 equal divisions of one degree each. Each degree consists of 60 minutes, and each minute consists of 60 seconds. Remember not to confuse minutes and seconds of *angular measure* with minutes and seconds of time. Fortunately, minutes and seconds of angle and time are usually written differently as follows:

Angle: Ten degrees, fifty minutes and eight seconds is written
    10° 50' 08"
Time: Ten hours, fifty minutes and eight seconds is written
    10:50:08 or *10 hr. 50 min. 8 sec.*
Navigators have used certain conventions for several centuries. The **north pole**

Parallels of Latitude and Meridians of Longitude

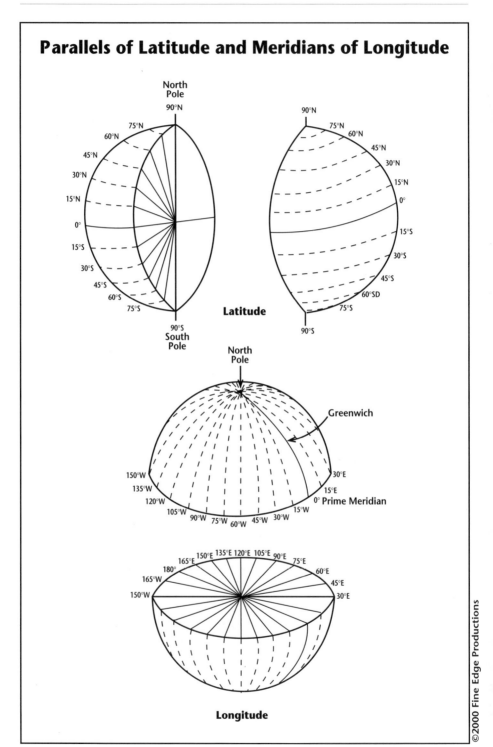

Figure 2.2

and the **south pole** are the points on the earth's surface around which the planet spins. Halfway between the poles lies the equator, an imaginary line dividing the earth into two halves—the north and south **hemispheres**.

Figure 2.2 shows an imaginary earth sliced into two halves along its north-south axis. The two poles lie 90° from the equator. Lines parallel to the equator, called **latitude lines** (or **parallels of latitude**), can be identified by the number of degrees, minutes, and seconds north (or south) of the equator.

Any line drawn from the equator to the north or south pole is known as a **meridian of longitude**. These meridians are identified by the number of degrees they lie east or west of the Prime Meridian which runs through the Royal Observatory at Greenwich, England.

If you draw lines of latitude and longitude at 15-degree intervals on the globe, you will see something similar to Figure 2.3. As a whole, the system of latitude and longitude forms a **co-ordinate system**; the unique latitude and longitude of any point on the surface of the earth are known as the **co-ordinates** of that point.

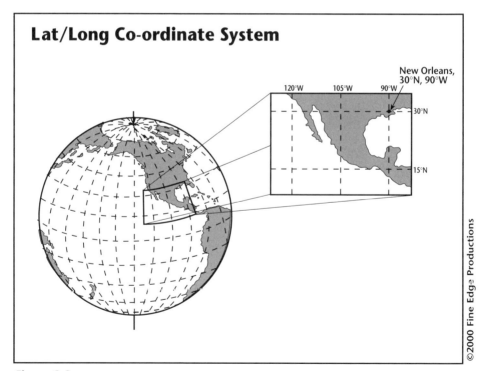

Figure 2.3

When a flat chart is prepared to represent a portion of the surface of the earth, selected parallels of latitude and meridians of longitude are shown to assist you in taking positions. New Orleans lies exactly at the intersection of 30°00.0' N, 90°00.0' W. To find the co-ordinates of any point lying between the printed lines, you must measure using dividers. (See also Figure 2.4.)

A map or nautical chart is merely a flat representation of a portion of the surface of this globe. The mapmaker (hydrographer) draws lines of latitude and longitude on the chart at convenient intervals, perhaps even-numbered degrees; for a chart of a smaller area, perhaps every five or ten minutes. (There is no fixed rule for the interval chosen.) Most charts show the intervening degrees and minutes along the margins [Figure 2.4]. Using these margins, you can find the latitude and longitude of any position on the chart.

By convention, **one minute of latitude equals one nautical mile (Nm)**—approximately 1,852 meters or 6,076 feet. (A nautical mile is 1.15 times greater than a statute or land mile.) **One degree of latitude equals 60 nautical miles**, so it is easy to measure distances along the **latitude scale** on the sides of the chart. *Note:* Always take your measurements from the *sides* of a chart adjacent to the point measured; do not measure distances along the top or bottom of a chart!

It is only at the equator that one minute of longitude equals one nautical mile. In Figure 2.2, you can see that as the lines of longitude (meridians) move from the equator toward either pole, they draw closer together until they converge at the pole, and the length of a minute of longitude becomes zero. At latitude 45°, a minute of longitude is just 0.7 Nm.

In the past, charts were commonly printed with margins graduated into minutes and seconds. Now it is more common to dispense with seconds and to divide the latitude and longitude scales into degrees, minutes, and **tenths of minutes**. By this convention, a position located at 58°47'24" becomes 58°47.40'.

Occasionally, when you work with a chart drawn to the older format, you will have to convert from degrees, minutes, and seconds to degrees and decimal minutes or vice versa. (Refer to Appendix A for tables and formulae for converting one system of measurement to the other.)

Taking a Position off a Chart

Suppose you wish to find the co-ordinates of a feature on a chart. You will need a pair of dividers. If the feature lies at the intersection of latitude and longitude lines printed on the chart, you have no problem. In Figure 2.3, New Orleans is located precisely at the point where the lines 30° N latitude and 90° W longitude cross. Thus, the co-ordinates of New Orleans are 30°00.0' N, 90°00.0' W. Unfortunately, few charted features are so conveniently located.

When a feature lies between the printed lines, you need to make precise measurements. To practice these measurements, study the graphic display in Figure 2.4 along with the following directions.

To find the **latitude** of Longships light:
1. Place one point of your dividers on the nearest line of latitude, directly to the north of Longships, 50°05' N.

Taking a Position Off a Chart

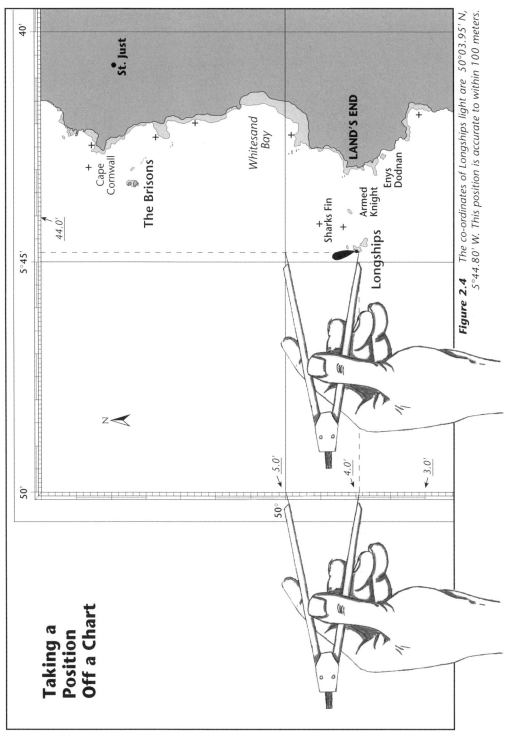

Figure 2.4 *The co-ordinates of Longships light are 50°03.95' N, 5°44.80' W. This position is accurate to within 100 meters.*

2. While keeping one point of the dividers on the line of latitude, move the other point to the base of the symbol representing the exact geographic position of Longships light. Work as precisely as you can. Any errors you make here will show up later as an error in position.

3. Once the points of the dividers span the distance from the latitude line to Longships light, transfer this distance to the nearest latitude scale at the side of the chart. (Dividers are normally fairly stiff and do not flex easily which helps avoid slippage when you move them.)

4. Place one point of the dividers exactly where the latitude line meets the latitude scale. The other point will mark a point on the scale south of this latitude line. With a sharp pencil, mark the point which defines the latitude of Longships light, reading the latitude off the scale.

5. Notice that on both the latitude and longitude scales, even though each minute is divided into tenths, the lines are drawn every 5 minutes. These are the only major divisions numbered, so you must count the intervening minutes to determine their individual numerical values.

6. Notice that the mark you made on the latitude scale is a bit more than one minute away from the 5' line. Since the chart covers an area of the northern hemisphere, *remember* that the numbering diminishes as you go south—the next division to the south of the 5' line will be 4'; south of 4' will be 3'. The mark you made falls somewhere between 3.9' and 4.0'. You have to estimate by eye, but since the pencil mark is approximately halfway between, 3.95' is pretty accurate. Next, be sure you can find the correct number of whole degrees of latitude along the side of the chart.

7. To put it all together, the latitude of Longships is approximately 50°03.95' N, accurate to within 0.05' or 100 meters. (If you were working with a chart of a smaller area, the latitude increments would be farther apart and you could estimate the latitude more precisely.)

To measure the **longitude** of the light at Longships:

Follow the same procedure you used to find its latitude, but use the longitude scale at the top or bottom of the chart. In this case, we recommend that you measure from the 40' longitude line rather than the 45' line because it is so difficult to measure a small distance with dividers. The longitude of Longships light is 5°44.80' W.

Write the co-ordinates of Longships light as: 50°03.95' N, 5°44.80' W.

Remember: The latitude designation *always* comes first, followed by the longitude. Note that leading zeros are not included in the number of degrees, but only in the number of minutes and seconds.

As we mentioned in Chapter 1, when you read the latitude and longitude co-ordinates (**lat/long**) aloud, read them as: "Latitude five zero degrees, zero three point (or decimal) nine five minutes north; longitude five degrees, four four point (or decimal) eight zero minutes west."

Each of the ten divisions between minute marks represents six seconds or one-tenth of a minute. So, if you want to read the position in seconds, visualize six parts between the smallest divisions on the latitude or longitude scale. Generally, we prefer to convert the decimal minutes to seconds using the Tables or Formula in Appendix A. Once converted, the position is 50°03'57" N, 5°44'48" W and is read as follows:

"Latitude five zero degrees, zero three minutes, five seven seconds north; longitude five degrees, four four minutes, four eight seconds west."

Plotting a Position on a Chart

Although GPS equipment displays a position in lat/long co-ordinates, to know where you are you must be able to plot the co-ordinates on a chart. When we talk about *instant navigation,* we mean that the GPS instantly calculates its own position in lat/long co-ordinates. To take advantage of this position information, you often have to plot your own position; the faster you can do this, the more *instant* will be your navigation.

Suppose your GPS display shows your position at 51°14.23' N, 127°47.80' W. With a set of parallel rules, find 14.2' on the latitude scale [Figure 2.5].

1. In this example, 14' is marked on the chart. Find 14.23' which lies approximately one-third of the distance between 14.2' and 14.3'. Estimate this distance by eye and mark the point with a sharp pencil.

2. Find 47.80' on the longitude scale and make a pencil mark.

3. Now, place your parallel rules with one edge exactly on any nearby latitude line. Hold this edge of the rules firmly on the chart with one hand while you swing the other edge down until its edge lies along your pencil mark at 14.23'. *Make sure that the rules do not slip away from the latitude line. If they move at all during this process, repeat the procedure.*

4. Draw a line along the edge of the parallel rules at the 14.23' mark. Now release your death grip.

5. To draw the longitude line, repeat the last step using a nearby longitude line, or the side of the chart as a starting place. Draw another line at the 47.80' position.

6. The intersection of these two lines is your **position** on the chart. You can draw a little circle around this intersection and erase the rest of the lines. Make a notation of the *time* beside the position; it will come in handy later.

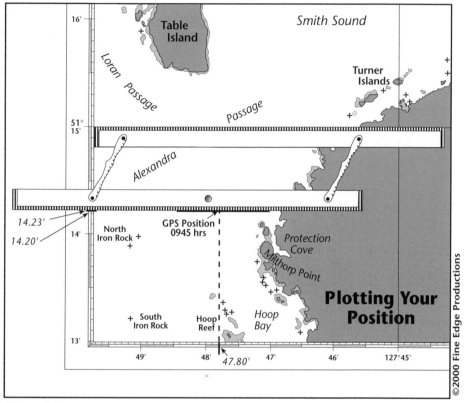

Figure 2.5

Although it's possible to use a compass in place of parallel rules to plot the position, you have to be more careful to achieve the same degree of accuracy. (A compass resembles a set of dividers but, instead of a needle, one of the points is replaced by a pencil). To use a compass, follow these directions:

1. Using the compass in much the same way you use a set of dividers, measure the distance from the latitude line to the mark you made on the latitude scale.

2. Move the compass along the latitude line to define the same line you drew with the parallel rules.

3. Repeat the procedure for longitude and draw another line that crosses the latitude line you drew. These two lines, essentially the same you drew with the parallel rules, define the same position.

Some navigators prefer to use one or two dividers and a sharp pencil, finding this to be the quickest method to plot position.

With a little practice, you will need to draw just a short segment of the line in the appropriate area of the chart. Many mariners prefer to use a compass for this procedure since it requires so little space on a chart table and is therefore suited to small-boat navigation. *Note:* Whichever technique you use, take great care and be sure to maintain accuracy. If you have any doubts, repeat the procedure and see if you arrive at the same position on the chart.

Conventions

In this book we use the standard conventions for nautical measurement: distance is measured in meters (m) and nautical miles (Nm) and, where appropriate, we include feet in parentheses. Since one nautical mile is equal to one minute of latitude, this unit is universal.

1 Nm	=	1852 meters
	=	6076 feet
	=	1.15 Statute miles (the land mile most readers know best)
	=	2025 yards
1 m	=	3.28 feet (just over one yard)

To indicate speed, we use nautical miles per hour or knots (kn)—but *never* knots per hour.

1 kn	=	1.15 Statute miles per hour
	=	1.85 kilometers per hour

At present, most of the world's hydrographic agencies are converting their charts to the metric system. Due to budgeting concerns, this process may take years if not decades in some areas. At this time most *offshore* charts are still in fathoms. In the interim, you will continue to encounter charts using fathoms (fm), meters, or feet for soundings. Depending on the units used in a local chart, we use any of these units for depth measurement.

1 fm	=	1.83 meters
1 fm	=	6 feet

One unit of measurement we do not use is the cable—one-tenth of a nautical mile or 100 fathoms (600 feet), and this is our only mention of the term in this book.

For time, we use the twenty-four hour clock. Thus 1:32 a.m. becomes 0132 hrs and 2:45 p.m. becomes 1445 hrs.

For direction, compass bearings, etc., we use 360-degree notation. (To the joy of most boaters, the practice of *boxing the compass*—"East by north by a quarter north"—has recently disappeared. It reveals nothing to the average recreational boater except that the direction is somewhere between east and north.) We do sometimes use *approximate* directions such as north, east, southeast, etc. But where specific *measurement* of direction is concerned, we keep to 360-degree notation.

Except where otherwise stated, all directions, courses, bearings, etc., are given in true. True and Magnetic directions are written as follows:

145° T
145° M

Direction and Magnetic Variation

A magnetic compass does not point to the north pole! Instead, it points to the **magnetic north pole** which lies in the northern Canadian mainland over a thousand miles from the **true north pole**. Consequently, the direction of true north and magnetic north differs by a certain amount at any location. This difference, known as **magnetic variation**, differs at various places around the world, so be sure to check each chart for the variation applying to the area covered by that chart.

Every chart contains one or more compass roses. The compass rose has two concentric circles divided into three hundred and sixty divisions of one degree each. The outer circle represents **true directions** referenced to the true north pole; the inner circle represents **magnetic directions**.

Any two points on a chart can be connected by a straight line. The direction of this line can be measured with parallel rules [Figure 2.6] as follows:

1. Lay one edge of the parallel rules exactly along the line connecting the two points.
2. Walk the parallel rule across the chart until its edge crosses the exact center of the compass rose. (Practice this procedure until you are sure that the rule, when laid across the compass rose, is exactly parallel to the original course line.)
3. Draw a line through the compass rose. This line should be exactly parallel to the original line.
4. Read the true direction at the intersection of the line with the outer compass rose; for magnetic directions, read the inner compass rose.

To determine a direction from any position on the chart, reverse the procedure. If, for instance, you wish to lay out a course of 125° True from the position of your vessel:

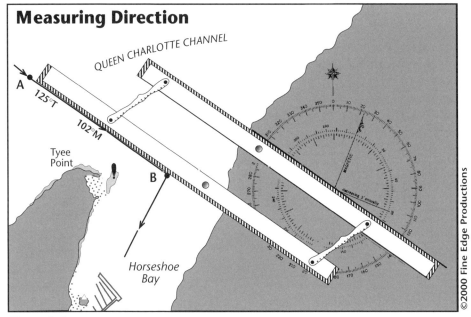

Figure 2.6

First lay one edge of the parallel rules exactly along the Course Line. Then swing the other edge around until it crosses exactly through the center of the compass rose. Often, it is not possible to span the distance in one step, so you must move the rule in a series of steps. Be careful to avoid slipping. If you do, the line transferred across the chart will no longer be parallel, and you will have to start again. Note that the compass rose reads 125° T or 102° M. Also note that the line has been extended to the opposite side of the compass rose in case you wish to follow the course in reverse when leaving the harbour.

1. Align the parallel rule with the center of the compass rose and the 125° mark on the outer circle.
2. With the parallel rule, transfer the line to the vessel's position on the chart.
3. Draw a line in the appropriate direction.

Plotting an Approximate Position

The first rule of navigation is to plot your position frequently. It is good discipline to plot your exact positions; however, under some circumstances an approximate position is adequate, especially if there is plenty of sea room. You should always know *approximately* where you are, where you are headed, and be aware of the *degree of accuracy* required in your particular situation. For proper use of the GPS, a paper chart is essential.

For a 30- to 40-mile crossing using a small-scale chart (covering a large area), it is enough to place an X on the chart every half-hour or so at your approximate position. Run your finger up the side of the chart until it falls on the approximate latitude co-ordinate; do the same for longitude. Your approximate position lies at the intersection of the two lines [Figure 2.7]. Note the time beside that point. In the event of a power failure or a change of wheel watch, your vessel's progress has been recorded and you can refer to it at a moment's notice.

When operating close to shore, refer frequently to your position and its relationship to navigational marks of interest, such as headlands, rocks, and lights. Know where you are at all times. *Remember:* If you cannot establish your position (especially inshore), stop your vessel and, using your depth sounder and any other means, determine your position and the depth of water before proceeding.

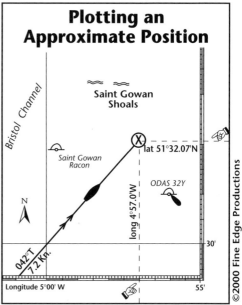

Figure 2.7

Dead Reckoning (DR)

A simple projection of your course and speed giving you an estimated future position is known as **Dead Reckoning (DR)**. Whether it is based on precise or approximate positions, dead reckoning allows you to determine where you *should be* and what you should be able to see or observe on radar.

Many of the techniques in this book require you to determine a dead reckoning (DR) position. To do so, project your course and speed ahead from your last well-known position (or fix) for a specific amount of time. This tells you where you *should* arrive assuming no current or wind is acting on your vessel.

A **Dead Reckoning vector (DR vector)** is an arrow drawn in the direction in which you are steering. Its length is equal to the distance you travel through the water in any given amount of time. The far end of the arrow is your DR position at the end of the projected time. This position may be fairly accurate or it may differ significantly from the position at which you actually arrive (see the next section). To find a good DR position, you must know your course and speed to a fairly high degree of accuracy. (See **Course and Speed** below.)

Course and Speed

In addition to position, a modern GPS receiver displays other information. Primary among these are **Course** and **Speed** which may be indicated as COG

(Course Over the Ground) and SOG (Speed Over the Ground). If you can't view course and speed data on the position display, you must switch to another display.

If you are travelling in calm water without the effects of wind or current on your vessel, and with a properly adjusted compass, your vessel should follow almost exactly the course line you have laid out.

In actual practice it is impossible to follow a compass heading closely in a small boat. Less expensive marine compasses are graduated in 5-degree increments, making it more difficult. Even with a quality compass, you may have difficulty following a heading to within a degree or two, and your vessel will wander back and forth across the projected Course Line. Over a period of time, the errors may cancel out, allowing your vessel to arrive close to its destination. However, you need to pay attention to the exact compass heading or your vessel may end up a significant distance from its intended destination.

Time, Speed, and Distance

Time, speed and distance are intimately related to one another. If you know any two of these values, you can easily find the third by using the following formula:

$$D = \frac{S \times T}{60}$$ where   D is the distance travelled in Nm
S is the speed of travel in kn
T is the time in minutes taken to travel that distance

Thus a vessel travelling at 6 knots for 20 minutes will cover

Distance $= \frac{S \times T}{60} = \frac{6.0 \text{ Nm/hr} \times 20 \text{ min}}{60} = \frac{6.0 \times 20}{60} = 2.0 \text{ Nm}$

To find the speed, transpose the equation to read:

$$S = \frac{60 \times D}{T}$$

If a vessel travels 11.5 Nm in 1 hour and 15 minutes (1 hour and 15 minutes = 75 minutes), then

Speed $= \frac{60 \times D}{T} = \frac{60 \times 11.5 \text{ Nm}}{75 \text{ min}} = 9.2 \text{ kn}$

To find time, again transpose the equation:

$$T = \frac{60 \times D}{S}$$

To find the time required to reach a marina 25 Nm distant when your vessel is travelling at a speed of 6.0 kn:

Time $= \frac{60 \times D}{S} = \frac{60 \times 25 \text{ Nm}}{6.0 \text{ kn}} = 250 \text{ minutes} = 4 \text{ hours } 10 \text{ minutes}$

These relationships are fundamental to any kind of navigation, so be sure to familiarize yourself with these calculations.

Wind, seas, and strong currents can also push your vessel off its intended Course Line by carrying it sideways. The greater the strength of current or wind, the greater the discrepancy between the course steered and the actual track followed. Some currents which are tidal in nature can rise to extreme values.

At Nakwakto Rapids in British Columbia, for example, tidal currents of 18 knots have been recorded during extreme spring tides. Other currents, such as the Gulf Stream, are a product of trade winds and the rotation of the earth. Whether tidal or otherwise, currents will carry a vessel laterally over the seabed.

Figure 2.8 illustrates an extreme example. Imagine that you are heading at 6 knots directly across a channel in which the current is running at 6 knots. With no external references, such as in dense fog, you assume you are advancing nicely toward your destination. However, if the fog lifted suddenly, you might find yourself far downstream of your intended destination, and that the course you steered was different from the actual track you followed.

The actual course followed, known as the **Course Made Good** (CMG), represents the *actual* direction a vessel moves in a straight line between any two points over a period of time. The **COG** indicated by your GPS is an *instantaneous measurement* of the direction a vessel is moving at any particular moment. The *average* COG will be fairly close to the CMG.

The **Speed over the Ground** (SOG) displayed by your GPS is also an *instantaneous measurement*. It does not necessarily provide you with the Speed Made Good (SMG) between two separate points. In Figure 2.8, the speed of 6 knots is measured by an impeller speed log that gives *speed through the water*, not over the ground. Since the vessel is carried downstream by the water, determining the

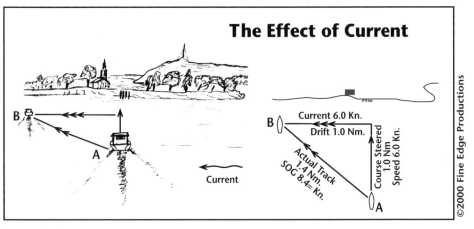

Figure 2.8

A vessel departing Position A steers directly across the river at 6.0 knots but is swept downstream by the current which is also running at 6.0 knots. The result is that the vessel follows a diagonal path across the river at a speed of 8.4 knots.

true SMG between points A and B requires calculation. [For a demonstration of how to calculate SMG, see Chapter 6, Figure 6.7.] For now, it is enough to understand that CMG and SMG can differ from the actual course steered and the speed through the water.

In the 10 minutes it takes to go from point A to point B in Figure 2.8, the current carries the vessel 1.0 Nm downstream (in one hour, 6 Nm). In the same time, the vessel advances through the water 1 Nm. However, the actual track followed (CMG) in the same 10 minutes was 1.4 Nm in a different direction than that steered by the helmsman.

If you calculate the SMG, you will find it to be 8.4 kn—more than the 6.0 kn through the water but fairly close to the average SOG given by the GPS while the vessel is in motion. The advantage of the GPS-derived SOG is that it gives the answer *instantly and continuously.*

In addition to current, wind and wave action cause a vessel to be carried off course. Large waves striking your vessel can cause your bow to turn away from the course steered. Heading upwind, the bow is pushed downwind; heading downwind, the opposite occurs. Although you may diligently correct your vessel's swing following each wave, after an hour or two you may find that you have been running with your bow pointed off course for a significant length of time! Thus the vessel's Actual Track differs from its Intended Track.

Wind, on the other hand, not only pushes the bow off course, but also pushes the *entire vessel* laterally through the water, leaving a wake that streams away from the stern at an angle— unlike a vessel under the influence of current alone. The force and direction of the wind either reinforce the drift due to current or counteracts some or all of that drift. When there is no wind pushing the vessel laterally, the direction steered and the direction of the wake do not differ. But when a cross wind pushes on the vessel, the line of the wake forms an angle to the course steered.

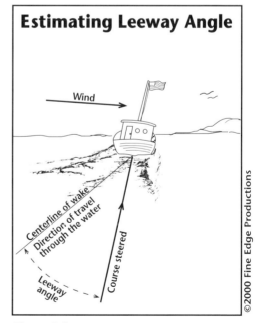

Figure 2.9

You can estimate the direction of the vessel's travel through the water by observing the direction of the wake.

This angle, known as **leeway angle**, can be roughly estimated by eye. [Figure 2.9 shows how to estimate leeway angle.]

In most practical applications, the effect of all three forces are counted as one and called **drift**. *Remember*: Tidal currents oscillate twice per day, so tidal current values remain constant for just a short time; on the other hand, a drift current, such as the Gulf Stream, is consistent for a longer time.

Search and Rescue

For the recreational boater, the topic of **Search and Rescue** may be unpleasant, but for fishermen and workboat skippers, it is a vital element of life at sea. If you are in trouble and need to call for assistance, your position at the time you call is the most important single piece of information needed by rescue agencies. Stories abound about crew who were unable to give an accurate position to coast guard vessels or others trying to assist them as their vessel was sinking, going aground or had caught fire. Where navigation is sloppy, or dead reckoning not maintained, vessels in distress may give positions that are in error by several miles, causing a critical loss of time in searching for the stricken vessel. Once a vessel sinks, people and rafts in the water are far more difficult to locate.

If you call for help when your GPS still displays position, include latitude and longitude co-ordinates in your call. If you can report an obvious nearby land-mark, do so. Don't feel compelled to read each minute of latitude or longitude to the third decimal place. A position given to one decimal place—one-tenth of a nautical mile—is sufficient. If you have time to do so, *write down the co-ordinates and the time of your call* in case you need to repeat your distress message.

If you are drifting, and help is a long time in arriving, the current will prob-ably sweep you away from your original position. If you can, broadcast new co-ordinates at regular intervals of fifteen or twenty minutes. Rescuing ships can then work out the exact conditions of the current and effect a much swifter res-cue. Although the search and rescue agency will estimate the force and direction of the current to establish a search datum, their estimations are prepared from generalized current information.

We sincerely hope that none of you ever has to undergo such an emergency, but it helps to be prepared if such a case does occur.

On a small recreational boat, be sure that *everyone* on board knows how to operate your radio and read aloud the position of your vessel. After all, you as skipper may be engaged in other critical tasks such as keeping your boat afloat!

CHAPTER 3

GPS Errors and Insights

Precision and Accuracy

As soon as you power up your GPS, you can see that the GPS position display gives your position in lat/long co-ordinates to three decimal places of a minute of latitude and longitude. Since each minute of latitude is equal to one nautical mile (1,852 meters or 6,076 feet), the third numeral after the decimal in the latitude line represents thousandths of a nautical mile (1.8 meters or 6 feet).

You have also learned that the nominal accuracy of GPS is 20 meters (65 feet), so to reconcile this apparently conflicting information, you need to understand the difference between **precision** and **accuracy** in fixing a position.

When a measurement is given in very small increments, it is said to have precision. Since its smallest increment of measurement is one-thousandth of a nautical mile, the GPS display is highly precise; but do not confuse this quality with accuracy!

For the *accuracy* of the GPS position fix to equal its *degree of precision*, it must be within 0.001 Nm (6 feet) of the true position; a degree of accuracy that is still not possible with GPS. Instead, the U.S. Coast Guard advertises that the accuracy of any position you obtain with the civilian GPS system will be within 20 meters (65 feet) of your true position.

Most of the time GPS accuracy will be better than 20 meters, but there may be occasions when it is not as good. Because we depend on our equipment to give reliable and repeatable results, we must assume that GPS error is at least 20 meters at all times.

GPS error is composed of atmospheric and ionospheric propagation errors and other small errors caused by shipboard and environmental influences.

The Dockside Test

If you watch your GPS display while your vessel is tied to the dock, notice that the last two decimal places of the lat/long co-ordinates are constantly changing. If you record the maximum and minimum readings for both latitude and longitude, the displayed position will vary by approximately 5 to 10 thousandths of a minute

New GPS Accuracy Standards

The signal and timing errors that affect GPS positioning vary in a random fashion. For this reason the U.S. Coast Guard has applied statistical analysis to the resulting GPS position fixes. Prior to May 1, 2000 the advertised accuracy of GPS was as follows:

100 meters (328 feet) 95% of the time;
50 meters (165 feet) 65% of the time;
40 meters (130 feet) 50% of the time.

Now that GPS signals are not intentionally degraded, the United States military states that GPS accuracy should fall within 20 meters (65 feet). But the specification does not state whether this figure is meant to replace the 100-meter figure (95% of the time) when selective Availability was active. The predicted figure of 20 meters depends on a scientific prediction of the degree of ionospheric activity. Just as there are many scientists, there are many predictions and there may be times during solar flares, etc. that ionospheric activity far exceeds the predicted average.

Certain tests conducted in Colorado Springs and in Canada and Australia in the days following May 2, 2000 seemed to indicate civilian GPS accuracy in the order of 5 to 10 meters. However, these tests were conducted using dual-frequency receivers which have access to the GPS military frequency. These receivers are able to eliminate a large portion of ionospheric error by comparing the interference on each frequency; but they are extremely expensive and are unavailable to the average recreational boater.

However, with the introduction of a second civilian frequency in 2003, this degree of accuracy may be available in the next generation of civilian receivers.

As this book goes to press, the formal accuracy specification of the new GPS has not yet been announced. The initial indications are very exciting, but further testing over the remainder of the year 2000 will be required to determine the exact limits to accuracy of the new GPS.

---

of latitude (0.005 to 0.010 Nm) and a somewhat greater amount of longitude. In other words, the latitude and longitude display might show:

| 52°47.685' N | or it might show | 52°47.675' N |
| 127°07.331' W | | 127°07.347' W |

| when the true position was actually | 52°47.680' N |
| | 127°07.339' W |

It is the random (and thus unpredictable) errors of the GPS system that cause the displayed position to vary like this, as if the GPS receiver itself were in motion. Let's perform an experiment in our minds and see what conclusions we can draw.

- While your boat is secured to a dock, power up your GPS receiver and select the "Position" display.
- Plot the displayed position on a large-scale chart or a plotting sheet.
- After 10 seconds, plot the displayed position again.
- Draw a straight line from the first position to the second.
- After another 10 seconds, plot the position again.
- Continue the process for 24 hours.

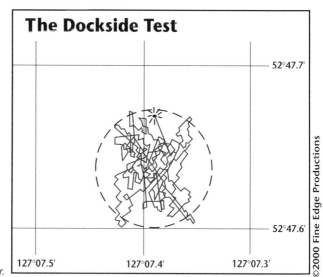

The Dockside Test

52°47.7'

52°47.6'

127°07.5'   127°07.4'   127°07.3'

©2000 Fine Edge Productions

Figure 3.1

The position at which you became tired of plotting was an extreme position at the north end of the pattern. The true position is near the center.

While we don't suggest that you actually carry out this procedure, if you have a GPS plotter, you can observe the experiment on the plotter screen. [See Chapter 10.] After a few hours, a pattern will develop that looks much like the diagram in Figure 3.1.

The total diameter of the pattern (except for a couple of extreme loops) will be no more than 0.02 Nm across (40 meters or 130 feet). The average diameter will be 40 meters and the average radius 20 meters. When we talk about GPS accuracy, it is the radius of this pattern that we refer to.

Since you know that your boat has not moved away from the dock, you know the true position of your vessel and, sure enough, the pattern is centered on the dock. In other words, the true position is at the center of the 20-meter radius error circle. [See Figure 3.2.]

Error Circles

You can develop this sort of pattern only on a vessel that is motionless for a long time. If the vessel is in motion, or if you observe the GPS display for just a few moments, you can be sure that the displayed position lies somewhere in a 20-meter radius circle centered on the true position of your GPS antenna.

When navigating with GPS, you will use the GPS error circle to estimate the consequences of possible positioning errors. In the past, navigators would have shed tears of joy to know their position with such a degree of accuracy. Now it is a common experience. But don't let this awesome accuracy lull you into complacency. When operating offshore, with no dangers in sight, you can comfortably assume your position to be **virtually exact**; but when navigating intricate channels, you must be constantly aware of the 20-meter radius error

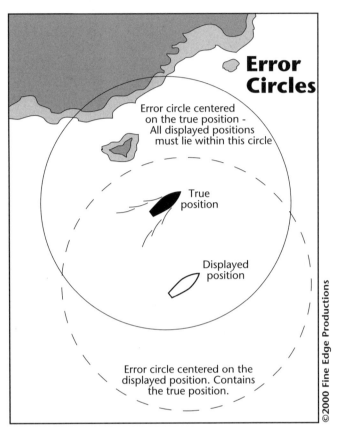

Figure 3.2

The displayed position may be anywhere within the solid circle. This is the same circle that enclosed the pattern in Figure 3.1. The displayed position lies at the center of the dashed circle. Since the displayed position is provided by the GPS, you must assume that the true position is somewhere within this 20- meter radius circle.

Within the figure:

Error Circles

Error circle centered on the true position - All displayed positions must lie within this circle

True position

Displayed position

Error circle centered on the displayed position. Contains the true position.

©2000 Fine Edge Productions

circle and the need to provide yourself with a margin of error above and beyond the 20-meter GPS error.

Repeatable Accuracy and Loran C

Fishermen with a long history of operating Loran C tell stories of using it to guide them back to their fishing gear with only 30 meters of error. Bear in mind, however, that the **predictable accuracy** of Loran C—its ability to take you to a position taken from a chart—is often poor. This predictable accuracy, best in near-shore waters, becomes poorer and poorer the closer inshore you go—precisely the opposite of what you need.

To understand the repeatable accuracy of Loran C, refer to Figure 3.3. In the diagram, you are alongside the dock at Klemtu. You leave your GPS running and plot your GPS position on the chart every 10 seconds. If you continue this for 12 hours, the characteristic pattern emerges.

Turn on a Loran C set and repeat the process, plotting the Loran C positions on the chart every 10 seconds for the next 12 hours. In our experience, the Loran C pattern is usually up to one and a half times the size of the GPS pattern and the pattern can be **offset** from the true position by up to a half-mile. In that case, the Loran C error circle will not contain the true position.

If you were to navigate back to the same Loran C co-ordinates at a later date using the same Loran C receiver, you would find yourself very close to the dock at Klemtu because *Loran C offsets do not change with time.* Consequently Loran C is said to have great repeatable accuracy, but the catch is that you have to have been at the dock in Klemtu at some previous time in order to know which co-ordinates to return to. If you use the lat/long co-ordinates of the dock taken directly from a chart, your position may be in error by up to 0.5 Nm.

The predictable accuracy of Loran C is comparatively poor *because the dis-*

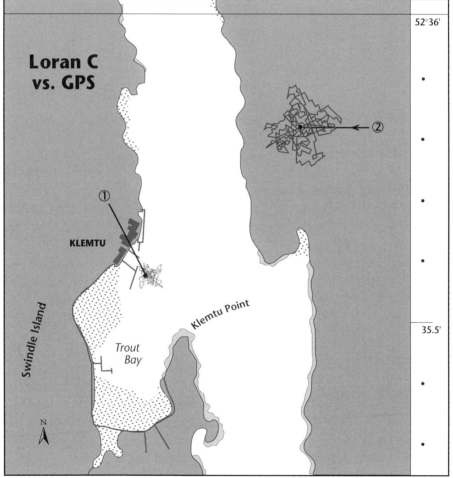

Figure 3.3

1. Pattern of GPS positions centered on true position.
2. Pattern of possible Loran C positions. The center of this pattern is offset from the true position by 3/8 Nm.

played position cannot be reconciled with a true geographic position. In fact, the offsets change significantly with location; a few miles away, they might be a completely different amount and *in a different direction.* In an extreme case, a Loran C receiver might read one-half mile to the south of the true position in one location, and three-eighths of a mile to the north just a mile and a half away. Consequently, it's pointless to compensate for the offsets by adjusting the displayed co-ordinates to match the true position.

Radio waves are slowed by diffraction effects when passing over water; they are further slowed over land, due to the decreased electrical conductivity of soil and rock. This variability of speed of propagation of radio signals is known as ASF (additional secondary factor), propagation delay or land path error. It is this variability that causes the **offsets** so common to Loran C in inshore waters.

Away from close proximity to land, Loran C offsets are usually less than 0.25 Nm and may be as little as 0.10 Nm, depending on your proximity to the transmitting stations.

The Loran C system has worked reliably for many years, but its future is by no means certain. Both the Canadian and U.S. Coast Guards are considering the discontinuance of Loran C in favor of Differential GPS (Chapter 9). However, U.S. Coast Guard policy on Loran C has been reversed temporarily; and Canada and the United States are continuing their review of Loran C policy.

In light of the new levels of accuracy of the new GPS, the fate of Loran C may seem to be a foregone conclusion. However, foreign governments may see Loran C as an essential backup to GPS, now that the United States has announced its ability to deny GPS signals locally in times of U.S. national emergency. Loran C may actually see a revival in the near future. At this point we can only suggest that you wait and see what the future brings.

The Workbook

When you set up your new GPS, you need to study your owner's manual and learn all the necessary procedures for handling waypoints and routes. To assist you, we have created a workbook in the back of this book with a prepared list of functions common to most GPS Navigators. As you work through your manual and come to a function listed in The Workbook, record the keystrokes necessary to achieve that function in the right hand column. *We recommend that you always record all relevant information in The Workbook.* At some future time, if you forget the keystrokes necessary to perform a task, your instructions will be accessible in a form you can easily understand, eliminating the need to search through your GPS manual for vague and confusing instructions.

Course and Speed Error

One of the consequences of the apparent movement of the GPS position over time is that your GPS receiver acts as if it is actually moving, even though it may be at rest. Since the receiver uses no outside reference except the coded satellite signals, it believes it is not only moving, but that it is also constantly changing course and speed.

When you watch the course and speed readout, you will notice that it may show a speed of up to one knot or more, and the course readout may indicate that the receiver is moving around in lazy circles, in almost every direction except the one the boat is actually pointing toward.

You can hardly blame the receiver for such apparently misleading information. After all, it is the receiver's job to constantly calculate position, course and speed. However, you must be aware that *when the vessel is at rest, the course and speed displays will always be erroneous.*

Now imagine you are proceeding out of Tucker Bay at 5 kn through the water on a northwesterly heading [Figure 3.4]. When the boat is at position A

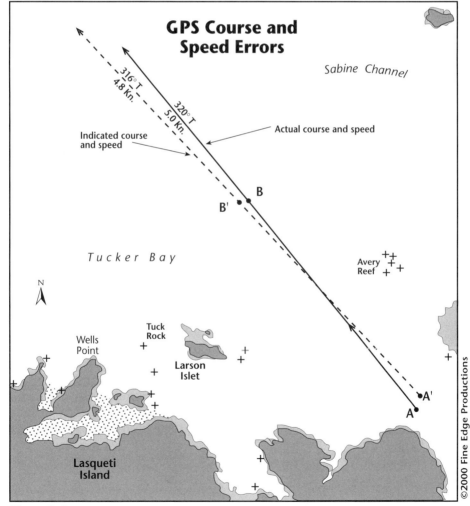

Figure 3.4

on the chart, the GPS receiver determines that you are at point A'. Six minutes later, when the boat is at position B, the GPS receiver indicates position B'. (GPS receivers update position, COG, and SOG much more frequently than every 6 minutes, but let's ignore that for now and use a 6-minute interval in the example.) Point A' is 40 meters to the north of the true position at A; point B' is 25 meters to the west of point B. The course actually followed in this situation is 320° T. The apparent course followed from A' to B', as determined by the GPS receiver, is 316° T, a difference of 4 degrees. Also, the receiver calculates that the distance travelled is 4.8 Nm, so the speed must be 4.8 kn, an error of 0.2 kn. Given the accuracy of the new GPS, the positioning errors described above may seem extreme, but there will probably be short periods of time when position errors reach these values.

This figure seems closer to the truth than a figure of 0.3 kn, shown when the receiver is at rest. But both fall within the generally observed limits of GPS speed accuracy. Though there are no formal specifications for **velocity** (course and speed) accuracy, our experience prior to May 1, 2000 suggests that an error of 1.1 kn is high but not uncommon. The course and speed errors you can now expect will probably be half of that. Obviously, 0.5 kn of error is relatively more important in a vessel travelling at 5 kn than it is in a high-speed vessel travelling at 32 kn. For a jet aircraft zooming along at 600 kn or more, the error is virtually irrelevant. Only for a vessel moving at low speed does the error become a significant percentage of the vessel's true speed.

Course accuracy, which is strongly influenced by vessel speed, becomes very undependable at speeds less than 2 to 3 knots. If the vessel is stationary, the indicated COG can vary between any and all possible directions. Consequently some GPS receivers will not display COG when the SOG is below a certain minimum value. In later chapters we show how this characteristic of COG can have profound implications.

GPS and the Nautical Chart

Even though your GPS receiver is properly installed and is set to the proper chart datum (see next section), when you plot your position you may find that the chart indicates you are aground. What has gone wrong?

Don't be alarmed. The error you are observing may not be an error in your GPS at all. It could be that chart errors are affecting your GPS position. Remember that the GPS receiver you use for fixing position is far more accurate than the instruments the chart-makers had at their disposal until a few years ago. The date of the original survey of the chart you are using—*not the date of printing or the date of the latest edition*—may pre-date GPS; if so, your GPS is probably more accurate than the chart itself. This problem is present everywhere, but in more remote parts of the world, the errors can be quite large. If you cannot find the survey date, you must assume that the chart is drawn to an unspecified standard of accuracy and act accordingly.

Even in developed countries, some charts made prior to 1990 may be problematic. Hydrographic agencies work to a standard of confidence that charted features shall be no more than 1 millimeter out of position at least 98% of the time—far less than the thickness of a pencil line. This level of accuracy is easy to maintain on small-scale charts, where 1.0 mm may represent more than 200 meters, but on large-scale charts, 1.0 mm may represent just a few meters. You cannot expect small-scale charts—especially those based on old surveys—to be that accurate. Now that high-accuracy GPS is a reality, mariners can plot positions with far greater accuracy than the original hydrographers did; thus you may not be able to reap the full benefit of the new GPS until the accuracy of large-scale charts is uniformly consistent with the new accuracy levels of GPS. In some parts of the world this may not happen for many years to come.

Chart Datum

Not only may charts be subject to small errors in the location of certain geographic features such as shorelines, isolated rocks, shoals and the like, but they may also contain large systematic errors due to inaccurate determination of latitude and longitude.

As an example, certain islands in the South Pacific Ocean actually lie up to seven miles from their charted positions because their discoverers made errors in computing latitude and longitude—especially longitude. When you consider that accurate determination of longitude depended on the ship's captain accurately tracking the error of his chronometer for two years or more, it is wonderful that we can make any sense at all out of these older charts. [See Figure 3.5.] In the Strait of Magellan, one of the authors noted discrepancies of 0.7 Nm to 1.1 Nm between the charts and his GPS position. On British Admiralty charts the largest known difference is 9 miles.

These errors developed because there was no single reference point to which charted features could be compared. For instance, when charting a South Seas lagoon, a nineteenth century surveyor could only reference the chart to a datum point somewhere on the shore of the lagoon; he could not accurately position that datum point in relation to the surface of the earth. What he needed was a single datum point somewhere on the earth's surface to which he could reference his charts. Although such a datum point did exist (the Royal Observatory at Greenwich, England), it was too far away to be used as an accurate reference for the chart, so the surveyor had to make do with a local datum.

Since that time, cartographers and hydrographers have continued to attempt to define local datums that are relevant over larger and larger areas. In order to do so, they have used measurement systems that maintain accuracy over greater distances but, when crossing bodies of water, these systems break down because there is no fixed ground in which to set survey stakes. Consequently until the arrival of satellite positioning, map datums were limited to continental-sized areas.

An additional problem arises when a hydrographer attempts to extend a datum over a large area. The earth is not a true sphere; it is flattened at the poles and has lumps, bumps, and depressions. The surface of the ocean, likewise, does not follow an ideal spherical shape. Local differences in the force of gravity cause parts of the world's oceans to be more than one hundred meters higher or lower than others, refuting the idea that there is a perfect "sea level" to which heights can be referred.

Hydrographers and cartographers must make assumptions about the shape of the earth when they draw their maps so, in 1927, North American hydrographers began to use a standard set of assumptions about the earth's shape which applied to all North American charts. This standard model is known as a "geodetic system," "chart datum," or "horizontal datum." In North America it is known as North American Datum 1927 or NAD27 (not to be confused with tidal datum which is the zero tide level). In other parts of the world, surveyors have established different datums.

Since 1927, cartographers have learned more about the shape of the earth, and in 1983, using satellite telemetry data they established a new datum (NAD83) in North America. Among its many features, it makes allowance for changes in their understanding of the shape of the earth's surface that introduced errors of up to 200 meters in NAD27. When charts were drawn to the new datum, cartographers discovered that the positions of geographic features on charts drawn to the older datum could not be reconciled with their positions on new charts—the lines of latitude and longitude on the older charts were in the wrong places. In many areas of the continent, these differences are minimal—just a few meters—but in other areas the difference between NAD27 and NAD83 is over 200 meters (more than 0.10 Nm). [See Figure 3.6.] Displacement of position due to datum differences is called **datum shift**.

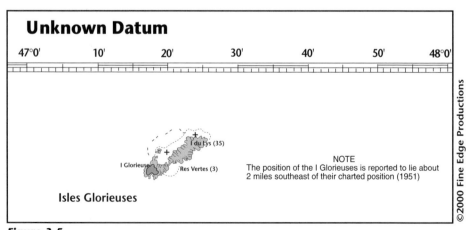

Figure 3.5

The Isles Glorieuses are not represented in their proper position relative to the north coast of Madagascar shown on the same chart. The area was surveyed between 1822 and 1826.

These discrepancies did not matter when navigation systems were less exact, but with the advent of precise positioning, cartographers began to take these datum shifts seriously. Notices suddenly appeared on charts indicating the datum to which the chart was drawn, as well as the degree of correction to be applied to older charts to reconcile them with the new navigation systems. Now that worldwide satellite positioning is available, GPS uses a truly universal chart datum—World Geodetic Survey 1984 (WGS84). In North America, WGS84 is equivalent to NAD83.

Boaters operating in northern British Columbia and southeast Alaska may find discrepancies of up to 200 meters. On older charts of Dover Strait, charted to the 1936 Ordinance Survey of Great Britain (OSGB), the shift is approximately 140 meters. Unless you resolve these differences, your GPS receiver will lose some of its usefulness.

Converting from One Chart Datum to Another

Since many parts of the world are charted using the old datums, hydrographic agencies are now adding notices on older charts indicating the horizontal datum and the required corrections to be applied to a GPS position before you plot it

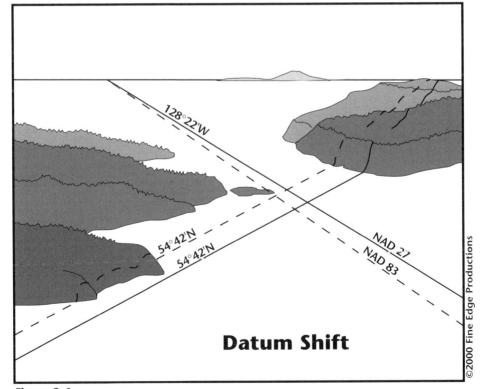

Figure 3.6

Latitude and longitude lines of one datum (NAD27) are slewed with respect to another (NAD83).

on a chart. [See Figure 3.7 for an example of such a note.] When new surveys are conducted and a new chart issued, it is drawn to WGS84, and a datum note is incorporated.

Before you plot GPS-derived WGS84 co-ordinates on a chart drawn to a local datum, you will have to apply corrections either to your plot or to the GPS receiver itself. If you decide to correct the co-ordinates manually, you will find it a cumbersome process. If you want to lift positions off a chart not drawn to WGS84 or an equivalent datum, and you wish to use the co-ordinates with a GPS set to WGS84, you will have to perform the conversion in reverse. (See examples in Figures 3.7 and 3.8 .) If no horizontal datum is noted, you may be able to find the corrections in the issuing agency's *Notices to Mariners*.

Manufacturers of GPS receivers are aware of chart datum problems and have gone to great lengths to include corrections for over 100 datums in their software. (See Appendix G for a list of 151 datums, of which approximately 100 are used on nautical charts.) If your receiver is fairly recent it probably has the proper software; simply select the correct datum when working with any particular chart and the receiver will then display lat/long co-ordinates consistent with the charted position. This is the method most skippers use, and it certainly simplifies things.

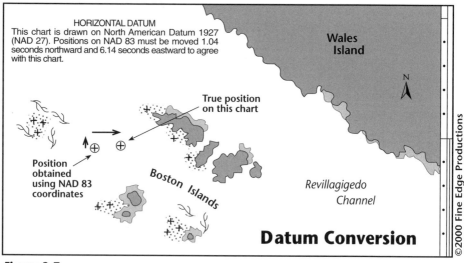

Figure 3.7

The + to the west represents the lat/long co-ordinates given by a GPS operating on NAD83.

Move this position north and east by the required amount to the position of the + to the east. You have now converted your position to NAD27 co-ordinates.

To convert seconds to decimals of a minute, note that each small division on the latitude scale represents 1/10 minute or 6 seconds. [Refer to Appendix A.]

Another method is to record the lat/long co-ordinates provided by the GPS and then add 1.04 seconds to the latitude and subtract 6.14 seconds from the longitude. (Moving north increases the latitude in the northern hemisphere; moving eastward decreases the longitude in the western hemisphere.)

One of the older hand-held GPS Navigators we used had only a few of the most common chart datums in its limited memory. However, it did include a user-defined datum, an option which allowed us to enter offsets from WGS84 datum. (These offsets were listed in the owner's manual.) By entering these offsets into memory, we were able to define the new chart datum. However, if another datum is to be entered, the previous user-defined datum must be erased. In a GPS Navigator with limited memory, this is an imaginative but cumbersome method of accessing the nearly 200 chart datums in use world-wide.

If you want to make the conversions with your GPS, you must ensure that the chart datum being used by the GPS at any one time matches that of the chart you are using. *This means that you must check every chart you use and, if necessary, reset the GPS every time you move from one chart to another.* The value of your GPS as a precision navigation tool will be seriously compromised if you fail to do so.

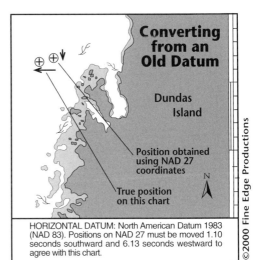

Converting from an Old Datum

Dundas Island

Position obtained using NAD 27 coordinates

True position on this chart

HORIZONTAL DATUM: North American Datum 1983 (NAD 83). Positions on NAD 27 must be moved 1.10 seconds southward and 6.13 seconds westward to agree with this chart.

©2000 Fine Edge Productions

Figure 3.8

Since this chart is drawn to NAD83, you do not need to convert a GPS position unless you previously recorded a fishing spot by latitude and longitude while using an older chart of the same area. You might have been using a GPS operating on NAD27 or you might have lifted the old co-ordinates directly from the older NAD27 chart. The new chart will match the datum in use on the GPS, but the old information must be converted to NAD83 before being recorded on the new chart.

Remember: Corrections used on one chart may not be the same as those for a chart of another nearby area drawn on the same datum. However, modern receivers include most of the common datums in use worldwide—some software packages contain over 100 choices.

In The Workbook, record the necessary keystrokes for changing to a new chart datum.

Unknown Chart Datum

When you use older charts that have no horizontal datum notes, you may have to guess at the datum in use. You cannot plot satellite-derived positions on a chart unless you know that the chart is compatible with WGS84.

However, the datum to which the chart is drawn may be unknown. Note the following quotation from the Canadian Notices to Mariners, Number 1996–546, in reference to Canadian Hydrographic Service Chart No. 7193 (Baffin Island).

HORIZONTAL DATUM: This chart is drawn on an unknown datum. Positions on North American Datum 1983 (NAD83) and those taken from GPS, SAT-NAV or Loran C co-ordinate conversion after ASF correction must be moved 2 minutes 11 seconds southward and 3 minutes 26 seconds eastward to agree with this chart. Even incorporating this data, positions plotted from navigation systems such as GPS, SATNAV, Loran C, Omega may be in error by 1.0 miles because the horizontal reference datum for this chart is unknown. Positioning methods such as range and bearing should therefore be used.

Of some 3,300 charts in the British Admiralty series of world charts, approximately 40% are drawn on unknown datums. Fortunately, in British home waters most older charts have been drawn to a datum—the 1936 Ordinance Survey of Great Britain (OSGB)—whose relationship to WGS84 is well understood.

Until these areas have been re-surveyed and charted to the new worldwide datum, mariners will continue to have difficulties obtaining the greatest accuracy out of their GPS equipment. Overhauling the collection of world charts of the major hydrographic agencies of the USA, Great Britain, and Russia is not only a huge undertaking, but it also involves such an expenditure of funds and manpower that many countries may be unable to convert existing charts of little-used areas. Instead, they will have to focus their efforts on major shipping routes.

Universal Transverse Mercator Maps (UTM)

The **Universal Transverse Mercator Projection**, or **Military Grid** referencing system, is not a datum, it is a completely separate co-ordinate system. Topographic maps are usually drawn with this grid superimposed, and many GPS units—especially handheld units for use on land—include a software option for UTM as if it were a chart datum.

Why describe UTM at all in a book on marine navigation with GPS? It may sound unlikely, but some coastal mariners could find themselves in completely uncharted waters. In British Columbia, for example, an area of 300-square-nautical miles that includes all of Spiller Channel and Briggs Inlet, remained uncharted until 1996. Other areas in British Columbia, especially in the Queen Charlotte Islands, remain uncharted to this day. This must certainly occur in other remote areas of the world, as well, so where topographic maps are available, they can provide limited information for skippers entering uncharted waters.

CBC Radio News: 21 Dec. 1998

A German couple out for a Christmas drive near Berlin ended up in a river. They had been relying on their luxury car's navigation system when they came to a ferry crossing at the Havel River. That information, however, was never stored in the satellite-steered system they were using. The driver kept going straight in the dark, expecting a bridge, and ended up in the water. They were not injured. A coast guard officer said: "You can't always blindly rely on technology."

The Transverse Mercator Projection accurately portrays the size and shape of areas near any specific reference meridian. The **Universal Transverse Mercator system (UTM)** uses 60 zones, each 6 degrees wide, to approximate a flat surface for the entire globe. Each of these zones is referenced to a central meridian. The problem is that, on a flat surface, the lines of latitude and longitude do not necessarily lie parallel to the edges of the map, so an arbitrary rectangular grid is superimposed.

Each grid square is one kilometer across. Since there are 1,000 meters in one kilometer (km), a grid reference given to three decimal places has a precision of one meter.

An appealing characteristic of the UTM system is that, travelling east or north, all numbers increase. In fact, the reference numbers are called eastings and northings. Let's look at a couple of grid references to be clear about how to read the eastings and northings.

Eastings

- Since the grid lines on the map are 1,000 meters apart, the grid designations actually represent metric units. Eastings are measured relative to the central meridian of any zone which is always designated $^{500}000$. An easting value of $^{595}360$, indicates that the position is 95,360 meters to the east of the central meridian of that zone, or 360 meters to the east of the line labelled 95. On each map there are one or two grid lines with the complete designation printed out, but it is usual for the intermediate lines to be labelled with only two numbers, i.e. 95. When combined with the zone designation, each easting value is unique. There are no others like it on the globe.

Northings

- Northings are measured from the equator, which is designated $^{00}00^{000}$ for positions north of the equator, or $^{100}00^{000}$ for positions south of the equator. This makes sense because the distance from the equator to each of the poles is ten million meters (10,000,000). In the southern hemisphere, it is the south pole that is designated $^{00}00^{000}$. Otherwise northings are measured in exactly the same way as eastings.

Zones

- The map may indicate that the northing is in the northern or southern hemisphere, or the zone itself may be divided into sub-zones of 8 degrees of latitude each, identified by a letter. Thus a map may be identified as Zone 9U, indicating that the grid reference is in Zone 9 and is between latitudes 48° N and 56° N.

Referencing positions to the grid in this manner achieves two objectives: 1) Each place on the earth's surface has a unique letter/number identifier; you need not specify north or south and east or west. 2) There is no need to indicate units used, such as degrees, minutes and seconds.

The GPS displays positions with a precision of one meter. Since the proper form of a full UTM position is the zone first, then easting, then northing, a grid reference may be displayed as follows:

9U 501^{363}m. E 5793^{062}m. N

or as

9 North 501^{363}m. E 5793^{062}m. N

Since a GPS receiver cannot fix a position to within one meter of accuracy, if you are operating with topographic maps, you should round off the last digits of the UTM co-ordinates, giving a precision of 10 meters which is consistent with GPS.

As long as the zone and sub-zone, or zone and hemisphere are known, and the proper map chosen, the previous grid co-ordinates should be abbreviated to:

01^4 E   93^1 N

01 E and 93 N can be read directly from the gridlines; tenths are estimated by eye to find a position.

GLONASS

GLONASS is the Russian Federation version of GPS and, like GPS, is composed of 24 satellites and the associated monitoring and control ground stations. GLONASS uses just three orbits instead of the six used by GPS. Each satellite broadcasts timing signals which can be converted to distance measurements for position fixing. Like GPS, GLONASS provides a high-precision frequency—the **Channel of High Accuracy (CHA)** for military use, and a lower-precision frequency for civilian use—the **Channel of Standard Accuracy (CSA)**.

Like GPS, the high precision (CHA) channel is scrambled in order to block access to civilian users. The Russian Government has disavowed any intention to degrade the accuracy of the CSA service by introducing Selective Availability. The system is so similar to GPS that combined GPS/GLONASS receivers are now available to the general public, though the price is still very high. Because of this similarity, the techniques and procedures outlined in this book apply equally to GPS and GLONASS navigation.

As of July 1996, the Russian Federation Ministry of Transport offered worldwide GLONASS coverage to the International Civil Aviation Authority for position-fixing purposes and guaranteed its coverage for the next fifteen years. However, it is unclear when the system will be declared operational. At the time this book went to press only 9 of the 24 satellites were fully operational.

Operating Near the Magnetic Poles

Even though the GPS satellite orbits do not cross over the polar regions, they are so inclined from the equator that from virtually anywhere in the world a GPS receiver will have a good view of several satellites. Therefore, GPS does not lose efficiency near the poles as do compasses and other navigation aids. However, to ensure seeing enough satellites, you may need to lower the mask angle of the antenna. [See Chapter 8.]

CHAPTER 4

Waypoint Navigation

Waypoints

Since waypoints are the basis of almost all GPS navigation, let's take a moment to review the concept. A **waypoint** is a virtual position that a GPS Navigator stores in memory as if it were an X on an imaginary map of the earth. This virtual position represents a real location which your GPS Navigator treats as a landmark. Since the GPS Navigator continuously determines its own changing position, it can calculate the distance and direction (range and bearing) to the waypoint's co-ordinates. These calculations are made continuously and in real time, 24 hours per day. When added to the other fundamental GPS data (course, speed, and time), the range and bearing data provide the basis for all GPS navigation.

Waypoints can be used individually or in groups, or even for other purposes. As demonstrated in Chapter 1, an MOB position is a waypoint, as is a GOTO destination. A waypoint is thus an "address" which defines your starting point, a point you hope to go, a place to avoid, or some intermediate position along the way.

The Destination Waypoint

A destination waypoint is the waypoint toward which you are navigating at any particular time (i.e., the GPS's active waypoint). *Remember:* When you initiate navigation *toward a new waypoint*, that waypoint becomes the new destination waypoint. At any one time, there can never be more than one destination waypoint.

For a detailed discussion of waypoint selection criteria, see Chapter 5, in particular the sections titled **Selecting Waypoints** and **Curvilinear Legs**.

Routes

A **route** is a series of waypoints which, taken together, define all the courses required to complete a passage. When navigating along a route, the GPS Navigator directs the vessel to the first waypoint, then to the second, and so on. Once a waypoint has been passed, it is said to have been *realized.*

Cecil's Style of Navigation

Cecil Varney was a retired dairy farmer from New York State who settled near my home in the Gulf of Georgia in British Columbia. During the years of his retirement, he discovered that his favourite form of relaxation was fishing for salmon. Almost any early morning of spring or summer would find him puttering along in his small open boat, a fishing rod gripped between his knees, his hearing aid unplugged. He became an excellent fisherman and brought home many fine coho and chinook, but his greatest difficulty was in finding the exact spot where he had caught fish the last time. He was no navigator.

One day, while explaining this problem to me, he said, " I've thought of painting a large X on the surface of the water every time I catch a fish, but of course that wouldn't work!" He winked at me. "I've painted it on the side of the boat instead." We both got a laugh and agreed that his solution would not find the fish. This conversation took place in the early 1970s and, sadly, a few years later Cecil died.

In the years Cecil was fishing, Loran A, although available, would have been no use to him. Its accuracy was not good enough for his purposes and the receivers were bulky and expensive. Even if he had used one of the cumbersome old units, obtaining a fix required the operator to match up two wave forms on an oscilloscope screen. It would have taken all the joy out of fishing for Cecil. I wonder now if the risk of getting lost in the fog was part of the fun of fishing for my dear friend. Access to a modern GPS Navigator would have ended Cecil's difficulties, but his own unique form of navigation appealed to him more; he never strayed too far and he always came home.   K.M.

Once a route has been set up in memory and your GPS Navigator instructed to follow it, the process is automatic, reliable, and instantaneous. The GPS Navigator operates in real time—except for a few unimportant milliseconds—and when it displays a position or other navigational data, the information is completely up-to-date.

Manufacturers are constantly changing the way they display information in order to differentiate their products; unfortunately this means they have been unable to agree on similar procedures for storing and recalling waypoints and routes, and for navigating to a waypoint. *Note:* Be sure that you become familiar with the way your particular unit handles these procedures.

MOB (Man Over Board) Revisited

The **MOB (Man OverBoard)** waypoint is a special type of waypoint that is often activated by a specific MOB key. [Refer to Chapter 1.] If an emergency occurs, a single stroke on the special function key saves the present position as a waypoint and immediately calls up steering instructions to guide you back to the position where you pressed the key. When somebody or something goes over the side, time is crucial in effecting a safe recovery. The procedure is so simple that even if the captain falls overboard, an untrained operator can begin the process of navigating back to the MOB waypoint.

Once MOB is engaged, a **steering diagram** directs you back to the site of the emergency. If the recovery of the man overboard takes some time, a simple procedure allows you to view the co-ordinates of the boat at the time the MOB key was pressed. These co-ordinates are vitally important to the local coast guard or other rescue vessels in the area.

Never delay activating MOB— lives depend on speed. If your vessel travels any distance before you activate MOB, its value can be compromised since the steering diagram directs you back to the point where you *activated* MOB, not necessarily to the person in the water. Once you reach the MOB position and recover your man overboard, deactivate MOB; this erases the MOB waypoint from memory and the GPS Navigator can revert to non-navigating mode.

It's always a good idea to stage a MOB drill by dropping a float in the water and practice returning to it using the MOB feature. Repeat the process until your crew understands how to carry it out correctly and speedily. A successful practice reduces the potential for making mistakes under stress, and it gives the crew confidence in the equipment. *Remember:* You, as skipper, should ensure that your crew and guests are familiar with the procedure for activating the MOB function. Record the MOB procedure on the Quick Reference page and in The Workbook if you have not already done so.

Authors' note: One particular model of GPS has a dual-function MOB/Save key requiring that the key be pressed for three seconds to invoke MOB. If your GPS Navigator has this type of key, be sure that you press it for the required time, and verify that your crew are fully aware of the procedures for activating MOB.

Navigating to a Single Waypoint (GOTO)

The simplest method of navigating is toward a single waypoint—a **GOTO** waypoint or one selected from a waypoint list. Many GPS Navigators have a special key for activating GOTO with a single keystroke so that all you have to do is enter the co-ordinates of the destination waypoint and press GOTO. GOTO is a real time-saver and the simplest method of navigating to a specific location. Each time you engage a new GOTO waypoint it becomes the new destination waypoint.

In an effort to make GPS easier to use, manufacturers have used different names for GOTO. In some units, it is called **Quick Waypoint**; in others, something else. Read your GPS manual to determine if your set has this feature and what it is called. In this book, we always refer to it as GOTO.

A typical GOTO procedure goes something like this:

1. Activate the GOTO display and enter the latitude and longitude of the new destination in the space provided. (Verify that the default latitude and longitude are correct for the hemisphere in which you are navigating.)
2. Press ENTER (or NAV or GOTO). The steering diagram should automatically pop up and give you instructions for navigating to the destination.

[See the section "Following the Steering Diagram" later in this chapter.]

3. Once you arrive at the GOTO waypoint, you can activate GOTO again to proceed to the next in a series of waypoints. Each time you engage a new GOTO waypoint, it becomes the new destination waypoint.

Most GPS sets allow you to select any waypoint from a waypoint list or choose a GOTO waypoint by entering a range or bearing from your present position. By setting the GOTO destination at a pre-existing waypoint, you can make a quick choice from all the waypoints in memory. In fact, in some sets, this may be the only way of activating navigation toward a single waypoint. (Each software package is unique, so check your GPS owner's manual for the section dealing with navigation to a single waypoint.)

When the GPS computer navigates to a single waypoint, your present position automatically becomes the **departure waypoint** of the Course Line. (If your unit asks you to select two waypoints, read the section of your GPS manual that describes routes. When you select two waypoints, you are actually setting up a route—a subject we cover later.)

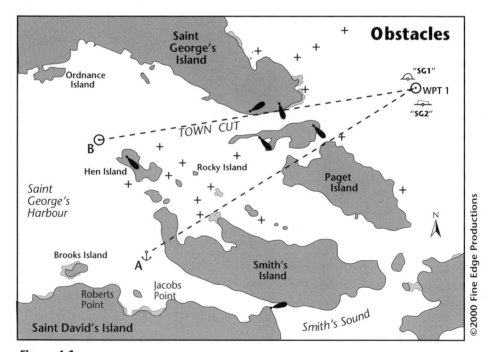

Figure 4.1

From the anchorage at Position A, it would not make sense to navigate directly to a destination waypoint at the east end of Town Cut (WPT 1). Even from position B at the west end of Town Cut, it would not be safe to choose WPT 1 as a destination waypoint.

Caution: The GPS computer navigates from your present position to the destination waypoint, oblivious to any intervening danger such as twenty miles of solid rock, so be sure that your Intended Track passes through safe water [Figure 4.1].

If you find that the Intended Track will indeed take your vessel into a rock pile, you can ignore the steering diagram or turn off the navigation function and proceed visually, engaging it later when no further dangers lie in the way. When

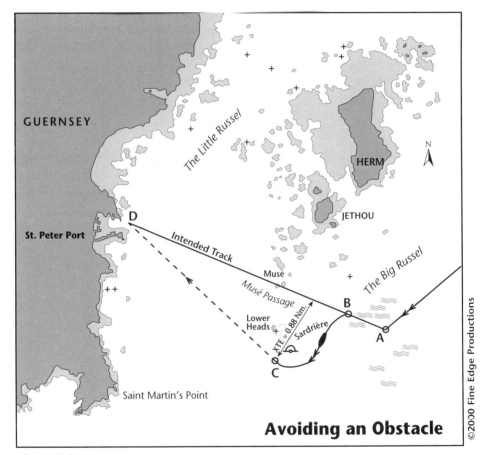

Figure 4.2

While heading southeast through The Big Russel (position A), you instruct the GPS Navigator to begin navigating toward the destination waypoint D. Suddenly, at position B, you realize your Intended Track crosses Musé rock which is covered by tide at the present time, with only its beacon visible. You must alter course to pass south of the buoy at Sardrière. By the time you reach position C, XTE on the steering diagram has reached 0.88 Nm.

    If you restart navigation to the same destination waypoint, a new Course Line is established with the vessel's present position designated as the new point of departure. XTE is reset to zero because your vessel is beginning navigation to the same destination completely afresh.

you re-engage navigation, your GPS Navigator will most likely draw the new Course Line from your present position. As shown in Figure 4.2, this new Course Line will differ significantly from the previous one.

Author's Note: The difference between the GOTO function and MOB is that GOTO places a waypoint at a distance from the present position and directs the operator to that waypoint; MOB places a waypoint at the present position, allowing the operator to return to that position.

Keeping a Waypoint Log

It is essential that you record the relevant details of your waypoints in a Waypoint Log. In addition to allowing you to refer quickly to the waypoints, the log permits you to record information not in the GPS Navigator's memory. (Some of this additional information is extremely useful!)

Group the waypoints according to their general location and include obvious details such as latitude and longitude, chart number, chart datum, and even sketch-maps of the area. If your GPS Navigator should fail, whatever details you choose to include in your Waypoint Log will be easily accessible. The process of taking positions and converting them to waypoints in memory is a tedious process; if you don't record the waypoints on paper or download them to a PC, you may be forced to recalculate them. [See Figure 4.3 and Appendix E for a suggested Waypoint Log.]

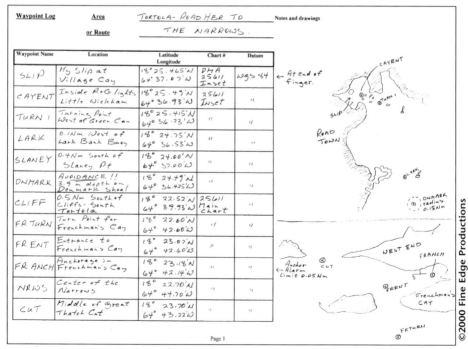

Figure 4.3   A Sample Waypoint Log

The Saved Waypoint and Waypoints Entered by Present Position

The Saved Waypoint is also known as **quicksaved waypoint**, or **temporary waypoint**. It is the easiest type of waypoint to store since it is normally entered by a single keystroke that stores the present position in memory.

In many cases, this waypoint is stored in *temporary* memory which holds a limited number of waypoints. When the temporary memory is full, the navigation computer begins to delete the oldest saved waypoints from its internal waypoint list to make room for new ones (a function based on the premise that you may wish to store a saved waypoint temporarily, having no long-term use for it).

If you want to convert a saved waypoint to permanent memory, you must go through the process dictated by your own particular GPS. *Note:* Record in the **Workbook** both the process of *storing* saved waypoints and the process of *converting* a saved waypoint to *long-term memory*.

If your GPS does not have a **saved waypoint** function, it will have some other procedure for entering a waypoint by present position. *The difference is that waypoints entered by present position are placed into permanent memory.* Some GPS Navigators have both functions. Every manufacturer (if not every model) of GPS Navigator has different options and may specify a different sequence. Familiarize yourself with the process given in your GPS manual and record it in the Workbook.

Initially, when you activate the function, you are prompted with a message such as "Enter present position as waypoint?" Press enter for "yes." You are then asked to name the waypoint and press ENTER again. This will enter the waypoint into permanent storage.

In the fairy tale, Hansel and Gretel went into a dismal forest to find the witch's home, leaving behind them a trail of bread crumbs as a guide in case they got lost. There are numerous times when you might want to leave such a trail behind your boat, but seagulls would eat most of the crumbs and the remainder would sink or drift away. However, a route constructed of waypoints based on the present position leaves a trail of waypoints behind you, allowing you to retrace your route at a later time. This function is particularly useful in areas of numerous shoals or branching channels. Once you have found a good route, you can use it again and again by converting it to permanent memory.

Another advantage to using waypoints based on the present position is that chart datum is essentially irrelevant. If you change the datum in the GPS Navigator, the computer changes the co-ordinates of all stored waypoints to the new datum. (See the sidebar "Chart Datum Conflicts" at the end of this chapter.) But since a saved waypoint is not referenced to any particular co-ordinate system, even though the co-ordinates may change in the GPS Navigator's memory, they continue to refer to the same physical position.

Returning to a Saved Waypoint

Though a saved waypoint may represent the easiest way to store a GPS position, be aware that when you return to a saved waypoint, you are depending on the repeatability of GPS, which may not be as accurate as the predictability of a waypoint taken directly from a large-scale chart.

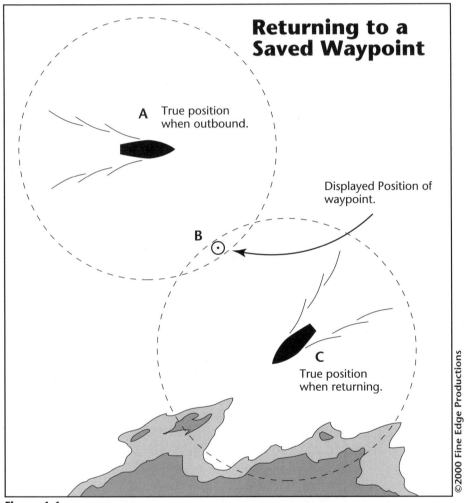

Figure 4.4

When outbound, the skipper saves a waypoint at Position A. At this time, the GPS error is at an extreme value of approximately 30 meters to the southeast, and the GPS Navigator saves the co-ordinates of the displayed position (Position B). When the vessel returns to the saved waypoint, the GPS Navigator shows the lat/long co-ordinates of Position B. However, in the time between the outbound and return trip, the ionospheric error has changed and is now approximately 20 meters to the northwest. Thus the true position of the vessel is at Position C—almost 60 meters away from the place where the skipper saved the waypoint— even though the GPS Navigator shows that the vessel has returned to exactly the same place.

Because the GPS Navigator saves the waypoint without reference to a chart, you have no way of knowing how close the lat/long co-ordinates entered into the GPS memory are to the true co-ordinates of your position. [See Figure 4.4.] When you return to the same position as indicated by your GPS, the error could be cumulative—in other words you might be the same distance from the waypoint, but in the opposite direction. Thus the 20-meter GPS error could accumulate to 40 meters, and in times of extreme solar activity, this figure could be even larger.

We strongly recommend that if you save waypoints based on the present position, you allow a large margin for error and that, when you first return to the waypoint, you visually verify that the waypoint has been placed exactly where you want it.

Entering a Waypoint by Latitude and Longitude

The most common method of entering a waypoint into a GPS Navigator is to enter its latitude and longitude and give it a name by which to store it. Refer to your GPS manual for instructions. Once you are familiar with the necessary keystrokes, record them in The Workbook.

Mark the desired position of the waypoint on the chart, using a fine pencil. Write down the co-ordinates immediately *before* you enter them into the GPS memory. Recording them reduces keystroke errors to a minimum—after you enter twenty or thirty waypoints in a row it's easy to make a mistake! (Long strings of numbers are impossible to remember while you are pressing the buttons!) Remember: When you have completed entering the co-ordinates, record them directly into your Waypoint Log.

Practicing With Your GPS Navigator

Even if it is disconnected from its antenna, your GPS may still be able to accept waypoint entry. You may be able to disconnect the antenna, remove the body of the GPS from your wheelhouse and plug it into a power supply at home. In this way, you can practice using all its functions and enter waypoints into its memory in the comfort of your own living room.

Don't be concerned if you need to change a few waypoints later or add a number of them en route; your preparations will give a big head start to your cruising season. Although you may have to make modifications to the waypoints you entered, by practicing at home you can reduce your potential for error and gain confidence in yourself and your equipment.

Caution: Although GPS navigation can offer instant results, you must take time to properly plan your passages!

Default Hemisphere

The two hemispheres of longitude and the two of latitude divide the globe into four quadrants. Unless you specify N or S for latitude and E or W for longitude on your GPS, there will be four possible positions on the surface of the globe with the same lat/long co-ordinates.

A GPS Navigator will supply **default hemispheres** for latitude and longitude. Whether the defaults are N or S latitude and W or E longitude depends on where you purchased your set. GPS Navigators sold in North America use N latitude and W longitude as defaults. Each time you enter a waypoint into memory by latitude and longitude, be sure to identify the correct hemispheres. If you are far from your home waters, in a different quadrant of the globe, change the default hemispheres in your GPS Navigator so you do not have to change N to S and W to E every time you enter a waypoint. (You could easily forget and enter your home hemispheres, creating waypoint position errors of several thousand miles.)

When operating either near the equator or near the 0° or 180° meridians of longitude, be careful to specify the correct hemisphere when you enter a way-

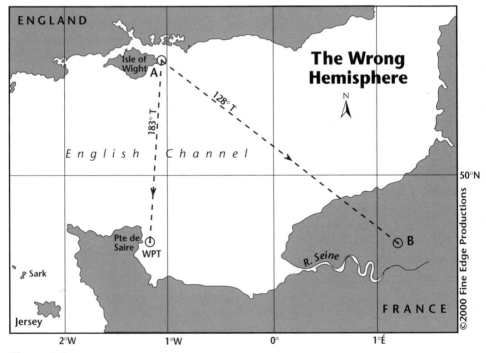

Figure 4.5

Prior to crossing the English Channel from the Isle of Wight (point A) the skipper assigned the waypoint to the east of Pte. De Saire. However, when entering the waypoint in his GPS Navigator, he selected the wrong hemisphere. Instead of entering the position as 49°37' N 1°08' W, he entered 1°08' E, which placed the waypoint at position B, several miles inland.

By activating the GOTO function at position A, it is immediately obvious that the bearing of the waypoint is 128°T, when it should be approximately 183°T.

point. One way to check yourself is to select the waypoint as a GOTO destination and observe its bearing. If the indicated direction doesn't seem correct, you have probably entered the wrong hemisphere [Figure 4.5]. If your software allows you to take the range and bearing of a waypoint from your present position without actually selecting it as a destination waypoint, you can easily check this out.

Entering a Waypoint by Range and Bearing from the Present Position

Entry by range and bearing is a function most commonly used on chart plotters. [See Chapter 10.] If your GPS Navigator offers this option, select the appropriate display, and enter the range and bearing to the proposed waypoint. Your GPS Navigator then displays the latitude and longitude of the resulting position. Name the waypoint and enter the name.

Since the waypoint position is referenced to your present GPS position, these types of waypoint are subject to the same repeatability errors as saved waypoints (see **Returning to a Saved Waypoint**). In addition, when you choose a range and bearing—probably derived from radar—you will be including the inherent errors of the radar as well. Waypoints chosen by this method are generally more unreliable than waypoints chosen by present position; check these waypoints against a large-scale chart before you use them in navigation.

Entering a Waypoint by Loran C Time Differences (TDs)

If you have purchased a GPS Navigator to replace a Loran C receiver, you may have numerous waypoints already stored as **Loran C** co-ordinates or **time differences (TDs)**. Some GPS Navigators allow you to transfer your Loran waypoints; if you have such a unit, you can access the relevant screen or menu function and enter the GRI (Loran C chain) and TDs directly into the Navigator. The TDs will then be converted into lat/long co-ordinates in the GPS memory and the waypoints treated as any waypoint in the GPS waypoint list.

Caution: Due to the fundamentally different methods by which GPS and Loran C obtain position fixes, positions determined with one system do not accurately match those taken from the other

In order to display a Loran C position as lat/long co-ordinates, the Loran C uses conversion software to model the radio propagation delays that are the true cause of its offsets. Offshore, the effect of these propagation delays is well understood and converted positions are often quite accurate, but this is not true for inshore areas.

If you plan to enter the TDs, or the lat/long co-ordinates of those waypoints as given by a Loran C (a miserable task), convert only those waypoints which you can assume to be the most accurate. As a general rule, *enter only those waypoints from TD co-ordinates that actually lie in an area of the chart that is over-*

printed with the Loran C lattice. Also, be aware that equipment manufacturers use different algorithms for modelling Loran C errors so you may be introducing an additional error of up to 150 meters. The irony is that offshore—where accuracy is least important—Loran C and GPS positions are most likely to agree.

Updating a Waypoint

Suppose that, as you navigate to a waypoint, once you actually see the lay of the land, you decide you are not happy with the waypoint position. Rather than deleting it from the waypoint list and entering a corrected waypoint, you can use a simpler method called **Updating** (or **editing**) **a Waypoint**, a feature available in many GPS Navigators.

By calling up the correct screen, you can edit the existing co-ordinates for any particular waypoint. But to do so, you must know its correct co-ordinates.

- Proceed to the correct waypoint position.
- Enter your present position using a single keystroke if your set allows you to update in this way.
- If not, scribble down the co-ordinates of the present position and enter those figures *manually* to update the waypoint.

If your GPS does not permit *either* of the above procedures, proceed to the new waypoint position, delete the existing waypoint, and enter the new waypoint by present position or as a saved waypoint.

Note: If you need maximum accuracy in a waypoint position, enter the waypoint by present position or as a saved waypoint. Lifting positions from a chart is always subject to error and seldom yields a position as precise as a GPS-derived position.

En-route Functions

Before we go deeper into the subject of navigating with waypoints, let's take a look at the information that becomes available once you activate waypoint navigation.

When you initiate navigation toward a destination waypoint, a steering diagram displays various types of information, most of which the computer derives from measurements of its own position relative to any waypoint in effect at the time. These functions are called **en-route functions**, **derived functions**, or **navigation functions**. Your GPS Navigator may display some of these functions, but not all of them—the software writers make the choices.

Below we list a series of definitions of various derived functions [Figure 4.6]. Since British and American conventions differ, we have included both. For certain functions that play no part in traditional navigation—having made their first appearance on the screens of Loran C and GPS Navigators—we do not identify their country of origin.

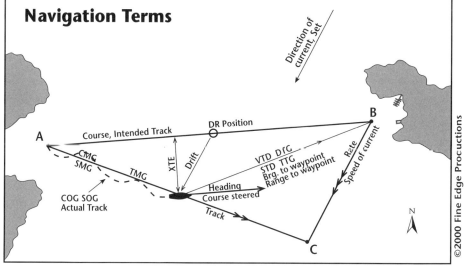

Figure 4.6

Track or **Actual Track** (U.S.): The true path the vessel actually travels.

Brg (Br., U.S.) **Bearing**: The direction of a line joining any two points on the surface of the earth; may be expressed in degrees True or Magnetic. In GPS navigation, it is usually the Bearing to a waypoint from your present position.

Course (Br., U.S.): The direction in which a vessel intends to travel along the **Course Line**. (Some electronic Navigators confuse this with **COG**.)

Course Line (Br., U.S.): Also known as **Intended Track**. The line laid down on the chart to represent the course you wish to follow. It is this **Course Line** that the GPS sets up as the ideal path to follow between two waypoints.

Course to Make Good (Br.): A direction over the ground to be followed by counteracting the effect of current. When counteracting the current, the **Heading** always differs from the **Course to Make Good**.

Course Steered (Br., U.S.): The direction a vessel is steered.

Course to Steer (Br., U.S.): The specific **Course** or **Heading** to steer to ensure that the vessel will counteract the current and follow a particular **Course to Make Good**.

COA (U.S.) **Course of Advance**: (See **Course to Make Good**.) The intended direction over the ground to make good from a vessel's present position to the destination. (Sometimes confused with **COG** and **CMG**.) In the navigational triangle, designated by a double arrowhead.

COG (Br, U.S.) **Course Over the Ground**: The direction of travel at any moment along the **Actual Track**. Since currents can deflect a vessel from its **Intended Track**, this **COG** may depart significantly from the **Course Line**

laid down on the chart. The COG displayed by a GPS Navigator is an *instantaneous value* that changes as the forces acting on the vessel change, thus it does not give an average for the entire run. (It is sometimes confused with CMG.) The difference is subtle; COG is an *instantaneous value;* CMG is calculated over a period of time.

CMG (Br., U.S.) **Course Made Good** (or **Track Made Good [TMG]**): The direction of a line from the point of departure to the position of the vessel. (Sometimes confused with **COG**.) In the navigational triangle, designated by a double arrowhead.

DTG (Br., U.S.) **Distance To Go**: The distance between the present position and the destination measured along a straight line connecting those two points. DTG may refer to the destination waypoint or to the eventual destination, the final waypoint of the route.

Drift (Br., U.S.): The distance, in a direction parallel to the direction or **Set** of the current, that the vessel has been carried from its **DR (Dead Reckoning) position**. If the vessel is stopped in the water, the **drift** is the actual distance travelled over the ground; also, in U.S. usage, the speed of the current. It may also refer to the total movement caused by current and wind.

DR Position (Br., U.S.): The point at which the vessel would have arrived had there been no current or wind; projected by advancing the vessel's position along the **Course Line** a distance equivalent to the distance the vessel travels at its **Speed** through the water over a specific time period.

ETA (Br., U.S.) Estimated Time of Arrival: The time at which it is calculated that the vessel will arrive at the destination based on present speed and Distance to Go. ETA may refer to the destination waypoint or the final waypoint of the route. In some sets, the speed value used may be the SOG, but most likely it is based on the **Velocity Toward Destination** (sometimes called **VMG**).

ETE—**Estimated Time En-route**: The number of hours to complete the trip to the destination; it usually refers to the final destination of the route.

Heading (Br., U.S.): The direction in which a vessel is pointing at any given time. The heading will vary over time and may differ from the **Course** or **Intended Track** if an attempt is made to counteract the force of the current.

Intended Track (U.S.): (See **Course**.)

Rate (Br.): The speed of the current. (See **Drift**.)

Range (Br., U.S.): A distance to a pre-selected target; in GPS navigation this is usually, but not always, the **Range** to a waypoint measured along the line of **Bearing** from the present position.

Set (Br., U.S.): The direction of the current. Unlike measurements of the direction of the wind, identified by the direction it is blowing from, **Set** is identified by the direction the current is moving toward; in a tidal triangle it is designated by a triple arrow head.

Speed (Br., U.S.): The speed of the vessel through the water as measured by a speed log.

SMG (Br., U.S.) **Speed Made Good**: The speed of the vessel along the **Course Made Good**; i.e., along the straight line joining the point of departure and the present position.

SOA (U.S.) **Speed of Advance**: (Also known as **Speed to Make Good**. Sometimes confused with **SMG**.) The speed required to make good an intended speed over the ground in order to arrive at an intended time or position.

SOG (Br., U.S.) **Speed Over the Ground**: The speed of the vessel at any instant along its **Actual Track** over the ground. The **SOG** may differ significantly from the **Speed** through the water. For instance, a slow vessel working against a strong current may have its **SOG** reduced to almost nothing. **SOG** will change as the forces acting on the vessel change, thus it will not give an average for the entire run. Sometimes it is confused with **SMG**, especially when all the forces acting on the vessel are constant. The difference is subtle: **SMG** is calculated over a period of time; **SOG** *is an instantaneous value.*

STD—Speed Toward Destination (also known as **VTD**, **Velocity Towards Destination**): The speed at which the vessel closes on the destination waypoint. It is measured in one of two separate ways and may differ significantly from any other speed value (see below).

VTD—Velocity Toward Destination: [Figure 4.7]. (See also **STD**.)

VMG (Br., U.S.) **Velocity Made Good**: another version of **STD**.

XTE (Br., U.S.) **Cross Track Error**: The perpendicular distance of the vessel at any time from the **Course Line**. This value is displayed on the steering diagram.

Some, if not all, of the above information becomes available once the GPS Navigator begins to navigate toward a specific waypoint.

Note: Be aware that there are subtle differences between some of these functions, for example, **COG** and **CMG**, or **SOG** and **VTD**. Although the differences may seem inconsequential, it is a good idea to study your GPS owner's manual thoroughly for the definitions of your particular software. (Some manufacturers do not follow these naming conventions and may even use terms interchangeably.)

Because manufacturers of GPS units build their products for a number of different uses, such as aviation, mountaineering, and backpacking, they have not yet standardized their terminology. We have been told that the terminology will

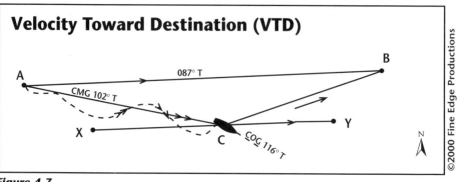

Figure 4.7

Some GPS Navigators calculate VTD based on the speed at which the distance reduces along a line (CB), drawn from the present position to the destination waypoint. Others calculate VTD based on the speed of progress of the vessel along a line parallel to the original Course Line (XY).

soon settle into a common standard as marine, aviation, and land navigation terms are combined into a single electronic navigation language. That will certainly make life simpler for all of us.

The Steering Diagram

There are two types of steering diagrams in common use; some GPS Navigators are capable of displaying both or more. The traditional style, the **Course Deviation**

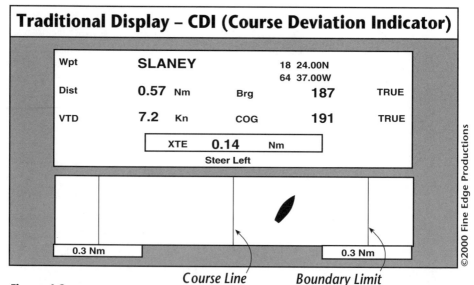

Figure 4.8

In this example, the steering diagram indicates that you should steer left to bring the vessel back on to the Course Line. Note that the COG is 191°, and the XTE is 0.14 Nm to the right of the Intended Track. The vessel icon in the lower screen is clearly a few degrees off the proper heading.

Indicator (CDI) [Figure 4.8], is available in one form or another in virtually all GPS Navigators. Navigation information, which normally appears at the top of the screen, may include the name of the destination waypoint, its bearing and range and other information considered important. *Note:* All steering diagrams display the Cross Track Error (XTE) and the direction in which to steer to regain the Course Line.

The lower portion of the screen displays a simple horizontal bar with the vertical Course Line centered in the middle. Somewhere along the bar is an icon of a stylized ship; to either side are the boundaries of the XTE limits. You can usually adjust these XTE boundaries by calling up another screen.

In recent years, the **Perspective Display (Road Display)** [Figure 4.9] has become the most popular type of display. A perspective display provides a 3-D representation of the Course Line to be followed. The destination waypoint, represented on the center line (the Course Line), appears to advance toward the ship icon as the vessel advances toward its destination waypoint.

The vessel in the display is shown heading in the direction indicated by the COG. The clear lane, shown in perspective—with the waypoint apparently in the distance—represents the area in which the vessel can operate without exceeding the XTE limits. (These limits are indicated at the lower left and right of the display.) The entire display is graphic and intuitive; we prefer it to the traditional display.

The most important pieces of information in either type of display are Cross Track Error (XTE) and Bearing to the Waypoint (Brg to Wpt).

Customizing the Steering Diagram

Once you identify your destination waypoint and begin navigating to it, the steering diagram should supply you with en-route data. Some GPS Navigators, however, force you to switch to another display for this important information;

Figure 4.9

A perspective display provides information in graphic form, making it easier to understand. The vessel is shown in relationship to the next waypoint and any other waypoints in the vicinity.

Photograph courtesy of Northstar Technologies Ltd.

others allow you to customize the steering diagram to display *any* information you desire. If you have a unit that allows customizing, we suggest you include the following: COG; SOG; VTD; range and bearing to the waypoint; XTE; name of the destination waypoint and its latitude and longitude; latitude and longitude of the present position; the correct time. With most GPS Navigators, you cannot display all this information on the steering diagram, so be sure you are familiar with the procedures for calling up the displays which show these useful data. Enter the procedures in The Workbook.

Following the Steering Diagram

As you move along the Course Line, your vessel inevitably drifts off the Intended Track. It is impossible to tell immediately whether the drift is due to small variations in steering or to current or wind. Watch the bearing to the destination waypoint for a while before you take any action. Small variations of one or two degrees are not important (not even the most experienced helmsmen on the largest ships can steer a course to within one degree). In fact, on a small vessel where the compass may be graduated in five-degree increments, steering performance is inevitably far less exact. Your position wanders back and forth from one side of the Course Line to the other unless there is current acting on your boat; the bearing changes in a corresponding manner, as well. Watch your bearing for a while; if it continues to change more than one or two degrees, you should change your heading by small increments until your heading matches the bearing to the waypoint. *Remember:* The COG will wander by several degrees due to the inherent GPS error, especially at low speeds. If the bearing remains constant and matches your compass heading within one or two degrees, you are doing well and should maintain your heading. If the bearing begins to change again, repeat the procedure.

A quick check of XTE tells you how far you have drifted from the Intended Track. If XTE is extreme, or if you are navigating in tight quarters, you should compensate for the current.

The simplest way to compensate for current is to alter your heading in small increments until the COG matches the bearing to the waypoint. However, this is not as easy as it sounds since the COG is not usually very stable, and the change in COG lags behind the changes in heading. After a while you may find you have over-steered and are now on the opposite side of the course line. This is why manufacturers have included the Cross Track Error display in virtually all GPS Navigators.

The steering diagram will indicate that you should steer right or left, as the case may be. But by how much? In this situation, use the rule of thumb illustrated in Figure 4.10.

Suppose that your vessel, starting at Point A, heads 150°T to follow the Intended Track toward Point B. Since the COG readout always varies a few

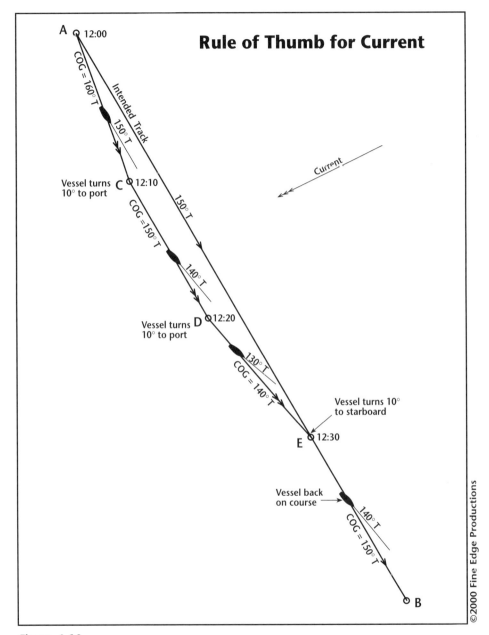

Rule of Thumb for Current

A 12:00

COG = 160° T

Intended Track

150° T

Vessel turns C 12:10
10° to port

COG = 150° T

150° T

Current

140° T

Vessel turns D 12:20
10° to port

130° T

COG = 140° T

Vessel turns 10°
to starboard

E 12:30

Vessel back
on course

140° T

COG = 150° T

B

©2000 Fine Edge Productions

Figure 4.10

A boat departs position A at noon, heading 150°T for destination waypoint B. By 1200 it is apparent that the boat has been deflected from its Intended Track by 10°. At position C, the heading is altered to 140°T, keeping the vessel on a track that parallels the original Course Line. At 1220, position D, the heading is again altered to 130°T. By 1230, the vessel has regained the Course Line, and by altering the heading to 140°T, the boat follows the Intended Track.

degrees, it is no surprise that it varies from 158°T to 163° T. Since you cannot observe the CMG directly, you infer that it is best represented by an *average* of the various COG values over a few minutes. You arrive at an average figure of 160°T, concluding that the current is forcing the vessel 10 degrees to the right of its Intended Track.

At 1210 hours when XTE is at a value of 0.3 Nm, you alter your heading 10 degrees to the left to 140°T in an effort to cancel the effect of the current.

However, after a while you notice that your boat is not regaining the Intended Track. Rather, it is paralleling the Course Line as laid out on the chart, and XTE remains more or less the same at 0.3 Nm. Although you have succeeded in negating the effect of the current, you are no closer to regaining the Intended Track and reducing XTE to zero. So, you must alter the heading even more to the left to bring your vessel back on the Course Line.

By doubling the amount of **deflection (drift angle)** caused by the current, you achieved your goal in 10 minutes, approximately the same amount of time spent being driven off course by the current. In other words, at 1220, by altering an additional 10 degrees to the left to 130°T, you regain the track by 1230. This tells you that you must apply opposite helm to counteract the deflection. The degree of opposite helm you must apply is known as the **lead angle**, which under these current conditions is 10 degrees. Thus, by heading 140°T, once you regain the Intended Track you should be able to maintain the proper CMG.

Unfortunately, current conditions caused by tidal action never remain stable, and the corrections you apply by rule of thumb are only approximate. By observing XTE, however, you can make good the proper course by adjusting the heading a little to the left or right to keep XTE within reasonable limits.

Do not attempt to follow every slight variation of the XTE. With a little practice, you should be able to perform these calculations almost unconsciously, without having to plot positions on a chart (advantageous on small boats where there is often a lack of a decent chart table). The chart should be available for quick reference, but the primary work of navigation is done in your head and by the GPS Navigator.

[For a more detailed look at the effects of current on navigation, see Chapters 6 and 7; for a more precise procedure for determining the magnitude of the required course alteration to regain the Intended Track, see Appendix F.]

The One in Sixty Rule

A change of bearing at relatively close range represents a small XTE, but a change of bearing at long range represents a much larger XTE. The **one in sixty rule** is a simple guide. Simply put, an angle of one degree represents a difference of one mile at a distance of sixty miles. An angle of five degrees represents a difference of five miles at the same distance, and so on.

Waypoint Realization

Most GPS Navigators allow you to specify an **arrival radius** that defines an arrival circle—an imaginary circle drawn around the destination waypoint. When your vessel enters the arrival circle, the waypoint is said to be **realized** or **arrived**; navigation ceases, and the display either freezes or clears itself of all references to that particular waypoint.

If you are slightly off course when approaching a destination waypoint, notice that the bearing to the waypoint begins to change rapidly until the waypoint passes abeam and begins to draw astern. Do not try to follow this bearing once it begins its rapid swing. There is no point in trying to cross a GPS waypoint exactly; you will rarely succeed in doing so.

Avoidance Waypoints

Most modern GPS Navigators allow you to select certain waypoints as **danger** or **avoidance** waypoints around which you can set an avoidance alarm limit. The geographic features you choose as avoidance waypoints can be as varied as buoys, submerged rocks or shoals, drying or exposed rocks, or even points of land [Figures 4.11 and 4.12].

When you choose an avoidance radius, allow for a margin of safety. We recommend using a standard margin of 0.10 Nm. As an added precaution, most GPS Navigators do not permit you to use an avoidance waypoint as a destination waypoint.

Caution: If your GPS Navigator does allow you to choose an avoidance waypoint as a destination, be sure you identify avoidance waypoints as such in your Waypoint Log, and be aware that you approach the waypoint at your peril.

Some GPS Navigators display the avoidance circle on a perspective steering diagram, which is an excellent feature. If yours has this feature, a quick glance at the display tells you if you are in danger of entering an avoidance zone. For example, in a perspective display,

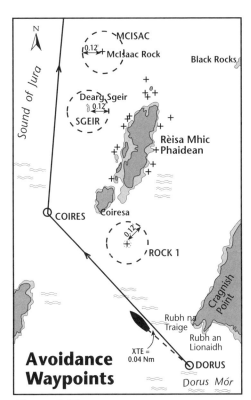

Figure 4.11

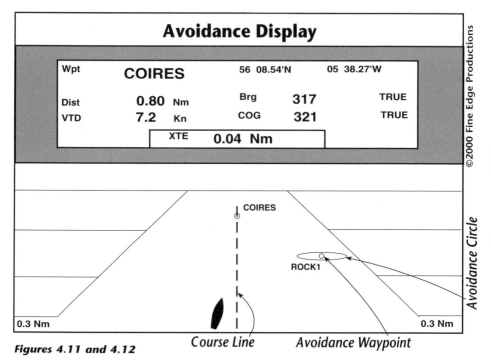

Figures 4.11 and 4.12

In Figure 4.11, avoidance waypoints have been selected for three navigational hazards. Each has an avoidance radius of 0.12 Nm. During the transit from wpt DORUS to wpt COIRES, the perspective display will show a diagram similar to that in Figure 4.12.

if an isolated rock previously identified as an avoidance waypoint lies on your Intended Track, the danger will appear directly in line with the destination waypoint.

Rather than setting up new waypoints to navigate around the danger, you can simply steer around the avoidance area and come back onto the Course Line [Figures 4.13 and 4.14].

Waypoints and Chart Datum

As noted in the previous chapter, to get maximum performance from your set, you must take into account the horizontal datum used in each chart. This is particularly important where a route consists partially of saved waypoints and partially of waypoints taken from a chart. For this reason, when you enter waypoints into memory, *be sure that the datum shown on the GPS and that of the chart are the same. Record the datum in your Waypoint Log beside each waypoint entry.*

When navigating to a destination waypoint, be sure that your GPS is switched to the correct datum for that destination. Since a route can span several charts, each with its own datum, you may have to switch once or twice while transiting a route.

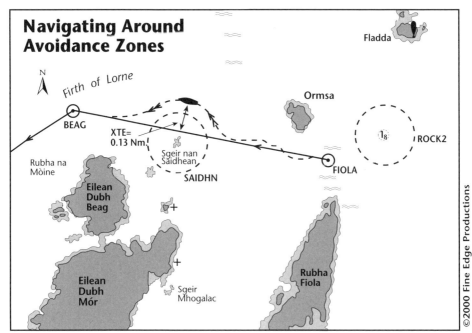

Figure 4.13

Avoidance waypoints have been selected at the 1.8 meter rock, east of Ormsa, and at Sgeir nan Saidhean. During the transit from wpt FIOLA to wpt BEAG, the Intended Track passes through the avoidance zone around SAIDHN. In these confined waters there are heavy tidal currents at spring tides so you must pay particular attention. While going around the avoidance zone, the steering diagram would appear as shown in Figure 4.14.

Every so often a new chart consistent with WGS 84 is issued to replace a chart that was drawn to an older datum. If you are navigating with a new chart, and the waypoints in memory were taken from the old chart, it is still safe to set your GPS to the new datum. The old waypoints were accurate before, and when converted to WGS 84, all that changes are the co-ordinates describing the waypoint. *Make a note in your Waypoint Log that it is safe to convert to the new datum on the new chart.*

As demonstrated in the sidebar "Chart Datum Conflicts," GPS waypoints are a matter of personal choice and, if more than one person is inputting waypoints, confusion can develop. When you use a destination waypoint selected by someone else, *verify that it is positioned exactly where you want it*. If you share the same GPS Navigator with others, keep your own personal waypoints in a separate section of the GPS memory to ensure that you know exactly where you are headed!

Alarms and Alarm Zones

Most modern GPS receivers allow you to set different types of alarm zones, such as avoidance alarms, arrival alarms, anchor watch alarms, loss of signal alarms,

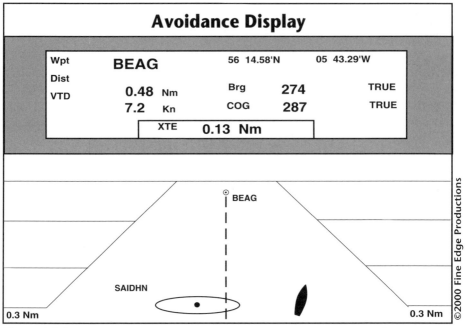

Avoidance Display

Wpt	**BEAG**	56 14.58'N		05 43.29'W
Dist		Brg	**274**	TRUE
VTD	**0.48** Nm			
	7.2 Kn	COG	**287**	TRUE
	XTE	**0.13 Nm**		

©2000 Fine Edge Productions

0.3 Nm   0.3 Nm

Figure 4.14

and XTE alarms. Below is a discussion of the two most common alarm features. The rest are self-explanatory. All alarms should provide visual and audible indications of an alarm condition.

Anchor Watch Alarm

By activating the **anchor watch alarm**, your GPS Navigator establishes a temporary waypoint at your present position, then monitors your vessel's movement as it swings about the waypoint. When you set up the anchor watch alarm, you are prompted to enter an anchor alarm radius. If your vessel moves beyond this radius, the GPS Navigator detects that the limit has been violated and sounds the alarm. This feature can help skippers avoid spending sleepless stormy nights watching radars and depth sounders.

The anchor watch alarm does have limitations, however. When your vessel swings at anchor, it describes a circle around the anchor in response to wind and tide; the shallower the anchorage, the smaller the circle. The radius of the alarm zone must be equal to the *expected horizontal distance* the vessel can swing in any one direction plus the GPS potential error of 20 meters, plus a little margin—perhaps 50 meters. If your anchorage is only 100 meters or so in its smallest dimension, the alarm circle will be larger than the anchorage area itself. In this case, if you were to set the radius to less than 100 meters, the alarm would go off all night as GPS errors and the swing of the vessel at anchor continually vio-

Chart Datum Conflicts
[Figures 4.15 A-F]

One day, shortly after a crew change, I discovered a waypoint named FOGRKS in the waypoint list. I did not recall having entered it myself, so as I travelled north through the area I decided to do some checking.

The meridian 127°55′ passes almost exactly through Fog Rocks on Chart 3785 (NAD27). At that time, my GPS was set to NAD27. I brought the boat onto the meridian, headed due north and sighted the light on the rocks dead ahead. I activated GOTO toward waypoint FOGRKS, and the GPS indicated the longitude as 127°55.007′ W [A]. Once settled into the new heading, I checked the steering diagram [B] which indicated I would pass to the west of FOGRKS with about 0.1 Nm to spare [C]. Obviously something was wrong.

When I switched the GPS Navigator to WGS84 datum, nothing changed except the displayed latitude and longitude of my vessel and the waypoint FOGRKS [D]. The indication was that I would pass to the west of FOGRKS by about the same distance [E]. By switching datums all I had achieved was to shift both the vessel's present position and the waypoint FOGRKS to the west by about 150 meters. I confirmed this by observing the change in my longitude, which now read 127°55.172′ W. But when I checked the co-ordinates of the waypoint, the longitude of FOGRKS was displayed as 128°55.000′ W, significantly to the east of my heading line, but right where it should have been on an NAD27 chart.

Neither the waypoint nor my boat had actually moved, nor had Fog Rocks of course. Instead, the lat/long grid had been shifted to the east so that the position co-ordinates of both my boat and the waypoint had changed. I could tell the boat was still heading directly for Fog Rocks even though the GPS indicated that my heading was to the west of the danger. I turned the boat away from the rocks and continued to think about the situation.

It became clear to me that, when the co-ordinates were taken from the chart and the way-point entered into memory, the GPS had been set on WGS 84. But the co-ordinates of the waypoint had been taken from a chart drawn to NAD 27. Consequently, the GPS assigned the position of the waypoint to the east of the rocks by almost 150 meters. When I switched the GPS to WGS 84, the co-ordinates of the waypoint in memory were adjusted so that the position matched that of Fog Rocks on the chart, even though the chart was drawn to a different datum. The relationship between the vessel and the waypoint had not changed. But no matter which datum I switched to, the problem remained, because whoever had originally entered the waypoint had not correctly identified the position and chart datum in the first place; correcting the datum in the GPS Navigator had not resolved the situation. An additional problem was that the waypoint—probably selected to represent the danger of Fog Rocks—had not been entered as an avoidance waypoint.

Since it was a clear day, I could see that we were headed toward Fog Rocks. It took time, however, to figure out the problem—time I might not have been able to afford under different conditions. At a time when GPS was still quite new, the situation did nothing to bolster my confidence in GPS until I had resolved the problem!

Caution: To avoid such problems, always select and enter waypoints using the same datum as the chart you are using, and always navigate to that waypoint using the same datum. Where two charts drawn to different datums cover the same area, be sure to record both the datum of the chart and its number. (That is why there is a space for the chart datum and number in each entry of your Waypoint Log.) If you don't know which datum was used when the waypoint was entered, provide enough margin for error. In this case, the margin should have been GPS error (20 meters), plus the datum difference (150 meters), plus 100 meters margin for a total of 270 meters, almost 0.15 Nm.

Chart Datum Conflicts

A. The True Situation

B. The Steering Diagram while Set to NAD 27

C. Situation That Might Be Assumed from the Steering Diagram

D. The Steering Diagram after Switching to WGS 84

E. Situation That Might Be Assumed from the Steering Diagram

©2000 Fine Edge Productions

Figure 4.15 A–E

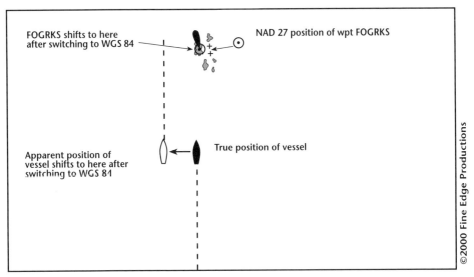

F. What Actually Happened

Figure 4.15 F   Chart Datum Conflicts

lated the alarm circle limits. If you set the radius too high, your vessel would drag anchor and beach itself long before your alarm was triggered!

The alarm is useful for small boats in spacious anchorages, as well as for larger vessels that keep an anchor watch at night. Since most anchor alarms are not strong enough to awaken you from a deep sleep, you might consider having it connected to a loud buzzer.

Note: The anchor watch alarm must be engaged *when and where you drop your anchor* (not after your vessel has settled into position), otherwise the alarm zone centers on the vessel itself, not on the anchor which is the actual center of the vessel's swing.

Cross Track Error (XTE) Alarms and Boundary Limits

The XTE Alarm is designed to indicate that your vessel has strayed beyond the limits of Cross Track Error. XTE Boundary Limits are chosen with safety in mind to draw attention to the fact that your boat may have entered an unsafe area and needs to be brought within safe boundaries. When this alarm sounds, pay attention!

If XTE limits are irrelevant to the leg you are navigating, you can turn off the alarm sound, not the alarm itself, and your GPS Navigator should still display a visual indication of an alarm situation.

Caution: To allow for possible GPS error and still provide a margin of safety, always set XTE limits so that the XTE boundary is at least 0.1 Nm from any danger.

Anchor Watch Alarms

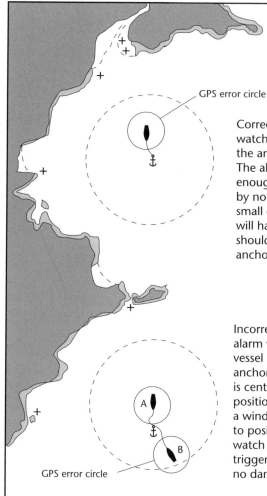

GPS error circle

Correct — the anchor watch alarm is centered on the anchor, not the boat. The alarm circle is large enough not to be triggered by normal GPS error, but small enough that the crew will have time to react should the vessel drag anchor.

GPS error circle

Incorrect — the anchor alarm was engaged once the vessel had settled on the anchor. Thus the alarm circle is centered on the boat's position at that time. When a wind shift moves the vessel to position B, the anchor watch alarm will eventually trigger, even though there is no danger.

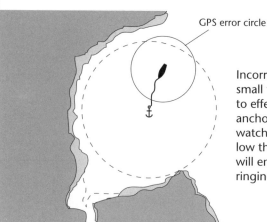

GPS error circle

Incorrect — this cove is too small to allow the skipper to effectively use the anchor watch. The anchor watch limit has been set so low that normal GPS error will ensure the alarm is ringing all night.

When setting up a route, most GPS Navigators apply the same XTE limits to every leg of a route, so you must choose a XTE limit for the entire route equal to the smallest *safe* XTE associated with any leg of your route.

Some GPS Navigators allow you to select different XTE limits for each leg, so if you choose this feature, *record the safe XTE limits associated with each leg of the route.* (We suggest using this feature sparingly; it is best not to resort to setup procedures when you switch waypoints, especially in tight quarters or under stressful circumstances.)

Different steering diagrams handle boundary limits differently. Some show the actual XTE boundary as the width of the clear lane in a perspective display. Others show only a standard lane width no matter what boundary limits have been chosen, in which case the steering diagram gives you no visual indication of the boundary.

The clear lane shown in Figures 4.12 and 4.14 implies that XTE boundary has been set at 0.3 Nm, but this may not be the case at all—it may be 0.25 Nm or 0.40 Nm. The only indication that you have strayed outside the boundary is a flashing symbol or the sounding of an alarm buzzer, so be alert to the XTE display and ensure that it does not exceed the pre-set limit. *Caution:* If your GPS is configured in this manner, never turn off the alarm sound or you may forget and think that the displayed boundaries are real boundaries when in fact they are not.

To determine how your GPS configures the boundary function, begin navigating to a waypoint while testing several different alarm widths. Each time, return to the perspective display to see if the actual XTE boundary limits are displayed at each edge of the clear lane. If the indicated widths remain the same, your GPS Navigator does not display selected boundary limits and you must depend on the XTE alarm.

Figure 4.16   Anchor Watch Alarms

Upper
Correct—the anchor watch alarm is centered on the anchor, not the boat. The alarm circle is large enough not to be triggered by normal GPS error, but small enough that the crew will have time to react should the vessel drag anchor.

Middle
Incorrect—the anchor alarm was engaged once the vessel had settled on the anchor. Thus the alarm circle is centered on the boat's position at that time. When a wind shift moves the vessel to position B, the anchor watch alarm will eventually trigger, even though there is no danger.

Lower
Incorrect—this cove is too small to allow the skipper to effectively use the anchor watch. The anchor watch limit has been set so low that normal GPS error will ensure that the alarm is ringing all night.

Data Input

We have mentioned many times in this book that there is no standardization in GPS software. Each manufacturer has experimented with software configurations, keyboard layouts and extras. The resulting polyglot "GPS-speak" can be discouraging to the beginner. However, once you have mastered one GPS Navigator, you will find that accessing the functions of another is much easier because you know what to look for.

As if to prove that GPS manufacturers can come up with a standard when they want to, one trend has become common: sets devoid of alphanumeric keys where a cursor or collection of arrow buttons is substituted instead. This not only saves money, but allows the manufacture of smaller GPS Navigators—some no larger than a cellular telephone. Although the reduced size of these units is an advantage [Figure 1.4], when you attempt to enter numbers or letters, the arrows and menus you have to negotiate are cumbersome. *Lack of input keys can make data entry a time-consuming experience!*

Alphanumeric keyboards were the standard for past generations of GPS Navigators [Figure 4.17] and mariners found them completely adequate for entering data.

As the capabilities and functions of GPS equipment become more complex, and more choices are offered to the user, the problem of how commands should be entered arises—by menus or by special function keys, or by both?

Menus are best kept simple and only one or two levels deep. They obviously work best with arrow keys; thus the use of menus in the software structure works well with the simple keyboards found in much of the more inexpensive equipment. Special function keys, on the other hand, reverse the trend toward miniaturization because they take up extra space on the keyboard—not a popular option with manufacturers.

The ideal system uses a combination of the above in a manner which is easily understandable and which allows the user to operate the unit with little reference to a manual. Where ambiguities exist, the display itself prompts the oper-

Photograph courtesy of Magellan Systems Corporation

Figure 4.17 GPS Navigator with Keyboard

This older model of a hand-held GPS has a well-organized alphanumeric keyboard, a waterproof casing, and general ruggedness, which account for its popularity.

ator to press the correct button. This requires a screen large enough to display the prompts, with context sensitive soft keys—the most recent innovation— arranged around the edges of the display. Soft keys are not labeled at all. As you access one display, the labels for the keys appear on the display beside the key. When you choose another display, each soft key assumes a new label and a new function. By an intelligent mix of soft keys, menus, special function keys, and alphanumeric keyboards, some manufacturers have been able to create a GPS Plotter/Navigator which is easy to use and requires very little reference to the owner's manual [Figure 10.11]—a notable feat!

CHAPTER 5

Route Navigation

What Is a Route?

A route is a collection of two or more waypoints that describes a path of travel between an initial waypoint and a final waypoint. It can be as simple as the direct-line path from your favourite fishing spot to a harbour entrance, or as complex as a course along the coast to a distant harbour. The simplest route (navigation to a single waypoint) always begins at your present position and proceeds in a straight line to your destination. A more complex route requires numerous intermediate waypoints between the initial waypoint and the eventual destination. Your GPS Navigator calculates the Course Line (or Lines) and the distance between waypoints. The Course Line between two successive waypoints is called a **leg**.

Depending on the age and model of your GPS Navigator, you may be able to create and store as many as a hundred routes or more, each consisting of several legs. Your GPS owner's manual contains information regarding the route capability of your unit. For an example of a route see Figures 5.2 and 5.3.

Each route is a unique trade-off of many factors that reflect the needs of each individual. The more complex the natural environment is, the greater the possible number of routes between starting and ending points. A prudent skipper develops multiple routes to the same destination to take into account different weather conditions or places of interest along the way. A route can be used just once then deleted from memory, or it can be used numerous times. It can also be reversed to end at a starting waypoint such as a dock or a slip where the vessel is moored.

Some skippers find the route set-up process tedious and are satisfied to use GOTO to navigate to a series of single waypoints. However, using the route capability of your GPS can significantly simplify your voyages.

Creating a Route (Setting up a Route)

The first step in **creating a route** is to identify the waypoints you wish to use. Select the waypoints from the ones you previously stored in memory and which appear in the GPS Navigator's waypoint list. If you did not previously store these waypoints in memory, you must do so now before you include them in the route.

Some GPS Navigators allow you to enter waypoints into the waypoint list during the route set-up process—a handy feature.

All GPS Navigators use the same basic principles, but the actual procedures and options associated with creating a route are as varied as snowflakes; there is no standard. Refer to your GPS manual to determine how your unit handles routes. Be sure you understand all the options, then record what you have learned in The Workbook.

To create a route, the usual procedure is to call up a specific route-creation display. The initial prompt may ask for a route name of your choice. Next it prompts you to enter the names and numbers that identify the waypoints you wish to include. (Your GPS Navigator will not allow you to enter avoidance waypoints into a route.) Enter the waypoints in the order in which you wish to travel, verifying that the sequence of waypoints is correct before you proceed to the next step.

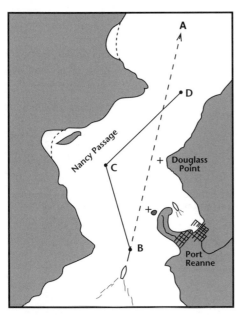

Figure 5.1
Mid-Channel Fever

When the skipper says "Steer a mid-channel course," the natural tendency for an inexperienced helmsman is to steer for point A, which appears to be correct. A glance at the chart however, will show that this heading will place the vessel perilously close to the rock off Douglass Point. Also, the helmsman may suddenly encounter another vessel at close quarters departing Port Réanne.

By assigning waypoints at points B, C and D, the skipper has created a truly mid-channel route for the helmsman to follow.

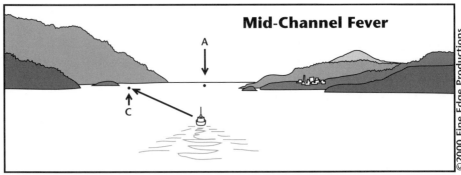

Mid-Channel Fever

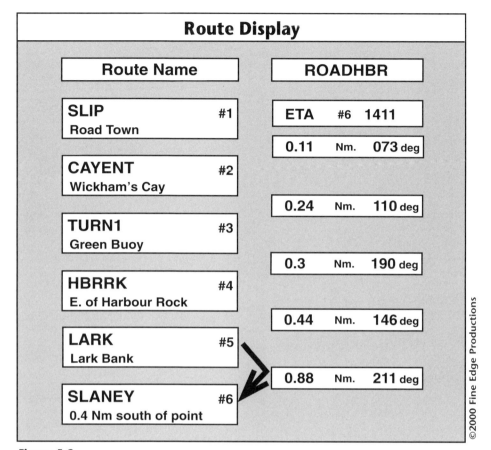

Figure 5.2

A route as shown in a Routes display. The arrow-shaped symbol in the center column indicates the leg being navigated. The same route is shown in Figure 5.3. This route uses the waypoints listed in the waypoint log in Chapter 4, Figure 4.3.

The route name is located at the top of the right hand column. Just below is a box indicating the Estimated Time of Arrival at waypoint #6, SLANEY, the final waypoint. In the right hand column below the ETA, are the ranges and bearings between waypoints. Thus, leg 5, (LARK to SLANEY) is 0.88 Nm in a direction of 211°. When you instruct the GPS Navigator to reverse the route, it automatically displays the corrected new bearings.

Verifying Waypoints in a Route

Since data entry errors frequently occur when you set up a route, pay careful attention to the numbers and letters as you enter them. It is good practice to keep a Route Log in which you record all the details of the routes you create; *this is not the same as a Waypoint Log*, since it includes only the waypoints that define the legs of the route. (We provide a sample Route Log in Appendix F; this log is similar to the route display of many GPS Navigators.)

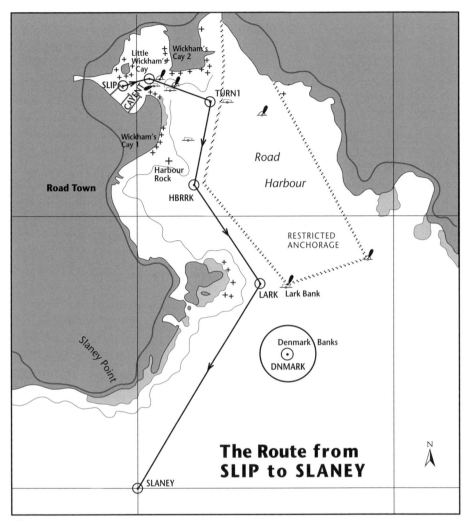

The Route from SLIP to SLANEY

N

Figure 5.3

On your chart, using dividers and parallel rules, measure the range and bearing from the first waypoint to the second, the second waypoint to the third and so on, until you have completed the entire route. Record the co-ordinates and the ranges and bearings in your Route Log.

Once you have created the route in memory, call up the "Routes" display and compare the bearings and distances with those in your Route Log. If they match closely, you do not need to check for errors. If the bearings and distances between any two waypoints do not agree with your Route Log, you probably made an error in data entry.

In case you find an error, check the latitude and longitude of the waypoints by switching to the waypoint list. If you made a mistake entering the co-ordinates of one or more waypoints, edit the information.

Return to the "Routes" display; you should now find that the ranges and bearings agree with those taken from the chart. If not, continue checking the co-ordinates of the other waypoints in your route and verify that you entered the correct hemisphere. Once you have set up and verified a few routes in this manner, errors will literally jump out at you. This is a quick and easy way to double-check any route and its constituent waypoints.

Waypoints within a Route

Once a waypoint is placed within a route, the GPS Navigator treats it as a fundamentally different type of waypoint. Depending on its placement within the route, a waypoint may be an initial waypoint, a departure waypoint, a destination waypoint, an intermediate waypoint, or a final waypoint.

An **initial waypoint** (origin) is the first waypoint in the route and is usually, but not always, your present position. **Intermediate waypoints** fall between the beginning and end of a route. For each leg being navigated, there is a "from" or **departure waypoint** and a "to" or **destination waypoint**.

Each intermediate waypoint becomes a destination waypoint and, as your vessel completes the leg joining any two waypoints, each destination waypoint becomes the departure waypoint for the next leg.

The **final waypoint** (end) is, of course, the last in the series. Once your vessel reaches the final waypoint, route navigation is complete and electronic navigation ceases.

Starting Route Navigation

There are four methods to begin navigating a route—two for starting a route at the beginning, two for joining somewhere in the middle. In all likelihood, these four methods will be handled differently by the various models of GPS Navigators and only some will offer all of the following methods. Read your GPS manual to be sure you understand the options offered by your GPS, as well as how to use them. Record the procedures in The Workbook.

From the Beginning

Method 1. From the Present Position [Figure 5.4]

This is the most common method for starting a route and is chosen as a default by virtually all software writers. In this method, the GPS draws the Course Line from your present position to the first waypoint of the route. Your present position then automatically becomes both the initial waypoint and the first departure waypoint. When you activate navigation, XTE is zero because your position already lies exactly on the Course Line. *Caution:* The Course Line may cross a landmass so, before you engage this function be sure that the route to the destination waypoint is clear of obstructions.

If your vessel is located near the first waypoint of the route, the GPS Navigator automatically navigates directly to the first waypoint. When you enter the arrival circle of the first waypoint, the GPS begins navigating to the second. However, if you were already in the arrival circle of the first waypoint when you initiated navigation, the GPS recognizes this fact and immediately draws a Course Line to the second waypoint.

Method 2. From the First Waypoint [Figure 5.5]

If your GPS Navigator gives you this option, when you instruct it to start navigating it prompts you "from present position or from the first waypoint?" Select the first waypoint; when you have done so, the Course Line is drawn from the first waypoint to the second. Now, the first waypoint becomes both the initial waypoint and the departure waypoint, and the second waypoint becomes the destination waypoint.

In this situation, since the Course Line does not originate at your present position (which lies some distance off the Course Line), XTE will start at a high value. How high depends on your distance from the Course Line.

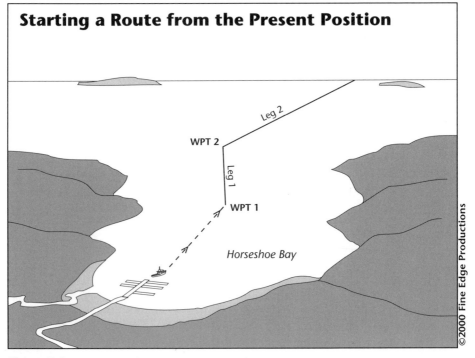

Starting a Route from the Present Position

WPT 2
Leg 2
Leg 1
WPT 1
Horseshoe Bay

©2000 Fine Edge Productions

Figure 5.4

Departing a slip at Horseshoe Bay, heading northeast the first waypoint lies in the middle of the bay. When the GPS Navigator begins following the route, it automatically begins from the present position, and selects the first waypoint as the first destination waypoint of the route.

Joining a Route

If you wish to join a route at some point other than at its beginning, you must follow these procedures:

Method 3. Along a Designated Leg [Figure 5.6]

In many GPS models the procedure for joining a route begins at the display which initiates route navigation. If this procedure applies to your unit, select the route you wish to join then initiate route navigation. When prompted "*from* present position or from waypoints XXXXX," select the name or number of the departure (from) waypoint of the leg you wish to join. As in Method 2 above, the GPS draws the Course Line from your selected departure waypoint to the next waypoint in the route.

Again, since your vessel is probably located some distance from this Course Line, XTE will have a high initial value, but as you approach the Course Line, it will reduce to zero. Once you observe XTE=0, follow the bearing to the destination waypoint and navigate the route in the normal manner.

Method 4. From Present Position [Figure 5.7]

You may be able to start route navigation from your present position to any intermediate waypoint in the route. If your unit has this option, it prompts you to identify the destination waypoint, then defaults to your present position for the departure waypoint, drawing a Course Line *from* your present

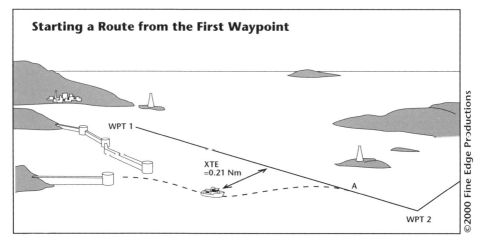

Figure 5.5

Departing the port, the first waypoint lies outside the harbour. When the GPS Navigator begins navigating from WPT 1, it draws the Course Line from WPT 1 to WPT 2. Initially a large XTE is displayed, but as you head east, the XTE will diminish until you join the route at position A.

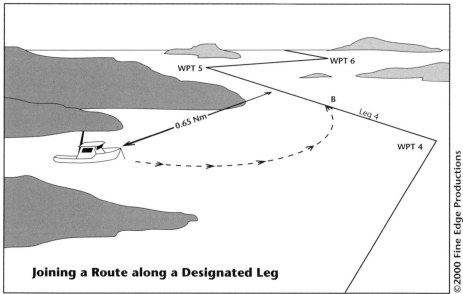

Figure 5.6

Having exited the route the night before between WPT 4 and WPT 5, you now intend to join the route and continue with the voyage. You can activate navigation while still at anchor and select WPT 4 as the departure or "from" waypoint. The display will immediately show an XTE of 0.65 Nm, the perpendicular distance of the vessel from the Course Line, but as you approach the Course Line, the XTE will steadily diminish and, by position B, the XTE will be zero. Once this occurs, it is simple to follow the route and continue the voyage.

position. As in Method 1 above, when you begin route navigation XTE will be zero. The GPS may draw a new Course Line that crosses a landmass, so be sure the route to that waypoint lies in safe water before you initiate this function.

Following the Route

Once you select a method to begin navigation, following a route is essentially the same as navigating to a single waypoint. The steering diagram provides you with the same information as GOTO or single-waypoint navigation. Additional information relating to the route may also be available, such as ETA, ETE, DTG and VTD (Estimated Time of Arrival, Estimated Time En-route, Distance to Go, and Velocity Toward Destination). Some models may even allow you to apply these functions to an intermediate waypoint, as well as to the final waypoint. Times may be based on the vessel's SOG or VTD, or on any predicted speed you enter.

When your GPS is in route navigation mode, it may display range and bearing to the next waypoint after the destination waypoint. When you are concerned about the direction to turn at an intermediate waypoint such as navigating in fog or in a harbour with a lot of traffic and must repeatedly take avoiding action, it is reassuring to see at a glance the direction of your next leg.

Joining a Route from the Present Position

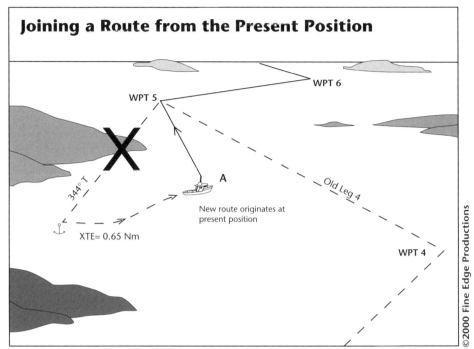

Figure 5.7

If you initiate navigation from your present position at the anchorage, the steering diagram will direct a course of 344° T to WPT 5, obviously not a good idea. Even if you head west, you must wait until your boat is at position A before joining the route from present position. At this point the Course Line is drawn from the present position and the XTE is reset to zero.

A simple readout of bearing and range of the next waypoint will assist you in resolving any uncertainties that arise as you near a destination waypoint. Prior to arrival, simply call up the route display and read the bearing and range of the next waypoint.

Other route navigation features that may be included in GPS software are described below. Be sure to record the procedures in The Workbook—you will use each of these frequently.

Reversing a Route

Your GPS Navigator will follow a route in either direction; otherwise its usefulness is severely limited. Some units allow you to reverse a route while you are still following it. When you reverse the route, the distances in the route do not change, but the bearings will differ by 180 degrees since they are calculated from the opposite end of the leg; the sequence of numbering the waypoints may be reversed as well.

Exiting a Route

At any time you are following a route, you should be able to exit by disabling route navigation. Diversions from a route are frequent and necessary to your enjoyment (you may need to proceed to an anchorage for the night or decide to visit a small harbour off your route), so the procedure for exiting should be simple and intuitive. If you have trouble deactivating the route, you cannot use your GPS Navigator to guide you to the anchorage. Learn how to exit a route, and record the procedure in The Workbook.

Manual/Automatic Waypoint Switching

Most GPS Navigators offer you the option of manual or automatic switching.

In manual switching mode, the GPS Navigator will continue to track the destination waypoint even after the waypoint is realized. In older units, the display may freeze up completely. In either case you must instruct the GPS Navigator to switch to the next waypoint in the route.

With automatic switching enabled prior to arrival at the destination waypoint, the GPS Navigator automatically switches to the new destination making the process seamless. A good GPS Navigator provides an audible or visual warning when a destination waypoint is realized and then switches to the next leg of the route. *Note:* Use manual switching only if automatic switching fails.

Re-starting a Route

Having exited a route, if your GPS Navigator has a re-start feature, you can use it to activate the original route on re-start command even if you have activated GOTO or another route in the meantime. This feature draws the Course Line from your present position to the next unrealized waypoint in the route, resetting XTE to zero. The procedure is essentially the same as joining a route from present position as described in Method 4 above [Figure 5.7] except that you have no choice of destination waypoint. Just one keystroke starts the process, making the re-start option simple to operate.

Since the Course Line now originates from your present position, you cannot continue on the leg you last followed, so the re-start feature is useful only when you are fairly close to the original route.

Suspending a Route

The re-start feature alters the leg you are presently navigating, so it is not always your best option. Some GPS Navigators allow you to suspend route navigation, in which case the route remains selected in memory, and the next unrealized waypoint becomes your first destination waypoint when you reactivate route navigation.

The difference between reactivating a suspended route and re-starting a route is that the computer does not re-draw the last leg; instead, it draws the Course Line from the last departure waypoint, preserving the route in exactly the same form as when you suspended navigation. This procedure is essentially the same as joining a route along a designated leg as in Method 3 above [Figure 5.6]. In the meantime, you may be able to use GOTO or other navigation functions without interrupting the route in memory.

Inserting a Waypoint into a Route

If your Intended Track takes you too close to a shoal or another danger, you may decide to insert a new waypoint into the middle of a leg, creating two new legs where just one existed previously. Be careful to choose your new waypoint to ensure that the new legs pass through safe water. Most GPS software requires you to select a waypoint from the waypoint list, so you must first enter it in memory before you can insert it into the route.

Other software configurations have a convenient feature that allows you to insert a new waypoint *directly* into a route without first entering it into the waypoint list—the GPS Navigator automatically updates the waypoint list.

Most models, however, update the route in memory, but not in the copy of the route you are following. So in order to follow the amended route, you may have to start navigation again [Figure 5.8]. When you do so, follow the procedure in Method 3 for joining a designated leg of a route [Figure 5.6].

Skipping a Waypoint

If you wish to ignore a certain destination waypoint and pass, for example, to the opposite side of a landmass, you must draw new Course Lines, a process called Skipping a Waypoint. It is critical that you learn how your receiver handles this process.

If the GPS Navigator creates a new Course Line from *present position*, it resets XTE to zero [Figure 5.9]. When the new Course Line is drawn from the previous waypoint to the next, XTE may jump to extreme values [Figure 5.10]. In either case, since new Course Lines are drawn, be sure that no obstacles lie in your path!

If your GPS does not have the option for skipping a waypoint, try exiting the route and starting navigation again. You can choose to steer to the next waypoint from present position ("Joining a Route"—Method 4), in which case, XTE will be reset to zero. Or you can join the next leg of the route ("Joining a Route" —Method 3).

As usual, there is no standard procedure for skipping a waypoint. Study your owner's manual to determine which method your particular GPS Navigator uses and perform a few experiments, if necessary. Once you know how to skip a destination waypoint, record the procedure in The Workbook.

Inserting a Waypoint

9
11

Squash Meadow

LONE

Leg 5

XTE = 0.6 Nm

B
Join Leg 5 here

A

Leg aborted here

New leg here could
be dangerous

R2

11
11

INSERT

Leg 6

N

Soundings in feet

Original leg passes through rocks

Nantucket

Sound

Allen
Rock   4

Hatsett Rock   3   6

5   Monohanset Rk

5   7

Mill
Rock

4

3

2

3

TURN1

3
Edgartown Beach

5

5

2   2

Middle Flats

5

1

Little Beach

Eel Pond

2

2

4

5

4

2

6

4

Leg 7

Edgarton Harbor

Sturgeon Flats

EDGARTOWN

5

EDGAR

Arrival Radius and Waypoint Realization

What happens when your vessel arrives at the destination waypoint?

The computer compares its present lat/long co-ordinates to those of the waypoint. If the co-ordinates match exactly, the computer considers the vessel

Figure 5.8 (opposite)   *Inserting a Waypoint*

You are in a sailing boat proceeding under power from waypoint LONE to waypoint TURN1. Unfortunately, you didn't notice the 3-foot depth over Hatsett Rock when laying out your route. This is far too shallow for the sailboat's fin keel. So a new waypoint, named INSERT, must be entered into the route.

Remember, the GPS Navigator may not recognize the new destination waypoint until you refresh its memory by exiting navigation and initializing navigation again. If you re-start the route from point A (the present position) to waypoint INSERT, the projected course takes the vessel very close to the rocks near bell buoy R "2". Instead, when you re-initiate route navigation, you should join the route along Leg 5 (Method 3). Initially, the XTE = 0.60 Nm, but this gets less as the vessel approaches Leg 5 until at position B the XTE is zero.

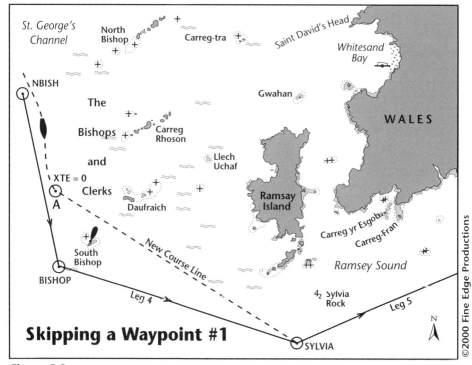

Figure 5.9

At position A you decided to transit east of South Bishop to waypoint SYLVIA, skipping destination waypoint BISHOP. When you exit the route and re-start navigation, the GPS Navigator chooses to navigate directly to waypoint SYLVIA from the present position. It draws the Course Line from the present position to the next waypoint and resets the XTE to zero. You must take care that the new Course Line does not pass over or near any navigational dangers.

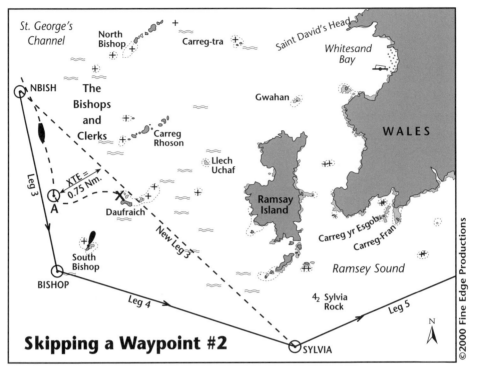

Figure 5.10

This time, when you instructed the GPS Navigator to skip destination waypoint BISHOP, it drew the Course Line from waypoint NBISH directly to waypoint SYLVIA. Consequently the XTE is not reset to zero, but reads 0.75 Nm. The steering diagram instructs you to steer left on a course that may take you directly over rock Daufraich. You must take great care in this situation to avoid grounding.

to have "arrived." However, due to various errors, the co-ordinates rarely match precisely. (Remember that the third decimal place in the displayed position indicates two meters precision.)

Manufacturers have resolved the problem by allowing you to set an arrival radius. If you set the arrival radius to 0.10 Nm, the computer draws an imaginary circle (with a 0.1 Nm radius) around that waypoint, and when your vessel enters any area within this arrival circle, the destination waypoint is realized; your GPS Navigator then automatically switches to the next waypoint.

In cases where you have lots of sea room and long route legs, you can set the **arrival radius** to a high value—perhaps a half-mile or more. But inshore navigation requires smaller radius values in the order of 0.10 Nm. As in the case of XTE boundaries, your unit may apply one arrival radius to every waypoint on the route. If it is possible to select a separate arrival radius for each waypoint, you should do so.

Note the manner in which your GPS indicates it is switching waypoints. The time of waypoint switching may be confusing, especially if no other references are available, such as in thick fog. If your GPS display gives no indication that it is navigating to a new waypoint, you may not even be aware that the time to alter course is long past. On close approach to a waypoint, the bearing should start to swing rapidly to one side or the other; at the moment of switching to another waypoint, the bearing will suddenly jump to a different direction and stabilize. When you near a destination waypoint, pay close attention to the steering diagram.

Missing the Arrival Circle

When currents and wind force your vessel off its Intended Track, you may totally bypass an arrival zone [Figure 5.11]. If you miss the arrival circle by a small distance, your GPS may not switch to the next destination waypoint. Instead, it may continue to track the waypoint you have just passed. The only way to bypass this waypoint will be to manually switch to the next in the series. *Note: Don't forget to re-engage automatic switching once you pass the destination waypoint*, otherwise the GPS will not switch automatically when you reach the end of the next leg. As mentioned above, we don't recommend leaving your GPS Navigator set to manual switching—it draws your attention away from more important aspects of navigation.

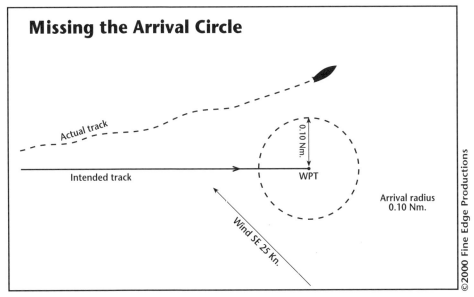

Figure 5.11

Due to a 20 knot SE wind, the vessel completely misses the arrival circle at WPT. Consequently the GPS Navigator will not switch over to the next waypoint. You must manually switch to the next destination waypoint.

Manual switching does not alter Course Lines: once you switch to the next waypoint, XTE is measured from the Course Lines originally laid out, and your vessel can follow the original route.

You may also miss the arrival circle if it has been set to too small a value. In that case, it may be impossible to realize the waypoint. For instance, if you previously set the arrival radius to 0.01 Nm, your true position may exactly coincide with the true position of the waypoint, but GPS errors may cause the displayed position to fall outside the arrival circle. In that case, the GPS would fail to realize the waypoint.

In our opinion, you should never set the arrival radius lower than 0.10 Nm Once within 0.10 Nm of your destination waypoint, visually determine whether the level of precision is adequate.

Arrival Radius Set Too High

If you have set the arrival radius too high, your computer will switch to the next waypoint long before you reach the destination waypoint [Figure 5.12]. In restricted quarters, this could cause difficulties.

Other Methods of Waypoint Realization

So far we have considered only one method of realizing a destination waypoint —by arrival radius. However, recognizing that arrival radius may not always pro-

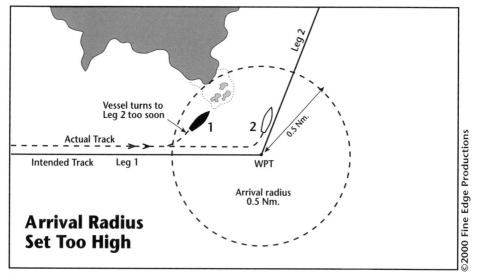

Figure 5.12

Your vessel is following the Intended Track along Leg 1; XTE is less than 0.1 Nm. However, at the perimeter of the arrival circle, the GPS switches to the next destination waypoint, and the XTE, measured from Leg 2, is 0.50 Nm. If you alter course at this point, you could have problems with the rocks off the point as shown (vessel 1). In this situation, you should continue on your easterly heading until XTE - 0 before turning to the new heading (vessel 2).

vide the best method of waypoint realization, most manufacturers now offer other methods of waypoint realization.

Imagine a vessel that has missed the arrival circle of a waypoint, and consequently the GPS Navigator is unable to realize the waypoint. However, by tracking the bearing to the waypoint, a GPS Navigator can determine when the vessel is abeam the waypoint and switch to the next destination, whether or not the vessel has entered the arrival circle. Since the GPS Navigator compares the bearing to the original Course Line, and not the vessel's COG, it is able to determine the proper moment of waypoint realization, no matter what the vessel's actual COG at the time [Figure 5.13].

Your GPS Navigator may offer you a choice of waypoint realization by arrival radius or by abeam passage, but in other sets the selection is automatic—*even if you enter the arrival circle of the destination waypoint, the computer refrains from realizing the destination waypoint until the waypoint is directly abeam* [Figure 5.14].

If your GPS Navigator does not offer a choice, try the following procedures to determine which waypoint realization method it does use:

1. Set up a route consisting of three waypoints with a 90-degree course change at the second waypoint. Orient the two legs exactly north-south and east-west, then set the arrival radius of the intermediate waypoint to 0.1 Nm.

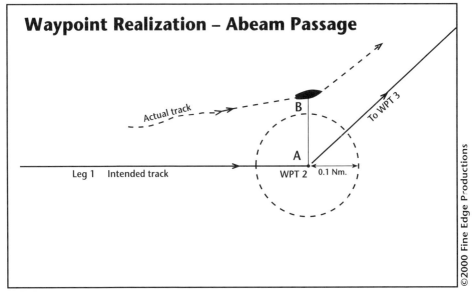

Figure 5.13

A modern GPS Navigator using abeam passage waypoint realization. If the vessel misses the arrival zone, the computer switches to WPT 3 when the vessel passes a perpendicular to the destination waypoint.

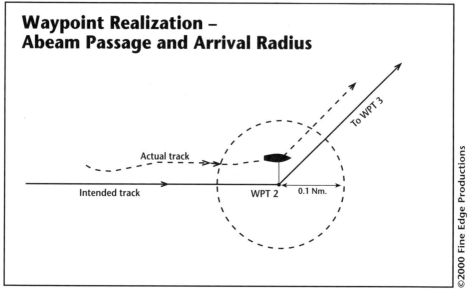

Figure 5.14

Using the same modern GPS Navigator as in the previous diagram, the vessel has passed within the arrival circle but the computer does not switch to WPT 3 until the perpendicular is passed, ensuring that the vessel approaches the destination waypoint as closely as possible.

2. Set your GPS Navigator to automatic waypoint switching and begin navigating the route from Waypoint 1, but be sure to remain more than 0.2 Nm from the Course Line (XTE greater than 0.2 Nm).

3. Continue on a track parallel to the Course Line until you are abeam the destination waypoint.

   Does your GPS Navigator automatically switch at the abeam point? If not, or if it remains locked onto Waypoint 2, it probably performs waypoint switching by *arrival radius alone*, in which case, you need to switch waypoints *manually* when you miss the arrival zone of a destination waypoint.

Another method of waypoint realization—by the bisector of the angle—is fast becoming the standard in many modern GPS Navigators. It is a suitable method when the angle between Course Lines is significantly greater than or less than 90 degrees [Figure 5.15].

Saved Routes

A **Saved Route** is a route made up of a series of saved waypoints which the GPS Navigator automatically assembles into a route as you proceed using the "Save Route" function.

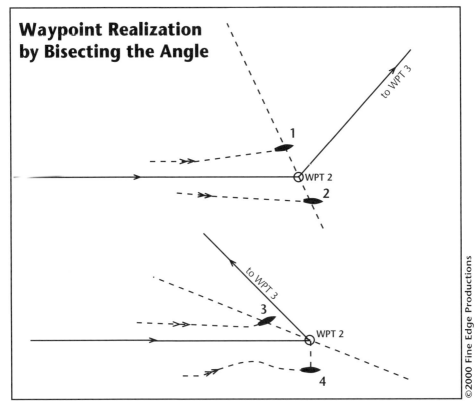

Waypoint Realization by Bisecting the Angle

Figure 5.15

When the vessel crosses an imaginary line bisecting the angle between Leg 1 and Leg 2, the destination waypoint is realized, whether or not the vessel actually enters the arrival circle. However, where the angle between the two legs is less than 90°, and the vessel is on the opposite side of the active leg from WPT 3 (vessel 4), better GPS Navigators may default to realization by abeam passage.

To save your route as you proceed, initiate **Save Route** or **Quicksave Route**, then save a waypoint each time you make a significant alteration of course. The procedure is subtly different from saving individual waypoints since you are constructing a route as you go. The GPS does all the work for you automatically without requiring you to key in a string of numbers or assemble the waypoints into a route at a later time. When you have completed transiting the area, the route will already be stored away for future use.

Marshes, river deltas, island archipelagos and reservoirs are all characterized by numerous trails or branching channels and, after two or three turns or branches in the channel, it can be difficult to determine a position or a new course to follow. In these confusing areas, it's a good idea to save your route as you proceed. Although in fine weather and good visibility, you may not need the

GPS during your first passage, by saving your route at this time, you will be glad later that you did.

By using the Saved Route function you do not need to lift positions from a chart or lay out Course Lines. The advantage to using the Saved Route function is that it places waypoints where you want them. Saving a route eliminates the possibility of additional errors caused by:

- Mistaken reading of latitude and longitude scales
- Slips of the fingers when transferring dividers to latitude and longitude scales
- Errors caused by the thickness of your pencil
- Incorrect chart datum
- Errors in the chart itself

Consult your owner's manual to see if your GPS Navigator has a Saved Route capability; if so, familiarize yourself with the procedure. If your set does not allow you to save routes, you can at least save individual waypoints as you proceed and assemble them later into a route.

Selecting Waypoints

Selection of waypoints must be done with forethought and care: you should select waypoints that define a safe, comfortable, and efficient route. The best navigation system in the world won't help you if you foolishly select waypoints that put your vessel at risk; on the other hand, waypoints selected with too much caution may extend your trip and make navigation more time-consuming.

To initially define the route, use the following procedures:

1. Waypoints and the Course Lines joining them must be sufficiently clear of dangers. Select the Intended Track by first laying parallel rules on the chart in the general direction of the intended leg and adjusting them till the edge of the rule is clear of all dangers. If a leg terminates at a saved waypoint or at another location that needs to be included in the route, adjust your parallel rules so that the Intended Track includes that waypoint.

2. With a set of dividers, measure the minimum distance from the Track Line to any rocks, shoals, or land—we suggest a minimum distance of 0.2 Nm where possible. A clearance of 0.10 Nm or less could be safe, but if you experienced a sudden steering failure and your vessel took a sheer toward shore you might not have time to keep it off the rocks with such limited clearance. The size of your boat and its steering characteristics play a part, too, in determining a safe clearing distance, so decide for yourself what constitutes a safe distance.

3. Once you are satisfied with the Intended Track, draw a line along the edge of your parallel rule and transfer it to the compass rose. Write the direction, either Magnetic or True, along the Course Line. This will prove valuable if your GPS goes "on strike."

4. Now examine the projected course for off-lying dangers that you may not
   have noticed previously. If you do notice any dangers, redraw the leg or
   assign an intermediate waypoint to allow ample clearance.

   As you lay out your route, pay close attention to the following guidelines:

• If you cannot avoid placing your Course Line near a hazard, such as a rock
  or shoal, be sure to assign an avoidance waypoint or **boundary alarm
  radius** to the hazard. Draw a circle around it with a radius that provides an
  adequate margin of safety. Enter that radius as the **avoidance radius**. If
  your GPS Navigator does not offer this feature, be sure to allow sufficient
  clearance between the Course Line and any charted danger. (For reference,
  note the clearance when you set the XTE boundary limit of that leg.)

• Consider the placement of the waypoints which define the ends of each
  leg—they should be placed in safe water and provide a good departure
  point for the next leg of the route.

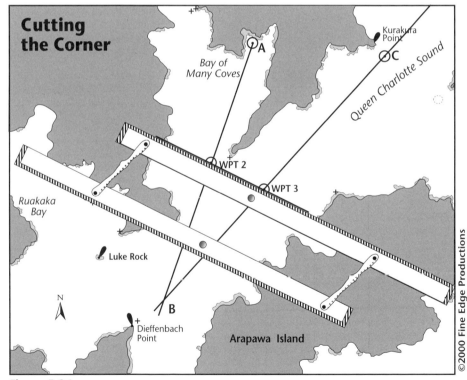

Figure 5.16

*When you lay out a route from position A to position C, you discover that the intermediate
waypoint should not be assigned at position B. Instead, insert a short leg between WPT2 and
WPT3 to "cut the corner".*

- Before assigning waypoints, it is good practice to lay out several legs. In some cases you can simply assign the waypoint at the intersection of two legs; in other cases you may have to insert a short leg to "cut the corner" [Figure 5.16].

- If possible, avoid placing two waypoints too close together.

Figure 5.17   Proceeding with the General flow of Traffic

From Proven Cruising Routes Volume 1 *by Kevin Monahan and Don Douglass. First Narrows in Burrard Inlet is the only entrance to busy Vancouver Harbour. The outgoing route (solid line) is in the outbound traffic lane, and the inbound route (dashed line) is in the inbound lane. Both are to the starboard side of the channel when viewed from the direction of travel, so they do not interfere with major shipping.*

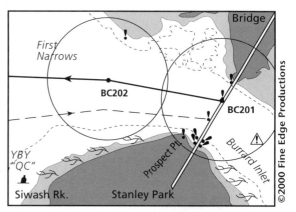

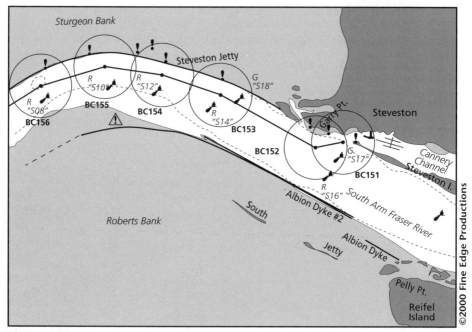

Figure 5.18

From Proven Cruising Routes Volume 1 *by Kevin Monahan and Don Douglass. This route has been laid down in the middle of the navigable portion of the South Arm Fraser River. The waypoint range circles have a radius of 0.20 Nm. Here it is impossible to place the route down the starboard side of the channel. Use the route as a guide only, and remain on the starboard side of the Course Line.*

- In narrow channels, place the Intended Track where it permits the vessel to proceed with the general flow of traffic (usually the starboard side of the channel). Where traffic lanes are wide enough, it is a good idea to construct separate routes for the incoming and outgoing portions of your trip. [Figure 5.17].

- If there is not enough width for two separate routes, you have no choice but to place the waypoint in the center of the channel. When navigating that portion of the route, keep your vessel to the starboard side of the Course Line by maintaining a constant XTE, and be aware of the possibility of GPS errors [Figure 5.18].

- When planning a waypoint near a point of land that lies on your starboard side, allow extra clearance. As you begin to round that point you could be surprised by a vessel coming toward you. The rules of the road call for each vessel to turn to starboard, but if you are already close to the point you may not have room to maneuver [Figure 5.19].

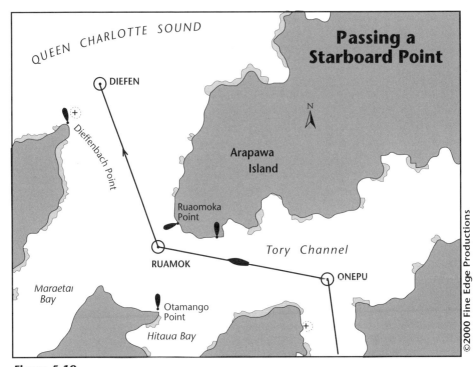

Figure 5.19

When travelling north past Ruamoka Point, assign the waypoint well clear of the point. At no time should a vessel be so close to shore that another vessel rounding the point will crowd it into a dangerous situation at the base of the cliffs. Remember that two vessels meeting head on must each alter to starboard to avoid each other.

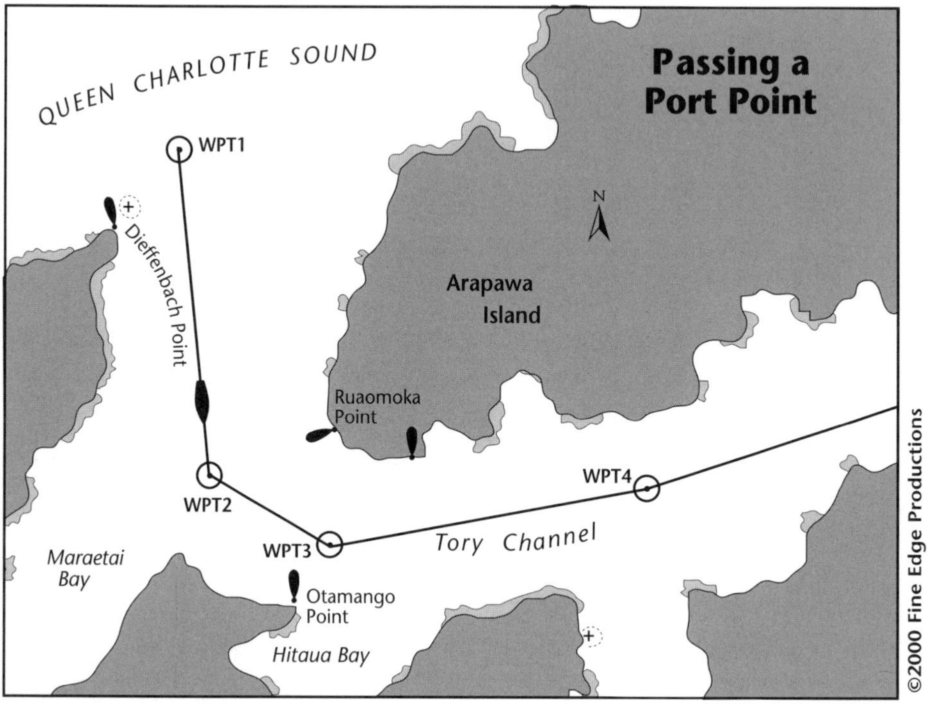

Figure 5.20

This vessel, heading south around Ruamoka Point, will pass well clear of the point and will not be likely to crowd another into the shore. If it passes too close to the point and encounters another vessel at close range, the opposing vessel, lacking sea room, might alter to port, thus passing across the southbound vessel's bow, creating extreme risk of collision.

Figure 5.21

For a vessel heading southwest along the route depicted by the solid line, the shoal to the east of Eilean na h-Eairne is less than 0.10 Nm in a direct line past destination waypoint A. If the vessel overshoots the waypoint, it is in extreme danger of running aground on the 1.8 meter drying rock. A vessel travelling at 10 knots covers the distance from WPT A to the rock in 28 seconds, so a moment's distraction could cause a disaster.

Instead, assign the waypoint at position B and follow the dashed Course Line.

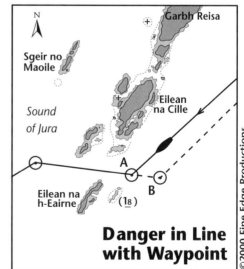

- When planning a waypoint near a point of land that lies on your port side, allow even greater clearance. If you encounter an oncoming vessel, you will be on the outside of the turn. The clearance you allow is for the advantage of the other vessel. Suddenly seeing you at close range and lacking room to turn to starboard, it may turn to port, crossing your bow and placing you in danger [Figure 5.20].

- Whenever possible, avoid placing a waypoint in a position where a hazard is directly ahead of your vessel as you approach the waypoint. You could overshoot the waypoint and run aground [Figure 5.21].

- If possible, arrange for another means of checking a waypoint

Figure 5.22

In the entrance to Shelter Bay, a waypoint has been placed in line with Evans Point and the next point to the west. When you arrive at the waypoint, the two points will be in line, and the small island to the northwest will lie abeam. These two references allow you to verify the GPS position before entering the bay.

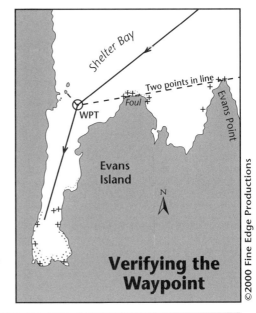

©2000 Fine Edge Productions

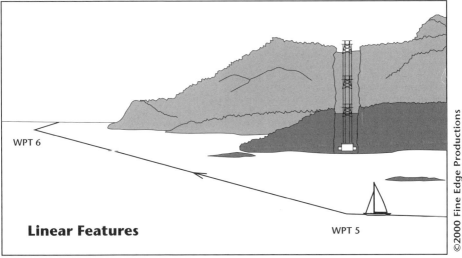

©2000 Fine Edge Productions

Figure 5.23

Assigning a waypoint in line with a power line cut makes it easy to verify the position of the waypoint.

position. For instance, place it so that at the waypoint, you can see two landmarks in line [Figure 5.22]. You may be able to place the waypoint so that it lies in line with a linear feature such as a road or power line cut. These features are especially valuable for verifying that you have arrived at the waypoint—the line of position you derive will be highly accurate [Figure 5.23]. Record these details in your Waypoint Log.

- If possible, place waypoints so that the leg runs along a line of position, such as a depth contour, but NEVER along a parallel of latitude or a meridian of longitude that is part of the lattice printed on a chart. Following a printed lattice line is known as "lattice homing" and is extremely dangerous. If you have chosen to follow the lattice, especially in crowded waters, then it is almost certain that some other vessel will do the same. If you both do so at the same time in opposite directions, you have set yourselves up for a close-quarters situation. In poor visibility, this could lead to a disaster.

- If you must assign a waypoint near a dangerous rock, keep your vessel on the side farthest from the danger [Figure 5.24]. This is especially important if your GPS Navigator lacks avoidance waypoint features.

- Don't place a waypoint in the middle of a narrows. This is the last place you want to be bothered by the intricacies of waypoint realization. Instead, place waypoints at either end of the narrows, where you have time and sea room to spare. [See the next section "Curvilinear Legs" and Figure 5.25.]

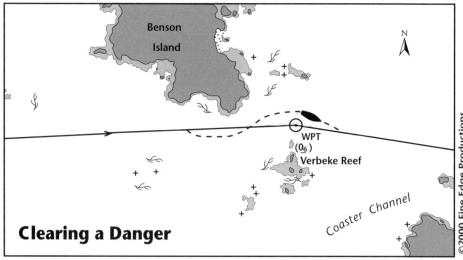

Figure 5.24

When you have placed a waypoint close to a navigational danger, especially one that is not visible, keep to the side of the Course Line farthest away from the danger.

- Set up an alternate heavy-weather route for open water passages which experience the roughest weather. You may need it. Make due consideration for the prevailing wind and wave direction. If, for instance, the prevailing storm winds are from the southwest, don't place waypoints so that the leg runs from southeast to northwest (perpendicular to the wind and swell), especially in shallow water. Instead, select a route that places the prevailing storm weather on your vessel's most comfortable point of sailing.

- When making longer passages, or with legs that are over 50 Nm, make sure the GPS Navigator is set up to use great circles.

Curvilinear Legs

Sometimes you may need to transit a narrow, twisting channel where a normal route leg (**Straight Line Leg or SLL**) between the departure and destination waypoints [Figure 5.25] would inevitably pass over a land mass or some other danger. If the channel is less than 100 meters wide, the GPS error alone may introduce enough ambiguity into the situation to render the Course Line useless.

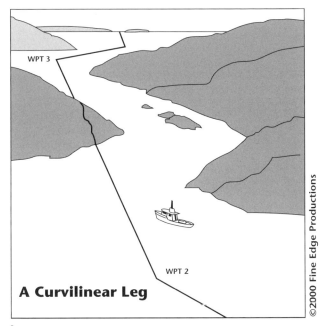

Assign waypoints at the beginning and end of the passage, instead, and navigate by visual transits or radar Lines of Position (LOPs) to follow the proper curving track required by the circumstances. By all means use the range

A Curvilinear Leg

©2000 Fine Edge Productions

Figure 5.25   A Curvilinear Leg

The vessel is approaching a passage that has a navigable width of less than 50 meters. One look at the chart should convince even the most optimistic novice that placing waypoints along its length is a hopeless task. Instead, the skipper has placed waypoints at either end of the passage and treated them as approximate guides to direct him in the correct general direction. The leg between the Turning Points passes over the port-hand shore, but that is irrelevant, because the skipper will not follow the steering diagram until he reaches the waypoint at the other end of the channel. This leg is a Curvilinear Leg. During this short passage, waypoint navigation is suspended, and the skipper transits the passage using the most reliable instruments of all, his own eyes, and an alert lookout.

and bearing to the next waypoint as a general guide, but do not follow the steering diagram. We call this type of leg that must be navigated with special procedures a **Curvilinear Leg (CLL)**.

When you follow a CLL, continuously modify your course according to what is required at the moment. Once you have completed the leg, you may follow the next one in the normal manner. Readers who pilot airplanes will find this analogous to reverting to visual flight rules (VFR) from instrument flight rules (IFR).

Where a narrow channel lies between submerged shoals, your problem becomes considerably more difficult and you should not attempt the passage unless you can safely navigate it without your GPS Navigator. *Remember:* It is your responsibility to properly identify any leg that presents special navigational challenges. When using a CLL, mark it clearly so that confusion with an SLL is not possible.

Curvilinear Legs often occur in coastal navigation. If you intend to navigate to CLLs, you must clearly identify these exceptions to the guidelines for selecting waypoints, and proceed with particular caution.

CHAPTER 6

Navigation Techniques Using Position, Course, and Speed

In classical navigation, a seaman rarely knew his actual present position, and the process of navigating with charts and sextants was time-consuming and laborious. Even when it was possible to obtain two lines of position, half an hour or more might pass between the taking of a sight and plotting the position on a chart; by that time the position was no longer valid. In coastal waters, although bearings of prominent landmarks provided simple position lines, laying these out on a chart still took time in regions where time and space were sometimes severely limited.

Using the fundamental GPS data (position, course, and speed) generated by any GPS receiver, you can quickly and confidently use the techniques described in this chapter to solve navigation problems without having to resort to the time-consuming waypoint and route functions of GPS Navigators.

Using Lines of Latitude and Longitude as a Quick Reference

Every shoreline has a distinctive character. Some are unbroken and low-lying without distinguishing features, where landforms look similar and it is easy to get lost. Other inshore areas are so convoluted with rockpiles, islands or mangrove thickets that it is often difficult to relate the landforms to their appearance on the chart. In areas like these, you can use your GPS equipment to find a position quickly without having to plot it on the chart.

In Figure 6.1, your vessel has passed De Wolf Island heading approximately south. Four possible channels lie ahead. You intend to pass south through Brown Narrows, but in light rain and poor visibility, you have difficulty determining one channel from another. A quick check of the chart shows that once you are south of 52°05' N, the port-hand channel ahead should be Brown Narrows.

This particular passage may confuse you if you have not navigated the area before, but by referring to the GPS latitude readout, the problem disappears. Once

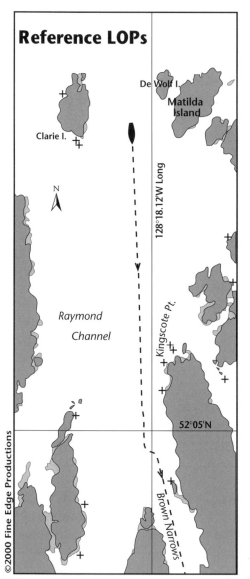

Reference LOPs

De Wolf I.

Matilda Island

Clarie I.

128°18.12'W Long

N

Raymond Channel

Kingscote Pt.

52°05'N

Brown Narrows

©2000 Fine Edge Productions

Figure 6.1

By determining the longitude of the point at the entrance to Brown Narrows, this skipper has ensured that he will not become confused by the numerous branching channels ahead. Once south of latitude 52°05' N, all he has to do is turn to port and cross the controlling longitude (128°18.12' W). Once his vessel passes east of the controlling longitude, he can safely turn south to enter Brown Narrows.

again, your seaman's eye, coupled with the instant real-time lat/long display, makes navigation a breeze.

Since all geographic features lie on some latitude and longitude, you can quickly check your progress along a coastline by noting the latitude or longitude of a geographic feature and checking your position visually relative to that feature.

When navigating in a river channel, especially in deteriorating visibility, you may lose count of the buoys you have passed. Check the latitude or longitude of a buoy by glancing at your GPS receiver, then quickly match the buoy's co-ordinates to its position on the chart. This is especially convenient if you are preparing to turn at a buoy that lies somewhere ahead.

When travelling along a shoreline that trends either north-south or east-west, you can find a quick position by referring to either latitude or longitude. Figure 6.2 shows the south shore of Martha's Vineyard (a featureless coastline). When the GPS shows the longitude to be approximately 70°35' W, your position is clearly to the south of Job's Neck Pond (position A). If a sudden change of plans requires you to alter course to the southeast, you won't have to worry about offshore shoals. However, if the GPS lat/long display places you at longitude 70°30' W (position B), it would be a mistake to make an alteration to the southeast. To assure your safety, *stop your boat immediately, obtain an exact GPS position, verifying it with a depth sounder*

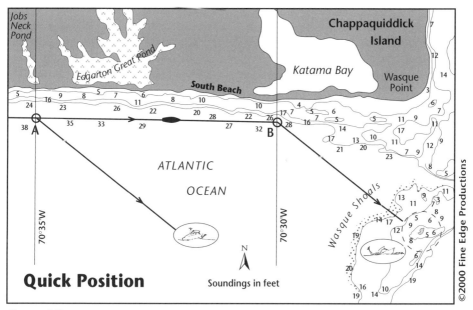

Figure 6.2

Steaming easterly along the south shore of Martha's Vineyard, a quick check of the GPS shows the longitude to be 70°35' W. If the depth at this point is 35 feet, the vessel is obviously very close to position A. It is time to think about making a turn to the southeast. If the skipper delays until longitude 70°30' W (position B), he will have to head almost due south to avoid Wasque Shoals.

reading, then carefully determine a safe course. Otherwise you risk grounding on Wasque Shoals.

It may seem unnecessary to dwell on such basics, but these are examples of *instant decision-making,* based on real-time information; you do not need to perform any calculations or lay out any courses. Using reference latitudes and longitudes is simple and intuitive and leads logically to the next step in navigating with GPS.

LOPs and Safety LOPs

No matter what method you use, if you determine your location somewhere along a specific line, that line is a **Line of Position** (**LOP**).

A meridian of longitude is a Line of Position. If the GPS readout places you on a specific longitude, that meridian becomes an LOP. If you determine your position on any other LOP—such as a parallel of latitude—your position must lie where the two LOPs intersect. In Figure 6.2, you used two LOPs to define position A: the meridian of longitude, and the line of soundings at 35 feet.

The following are all Lines of Position:

- A line of soundings (especially if the seabed is regular in slope and the soundings are close together on the chart)

- A bearing to a landmark
- A transit line where two identifiable features line up visually
- Range marks in narrow channels (by keeping one range mark directly above or below the other, you can follow the center of a narrow channel).

Other Lines of Position can be obtained from the sextant altitude of a celestial body or by the angular height of a tower. In reality, the last two examples are Circles of Position, as are distances determined by radar and GPS range measurements, but for practical purposes LOPs and Circles of Position are equivalent.

A **Safety LOP** is simply a line of any sort that allows you to avoid a danger by staying on the side away from that danger.

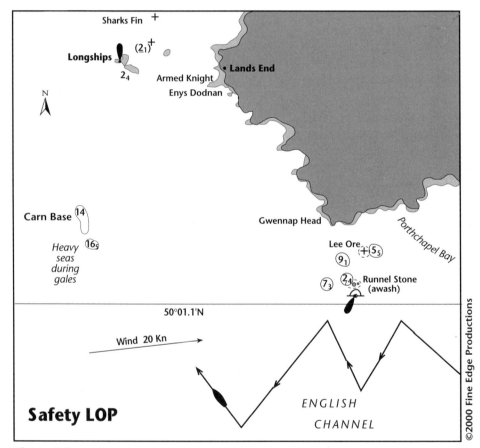

Figure 6.3

A sailboat making a passage west about Lands End and beating against a stiff 20 kn wind has established a safety LOP at latitude 50°01.1' N. By remaining south of the LOP, the skipper and crew can concentrate on efficient handling of the sails. It doesn't matter what course they follow as long as they don't violate this controlling latitude. If the skipper wishes, he can use this same safety LOP to stay clear of the shoal at Carn Base where the chart notes "Heavy seas during gales."

Single Safety LOPs are easy to use. Consider Figure 6.3. If you anticipate an offshore danger, such as Runnel Stone to the south of Gwennap Head, draw a line along the latitude of 50°01.1' N, which is approximately 1/4 Nm south of the awash rock. Since the buoy at Runnel Stone is likely to drift and may not remain in its charted position, it would be foolish to depend on that buoy to keep your vessel off the rocks. Also, if fog were to set in, you might have difficulty determining the direction of the sound of the whistle buoy. Be sure that when you round Runnel Stone you remain south of the Safety LOP.

Limiting Lines of Latitude and Longitude

Safety LOPs as determined by GPS equipment are also known as **Limiting Lines of Latitude and Longitude**, distinguishing them from LOPs which may follow

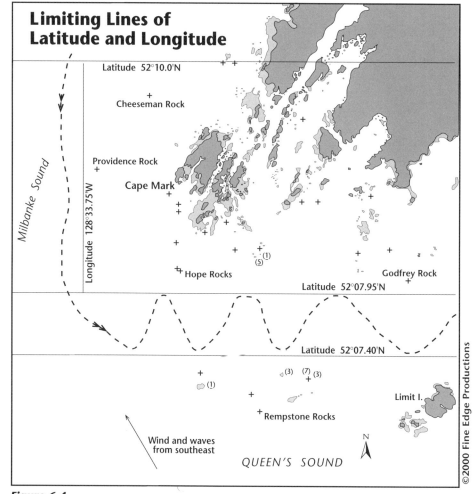

Figure 6.4

any true direction. Limiting Lines of Latitude and Longitude must lie in either a north-south or east-west direction.

The passage around Cape Mark [Figure 6.4] can be difficult during heavy weather due to the numerous off-lying dangers. Reference points chosen for radar ranging appear to move north and south as the tide covers or uncovers them. With the wind and seas from the southeast, most powerboats roll violently in the troughs on the passage from Cape Mark to Godfrey Rock, making chart work almost impossible. By following the approximate headings shown in the diagram, you can avoid setting your boat broadside to the weather (which would happen if you were using waypoints and routes). Instead, you take the seas at an angle that affords the most comfortable ride—on the bow or starboard quarter. But in order to take advantage of this route, you must be prepared in advance.

First, identify the various dangers (many of which do not show above the surface even at low tide).

North and west of Cape Mark, all the dangers lie between latitudes 52°07.95' N and 52°10.0' N and to the east of longitude 128°33.75' W.

To the south of Cape Mark, you can follow a lane of clear water between latitudes 52°07.40' N and 52°07.95' N from Cape Mark to Godfrey Rock.

Once you have identified all the dangers, draw the limiting LOPs on the chart. As you head south, be sure that the displayed GPS longitude does not drop below 128°33.75' W until the latitude falls below 52°07.95' N.

Once you reach latitude 52°07.95' N, you no longer need to follow the controlling longitude. Instead, you must now control your latitude to be sure you remain within the safe corridor.

Turn your vessel's head to the east as much as possible given sea conditions. Inevitably, you will have to head somewhat south of east because your vessel will roll violently if you take the weather on the beam. When the limiting latitude of 52°07.40' N approaches, turn your vessel to the northeast, heading easterly as much as possible while still maintaining a relatively comfortable ride. Repeat this procedure as many times as necessary until you have passed Godfrey Rock. As long as you do not cross the limits of latitude or longitude, your vessel will be perfectly safe. Remember to set up the LOPs to allow a reasonable margin for error, so that if you initiate your turns prior to crossing the LOPs, your vessel never strays into danger.

Determining Course Made Good (CMG) and Speed Made Good (SMG)

For any vessel, **Course Made Good (CMG)** and **Speed Made Good (SMG)** represent the average course and speed attained over any given period of time, possibly a period of several days. Whatever the length of time, CMG and SMG will often be of more interest to you than the COG and SOG displayed on your GPS. This is because COG and SOG are instantaneous values that may vary signifi-

Making a Landfall

Sometimes it is better to arrive near, but not exactly at, your destination: for example, a narrow inlet in a continuously fog-shrouded coast. If you attempt to arrive exactly at the mouth of the inlet—which seems to be the most logical course—you may find that you have erred to one side or the other, due to GPS error or some other cause. If fog or heavy rain limits visibility, you will want to stay close to shore in order to search for the inlet, but you may become disoriented since you don't know which way to turn. Should you turn right, or left? If you make the wrong choice, you will stray far from the inlet. If you had deliberately offset your landfall from the mouth of the inlet, then it would be immediately apparent that you must turn left (or right as the case may be).

Nitinat Narrows on the southwest coast of Vancouver Island is just such a place; in spring and fall the area is often shrouded in fog, and (to make life even more interesting) the narrows are difficult to see from a distance, blending subtly into the hard, unforgiving coast line and its off-lying dangers. When approaching the narrows,

using the lat/long display alone, it is still possible to arrange your course so that you arrive to the east or west of the narrows [see Figure. 6.5.].

Be sure to arrange your landfall to avoid serious offshore dangers such as the reef at Dare Point.

Even when navigating to a waypoint, it is often appropriate to offset the waypoint from the entrance of Nitinat Narrows. Strong currents flowing into or out of the narrows can set up large breaking waves over the bar at the entrance of the narrows. Imagine how uncomfortable it would be to arrive at the waypoint, emerging from the fog, only to suddenly find yourself in the middle of an angry surf. This can easily happen if you don't allow yourself enough margin for error. Instead, offset the waypoint to the east of the entrance a couple of hundred meters. As you approach the waypoint, reduce speed and proceed cautiously until the shore becomes visible, and then turn left along the shore until you can see the entrance.

By deliberately missing the entrance to your destination, you may save time—and anxiety—by eliminating uncertainty from the landfall.

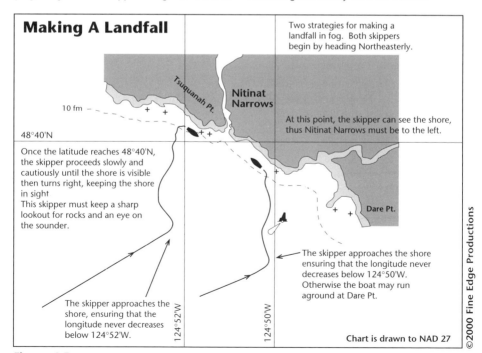

Figure 6.5

cantly over a period of time due to GPS errors and other factors. [For definitions, please refer to the Glossary and to the section En-route Functions in Chapter 4.]

If your GPS updates position, COG and SOG once every second, sea conditions may cause wild variations in the instantaneous value of SOG. For instance, consider a small fishing vessel heading downwind in large seas making eight knots through the water [Figure 6.6]. When a wave overtakes the boat, the displayed SOG will cycle as follows:

1. *As the leading face of the wave overtakes the boat,* it tilts forwards and the stern rises; but because the water supporting the boat is rushing forward and the boat is powering downhill, its Speed Over the Ground increases. As the vessel becomes more unmanageable, the bow may fall off to one side or the other, resulting in a rapid uncontrolled turn. To avoid broaching, the helmsman must counteract this tendency. In heavy seas, a vessel may gain 5 to 8 kn at this point.

2. *As the crest of the wave overtakes the vessel,* the propeller may lift partially out of the water, and aerated water may surround the propeller resulting in less efficient propulsion. Simultaneously, the vessel's bow rises, downward momentum reduces, and the vessel's forward speed begins to fall off. But because the wave is still rushing forward, the vessel's forward Speed Over the Ground is still greater than its speed through the water. Just before the crest of the wave passes the midsection of the vessel, speed reaches a maximum.

3. *As the crest of the wave passes the boat,* the situation in Number 1 is reversed. The bow rises and the boat attempts to travel uphill, thus travelling over the ground at a slower speed than its speed through the water.

Fishing Boat Being Overtaken by a Wave

Figure 6.6

Vessel's speed through the water is 8 kn; SMG 9 knots.

1. *When the leading face of the wave overtakes the boat, SOG increases to 11 kn.*

2. *When the crest of the wave overtakes the boat, SOG decreases to 9 kn.*

3. *When the trough of the wave approaches the boat, SOG decreases to 7 kn.*

The cycle repeats with each overtaking wave which can result in significant fluctuations of the displayed SOG.

©2000 Fine Edge Productions

This condition continues until the face of the next wave begins to overtake the boat.

During this cycle, SOG displayed by the GPS varies from 6 kn to 12 kn, making any navigational calculations based on the indicated SOG values very difficult. What you need, instead, is a value for your vessel's Speed Over the Ground over a longer period, perhaps an hour or more; in other words, SMG.

Figure 6.7 shows the position of Vessel A at both the beginning and end of a one-hour period (determined by the GPS receiver). Measure the distance between the two positions with a pair of dividers; this distance represents the vessel's average speed in knots over that period, or the Speed Made Good (SMG). Since the vessel has travelled 8.0 Nm in one hour, the SMG is 8.0 kn.

Determining SMG over a fraction of an hour requires a little calculation. Referring again to Figure 6.7, the position of Vessel B is fixed first at 1215 hrs, then again 39 minutes later. Vessel B has travelled 5.2 Nm, a significantly shorter distance than Vessel A. To calculate SMG of Vessel B, use the following formula:

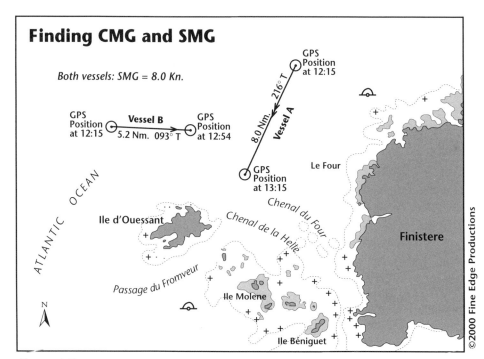

Figure 6.7

Vessel A travels 8.0 Nm in one hour. The SMG is 8.0 knots.
Vessel B travels 5.2 Nm in 39 minutes.

$$SMG = \frac{Distance\ in\ Nm \times 60}{Minutes\ of\ time} = \frac{5.2\ Nm \times 60}{39\ minutes} = 8\ knots$$

To find the CMG transfer the line joining the two positions to the compass rose on the chart.

$$\text{SMG} = \frac{\text{Distance in Nm X } 60}{\text{Minutes of time}} \quad \text{Therefore} \quad \frac{5.2 \text{ Nm X } 60}{39 \text{ minutes}} = 8.0 \text{ knots}$$

Vessel B is proceeding at exactly the same speed as Vessel A.

If the plots are taken over 6 minutes (one-tenth of an hour), the distance travelled in one hour will be 10 times the distance travelled in 6 minutes. We know that SMG in knots is equal to the number of nautical miles travelled in one hour, so if the vessel travels 0.8 Nm in 6 minutes, the SMG must be 8.0 knots.

Obviously, the longer the period of time, the more accurate the results; however, the 6-minute plot is such a convenient technique it is commonly used by all mariners, both amateur and professional.

The Course Made Good (CMG) is determined by measuring the angular direction of the line connecting the two positions, either in degrees True or degrees Magnetic. It does not matter whether the time period is a whole number of hours or not.

Checking Your Compass

Although any good book on navigation includes numerous methods for determining the error of a compass, we offer the following method which uses the precise position-fixing capability of your GPS.

1. Fix your position as accurately as possible on a small-scale chart.
2. Select a point of land or some other landmark, at least 5.0 Nm distant, that is clearly identifiable on the chart (a lighthouse or the peak of a steep mountain serves well). Otherwise, select a point of land that is visually clear and distinct. (Obviously, you need to perform this exercise on a clear day!) Draw a bearing line from your fixed position to that landmark.
3. Once you have completed 1 and 2, steer directly for the landmark.
4. Note the compass heading as you steer for the landmark and compare it to the bearing line you previously drew on the chart. If your compass reads higher than the magnetic bearing, it has a westerly deviation. If it reads lower, the deviation is easterly.
5. In the future, when you steer a heading in that quadrant of the compass, if your compass deviation is 5° W, simply *add 5°* to any course indicated on the chart. In this case, *before you plot a heading or a bearing taken from your compass,* you must *subtract 5°.* However, since deviations change depending on the heading of your vessel, do not assume that your compass error will remain the same on other headings.

We suggest that you repeat this process on different headings until you have more than a half-dozen measurements of deviation equally spaced around the compass rose. Recording this data for future use will give you an idea of the errors inherent in your compass. If the errors are extreme, make it a priority to have your compass readjusted by an expert.

Determining Speed Through the Water and Checking the Speed Log

Before you can make any navigation calculations, you must first know the speed of your vessel through the water. Until now, we have provided speed through the water for all the examples shown. But in order to make practical use of the knowledge you have gained, you must be able to find your own speed through the water. Simply taking two positions and calculating the speed between the two does not suffice, because the calculation gives Speed Made Good *relative to the land*, not through the water. If your boat is not equipped with a knotmeter or a speed log, you will have to construct a speed table. If you do possess a speed log, you can check its accuracy with the method described below.

The speed of a power vessel is a function of both engine RPM and the amount of load the boat carries. A small speedboat runs slower with four people aboard than with just one, even though engine RPM remains the same. Engine RPM and loading affect the final speed of a boat whether it is the tiniest dinghy or the largest supertanker.

You don't have to perform hundreds of calculations in order to determine speed through the water under all possible conditions. But we do suggest that each time you begin a long trip, you perform a few simple procedures to provide an approximate value for your boat's speed through the water. Record the speed through the water for the given loading of your vessel, and you will soon have a record you can use to perform calculations in the future.

Since tidal and oceanic currents are almost always present, either assisting or retarding your vessel's progress, you must take these currents into account when measuring your vessel's speed. The method described below, used during initial sea trials by vessels of all sizes, is reliable and it automatically compensates for the effect of a current.

Perform the following experiment in open water where currents are likely to remain constant for the duration of your trials, following the example shown in Figure 6.8. To do this you will need a stopwatch or a good watch with a second hand. In addition, it is essential that you maintain the same engine RPM throughout the experiment.

Parallax

Steering positions are often offset from the centerline of a vessel. If such is the case with your helm, when you look forward across the bow, your line of sight crosses the bow at an angle. Under these conditions, if you use the center of your bow to sight objects ahead of you, you will introduce an error known as **Parallax**. To avoid this error and ensure that your line of sight continues directly ahead of the steering position, set a mark on the bulwark that is offset from the centerline by the same distance as the steering position. Then sight along the axis of the steering wheel to the mark you made. Your sight line will then be directly ahead of the vessel.

1. Begin by running your boat at a constant RPM (preferably your standard cruising speed) on a heading of either 000° T or 180° T. As you proceed you will notice that the latitude readout changes, while longitude remains almost constant.

2. When the GPS displays 51°01.0' N, start your stopwatch.

3. When the display shows that you have covered one minute of latitude (one Nm) and arrived at 51°02.0' N, stop your watch and record the elapsed time.

4. Next, reverse the course and, over the same minute of latitude, time your passage again.

5. Finally, reverse your course and repeat the passage a third time.

6. Using the speed/time/distance formula given earlier in this chapter, calculate SMG over each timed passage. *Remember:* One minute of latitude equals 1.0 Nm. (You can use a distance of two minutes of latitude [2 Nm] or even more for each pass, so long as you calculate SMG accurately. You can also use ranges or landmarks ashore to determine the distances involved.)

When the course is reversed, the influence of the current on your vessel is reversed also; by averaging the speeds of your first and second passes, the influence of the current is negated. But because the current may change during the

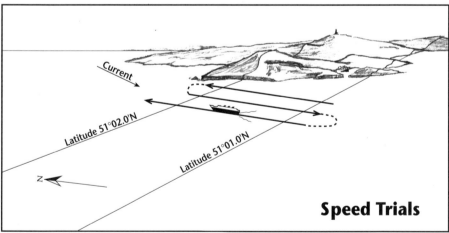

Figure 6.8

The ship is heading true north at constant engine RPM. When it passes latitude 51°01.0' N, the captain starts his stopwatch. When the ship reaches latitude 51°02.0' N, he stops the watch and notes the time. The ship then runs the course in reverse, then again in the original direction, all the while maintaining a constant RPM. By running the course in reverse, the effect of the current—first retarding the ship then assisting it—is negated. Though we have used a large ship for purposes of illustration, this technique works for vessels of any size.

process, we average the second and third passes as well. By averaging what are essentially two separate experiments, the average current value is incorporated into the calculations. The critical point is that you must travel over the same distance twice in one direction and once in the opposite, each time recording the times of passage and then determining the speed of each pass. Your figures will resemble the following:

1st pass   8.6 kn
2nd pass   9.2 kn
3rd pass   8.4 kn

7. The next step is to *average the averages*. Calculate the average of the first and second speeds, and the average of the second and third speeds. Then determine the average of these two averages. The result is the true speed of your vessel through the water.

Average of 1st pass & 2nd pass $= \dfrac{8.6 \text{ kn} + 9.2 \text{ kn}}{2} = \dfrac{17.8 \text{ kn}}{2} = 8.9 \text{ kn}$

Average of 2nd pass & 3rd pass $= \dfrac{9.2 \text{ kn} + 8.4 \text{ kn}}{2} = \dfrac{17.6 \text{ kn}}{2} = 8.8 \text{ kn}$

Average of the averages $= \dfrac{8.9 \text{ kn} + 8.8 \text{ kn}}{2} = \dfrac{17.7 \text{ kn}}{2} = 8.85 \text{ kn}$

The true speed through the water is 8.85 knots.

To check your speed log or knotmeter, simply keep track of your log readings while running the passages, then compare the average speed log reading to the speed through the water which you calculated.

Route Execution Using Combined Techniques

If you know where you intend to go, how to get there, and how to ensure that you are in the right place at the right time, you have a coherent plan. We have looked at a variety of techniques for planning and monitoring your routes as if every turn must be pinned down to some pre-assigned waypoint. In reality, you can choose to navigate using both waypoint and non-waypoint techniques.

Examine the route set up in Figure 6.9. At first glance, the passage from Codfish Passage west through the Tuft Islands seems daunting. However, by using your GPS intelligently, you can transit the area quite safely.

Assign Waypoints 3 and 4 near the ends of a line connecting the (140)-foot island to the southeast with the (21)-foot islet to the northwest. In the vicinity

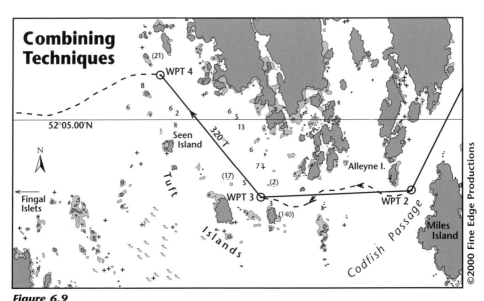

Figure 6.9

By combining techniques, you can complete the transit through the Tuft Islands in safety using only three waypoints.

of this leg there are only two dangers: the (2)-foot drying rock northeast of WPT 3 and the (17)-foot drying rock to the northwest. The rock to the northwest remains exposed at all but the highest tides, so the only real hazard is the (2)-foot drying rock.

Between WPT 2 and WPT 3, the Course Line passes close to two isolated rocks. Since the rocks are exposed at all conditions of tide, the only difficulty is in identifying them amid the numerous other reefs and islets. If you follow the steering diagram, however, you will see that one rock bears slightly to port, the other slightly to starboard. Caution: Be clear that since this is a Curvilinear leg (CLL), you should not follow the steering diagram precisely. Instead, pilot your boat visually or by radar past the two rocks, steering alternately north then south (right and then left of center of the steering diagram) until you clear the rocks. Then steer directly for WPT 3, staying slightly to the south (left) of the Course Line until the waypoint is fully realized.

Once at WPT 3, alter course to 320°T and follow the route to WPT 4—a Straight Line Leg (SLL) which you can navigate in the normal manner. On this leg, you will see the (21)-foot islet directly ahead and the (140)-foot island directly astern. By keeping them in a direct line fore and aft, you can regularly check for errors in your GPS Navigator.

At WPT 4 route navigation is complete. Approximately 1.5 Nm to the west lie the Fingal Islets [not shown on the diagram] which project almost as far north as latitude 52°05.00′ N. Steer westerly until you clear the rockpiles, at which point—if you stay to the north of this limiting latitude—you will clear Fingal Islets and their associated reefs. To the west of Fingal Islets is open water.

By combining techniques, you can transit this confusing area using only three waypoints, greatly simplifying the process of navigation.

When navigating without waypoints, you can use a combination of radar ranges, compass bearings, and limiting lines to ensure clearance of any hazard or to identify a turning point. The combinations and possibilities are endless, limited only by your imagination.

CHAPTER 7

Waypoint and Route Navigation—Advanced Techniques

Let's look at some of the more innovative ways to use waypoints and routes to enhance navigation. If this section seems a little too complex for you, just skip ahead to the next chapter and come back to it at a later time. When you are more familiar with your GPS Navigator, you will want to learn some of the techniques described in this chapter.

Navigating in Tight Quarters

When you navigate in tight quarters constrained by geographic features such as shoals and reefs, how can you work with precision and at the same time maintain a reasonable margin of error? Part of the answer lies in enhancing your understanding of GPS accuracy (see Chapter 8); you must also be constantly aware of your position with respect to land and use the information provided by your GPS to the best advantage. First, let's examine some of the limitations of the equipment.

Update Rate

By now you will have noticed that when you alter the heading of your vessel, the displayed COG takes a few seconds to catch up with the change in the compass heading. Higher quality receivers have a very small lag time; lower quality units demonstrate a significant lag. The difference is due to the update rate (the rate at which the GPS receiver calculates a new fix and sends the information to the display) and the speed of its processor. This is not an adjustable feature, but an inherent characteristic of your GPS.

What is true for the COG is also true of the SOG; it lags behind any actual changes in speed. However, since boats tend to accelerate and decelerate slowly, the effect may not be as noticeable.

If you use COG or SOG frequently in navigation, perform the following exercise to familiarize yourself with the characteristics of your own GPS Navigator.

- While maintaining a steady RPM, note the COG and compass heading.
- Rapidly alter course by 90°.
- Note the lag time before the COG catches up with the compass.
- While maintaining the same steady RPM, note the SOG.
- Bring your vessel to a quick stop by placing the engine in neutral, or even reversing it if necessary.
- Observe the SOG display and again note the delay.

Don't bother to record the lag times for each of these events, just remember that the delay exists and that it might be significant. This exercise should convince you not to expect accurate COG or SOG readings shortly after a turn or a change of speed. You must wait for the readouts to stabilize—the length of time it takes depends on your particular GPS.

Smoothing

If you could average out the more extreme errors inherent in GPS data, you could reduce the maximum errors to which your position, COG, or SOG are subject. Many GPS Navigators achieve this with a feature called **smoothing** control (also known as COG averaging, SOG averaging, etc.).

Most of the time the GPS error is far less than the advertised 20 meters; but on rare occasions it may approach 40 meters or more. These constant variations result in COG and SOG errors as well.

By using the smoothing feature of your GPS Navigator, you can instruct it to combine present data with data derived from a specific number of previous fixes, thus obtaining closer approximations of the true position, COG, and SOG. The processor may average just the last two or three fixes or many more than that. Since smoothing reduces the maximum errors in these fundamental data, you might think it is a simple fix for the problem of fluctuating GPS readings, but it also *increases the minimum errors*—when the position is most accurate. Remember that GPS errors tend to be more *constant* when smoothed, which is your true objective.

Smoothing averages not only errors inherent in the GPS Navigator, but also in SOG and COG due to sea conditions and variations in the heading of the vessel due to steering a variable course [Figure 7.1].

With some GPS Navigators you can vary the amount of smoothing by increasing or decreasing the number of previous fixes to average. For instance, a smoothing value of 5 will average more previous fixes (and COG and SOG measurements) than a smoothing value of 1. You may also be able to choose velocity (speed and course) averaging separately from position smoothing.

However, the constancy of COG, and SOG made possible by smoothing comes at a price. With smoothing, if you could instantly stop your vessel, the SOG readout would read zero only when each of the averaged fixes was zero or when your vessel had been stopped for some time—the length depends on the software in your GPS Navigator.

Though update rate may be a primary cause of the delay in recognizing changes in the display of position, course and speed, smoothing can actually contribute as well. If your set has a slow update rate, and you set smoothing to its maximum value, the combined delay might be excessive, especially when navigating in tight quarters.

For most situations, especially in slow moving vessels, we recommend that you set smoothing to a *moderate value* to provide stability in the displayed functions; but when you navigate in tight quarters, *deactivate it*. The quick response of the COG and SOG displays are more valuable to you than the GPS position when you navigate in confined waters. High-speed craft will find smoothing counter-productive, for at 20 plus knots you need quick response from your set to determine the slowing effect of turns and waves on your vessel. At higher

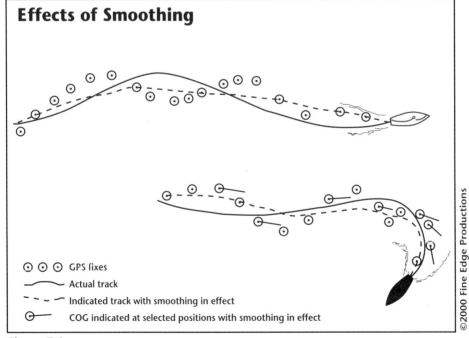

Effects of Smoothing

⊙ ⊙ ⊙ GPS fixes

⎯⎯⎯ Actual track

- - - - Indicated track with smoothing in effect

⊖⎯ COG indicated at selected positions with smoothing in effect

©2000 Fine Edge Productions

Figure 7.1

Both the sailing vessel (upper) and the powerboat (lower) are using GPS Navigators with quick update rates. The indicated positions with smoothing in effect will lie along the dashed line as smoothing averages the errors in position. (In the lower diagram, note that the COG lags behind the actual heading, even though the GPS positions closely follow the curved track of the vessel.)

speeds, the errors inherent in SOG and COG become proportionately smaller, so the values more closely match the true CMG and SMG.

Difficulties with Waypoint Realization

GPS Navigators that realize a waypoint by abeam passage have eliminated many of the problems associated with missing a waypoint (Chapter 5), but if your set recognizes only arrival radius, you will experience waypoint realization difficulties. In this section we provide a few techniques to help you.

In Figure 7.2, a vessel has missed the arrival circle—probably due to a strong tidal current that set it off its Intended Track—and it has passed on the port side of the waypoint. The skipper previously set the arrival radius at 0.10 Nm. Note the bearing and range to the waypoint at each location along the track and, specifically, that the vessel never approaches closer than the arrival radius.

Position	Time	Range to Waypoint	Bearing to Waypoint
A	1200	0.63 Nm	062° T
B	1201	0.53 Nm	064° T
C	1202	0.44 Nm	068° T
D	1203	0.35 Nm	075° T
E	1204	0.26 Nm	086° T
F	1205	0.20 Nm	105° T
G	1206	0.17 Nm	135° T
H	1207	0.20 Nm	166° T
I	1208	0.26 Nm	185° T
J	1209	0.35 Nm	196° T

You can draw two conclusions from your observations:

1. The range to the waypoint shortens at a steady rate as the vessel approaches. Near the waypoint, the range rapidly reduces until the waypoint is abeam (perpendicular to the heading). Once abeam, the range begins to increase, rapidly at first, then at a steady rate. Once the range begins to increase, the vessel has passed the waypoint.

2. The bearing to the waypoint remains stable until the vessel approaches the waypoint, then rapidly changes until the waypoint is abeam. Once you have passed the waypoint, the bearing continues to change, at first swinging rapidly astern, then more slowly until it once again stabilizes. Thus, in approaching a waypoint, a rapidly changing bearing indicates that the waypoint is near.

From these conclusions we can devise what could be called a manual method of waypoint realization by abeam passage.

If you are on one of the three vessels shown in Figure 7.3 and the bearing to the waypoint begins to draw away from your bow, be prepared to alter to the new

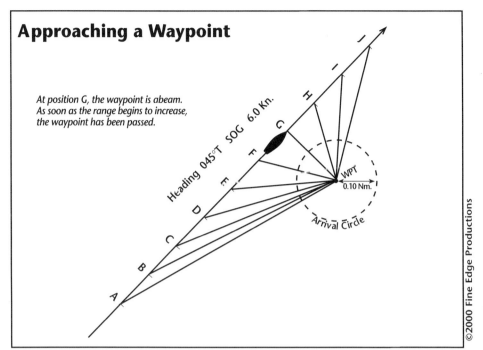

Approaching a Waypoint

At position G, the waypoint is abeam.
As soon as the range begins to increase,
the waypoint has been passed.

Heading 045°T SOG 6.0 Kn.

WPT

0.10 Nm.

Arrival Circle

©2000 Fine Edge Productions

Figure 7.2

heading—but don't do so yet. (You might enter the arrival circle or miss it completely, but as long as you have sufficient sea room to pass safely, you should not alter course.)

Vessel A

As you enter the arrival circle, the GPS Navigator rolls over to the next waypoint and indicates range, bearing, and XTE to WPT3, so you will not be able to monitor the range and bearing to WPT2 once you have entered the arrival circle. Watch the XTE instead; when it approaches zero, immediately turn to the bearing to WPT3. You are now close to—if not exactly on—the Course Line to the next waypoint.

Vessel B

Vessel B passes outside the arrival circle, so when you approach the destination waypoint, XTE will be greater than the arrival radius. Continue to maintain your heading, watching the bearing and range to the destination waypoint. If you know the bearing to the next waypoint in advance, you can be prepared to make the turn even if your GPS Navigator does not switch over automatically. As the bearing begins to draw away from the bow, prepare to make the turn. When the range reaches its minimum value and the bearing is nearly perpendicular to your

heading, it is time to turn. However, since the waypoint has not yet been realized (and may not be realized at all after you settle onto your new heading), follow the procedure for Bypassing a Waypoint [Chapter 5].

Vessel C

If you are in vessel C and have missed the arrival radius, another option is possible: Initiate the turn when the bearing to the destination waypoint is the same
as, the direction of the new Course Line; then closely follow the next Course
Line.

In tight quarters, the only way to navigate closely to a destination waypoint is to
set the arrival radius to a small value. But don't set the radius to less than 0.05
Nm. A small arrival circle makes a small target; if you miss an arrival circle your
GPS Navigator will fail to sound the arrival alarm.]

   If you attempt to pass directly over the destination waypoint before you
switch to the next (even though you've already realized the waypoint), you may

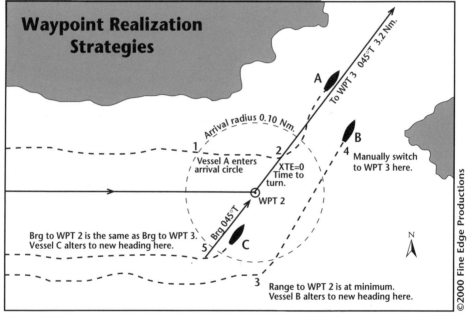

Figure 7.3

*When Vessel A enters the arrival circle, the GPS Navigator automatically switches to WPT3.
When the XTE reaches zero, it is time to make the turn toward WPT3.*

   *Vessel B misses the arrival circle completely, so the GPS Navigator does not automatically
switch to WPT3. At position 3, the range has stopped reducing and is just starting to increase.
At this same point, the bearing to WPT2 is approximately 90°different from the vessel's COG. If
the vessel begins to turn here, it will end up at position 4 when settled in on the new heading.
At this point, manually switch the GPS Navigator to WPT3 and follow the steering diagram.*

   *If Vessel C turns to the new heading of 045° T at position 5, when the bearing to WPT2 is
045° T, it will closely follow the new Course Line.*

find yourself chasing a will-o'-the-wisp as the waypoint wanders around under the influence of GPS error. Your GPS Navigator supplies all the information you need as you approach a waypoint; use this information to assist you in remaining oriented, even at the risk of missing the waypoint by some small amount.

Closely study the specific situation to reveal all available options. You can make an informed decision only by taking into account all aspects of the situation, such as proximity to dangers, the amount of course alteration, and your confidence in your own abilities. Do not attempt to navigate in tight quarters if you are unsure of any aspect of a situation.

Remember the rule! GPS is an aid to navigation only and should always be used with other sources of information. A Canadian Coast Guard officer once told us that she had been approached by a small-boat owner who said, "One hundred

A Close Encounter

One day, *Baidarka* left Seymour Inlet southbound in thick fog. By using pre-set GPS waypoints, radar, and a sharp bow lookout, we transited Nakwakto Rapids at slack water and worked our way slowly down narrow Schooner Channel to Queen Charlotte Strait.

The passage between the Jeanette Islands Group and the mainland of British Columbia—a half-mile wide and bordered with innumerable islets and rocks—is regularly used by small-sized commercial traffic, as well as the Alaska ferry. I headed for a waypoint in the center of the narrowest part of the fairway, and as we approached the waypoint in near-zero visibility, our radar showed a fast-moving target headed our way.

As I moved to the starboard side of the channel, the GPS started giving fluctuating steering information. (We were close to the destination waypoint and did not have Differential GPS.) At the same time, I tried without success to raise the unidentified target on VHF radio. I asked Vessel Traffic Services for help but they had no luck either.

By this time, the steering diagram indicated CLOSE and directed me to steer to port *toward* the radar target which was continuing to bear down on me. As I changed course, the radar target seemed to do likewise, maintaining a constant relative bearing. We were now in a critical situation that required rapid evasion on my part.

I chose to ignore the erratic steering diagram and, in the process, became confused about which compass heading would keep me off the rocks and clear me through the maze. With the compass card and radar display swinging at different rates, I continued to evade the radar target and lost track of which islet on the radar referred to which islet on the chart. It was white-knuckle-time until the radar target—a small, fast-moving tug—broke out of the fog for a few seconds and passed 100 feet away.

I moved the throttle into neutral and took a deep breath to regain my composure. Then, by manually switching to the waypoint located at the south side of the narrows, I was able to figure my way safely out of the maze showing on the radar screen.

This close call was an important lesson for me. Now I carefully pick a waypoint located at the *entrance* to a narrow channel; this allows the GPS Navigator to switch over and indicate the proper course and steering information to the far side waypoint *before* I enter tight quarters. This way, I don't get into an ambiguous situation when I need help the most—at the moment of waypoint realization when course and steering information become unstable.

—DD

meters accuracy is not good enough. How can I find the entrance to the Fraser River if I am limited to one hundred meters accuracy?" The officer replied, "We hope you occasionally look out your wheelhouse windows!" This continues to be true now that GPS accuracy has been significantly increased.

GPS tells you when to turn to a new heading by alerting you to the proximity of a realized waypoint, and by helping you remain oriented to the new waypoint. But if a passage is so fouled with dangers that it requires absolute accuracy to navigate safely, you must use other means—radar, a depth sounder, or visual clues—to determine your position relative to those dangers. If you have no radar or depth sounder, and visibility is seriously restricted, not even the best GPS Navigator can improve matters. In such a situation, you should never attempt to navigate a rocky, encumbered channel.

Using Turning Points

You don't always have to steer directly to a waypoint. (See Chapter 5, Figure 5.25 and Chapter 6, Figure 6.9). As long as your GPS Navigator displays the correct bearing and range, the destination waypoint can serve as a guide or beacon, even if the actual leg between the waypoints is impractical or impossible to follow. In this situation, follow a Curvilinear Leg as shown in Chapter 5. We call the waypoints that join CLLs **Turning Points** to differentiate them from standard waypoints. *A turning point is to be used for reference only and should not be considered a definitive destination.* You may assign Turning Points without the necessary margin of safety.

The use of Turning Points can be extremely useful in twisting channels where you are likely to become disoriented. It is futile to attempt to fully realize a Turning Point because your GPS Navigator may decide to switch to the next destination waypoint before your arrival at a safe turn. You must decide whether to activate manual waypoint switching or keep automatic switching and compensate for it in your head if your GPS Navigator rolls over to the next Turning Point before you are ready.

In very narrow channels, use the following guidelines:
- On approaching a Turning Point, don't place great reliance on waypoint realization. (Your GPS Navigator may even indicate that you have passed the turning point.) Judge for yourself, by means other than GPS, when to turn to the next leg. The bearing of the next Turning Point will indicate the direction to take.
- If there are obstacles directly in your path, you have either overshot your Turning Point or have not yet come to it. Once you are convinced that it is safe to turn, do so. *Remember:* You must ensure that your vessel remains on a proper course by referring to ranges and bearings to visible objects or by using radar, not the steering diagram. Failure to do so in channels narrower than 100 meters could lead to disaster.

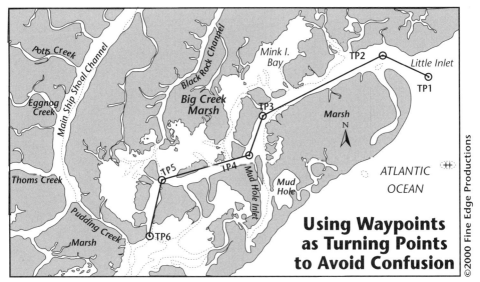

Figure 7.4

In this route in Big Creek Marsh, certain legs pass over land or shoals. You should consider this route to be comprised of Turning Points and Curvilinear Legs. Since this area is a labyrinth of shifting channels and creeks, on approaching TP 5, it helps to know that an alteration to the south to approximately 190° T will take you to TP 6. As long as the boat is in water deep enough to float and is headed in the right direction along a Curvilinear Leg, you don't need to follow exactly along the Course Line.

- Constantly refer to the bearing and range of the destination Turning Point to ensure that you have chosen the correct channel. If the bearing to the destination Turning Point draws significantly to port or starboard while the Turning Point remains distant, reassess your plans.

Determining CMG and SMG Using Waypoints

In Chapter 6, we discussed using GPS-derived positions to calculate SMG and CMG. Now that you are using waypoints, you can use several other easy methods for doing the same thing, without repeated plotting. In fact, some GPS Navigators allow you to construct a complete navigation triangle without resorting to a chart at all!

Method 1

The easiest way to establish CMG and SMG is by using the MOB function of your set which provides all the information you need for calculating CMG and SMG.

1. Once you have settled onto the correct course, activate MOB and wait a certain amount of time—one hour or one-tenth of an hour (six minutes), it doesn't matter.

2. Since the bearing to the MOB waypoint lies astern, it indicates a direction exactly 180° from the CMG. Simply add 180° to the MOB bearing to obtain CMG or look at your compass card and read the direction exactly opposite the indicated MOB bearing.

3. As your vessel travels away from the MOB waypoint, the distance increases. In six minutes, your vessel will travel one-tenth of the distance it covers in one hour (i.e., one-tenth of SMG in knots). Using this information, you can calculate SMG.

4. Once you determine these values, no matter the interval, simply re-start navigation along the route.

If you decide to use a time interval other than 6 minutes or one hour, you will have to resort to the time/distance formula. For example, if your vessel travelled 0.95 miles in 5 minutes, the calculation will be as follows:

$$\text{Speed in Knots} \quad = \quad \frac{60 \times \text{Distance in Nm}}{\text{Time in minutes}} \quad = \quad \frac{60 \times 0.95}{5} \quad = \quad 11.4 \text{ kn}$$

Caution: Be sure that when you re-activate navigation, you join the appropriate leg of the route. If your GPS Navigator allows you to restart navigation only from your present position, each time you re-start the route you will draw a new Course Line and XTE will reset to zero, giving you no indication that you have drifted from your original Intended Track. If your GPS Navigator does not allow you to join a specific leg of a route, you should never interrupt navigation to activate MOB—*except in a real emergency.*

Method 2

Some GPS equipment continually tracks the range and bearing of each waypoint in its memory. If this is the case with your receiver, you can tell by watching the waypoint list. As your own position changes while your vessel is in motion, the changing bearings and ranges to the listed waypoints will be apparent and the effect most noticeable with bearings to nearby waypoints. To determine CMG and SMG, record the range and bearing to the departure waypoint of the present leg *at the beginning and end of a specific time interval.* Once you have recorded the information, you can use it to calculate your SMG and CMG as if the departure waypoint was the MOB waypoint [Method 1]. On very long legs, save new waypoints by present position at regular intervals along the leg, then track the bearings and ranges to those waypoints.

Method 3

If your GPS Navigator does not have an MOB function or the capability to continuously track any waypoint in its memory, you can still find the CMG and SMG by *tracking the departure waypoint or another waypoint saved along the leg by engaging GOTO or single waypoint navigation.* Once the steering diagram appears, don't attempt to follow the steering instructions; simply record the range and bearing to that waypoint as if it were an MOB waypoint. Then you can re-activate the route you were originally navigating. Once you complete the leg, delete the temporary waypoints you used to calculate CMG and SMG.

Finding the Set and Drift of the Current Using a Dead Reckoning (DR) Waypoint

A Dead Reckoning (DR) waypoint is a waypoint placed at a DR position. If your GPS Navigator allows you to enter a waypoint by range and bearing from your present position, you can use a DR waypoint to find the set and drift of the current with the following procedure:

1. Enter your present position as a waypoint.

2. To project your position ahead to the DR position, simply enter the DR waypoint by range and bearing from your present position. If you are making 8.0 kn through the water and you intend to use a one-hour interval, use a range of 8.0 Nm (for six minutes, enter 0.8 Nm). To represent your Course Steered, enter your compass heading as the bearing.

3. Name the waypoint DR. The resulting waypoint will be your DR waypoint after one hour of travel [Figure 7.5].

4. After one hour (or six minutes) of travel at a constant heading and speed, your vessel will be at position B. If your GPS allows, call up the waypoint list and read the distance and bearing to the DR waypoint. Otherwise,

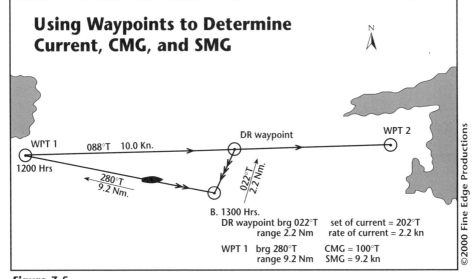

Figure 7.5

activate GOTO, select the DR waypoint as the destination, and read the range and bearing of the DR waypoint from your present position at B.

5. The distance from B to the DR waypoint represents the distance of drift caused by current (and possibly leeway due to wind) during the time interval. If the time interval is one hour, the drift distance in Nm equals the speed of the current in knots. Again, if you use calculations for only a portion of an hour, you need to perform a speed/time/distance calculation.

6. The set of the current will differ by 180° from the bearing to the DR waypoint.

At this point, you have found the direction and strength of the current without performing any chartwork. These procedures allow you to use the GPS Navigator as a navigational computer, freeing your hands and mind for more important tasks, but we suggest that you check your work with the chart until you are fully familiar with the procedures.

Routes and Currents—The Hooked Course Line

In Chapters 3 and 4 we discussed the effect of a cross-current on the progress of a vessel. The following example illustrates one of the problems you may encounter when navigating to a destination waypoint. A Hooked Course Line may develop even though you diligently follow the bearing to waypoint. [See Figure 7.6.]

In Figure 7.6 a vessel departs WPT 1 (between the Turner Islands and Chest Island) at 1200 hrs, heading 331° T at 10 knots. The skipper set the boundary alarm at 0.25 Nm. However, a 3-knot current setting westerly out of Smith Sound pushes the vessel to the southwest. By 1206 hrs, after only one Nm, the boundary alarm begins to sound as the XTE limits are violated. The skipper alters course to match the new bearing to WPT 2, but the XTE still increases; by 1212 hrs, the vessel is 0.58 Nm off its Intended Track.

The skipper again alters course toward the destination waypoint, but XTE increases to 0.6 Nm at 1218 hrs. At 1221 hrs, he makes another alteration and finally XTE begins to diminish; however, the vessel is now heading almost 045° to the right of the original compass course. (Of course, none of this really matters because, at 1215 hrs, the vessel strikes Edward Rock!)

What went wrong? The skipper of this ill-fated craft *failed to compensate for the 3-knot current* setting out of Smith Sound. Consequently he was unable to follow his Intended Track. Instead, he attempted to follow directly along the bearing to WPT 2, and a Hooked Course Line developed because of strong current. [Figure 7.7 shows a solution.]

Figure 7.6 (opposite)   The Hooked Course Line
As the vessel drifts off its Intended Track, the skipper corrects the heading to follow the bearing to WPT 2. A Hooked Course Line results which could cause the vessel to run aground on Edward Rock.

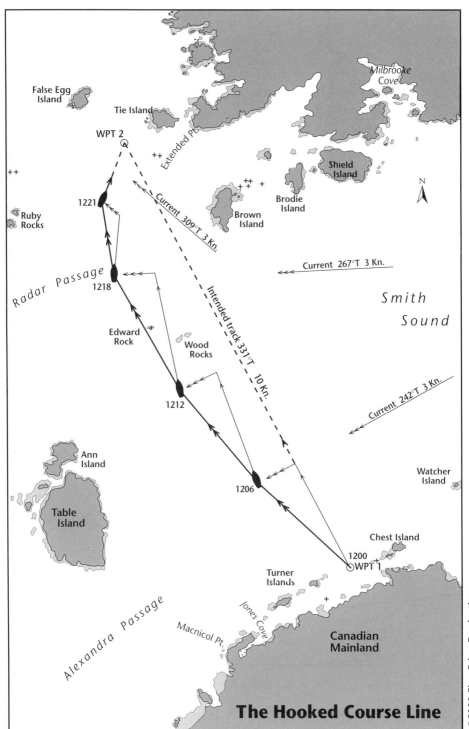

The Hooked Course Line

Any influence, however, that causes a vessel to deviate from its Intended Track will create the same problem if left uncompensated. For example, an unknown compass error might be responsible for the vessel's drifting off course, so, *it is extremely important that you maintain your magnetic compass in good operating condition.* Get it swung every six months if necessary, particularly when you add any electronic hardware to your wheelhouse. Without an accurate compass, you will find it difficult to follow the steering instructions provided by your GPS Navigator. (See "Checking Your Compass," Chapter 6.)

A Hooked Course Line may also develop if you continuously restart navigation to a destination waypoint from present position *as when using MOB to determine CMG and SMG.* If you use MOB or some other waypoint to get secondary navigational information, be sure that your GPS can put you back on the leg you were originally navigating, *not on a leg that originates at your vessel's present position.* If you have a second GPS Navigator on board, this is a good time to use it. Keep one unit for navigation only; use the second to derive other information.

Using Cross Track Error (XTE) to Fix Position

XTE can double as a position line and Distance to Waypoint can be used as an approximate circle of position. Provided you set up the solution in advance, you can easily find your position using these two en-route functions.

Follow these instructions to fix your position using XTE [Figure 7.8]:

- Once you have selected the departure and destination waypoints for the passage, draw the Course Line on the chart.

- Mark the Course Line every 5 Nm from the destination waypoint, creating a pre-measured baseline.

- Parallel to this line, draw lines 1.0 Nm apart.

- When you want to know your position, simply read the distance to the destination waypoint. Make a mark on the base line at this distance from the destination waypoint, then another mark at a point perpendicular to the baseline that corresponds to XTE.

On a long leg with lots of sea room, an approximate position is good enough for most purposes since you will probably be using a small-scale chart.

Figure 7.7 (opposite)   Solution to the Hooked Course Line

At 1206, the vessel has been set off its Intended Track such that a new straight-line course to WPT 2 will take it perilously close to Wood Rock. Instead, the skipper should overcompensate to starboard in order to return to the Intended Track, then slowly bring the vessel's head to port to maintain XTE=0. In this case, he must steer 017° T to bring the boat back on to the Intended Track by 1212, an alteration of 46° to starboard. Once back on to the Intended Track, he can maintain it by steering 350° T, an alteration of 21° to starboard of the original heading.

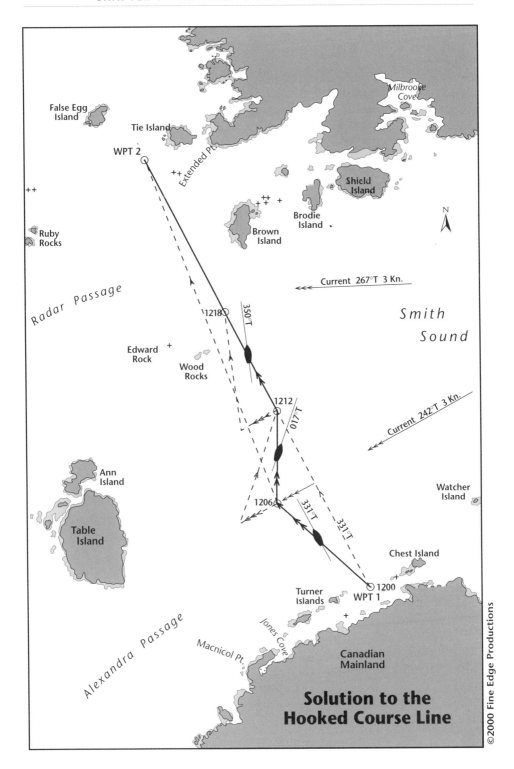

Solution to the
Hooked Course Line

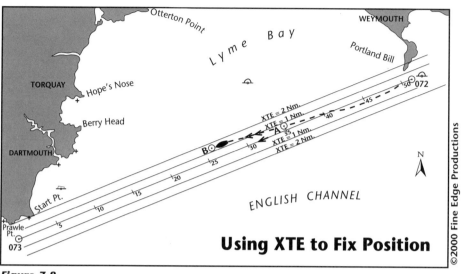

Figure 7.8

A passage from Portland Bill to Prawle Point is a total distance of 51.5 Nm. At 1345, the distance to waypoint 073 is 35.1 Nm and XTE = 0.8 Nm to starboard. Estimating quickly by eye, the vessel is at position A. At 1445, the distance to waypoint 073 is 26.2 Nm and XTE = 1.4 Nm. The vessel must be at position B.

Once you have recorded a second position, you can estimate Speed Made Good. Estimate visually the distance between the two positions along the baseline. If you make your observations an hour apart, no calculation is required.

In Figure 7.9, you are making a daytime crossing of the shoals at the entrance of Jurien Bay, intending to anchor at Waypoint 3. The channel has adequate depth but is not well marked; it shoals rapidly at the sides so your deep-keeled sailing vessel cannot afford to risk straying out of the channel. Though you have taken care to place the waypoints accurately, there are no external references to tell you how far you have travelled along the channel. If you prepare your chart ahead of time, you can instantly see how well you are following the Intended Track as well as your position in relation to navigation dangers.

The advantage of this technique is that it is quick to use and simplifies navigation of these tricky corridors. Try it a few times to gain confidence in your own navigation skills.

Using Range and Bearing of a Waypoint or GOTO to Fix Position

You can also obtain a position by range and bearing to any waypoint or by a combination of ranges and bearings to two or more waypoints. If your GPS Navigator displays range and bearing to any waypoint while in navigation mode, you are the owner of an extremely versatile tool.

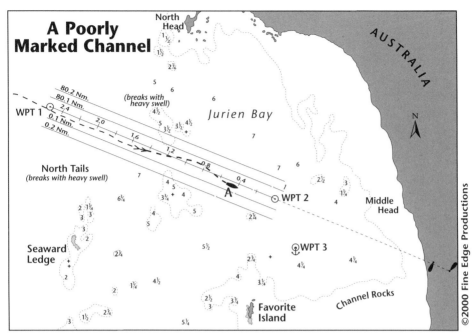

Figure 7.9

Entering Jurien Bay, the distance to WPT 2 is 0.45 Nm and XTE = 0.04 Nm. The vessel is at position A. Boundary limits should obviously be used to signal when the vessel strays more than 0.2 Nm from the Intended Track. The position is quickly and easily obtained from the GPS Navigator display and aids in building confidence in a somewhat tricky entrance.

- To find the vessel's position using the ranges of two waypoints, the waypoints must already be marked on the chart.

- Read the range to a specific waypoint and transfer that position circle to the chart, placing its center at the selected waypoint.

- Repeat the process with another waypoint. Your position is where the two circles cross. If the circles have two possible points of intersection, you must use a third waypoint. This is the same technique as radar ranging on three targets to find your position [Chapter 9, Figure 9.5].

If your GPS Navigator does not display the distance to the waypoints on the waypoint list, you must use either the destination waypoint as your reference, or quit navigation and engage GOTO in order to select the destination waypoint as a reference.

Using a Chart of Unknown Datum

Accepted wisdom suggests that you allow a sufficient margin for error to ensure the safety of your vessel at all times. Since many parts of the world are charted to unknown datums, this means your GPS Navigator will be of limited use in these areas unless you can somehow resolve the errors inherent in the unknown datum.

You may think that you can find the degree and direction of the datum shift

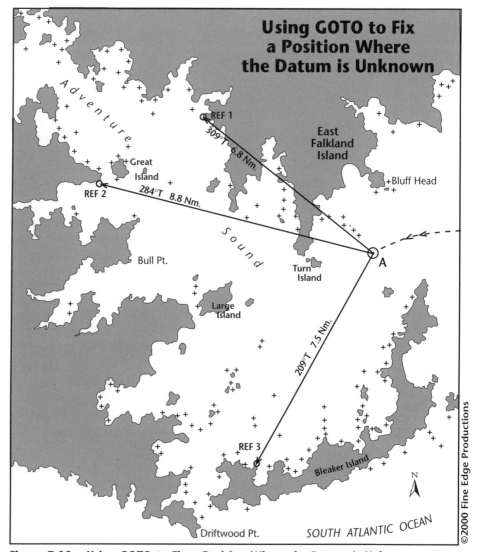

Figure 7.10   *Using GOTO to Fix a Position Where the Datum Is Unknown*

With the GPS set to WGS 84, save waypoint REF 1 near the rocky point at the northeast side of Adventure Sound. Save reference waypoints at two other points within the sound. Note that the co-ordinates of the GPS and charted positions do not agree. This is a result of an unknown datum shift.

On the following day, when re-entering Adventure Sound in a dense fog, activate each of the three reference waypoints as GOTO waypoints and note the bearing and range to each. This gives you three LOPs for fixing your position.

and apply an offset to your GPS position to find your true position. However, many charts are not only drawn to an unknown datum, but the relationships between landmasses and other navigational dangers on the chart may also be distorted. The entire process of calculating your own offsets is so fraught with possibilities of error that we suggest *you never attempt to do so.*

Instead, we suggest that you save reference waypoints at known locations; then use GOTO, or range and bearing of the waypoints, to fix a position.

• Identify the places where you wish to place reference waypoints.

• Proceed to each of the places and, using methods other than GPS such as radar ranges, transits, and compass bearings, plot your position on the chart.

• Save a waypoint at each position or enter the waypoint by present position.

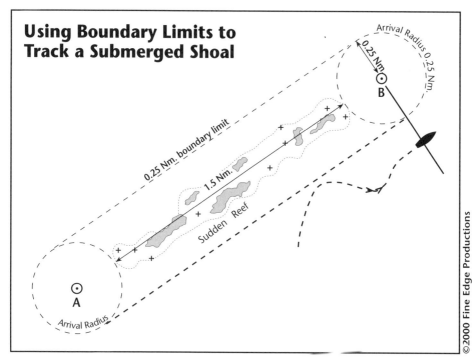

Figure 7.11   Using Boundary Limits to Track a Submerged Shoal

Assign two waypoints 0.25 Nm from the ends of the shoal; then instruct your GPS Navigator to join the route along the leg between waypoints A and B. Set the boundary limit and arrival radius to 0.25 Nm.

Having set up an avoidance zone around Sudden Reef, you can navigate in safety near the reef as long as you monitor XTE and keep the vessel out of the corridor between the two way-points. Since the GPS is programmed to trigger the boundary limit alarm whenever the vessel strays outside the designated corridor, the alarm will sound continuously unless you deactivate it. Also, set the GPS to manual switching to avoid the danger that the GPS will realize the way-point when near WPT B and quit tracking the avoidance zone.

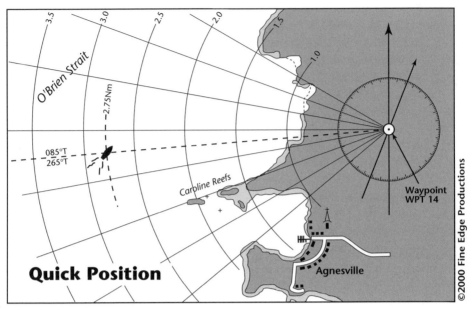

Figure 7.12

In many situations a single range and bearing is suitable for an approximate position. In this case, since the skipper often works out of Agnesville, she has prepared her chart in advance. She drew bearing lines from the center of the compass rose, 10 degrees apart, and range circles centered on the compass rose, 0.5 Nm. apart. Now when operating in the vicinity of Agnesville, she places a waypoint at the center of the compass rose, then activates it as a GOTO waypoint. As soon as the range and bearing to the waypoint are displayed, she can instantly determine the boat's approximate position on the chart. Since the GPS gives the bearing from the boat to WP14, she must reverse the bearing by adding 180°. In this case the GPS reads WP14 2.75 Nm. 085°T.

Since the datum is unknown, we suggest you set your GPS to WGS 84 datum.

- Once you record these waypoints in their proper locations on the chart, you can use the GOTO function—or range and bearing to a waypoint—to fix your position from any other point on the chart [Figure 7.10].

Before you place much confidence in these derived positions, double-check your position on a regular basis. Do not push your GPS to its limits of accuracy with a large-scale chart, since the procedure is subject to errors much larger than the error of the GPS itself.

Using Waypoints to Show Military Area, International, and Fishing Boundaries

You can approximate the position of any artificial linear boundary by creating route legs that follow the boundary. This works for any boundary such as an

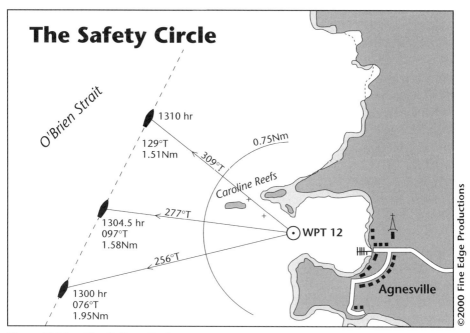

Figure 7.13   The Safety Circle

In this case the skipper has simply placed a waypoint at the entrance to Agnesville Harbour. By keeping track of the range and bearing to the waypoint WP12 (and remembering to reverse the bearings) the skipper can track the progress of her vessel. Also, by drawing a range circle with a radius of 0.75 Nm. around the waypoint, she can ensure that her vessel remains more than 0.75 Nm. away, thus obtaining a safety Circle of Position around Caroline Reefs.

international boundary, a fishing boundary, or even the boundary of a submarine cable zone.

If the boundary crosses the shore at an easily identifiable point, take your vessel as close to that point as possible, and save a waypoint. If you own a portable GPS, you can obtain greater accuracy by taking it ashore and saving the waypoint while standing next to the boundary marker. If the boundary crosses the shore in two places, save a waypoint at the second marker, and start navigation from one waypoint to the other. The GPS Navigator will continuously monitor your vessel's distance from the route leg and display that distance as XTE.

Where the boundary does not cross land, such as in a military exercise area [Figure 7.14], pick the lat/long co-ordinates of the corners of the area off the chart. Where a boundary crosses the shore at one place only, then heads out to sea, use a combination of the previous methods.

Always double-check the waypoints you have used. If it is critical that your vessel not cross the boundary line, *be sure to allow enough margin for error*. Crossing certain boundaries could result in large fines and inconvenience.

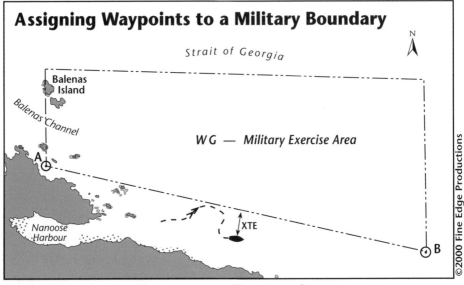

Figure 7.14   *Assigning Waypoint to a Military Boundary*

Military exercises are conducted in Area WG on a regular basis, during which time mariners are advised to stay out of the area. If you wish to spend a day sportfishing in the area east of Nanoose Harbour, assign waypoints at positions A and B and activate a route. This is a simple route, comprised of only two waypoints. Then instruct the GPS Navigator to join the route. From this time on, the GPS will track the route and display Cross Track Error. By monitoring the XTE, you can be sure to remain south of Military Area WG.

Using Two GPS Navigators

By using two GPS Navigators, you need not stop navigating a route to fix your position by GOTO. By using the second GPS Navigator, you do not need to exit navigation in order to find CMG and SMG, distances and bearings to other waypoints, and other useful data. Thus you will not run the risk of developing a hooked Course Line. In addition, a second GPS will allow you to enhance the accuracy of your position when your vessel is motionless. *Caution:* Two low-cost receivers next to each other may "jam" each other—check your system before critical uses.

Great Circles and Rhumb Lines

As any offshore sailor knows, a Great Circle is the shortest distance between two points on the surface of the earth. [Figure 7.15]. On a Mercator Projection chart, a great circle appears as a curved line; at any point along the great circle, the angle between the circle and the parallels of latitude and meridians of longitude is different. Consequently, it is difficult to follow a great circle exactly using traditional methods.

A **Rhumb Line** is any line that crosses parallels of latitude and meridians of longitude at a constant angle. On a Mercator projection, a rhumb line appears as a straight line. Where distances along any leg of a route exceed a hundred nautical miles, the differences between great circles and rhumb lines become significant.

Prior to the introduction of waypoint navigation, mariners on ocean crossings would plot the great circle route on a gnomonic chart (where the great circle appeared as a straight line) then choose intermediate points separated by perhaps five degrees of longitude. These intermediate points would then have to be transferred to a Mercator chart and rhumb lines drawn between them. The rhumb lines gave the navigator the compass headings by which he could steer to the next intermediate point.

The modern GPS Navigator, however, plots courses and routes on a virtual globe in its memory and continuously recalculates the proper heading to follow the great circle track. Any deviation from the great circle track increases the distance to be travelled, so great circle navigation saves a great deal of time. Since the equator is a great circle, as are meridians of longitude (represented as straight lines on Mercator charts), no advantage is gained from great circle navigation when you are heading approximately due north or south, or east or westbound near the equator.

For sailing vessels, following a great circle is less important than taking advantage of the route with the most favourable winds, so the quickest passage between two points may not entail the shortest distance. But when sailing downwind for more than a hundred miles, the great circle route can be useful.

Though most modern GPS Navigators allow you to select great circle or rhumb line navigation, the most common default is great circle. Select great circle navigation *only when there is a specific need*, such as:

- A long downwind passage in a sailing vessel
- A power vessel crossing of any body of water more than 150 miles in width
- An aircraft flying long distances
- Operating near an international boundary that is more than 50 miles between reference points; e.g., the A-B line between Canada and the United States in northern British Columbia. (On a Mercator chart, the A-B line is represented by a slightly curved line.)

Sailing with GPS

Sailing vessels do not act in the same manner as power boats. Consequently you may think that special techniques must be applied to sailing vessels. In fact, the differences are not that great. Specifically, sailing vessels are limited in the headings they can follow, since they are unable to lie close to the wind, and they make comparatively greater leeway than a power boat. With that in mind, we present

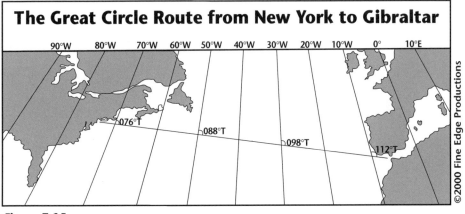

Figure 7.15

Note that the heading changes as the vessel proceeds eastward across the meridians of longitude. When set to great circle navigation, a GPS Navigator constantly recalculates the heading required to follow the Great Circle Route.

here a selection of techniques designed to make best advantage of your GPS Navigator when sailing.

The Windward Ability of a Sailboat

The **windward ability** of a sailboat is defined as the degree to which a sailing vessel can make good a course into the wind. The best, most agile sailing vessels can possibly bring their heading to within 45° of the wind, but since a vessel sailing so close to the wind must also, by necessity, make an unknown amount of leeway, the actual windward ability cannot be determined without plotting.

A GPS can provide significant assistance in finding windward ability. Consider the vessel in Figure 7.16.

1. On its first leg, it is heading 353°T, but only managing to make good a course of 008°T. This course can be determined one of two ways—by averaging the vessel's COG, or more accurately, by setting a waypoint in its wake (possibly a saved, or MOB waypoint) and using the reciprocal of the Brg to Wpt as the CMG. (See "Determining CMG and SMG Using Waypoints"). Also, by comparing the vessel's heading to the CMG it is possible to determine the vessel's leeway angle.

2. Once the vessel has come about onto the second leg, use the same procedure to determine the CMG and the leeway angle a second time.

3. If the leeway angle is significantly different on the two tacks, an unknown current, acting across the wind, may be amplifying the leeway on one tack while negating it on the other. If you suspect that the difference is due to the influence of a current, any values for windward ability of the

vessel will be in error when sailing under the influence of different current conditions.

4. The difference may be due to an asymmetrical sail plan. In that case, there will always be a difference in the leeway made between two successive tacks. You can find out if this is true of your boat by repeating this experiment in numerous different conditions.

5. The windward ability of the sailboat is equal to half the difference between

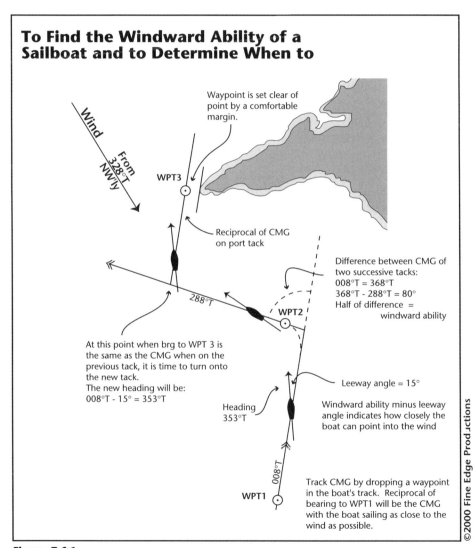

Figure 7.16

If the leeway angle is significantly different on opposite tacks, it indicates either an asymmetrically rigged boat or the presence of a current. Tidal currents may change or reverse with time and position.]

the two successive values of CMG. It is unique to the wind and wave conditions in existence at the time, so be careful to apply the windward ability value only under similar conditions. But by carefully recording the data from a series of tacks in different weather conditions, you can develop useful information on the performance of your boat for future use.

To Determine When to Tack

Once you have determined the windward ability of your vessel, it is possible to find the earliest point at which you can tack in order to round a buoy, clear a headland, etc. In racing this capability is essential.

1. Again refer to Figure 7.16. Once you have determined the CMG for the port tack (wind on the port side), select a waypoint that is in deep water, clear of the point by a comfortable margin.

2. Then extend a line toward your present leg, along the reciprocal of the CMG you determined when on the port tack. Where this line intersects your course line on the starboard tack is the earliest point where you will be able to bring the vessel about and still clear the point.

3. In practice, there is no real need to plot the reciprocal CMG on the chart. Just wait until the bearing to the waypoint is equal to the original CMG before you come about.

4. It is important to remember that in the vicinity of high cliffs and headlands, winds that have behaved with perfect regularity all day can suddenly

Sailing Into the Wind
(Figure 7.17)

When sailing into the wind from WP1 to WP2, there is just one leg between the waypoints. The skipper must make use of numerous waypoint and non-waypoint techniques to make the best use of the existing wind. On the first starboard tack, the skipper chooses to sail as close as possible to the wind and only tacks when she must in order to clear Joey Rocks at the south end of Kangaroo Island. As long as she gains the safety of the XTE boundary zone while still to the south of Latitude 48° 25′ N she will be in safe water. If she finds herself too far to the north, she can always fall off a little, and thus clear the rocks. While on the port tack, she determines her CMG, using an MOB waypoint.

For the next portion of the leg she must keep her boat within the XTE boundaries established between Kangaroo Island and Talon Rocks, tacking whenever she approaches the boundary limits. To do this she cancels MOB navigation, having established her CMG, and re-activates navigation to WP2, in order to display the XTE boundary zone.

Once north of Latitude 48° 28′ N, she can again exceed the XTE boundary limit, as long as she stays to the east of 123° 44′ W. As she approaches the limiting longitude, she determines that the bearing to WP2 is roughly equal to the CMG she found on the previous port tack. At this point she tacks for the last time, sailing as close to the wind as she can, and arrives very close to the final marker, having sailed the leg with the minimum number of tacks.

become gusty and unpredictable. Also, currents can behave very differently when rounding a point. Thus you must select your waypoint with care, making sure to allow ample margin for error, and closely monitor your progress along the Intended Track as you approach the point.

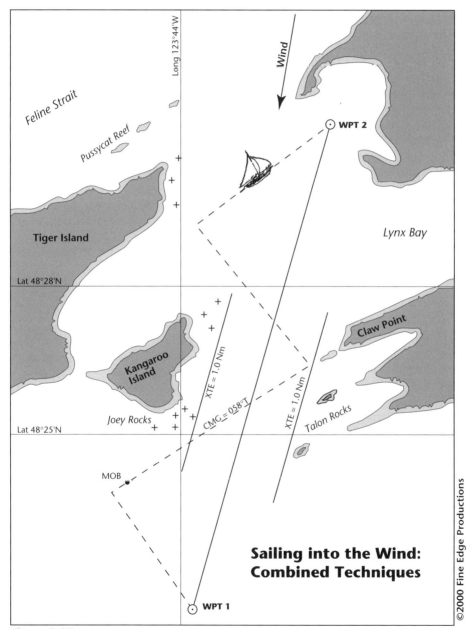

**Sailing into the Wind:
Combined Techniques**

©2000 Fine Edge Productions

Figure 7.17

When sailing upwind, sailboat skippers do not normally place a waypoint at each tacking point. Instead, they tack one way, then the other, taking full advantage of the wind to approach a specific destination. It is this destination that is of most interest and, consequently, it is usually selected as the destination waypoint. One result is that Cross Track Error boundaries are not nearly as important to a sailing skipper as they are to a power boat operator since the sailboat cannot sail directly toward an upwind waypoint.

Once you have determined the windward ability and have deduced the earliest point at which to tack in order to clear a point, you can use the same principles to determine the optimum tacking points anywhere along the leg to your destination. If necessary you can set a high value of Cross Track Error or establish boundaries from limiting lines of latitude and longitude to ensure you stay away from navigational hazards.

CHAPTER 8

Enhancing Your Understanding of GPS Accuracy

The accuracy of the new GPS is truly awesome. Having used the system for several years, the authors are still amazed that, using a small electronic instrument, we are able to pinpoint our position in the great expanse of the ocean to within 20 meters. This sense of amazement is healthy; begin to take the system for granted, and you can become complacent.

Even when you assume a 20-meter error in GPS position, it is still possible for the error to exceed 20 meters for a small portion of the time. When operating offshore, with no dangers in sight, you can safely assume that the position error is negligible, but when navigating inshore channels, you must protect yourself from the possibility of extreme errors by providing yourself with a suitable margin for error.

This chapter examines the various causes of GPS error, so that you may understand the factors that limit the accuracy of the system. Before testing GPS to the limits of it capabilities, you must first learn how much you can depend on those capabilities.

GPS Error Averaging

You can see the statistical distribution of GPS error by performing a dockside test over a period of time and plotting the resulting pattern on a plotting sheet. By taking GPS positions continuously over several hours, or by taking positions separated by several hours over a period of months, you can obtain useful information. Once again, we won't ask you to perform these experiments. [Refer to 8.1 and 8.2 for the results.] If your GPS is equipped with a plotter display, you can watch these results develop without any effort on your part.

Now perform the dockside test over a much shorter period [Figure 8.1]. Notice that the position wanders within a fairly well-defined area. Occasionally

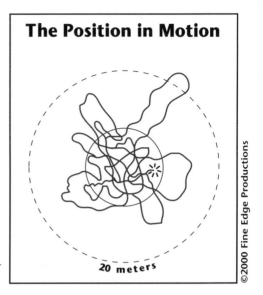

The Position in Motion

20 meters

©2000 Fine Edge Productions

Figure 8.1

Over a period of a few hours, the GPS positions obtained from a stationary receiver are continuously plotted. The position wanders primarily within the 20-meter circle. The error exceeds 20 meters for only a few minutes

it wanders significantly from the center of the pattern but rapidly reaches the extreme of its orbit and returns to a more central position. By observing this behavior, you can come to several conclusions:

1. Most of the time, GPS positions will be accurate to less than 20 meters.
2. Over the course of a few minutes, GPS errors will not vary much [Figure 8.2].
3. A certain percentage of the time, the error will be greater than 20 meters.
4. On rare occasion, the error will be far greater than 20 meters.
5. The duration of periods of excessive errors diminish as the errors increase.

Obviously there is a degree of error that is so transient and unlikely that you can ignore the possibility. Wild accuracy excursions of less than a few seconds are not worth considering—by the time you take notice of them, they will be over.]

[If you average all the positions you have obtained though, the average will be so close to the center of the pattern as to virtually eliminate the error. This "post processing" technique is used in science and surveying work to obtain sub-centimeter accuracies. Unfortunately you cannot average positions at sea, because the vessel is always in motion, so you will not be able to resort to this technique to help you navigate to close tolerances.

Ionospheric and Tropospheric Refraction

GPS signal paths through the ionosphere and lower atmosphere change over time due to changing environmental conditions. The ionosphere can be com-

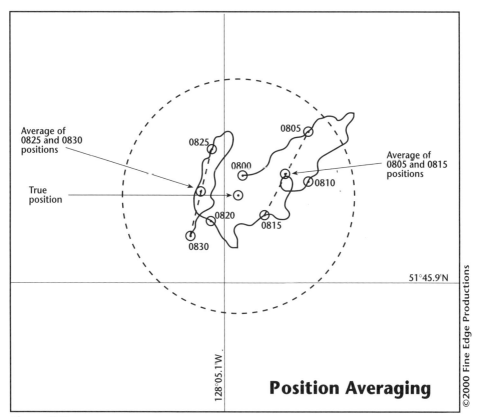

Position Averaging

©2000 Fine Edge Productions

Figure 8.2

Over a period of 30 minutes, the position displayed by a stationary receiver wanders significantly; but any two positions taken within 5 minutes are very close to each other.

If you draw a line between any two positions and take the center point of this line to be the average position, the average position will often be closer to the true position than either of the two indicated positions. In all cases it will be closer to the true position than the most extreme indicated position. If you average hundreds (or thousands) of positions, the result will be accurate within centimeters.

pared to a boiling electrical soup. It is this electrical influence that bends (refracts) the signals away from a straight-line path and thus the signal fails to follow the shortest path to the receiver. Because the signal follows a longer path, it takes a longer time to travel from satellite to receiver, introducing timing and position errors. At times, the ionospheric soup just simmers. At such times the ionosphere is fairly uniform in its electrical characteristics and GPS error is fairly uniform. But during periods of high solar activity, the ionosphere becomes more excited in a non-uniform manner, creating more and more localized areas of interference, especially toward the poles. This, in turn, causes the GPS error to change rapidly in a non-predictable manner. Watch the northern lights in high latitudes for a graphic demonstration of this localized activity.

Solar activity is at a maximum when the sunspot cycle reaches the peak of its eleven-year cycle. During minimum periods, interference is low but, most important, the interference is essentially uniform and consequently more predictable.

At the time of publication of this second edition of *GPS—Instant Navigation*, solar activity is near its maximum. As this solar activity diminishes over the coming years, we may expect to see improved accuracy in GPS receivers, especially during the daytime in equatorial regions.

Since the removal of Selective Availability on May 1, 2000, this refraction is the major cause of position errors. Military receivers using both the L1 and L2 frequencies can compensate for the ionospheric interference by comparing the differing amounts of refraction of the two signals, an option not available to the general boating public. *Author's note:* With the launch of Block III satellites transmitting the L5 frequency (expected in the year 2003), the next generation of civilian GPS receivers will be able to compensate for ionospheric refraction, resulting in significantly increased accuracy.

The refraction of the GPS satellite signal is most pronounced when the signal path travels obliquely through the ionosphere and lower atmosphere (this occurs when the satellite is near the horizon) and least pronounced when the satellite is overhead. At the present time there is no way to model the effects of the lower atmosphere (troposphere) on GPS positioning, so both civilian and military receivers make assumptions about its *average effect* on the GPS satellite signal.

However, an averaged model of atmospheric and ionospheric refraction cannot be accurate at all times and places, so the best we can do is to assume a certain amount of error and work within the limitations of the system.

Many GPS models allow you to set a limit in elevation below which your receiver ceases to track a satellite (the mask angle). Most receivers use a mask angle of 7.5 degrees. Below that the tropospheric model used in low-cost receivers causes considerable error. Generally, there are six satellites in view greater than 15 degrees, eight greater than 10 degrees, and 12 satellites greater than 5 degrees above the horizon. You may be able to set the limit to 10 or 15 degrees, increasing accuracy somewhat, but if you set it any higher, so many satellites may be blocked that your GPS won't be able to fix a reliable position.

How the New GPS Accuracy Affects Navigation

To watch the effect of GPS on navigation let's analyze the position co-ordinates on a GPS display. We noted previously that a latitude co-ordinate can be displayed to three decimal places of a minute, as in 56°24.245' N. The various numbers in this co-ordinate represent degrees, minutes and decimals of minutes as shown below:

56°	24	.	2	4	5
degrees	minutes	decimal	tenths of a minute (600 feet/ 180 meters)	hundredths of a minute (60 feet/ 18 meters)	thousandths of a minute (6 feet/ 1.8 meters)

Each digit in the series represents a magnitude ten times smaller than the digit to its left. Therefore, with the new accuracy of GPS, each change of the second numeral after the decimal place represents a distance equal to the GPS error. At last the precision of the display conforms to the accuracy of the position!

In the past, this was not the case, and you would have to wait for the second decimal place to change by several numerals before you could be sure that your vessel was no longer stationary. With the new GPS, you can be sure that if the second decimal place changes by more than one numeral, your vessel must be in motion. The third decimal place, however, will continue to change in a random fashion even when the vessel is still.

When you navigate near rocks, shoals, or other navigational dangers, be sure to maintain adequate clearances. If you were proceeding in deep water approximately 30 meters from the face of a cliff and your steering suddenly failed, could you react quickly enough to avoid a grounding? Once dead in the water, with an onshore wind, you might not have time to remedy the problem before you drifted ashore. So remember that when you are navigating with GPS, you cannot afford to eliminate your margins of error. We suggest that you always maintain a margin of 0.10 Nm (200 meters) unless you are navigating visually and with a good lookout.

Predicting Error Using Horizontal Dilution of Precision (HDOP)

HDOP is a term that simply means "quality of satellite geometry."

As we mentioned earlier, two-dimensional positioning requires that the GPS antenna "see" three healthy satellites at all times. The GPS receiver measures the range to each satellite and plots these distances (pseudoranges) electronically on its internal map. The GPS uses the same methods to define a position in its silicon brain as a mariner uses to plot a position on a chart using radar ranges [Figure 8.3A].

So let's examine the way radar determines a range. Since the accuracy of a range measured by radar is influenced directly by the length of the emitted microwave pulse, there is an inherent uncertainty (or possible error) in the measured distance. As a result, when plotted on a chart, the three circles or arcs of circles will not meet precisely at a point; instead they will form a triangular shape, in the center of which lies the true position [Figure 8.3B].

Do not consider the circles of position derived from these radar ranges to be fine lines. Instead, imagine that you drew them on the chart with a wide-tip felt pen instead of with a fine pencil. When you plot three ranges on a chart, a zone

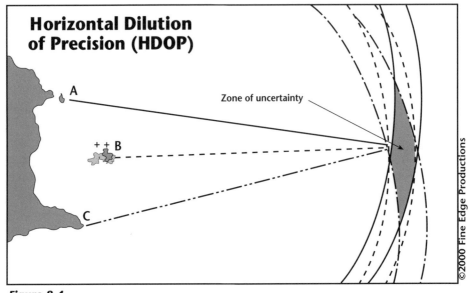

Figure 8.4

Where the objects being ranged are closely grouped [A, B, and C] the zone of uncertainty is stretched out and the accuracy of the derived position is affected.

of uncertainty is produced at their intersection which demonstrates in graphic form the error in position. The true position of the vessel must lie somewhere within the zone of uncertainty, but you don't know exactly where [Figure 8.3C].

Note that in Figure 8.4 the objects used for ranging are closely grouped. The result is that the circles of position cross each other at small angles, causing the zone of uncertainty to stretch out and the possible error in position to increase. Accuracy is enhanced when the objects being ranged are evenly distributed around the horizon. When just two objects are ranged, they should be 90° apart for maximum accuracy.

Since there is an inherent uncertainty in the pseudorange to a GPS satellite, the same principles apply to the distribution of GPS satellites. GPS software writers use HDOP to show the degree to which accuracy is degraded by a particular arrangement of satellites. HDOP values can vary a great deal with poor

Figure 8.3 (opposite)

Ranges to three prominent objects are determined by radar and plotted on the chart. If the three ranges do not intersect at a point, the true position is assumed to lie at the center of the curved triangle at the intersection of the Circles of Position [Panel B].

However, there will inevitably be some error present in the measurement of each range. Even when the three ranges meet at a point, the lines of position have a degree of inherent uncertainty themselves. It is as if each Circle of Position were drawn with a wide paintbrush instead of a fine pencil. Where these broad zones meet, a zone of uncertainty is produced [Panel C].

Radar Ranging on Three Objects

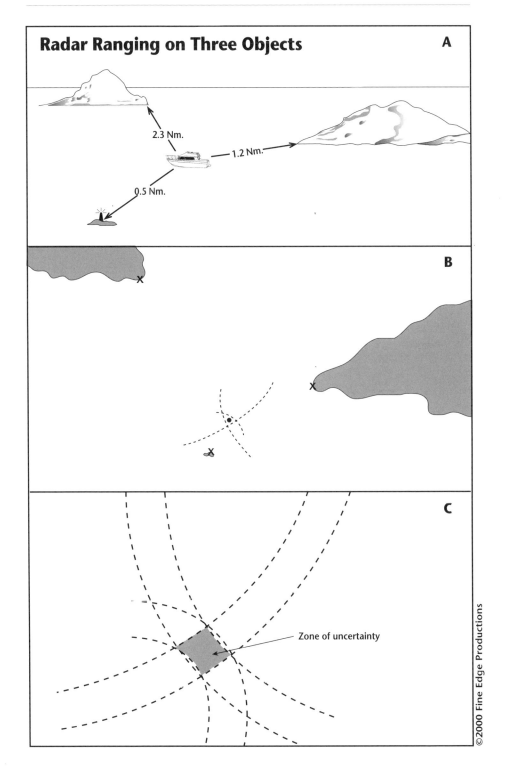

2.3 Nm.

1.2 Nm.

0.5 Nm.

Zone of uncertainty

quality represented by high numbers. When HDOP equals 1.0, the geometric relationship of the satellites is close to ideal, with three arranged around the horizon at 120° intervals and the fourth overhead.

HDOP values greater than 5.0 result in unreliable fixes so some GPS receivers suspend position-fixing if HDOP exceeds this amount. However, you should be aware that instead of HDOP, early GPS receivers use a value known as **Geometric Quality (GQ)** with higher numbers indicating higher quality—the exact opposite of HDOP. GQ is calculated differently than HDOP, which accounts for the difference in the way it is measured.

Since the satellites are in constant motion around the earth, HDOP values change as the geometric relationships between satellites change. At any time your GPS should be able to display HDOP. Record the instructions for displaying HDOP (or GQ) in The Workbook.

When the visible satellites are close to an ideal configuration, HDOP will have little effect on the GPS position, but as HDOP increases, the position loses accuracy. In order to predict potential errors, HDOP is used as a multiplier for other sources of GPS error. When potential propagation errors total approximately 20 meters and HDOP equals 1.5, you can assume that the *potential* error in the position will be 30 meters. But don't think this means the GPS error will be exactly 30 meters—it might be only 10 meters. Thus many modern GPS Navigators display the **Estimated Position Error (EPE)**, which is the product of HDOP multiplied by other GPS error values.

EPE predicts *potential* error or maximum expected error values. Although these predictions are a useful indication of the degree to which HDOP (and thus potential error) affects accuracy of position, you should treat them with caution since each software writer may be making different assumptions about signal propagation and SA errors.

Some receivers are equipped with a programmable threshold for high HDOP values, allowing position-fixing to be suspended when HDOP exceeds a selected value. With these units it is also possible to predict how position-fixing periods are affected by various threshold settings. If you choose a low HDOP threshold, the trade-off is that there will be predictable periods when the GPS suspends position-fixing. Unfortunately, unless your set has Dead Reckoning capability, the displayed GPS position will not change during these periods even if you travel a great distance.

Simultaneous or Multiplexing GPS

The new generation of twelve-channel receivers can track twelve satellites simultaneously (Simultaneous or Parallel Track GPS). Since there are now more than twenty-four operational satellites in orbit, there are seldom fewer than eight satellites visible to your GPS at any one time. Consequently, a twelve-channel GPS can dedicate a separate channel to each satellite, guaranteeing that it will calculate the pseudorange to each satellite simultaneously. This reduces update delays to a minimum and ensures that the GPS position is as near real time as is technologically possible.

Older sets, which utilize only five channels or fewer, are often forced to track more than one satellite on each channel; this results in positions that are less accurate and updated less frequently. In order to access signals from one or more satellites on each channel, these receivers switch from one satellite to another, and then back again. During this switching—a procedure known as **multiplexing** (or **sequencing**)—the satellites and the receiver move a certain distance, resulting in pseudorange measurements which may be out-of-date by a fraction of a second when the receiver actually calculates a position. Since the GPS satellites move at orbital speeds, and the receiver itself moves at over 900 kn as it is carried by the rotating surface of the earth, you can understand that these small time delays cause inaccuracies in the final calculated position.

Though it is doubtful you'll find any marine GPS Navigator manufactured later than 1998 to be a multiplexing type, if you're in the market for second-hand equipment you may come across older sets. Be aware of the limitations of multiplexing GPS sets.

Satellite Masking

Satellite masking occurs when your GPS antenna loses signals due to high land masses or buildings in the signal path. Masking may occur if your vessel is in a deep mountainous fjord, resulting in loss of signals from the satellites which would form the most accurate geometry. Even a nearby cliff or building can mask enough satellites that HDOP reaches extreme values. Consequently, use of the remaining satellites may result in a position fix with high errors due to poor HDOP values. When enough satellites are masked, position-fixing may be totally impossible.

Multipath Errors

Multipath errors are caused when a satellite signal takes a longer path to the antenna by bouncing off a cliff or a nearby structure, thus introducing further timing errors. If one or more signals from a group of four signal sources takes the longer route, the result is a longer measured range for those satellites which, when crossed with LOPs from other satellites, will create an error in position [Figure 8.5]. Normally, multipath errors are not a problem because the satellite signal which takes the direct path to the antenna drowns out the weaker reflected signal. But if that satellite is not clearly visible to the antenna due to masking by your vessel's structure, the reflected signal will be strong enough to overwhelm the direct signal.

This type of error generally amounts to far less than 100 meters since only nearby reflective surfaces can return a strong echo. If the cliff or other reflector is more than a few hundred meters away, the reflected signal is usually far weaker than the direct signal and does not effect the range measurement at all.

The only way you can control this multipath error is to move your vessel. To be safe, never rely on a GPS position taken close under a cliff or in a marina surrounded by large metal buildings. Positions taken in a crowded marina, full of metal masts and rigging, are often quite erroneous.

A special kind of multipath error is induced by satellite signals that bounce around in the rigging of your vessel before arriving at your GPS antenna. This causes "ghost" signals which at times are as strong as the direct signal from the satellite. An improperly installed antenna may have blind spots that can mask the direct signal path from the antenna so the receiver receives only multiple reflected satellite signals. In other installations, the receiver antenna may not be able to receive signals at all from a certain direction or the signals may be so weak that they become unusable.

The GPS receiver is a hard-working piece of equipment and, despite these problems, it can often use even the most meager of signals to work up a reasonable position.

Antenna Height

Although a modern GPS Navigator requires little or no initialization, you must enter a correct value for the height of your antenna. Skipping this critical step,

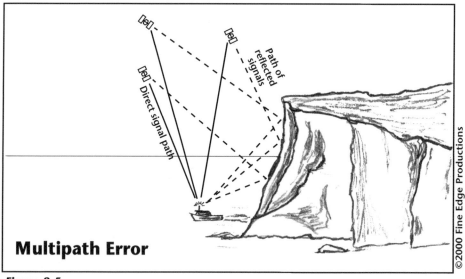

Multipath Error

©2000 Fine Edge Productions

Figure 8.5

The signal from one or more of the three satellites bounces off the cliff on its way to the GPS antenna on the small boat under the cliff. Normally these reflected signals are weaker than the direct signal, but when the direct path is blocked, or where the reflected signal arrives at such a strength that it overpowers the direct signal, pseudorange measurement to that satellite will be in error.

or incorrectly entering the height, could result in significant inaccuracies in your positions.

Though marine GPS navigation is concerned with the two-dimensional surface of the earth, we tend to forget that GPS operates in a three-dimensional environment. If your receiver antenna were located precisely at sea level, there would be no difference between a two- or three-dimensional position fix. But if your antenna is mounted 20 meters above sea level, it is that much closer to the satellites. Failing to enter the correct height might cause the calculated position to be off by several meters.

When using uncorrected GPS, an error of this scale is not extremely important. In fact, the rise and fall of the tide causes minor errors in positioning. But, in any case, you should set the proper height for your antenna; it pays to be as precise as possible. If there is no provision for setting antenna height in its set-up procedure, your GPS will operate at a disadvantage.

The Ideal Antenna Installation

To reduce or eliminate problems associated with shipboard shadowing, reflection, and electronic interference, manufacturers recommend some basic principles for antenna placement. Read the instructions in your user's manual and

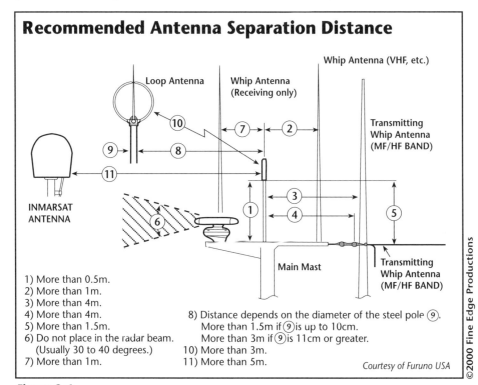

Recommended Antenna Separation Distance

1) More than 0.5m.
2) More than 1m.
3) More than 4m.
4) More than 4m.
5) More than 1.5m.
6) Do not place in the radar beam.
  (Usually 30 to 40 degrees.)
7) More than 1m.
8) Distance depends on the diameter of the steel pole ⑨.
  More than 1.5m if ⑨ is up to 10cm.
  More than 3m if ⑨ is 11cm or greater.
10) More than 3m.
11) More than 5m.

Courtesy of Furuno USA

©2000 Fine Edge Productions

Figure 8.6

follow them as best you can [Figure 8.6]. Here are six suggestions to keep in mind when you plan the placement of your antenna:

1. Locate your antenna high enough to obtain a clear, all-round view of the horizon.

2. Mount your antenna no higher than necessary. Remember that the position displayed by your GPS Navigator is the position of the antenna, not the position of the GPS Navigator itself. If your vessel rolls from side to side, the antenna will move in a different direction relative to the forward motion of your boat, thereby affecting COG and SOG [Figure 8.7].

3. For best results, locate the antenna above or below the radiation plane of any radar scanner and lower than any INMARSAT antenna.

4. Mount the antenna as far as possible from any high-powered transmitters such as MF or HF radio antennas.

5. Mount away from vertical metal surfaces and don't allow metallic rigging to shade or surround the antenna.

6. Mount the antenna where it is not likely to receive significant amounts of spray in sub-freezing temperatures; ice on the antenna can interfere with its ability to receive signals.

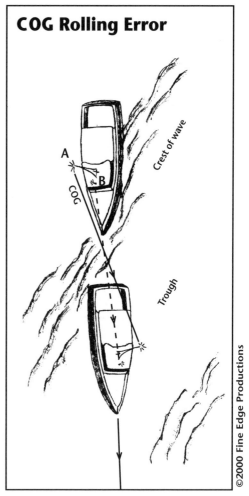

COG Rolling Error

Figure 8.7

As the wave crest passes, the boat rolls first to starboard and then to port. If the antenna is mounted high on the mast, as in the diagram (A), its displacement to port, as the boat rolls to port, is a significant portion of its forward motion. Consequently the antenna moves along the line labelled COG. This will be the COG the GPS receiver will display—significantly different from the true motion of the boat.

If the antenna is located lower (B), its transverse displacement is much less and the indicated COG (dotted line) is a closer approximation of the boat's true forward motion.

If the vessel is moving more slowly, the horizontal displacement of the antenna will be proportionally greater and the COG rolling error larger.

CHAPTER 9

Differential GPS (DGPS)

What Is DGPS?

Differential GPS (DGPS) is an innovation which allows civilian GPS users to achieve accuracy levels of less than 5 meters in DGPS coverage areas. DGPS achieves its phenomenal accuracy by using a network of fixed reference stations that broadcast error correction messages in the medium-frequency radio beacon band to nearby mobile users. Suitably equipped mobile GPS receivers can use these error correction messages to calculate refined position fixes accurate to within 2 to 5 meters and velocity to within 0.5 knots or less! [See Figure 9.1.] Prior to May 1, 2000, Differential GPS was rapidly replacing unassisted GPS in the coastal waters and major navigable rivers of the world's developed nations.

The original intent in establishing DGPS networks was to increase maritime safety for major commercial shipping in United States harbours, satisfying the requirements of the *United States Federal Radionavigation Plan* for 8-meter accuracy for commercial shipping operating in harbours and harbour approaches.

In addition to high degrees of accuracy, DGPS also provides real-time integrity monitoring of GPS satellite messages. Should a satellite message become unreliable, the DGPS reference station can broadcast a "do not use this satellite" message to your DGPS receiver within 10 seconds, thus eliminating a major source of system unreliability. However, now that unassisted GPS can resolve positions to within 20 meters, this integrity monitoring capacity may not hold enough interest in DGPS for the recreational boating community. For commercial shipping, surveying and other activities requiring precise positioning, DGPS will continue to be necessary into the foreseeable future.

DGPS achieves its remarkable level of accuracy by eliminating the errors caused by factors shared equally by the DGPS reference station and the user equipment at sea. Propagation errors caused by microwave signals transiting the ionosphere and troposphere are the primary causes of GPS error, but DGPS reduces them to a few meters or less. Orbit errors and satellite clock errors (generally from 1 to 5 meters) can be minimized or eliminated by the differential process. The theoretical accuracy of a properly-operating DGPS receiver close to a reference station is approximately 2 meters!

Since DGPS reference stations broadcast on medium-frequency radio waves that travel parallel to the earth's surface, DGPS is a local system with limited range. The farther you are from the reference station, the larger the error. Although the *maximum* reliable range is still unknown for many reference stations, you can safely assume that, within 60 nautical miles of the reference station, errors are limited to five meters or less. For each 60 Nm distance from the station, add another 4 to 5 meters error. Accuracy of course and speed data also benefit from the differential corrections, though not to the same degree.

Since solar activity is the primary cause of the ionospheric component of GPS error, this error is constantly changing. During the day, the ionosphere is subjected to continuous solar influence. As the GPS microwave signal penetrates this tumultuous environment, it is bent first one way, then the other. A few hours after sunset, ionospheric activity slows down (except during solar storms in the high latitudes) and creates yet a different electrical environment in the ionosphere. As a result, GPS error is characterized by continuous change. Not only does the differential process reduce GPS errors, but it also stabilizes the error. This stability may be of greater value than its absolute effect on accuracy.

Mobile DGPS receivers are passive—they do not transmit back to the reference station. Thus an unlimited number of mariners can use the signals simultaneously without draining the system's resources or degrading its accuracy.

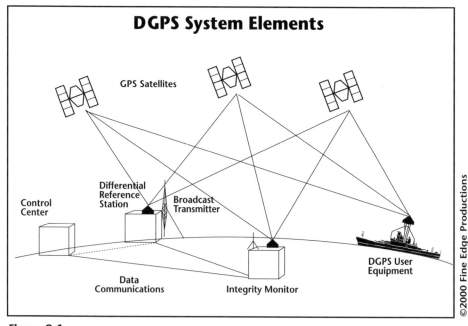

Figure 9.1

Some DGPS receivers may fail to recognize the "do not use this satellite" message and process it as a correction message instead; this can result in position errors of up to 10 Nm in DGPS mode. (If you think your equipment falls into this category, contact the manufacturer immediately for a software upgrade.)

To take advantage of DGPS, you need a separate receiver and antenna since the correction signals are broadcast on a different frequency than the satellite signals. Unfortunately, older GPS receivers may not be capable of "talking" to a differential receiver. Check your instruction manual or call the manufacturer to determine if your GPS is "differential ready." Newer DGPS sets come with both receivers mounted in one box, requiring just a connection to two external antennas. Hand-held GPS receivers may not be "differential ready," so be sure you understand what you are buying.

At this time there are no standards for evaluating DGPS receivers; claims for accuracy by various manufacturers vary anywhere from 2 to 10 meters. We know from experience that DGPS accuracy improves the closer you are to a reference station and within a few kilometers of the reference station, DGPS accuracy is closer to two meters than ten. However, without a single standard for specifying accuracy, comparing two different estimates of accuracy is like comparing apples to oranges, so until greater standardization exists, assume that all DGPS receivers are created equal.

DGPS networks are now being implemented for most of the coastlines of the developed world. In Europe and North America, most coastlines are now (or will soon be) within range of DGPS stations. Since authorities around the world are still in the process of establishing reference and monitoring stations, DGPS has not yet been declared fully operational in many jurisdictions. In the meantime, be aware that DGPS reference stations may go off the air without warning and reference stations moved to new locations.

Encoded in the GPS satellite signal is a highly precise description of the location of each GPS satellite (the ephemeris message), accurate to within 1 or 2 meters. The satellite also broadcasts an exact time signal which your GPS compares with the time in its internal clock. It then computes the amount of time it took the signal to reach its position. Since it knows the speed the signal travels, it can compute the distance to the satellite and draw a Circle of Position on the virtual map in its memory.

However, due to ionospheric and atmospheric interference, GPS receivers are unable to calculate the exact distance from the satellite to the GPS antenna. Obviously, it needs information from a second source to resolve this impasse.

This second source is the DGPS reference station. These stations have been established at specific locations whose latitude and longitude have been precisely surveyed. Knowing its own earthbound position and the precise position of the satellite (from the ephemeris message), the reference station can easily determine the exact distance to the satellite (the true range).

The differential reference station does not convert the transit time of the satellite signal to a distance, as a GPS receiver does. Instead, it calculates the time it should take for the signal to cover the known distance from the satellite and compares it to the *actual transit time*; the difference between the two represents the amount of ionospheric interference. The computer then broadcasts a *timing correction signal* on the low-frequency radio beacon band. Mobile DGPS receivers in its vicinity pick up these signals and correct the pseudoranges of all the satellites in view. Once the true range to each satellite has been determined, the DGPS receiver calculates its position in exactly the same way as a conventional GPS.

DGPS Coverage

At this time, 34 nations have established DGPS reference stations on coastlines and in major river systems, the areas of greatest concern to mariners. Because each station is designed to have different operating ranges, and some are still in the testing phase, it is impossible to state the *average* range of reliable DGPS signals. Published figures for some European DGPS stations are as low as 30 nautical miles, while differential GLONASS stations in the Russian High Arctic are said to have an effective range of 250 nautical miles. Some stations have been observed to have tolerable accuracy levels at more than 500 Nm where the signal travels a path over land. However, until more is known about the effective range of each of these stations, and in the absence of information to the contrary, you should assume that the signals are not reliable more than 100 Nm offshore. Remember that DGPS is intended for *coastal*—not offshore—navigation. You can find information relating to expected reliable ranges of specific reference stations in publications available from national authorities or the *Admiralty List of Radio Signals*.

DGPS for Land Surveying

You may have heard about highly specialized phase-measurement systems used by land surveyors that operate to accuracy of a centimeter and even a millimeter over small distances. These systems require specialized equipment and work on differential and phase or interferometer principles that continue to be developed as refinements to basic GPS signal processing. UHF local DGPS networks used for surveying (and hydrography) operate over baselines of just a few Nm and are dependent on reference stations established by the surveyors themselves. Other systems, capable of centimeter accuracy, require motionless receivers or post processing of the data and are thus outside the realm of marine navigation systems.

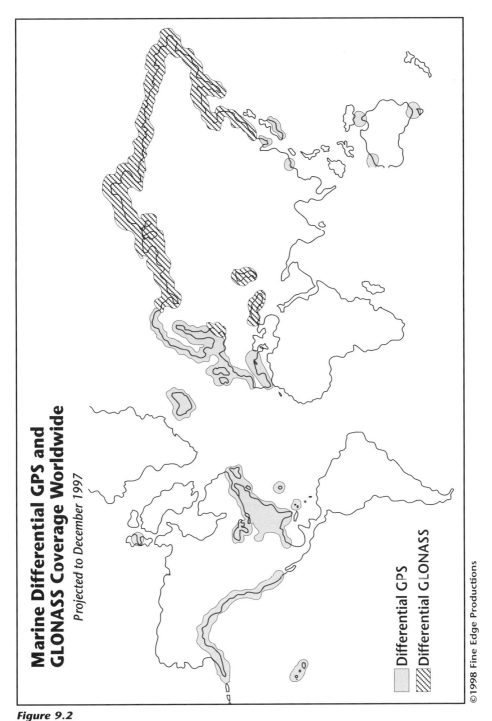

Figure 9.2

Compiled from information provided by IALA, 1997. Consult authorized publications from the respective jurisdictions for more complete information.

International standards have been established for marine Differential GPS broadcasts under the auspices of the International Association of Lighthouse Authorities (IALA). By following the IALA standards, nations are reassuring mariners that they can use their DGPS equipment *anywhere* differential broadcasts are available.

The Russian Federation has established differential GLONASS coverage for its entire coastline. In fact, the network of Differential GPS and GLONASS reference stations is now considered to form one single entity—the Differential Global Navigation Satellite System (DGNSS). Some jurisdictions are even considering the possibility of establishing facilities to transmit differential corrections to users of both GPS and GLONASS.

Caution: Since Differential GPS allows positioning of a vessel to within a few meters, you may be tempted to push the limits. If you do, *remember one universal rule:* Confirm navigation information from one source with that of another; never depend on one system alone to supply you with all the answers when accurate positioning is critical. A highly accurate DGPS Navigator—though it may seem like a miracle of science—can never replace common sense.

Another Dockside Test

Let's perform another dockside test as we did in Chapter 3. But this time, we will use a DGPS receiver. We don't expect you to actually plot out all the positions, but instead to imagine that you performed the test and arrived at the results we show in the diagrams.

Again, the dockside test begins with your vessel secured alongside a dock or wharf. If you plot the lat/long co-ordinates from your receiver for a twenty-four hour period at intervals of ten seconds, the displayed position will wander over a far smaller area than with unassisted GPS. [See Figure 9.3.] If you transfer the pattern of plotted positions to a nautical chart, it almost disappears. In fact, even on large-scale harbour charts, the DGPS pattern is so small you can consider it as a single point.

Fringe Reception Areas

As you travel away from a DGPS reference station, the correction signal becomes weaker and weaker, then completely fades out. In these "fringe reception areas," distance and intermittent signal loss significantly affect DGPS accuracy. Unless there is another reference station nearby, your DGPS receiver does not automatically switch to a stronger signal; instead, it reverts to non-differential mode.

In addition to attenuation (weakening) of the signal by distance from the

Comparing the GPS and DGPS Error Circles

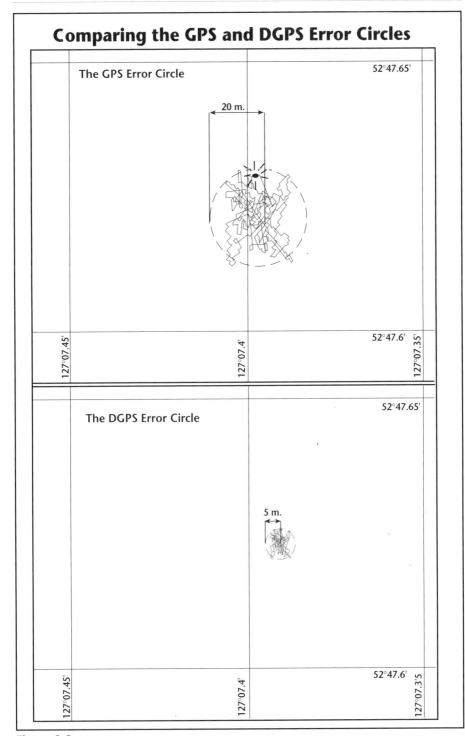

Figure 9.3

transmitter, similar difficulties of reception may occur when the signal path is blocked by land forms such as mountain ranges. Because the signal travels horizontally from the source, if your receiving antenna lies close under a land mass it may have trouble picking up DGPS broadcasts. If it can pick up signals from *two or more* DGPS transmitting stations (dual coverage), the receiver automatically switches to the signal with the greatest strength. If *both* signals are blocked by high land masses, DGPS corrections will be unavailable.

The same physical laws restricting the range of DGPS broadcasts allow the low frequency radio signals to bounce off the ionosphere and travel hundreds of miles. Since this occurrence is far more common at night, your receiver may be able to lock on to signals it cannot receive during the day. If you receive a DGPS broadcast at night that you cannot receive by day, treat the resulting positions with skepticism; the error corrections encoded in the broadcast will probably not be valid for your location.

Since a Differential reference station tracks and corrects only the signals of the satellites it can see, the corrections are valid only for those particular satellites. A DGPS receiver far from the reference station could actually be tracking one or more satellites that are below the horizon at the reference station. Also, satellites visible at the reference station could be below the horizon at the location of the mobile receiver.

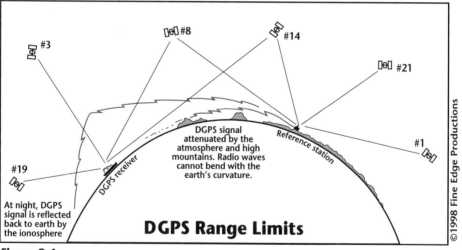

Figure 9.4

Both the DGPS reference station and the GPS receiver on board the boat are tracking four satellites each, but only two of the satellites are tracked by both stations. Satellites #3 and #19 are invisible to the reference station, and satellites #1 and #21 are invisible to the vessel at sea, so corrections for satellites #1 and #21 cannot be applied to any of the satellites visible to the mobile DGPS receiver. The DGPS receiver on board will also be unable to correct the signals from satellites #3 and #19 because no corrections for these satellite signals are available from the reference station.

As a result, the DGPS receiver may not be able to apply corrections to the pseudoranges of all the satellites it is tracking, and may correct some pseudoranges to DGPS accuracy but not others. The calculated position fix will thus be a hybrid and suffer in accuracy. Since the uncorrected satellite signals will probably come from one broad area of the horizon, the resulting position fix will have a bias either toward or away from the direction of the uncorrected satellite signals. [See Figure 9.4.]

When you perform a dockside test in a fringe area, the DGPS position may display a familiar tight pattern that—as a result of tracking different satellites— shifts to one side of the true position or the other or increases in size [Figure 9.5].

In fringe reception areas your GPS may lose and regain signal lock several times in the space of a few hours, switching back and forth between differential and non-differential mode and producing a pattern like that shown in Figure 9.5. However, when you lose signal lock, the resulting position should be no more in error than an unassisted GPS position. *Caution:* Our experience shows that when the DGPS signal is lost, a short period follows when displayed COG and SOG may be erroneous. This period can last 20 seconds or more while your receiver re-computes data from the received satellite signals. We have observed errors of up to 45° in COG at these times and, at the same time, have seen SOG drop from 10 kn to almost zero.

HDOP also plays a part in inducing errors in a DGPS position. Satellite geometry is subtly different for a roving DGPS receiver and a reference station, and as the difference increases with distance from the reference station, so does the error. This is why the transmitted power of the DGPS correction signal is carefully calculated to give the signal a limited range. Of course, your DGPS will still be subject to errors induced by antenna location, satellite masking, and COG rolling error.

There will always be remote areas where poorer nations cannot afford to establish DGPS networks, so you should become familiar with the characteristics of DGPS in fringe reception areas, keeping two important points in mind:

1. When navigating in DGPS mode, be sure your set is locked on to a differential correction signal before you assume that your position—or the course and speed displayed—has any greater accuracy than with unassisted GPS. A differential receiver should give some indication that it is operating in the Differential mode, otherwise your position may not be as accurate as you think. *Caution:* Be sure you are familiar with this indication and regularly check that Differential mode is still active. Remember that as your distance from the reference station increases, so will the DGPS error.

2. Never trust a Differential GPS position to be any more accurate than an unassisted GPS position unless you are sure your location is well serviced by DGPS broadcasts. Become familiar with the stations that service your area by consulting the national Radio Aids to Marine Navigation (or its

DGPS Dockside Test in Fringe Coverage Area

equivalent) or the Admiralty List of Radio Signals. Regularly check your set to determine which station's corrections your DGPS equipment is using. Late model DGPS receivers allow you to display the name and location of the reference station being used, as well as the frequency and baud rate. Once you have learned how to display this information, be sure to enter the procedure in The Workbook.

After you have navigated along a coastline for a while, you become familiar with the areas in which the DGPS broadcasts are reliable and learn where the fringe and shadowed areas are; in other words, you develop *local knowledge.*

DGPS and the Nautical Chart

If the charts you commonly use are less accurate than unassisted GPS, they are sure to be far less accurate than Differential GPS. If you are tempted to push the limits of accuracy of your DGPS receiver, you must also *continuously and scrupulously verify the indicated DGPS position with visual bearings and radar ranges.* Otherwise you may run into trouble. As shown in Chapter 3, unless the chart you are using was resurveyed in the last few years, the chart was probably not drawn to modern standards.

Hydrographers now collect data using local area UHF Differential GPS; therefore, new charts should avoid unacceptable errors. Unfortunately, government budgets are being cut everywhere and, with such a backlog of charts to update, even in developed countries it may be decades before all charts are brought to the accurate standard required by DGPS. The areas of highest priority for surveying are those of high-volume traffic where the consequences of chart positioning error are the most serious. *So explorers beware!*

Update Delay—High-Speed Navigation

After describing the wonderful accuracy that is possible with DGPS, it seems anticlimactic to report that the system has a flaw. This flaw is the inevitable result of employing two different receivers in order to obtain one position. It is only

Figure 9.5 (opposite)   DGPS Dockside Test in Fringe Coverage Area

At position 1, the DGPS is receiving valid corrections. A new satellite rises over the horizon but is not visible to the DGPS reference station. Consequently no corrections are available for pseudorange measurement to that satellite and the resulting fix is offset from the true position of the vessel by an amount greater than the normal DGPS error [position 2]. As the satellite rises higher it becomes visible to the reference station which broadcasts timing corrections for the satellite's pseudorange, returning the position indication to position 1. Another satellite rises and the process is repeated at position 3.

In this case, the receiver continues to lose and re-acquire the DGPS correction signal. When the DGPS receiver loses signal lock, it no longer applies corrections to any pseudoranges, reverting instead to <u>unassisted</u> GPS mode. In this case, the DGPS receiver has lost signal lock six or more times.

after several satellite navigation messages arrive at your GPS antenna, travel down the antenna cable, and are processed by your GPS receiver that a GPS position can be sent to your display. This process takes approximately one second. At the same time your GPS receiver processes this uncorrected message, the same message arrives at the reference station, where it is processed into a correction message before being broadcast on the beacon band.

Consequently, by the time your GPS receiver is ready to display the position, it is still waiting for the correction message from the DGPS reference station. The time taken to receive the correction message, feed it from the Differential receiver to the GPS receiver, perform the correction and display the finalized position, is the cause of the longer update delay of DGPS (up to two second in some models).

For a vessel travelling at 10 knots or less, this two-second update error amounts to 10 meters—not highly significant. However when travelling at 25 knots in a high-speed boat, the error can reach 25 meters. While this is not a large error by the standards of unassisted GPS, it represents a significant degradation of DGPS capability.

HM Submarine *Tireless*

In the early sixties, I was assigned to the submarine HM *Tireless*. We were bumbling along—or rather *under*—the English Channel, playing cat and mouse with a destroyer that was practising sonar search overhead. We were dependent for position-fixing on a dead reckoning plot that consisted of a point of light moving across a chart spread out on the control room table.

Everyone was in the ward room watching a film except the OOW (Officer of the Watch) who had drawn the short straw and was on watch in the control room. Guess who!

The plot showed the symbol for a *non-dangerous* wreck about two miles (twenty minutes) ahead. "Non-dangerous," I thought. "That's all very well, but non-dangerous refers to surface shipping not deep enough to be affected."

We were just a few feet above the seabed—a very different matter. A message to the wardroom, a minuscule compartment immediately ahead of the control room, brought the CO (Commanding Officer). "Well, Len, what's to do?" asked Lieutenant Commander "Sandy" Woodward. It was his first command and I expected some apprehension when I explained the position.

Nothing of the sort: immediate reaction, instant decision. I can still hear him: "Normal hazards of submarining. Altering course will cause cavitation and that destroyer will latch onto us for sure. No alteration of course or speed. Stand on." And he promptly disappeared to watch the film. So we stood on and were all right. Nothing happened.

I can understand his thinking, of course. The plot was a stone-age contraption driven by log and compass, and the wreck *probably* wasn't quite dead ahead. Any alteration of course might have done more harm than good. I wonder what his decision would have been if we'd had Differential GPS! . . . We shall never know.

Commander L.P. Fenner, R.D., R.N.R., former Trinity House Pilot

At the present time, military and coast guard agencies around the world are studying the problem in order to arrive at a resolution, but since it is inherent in the system itself, most operators of high-speed craft have been forced to live with it. Consequently we recommend that you don't expect pinpoint-accuracy out of your DGPS while travelling at high speed. Also, while operating at high speed, make sure the smoothing control is turned off.

In fact, the slower update rate of differential GPS is normally not a problem, given that the vessel operator requires at least three or four seconds to respond to the information provided by a DGPS display, thus making the human at the wheel the weakest link in the chain.

Navigational Notices

In many jurisdictions, DGPS reference and transmitting stations are still in a testing mode and may be shut down without notice. For example, a Canadian *Notice to Mariners* states that "users may experience service interruptions without advance notice." Further, Canadian Coast Guard advises that "DGPS broadcasts should not be used where sudden system failure or inaccuracy could

MH Submarine
Tireless

©2000 Fine Edge Productions

Figure 9.6

The plot placed the Tireless at a position and on a heading that would carry it directly into collision with a submerged wreck. However, the Tireless was not at the location indicated by the plot. Given the inaccuracies inherent in the technology of the time, the Commanding Officer considered it unlikely that the Tireless would approach the wreck and that an alteration of course might serve to place the submarine in danger.

constitute a safety hazard." Only when the service has been tested in operation and found reliable will national authorities announce Full Operational Service (FOS) in Notices to Mariners. Until the national networks are fully operational, the agencies responsible will attempt—but not guarantee—to provide warnings of station shut-down or failure.

Once in FOS status, national authorities will not alter or shut down DGPS stations without issuing a notice to the marine community in the following format:

- Announce planned shut down of DGPS reference stations through printed *Notices to Mariners* and *Notices to Shipping* broadcast by national coastal radio stations. (Notices to Shipping are normally announced on Channel 16 VHF and on 2182 kHz, as well as on Navtex.)

- Announce the sudden failure or unreliability of a DGPS reference station in *Notices to Shipping*.

For further information on the operational status of DGPS reference stations, consult the current *Admiralty List of Radio Signals, Volume 2*, or other national publications.

As DGPS Reference stations come on line they are subjected to a rigorous testing to ensure the quality of service. However, national hydrographic offices have become aware of intermittent anomalies in DGPS broadcasts. In the interest of perfecting their understanding of the actual operating characteristics of DGPS, most agencies are requesting that mariners forward their observations of DGPS anomalies. Report forms can be found in Notices to Mariners, or in the Admiralty List of Radio Signals, Volume 2. We encourage you to report any discrepancies you may note to the appropriate authority.

WAAS and NDGPS

On the horizon, the Federal Aviation Administration (FAA) plan called Wide Area Augmentation System (WAAS) will transmit continent-wide corrections on GPS frequencies and therefore will not require additional equipment. The plan calls for 35 ground reference stations which uplink the corrections to geosynchronous communications satellites then broadcast the navigation messages to any suitable receiver in North America. In addition to vertical and horizontal position accuracy of 7 meters for airport approaches in North America the system will provide integrity monitoring of the GPS satellites in much the same manner as marine DGPS.

The National DGPS network (NDGPS) is a plan to extend the U.S. Coast Guard DGPS system to all land surfaces in the contiguous 48 states in the next few years —not just near shores and rivers. This network will provide 2- to 5-meter positioning accuracy consistent with the rest of the Coast Guard's system, and may supercede plans for WAAS.

Anomalies in Canadian Waters can be reported over the internet at the following URL.

http://www.notmar.com/eng/services/notmar/notice.html

DGPS in the British Isles

As we reported in the first edition of *GPS—Instant Navigation*, differential corrections in the UK and Eire were the responsibility of Scorpio Navigational Services. Scorpio provided encrypted correction signals available for an annual fee. In August 1998, however, Trinity House and the General Lighthouse Authorities for Northern Ireland and Scotland began broadcasting free public DGPS signals that can be picked up by anyone equipped with a standard marine differential receiver.

Thus, marine DGPS is now a free service everywhere the signals are available.

Further information regarding DGPS in Great Britain, can be obtained from the Trinity House web site listed in Appendix B. (Trinity House is the authority responsible for lighthouses and navigational aids in English and Welsh waters.)

The Future of DGPS

Now that Selective Availability has been removed in accordance with the United States GPS policy statement, civilian GPS users can expect 20-meter accuracy from unassisted GPS. In light of this possibility, what are the implications for the future of DGPS? Will consumers still be interested in purchasing DGPS equipment and will governments still be interested in providing the service?

Even though removal of SA has not improved the accuracy of DGPS, we feel that DGPS will still play a valuable role in marine navigation.

The United States *Radionavigation Plan* calls for 8-meter positioning-accuracy for major shipping in U.S. harbours and harbour approaches. DGPS far exceeds this requirement, with accuracy in the 2- to 5-meter range in many harbours. Many other governments also feel that this is an appropriate degree of accuracy for busy shipping lanes and airport approaches. Even with SA removed, unassisted GPS cannot reach the degree of accuracy required by the *Federal Radionavigation Plan*.

While other governments are happy to use GPS and GLONASS signals for their own purposes, they are aware that the availability of GPS is dictated by the self-interest of a foreign government. In spite of policy statements to the contrary, other countries may fear that the United States could reintroduce Selective Availability at some future time. Consequently, by developing their own DGPS systems, foreign governments are serving their own interests in their own waters.

National authorities see in DGPS networks an opportunity to phase out many expensive aids to navigation maintained for the benefit of commercial shipping. Since the cost of a DGPS network is a small fraction of the cost of maintaining a system of buoys and lights, it is no surprise that governments are eager to pursue this technology.

As stated earlier in this chapter, DGPS provides a vital integrity monitoring capability for the Global Positioning System. Within 10 seconds of a satellite message becoming unreliable DGPS reference stations will broadcast a "do not use this satellite" message, and DGPS receivers will cease to range on the unhealthy satellite. While this capability may not be worth the expense to the recreational community, it provides a vital service to major commercial shipping. The environmental consequences of a large ship running aground in a busy waterway far outweigh the minimal cost of the DGPS receiver.

No other technology available now or in the near future appears to offer the same degree of positioning accuracy as DGPS. So, in the author's opinion, until some newer technology emerges that renders it obsolete, DGPS will continue to be the preferred method of precise positioning for commercial users in the foreseeable future.

CHAPTER 10

GPS Plotters

This chapter deals with fairly simple equipment compared to modern electronic charting systems (ECS), but readers who are interested only in electronic charting are still encouraged to read about the plotter interface since many of the basic functions of simple plotters are shared with ECS.

Simple Plotters

A plotter display is one that shows the vessel's track against a plain latitude/longitude grid without the benefit of even rudimentary electronic charts. Plotters are incorporated into almost all kinds of navigation equipment, even depth sounders and radars—at any boat show you will be astounded by the variety. Plotters are available now in many GPS Navigators as an additional display that can be used instead of traditional and perspective steering diagrams.

Whether they stand alone, or are incorporated into another piece of navigation electronics, plotters come with a huge range of capabilities. When purchasing any piece of navigation electronics that includes a plotter, learn the plotter's capabilities; many have full waypoint/route capability, while others that are integrated into depth sounders, etc. may only be able to display the waypoints/routes generated by an external GPS Navigator.

Early plotters were simple mechanical devices that plotted a vessel's movement on a plotting board or chart using dead reckoning instead of electronic positioning. Every so often the navigator would take a fix using a compass or sextant and update the position on the plotting board—a cumbersome process. At 12 knots, a vessel covers 1/10 mile (600 feet) in 30 seconds. It is seldom possible to resolve an accurate position in less than 15 seconds, and it often takes much longer—up to half an hour if you are taking sun or star sights. As a result, a position could be significantly out-of-date before it was ever placed on the plot.

Now that continuous electronic position updating is possible, driven by GPS or DGPS, the navigation plotter performs virtually *instantaneous* navigation. At least once per second, a GPS receiver fixes your position on the plot. As a result you can be sure that the position displayed by your plotter is fully up-to-date and that it displays events as they occur, not as they might be, based on obsolete DR projections.

The GPS Sensor

A GPS Navigator consists of four basic elements: an antenna, the receiver circuits, a console with keys for entering data, and a computer loaded with appropriate software. If the basic receiver and antenna were connected to another piece of equipment, such as a computer or a plotter which would provide navigation capability and a keyboard, the GPS receiver itself would not need its own keyboard and display. This type of equipment is known as a GPS sensor. Since it lacks any external controls and displays, it can be manufactured less expensively than a fully functional GPS Navigator.

This type of basic receiver first appeared when Loran C owners were switching to the new GPS technology. With a GPS sensor, a skipper could add GPS capability to his Loran C Navigator/plotter without purchasing another piece of electronic equipment that would have duplicated the displays and keyboards of his existing equipment. For those who already own some sort of electronic Navigator and wish to switch to GPS, this may be a reasonable alternative.

For skippers who own computers and electronic charting programs, the GPS sensor may also be a sensible solution. The raw GPS data goes directly to the PC which then becomes the navigating instrument for manipulating waypoints and routes. The only problem is that the GPS then depends on another piece of equipment to display its information and to receive commands. If that other equipment fails, you will have a perfectly functioning GPS receiver with no way to access its information. If you can afford a computer, you can surely purchase a fully functional modern GPS that will provide raw data to the computer but which can also stand alone as a GPS Navigator.

Figure 10.1
Si-Tex Combined GPS Sensor/Antenna

In the interest of reducing the number of pieces of equipment aboard your vessel, some enterprising manufacturers market a combined GPS or DGPS antenna combination with the GPS sensor built right in. This equipment transmits the appropriate data format directly to a computer, plotter, or compatible Loran C.

The Si-Tex GPS 10-A, a waterproof parallel channel receiver and antenna combination, continuously tracks six channels and is differential ready.

Getting Used to the Display

After powering up and initializing your GPS plotter, the first thing you notice is a flashing point or a small boat shape (**icon**) somewhere on the screen. This flashing point or icon represents your position displayed against a grid of latitude and longitude lines. [See Figure 10.2.]

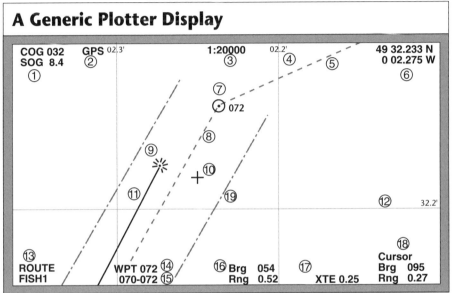

A Generic Plotter Display

Figure 10.2

Not all plotters display all this information; some may show more.
The primary features of a good plotter display are:
1. COG and SOG display
2. Positioning input (could be Loran C, GPS or DGPS)
3. Plotter scale (may also be given in Nm)
4. Designator of the number of minutes of longitude or latitude (the number of degrees is dropped)
5. Course Line to next waypoint
6. Latitude and longitude of present position
7. Destination waypoint named 072
8. Course Line to waypoint 072
9. Present position of vessel (a flashing point of light is used—other plotters may use a vessel icon)
10. Cursor
11. Track History
12. Latitude/Longitude Grid
13. Name of route being navigated
14. Name of destination waypoint
15. Leg being navigated (from waypoint 070 to waypoint 072)
16. Bearing and range of destination waypoint
17. Cross Track Error (XTE)
18. Bearing and range of cursor (it may be possible to switch to lat/long of cursor)
19. Cross Track Error (XTE) boundary alarm limits

Somewhere on the screen you will find an indication of the scale of the image which may be given in nautical miles or a scale ratio, such as 1.0 Nm or 1:5000. In the former case, the distance from one edge of the plotter screen to the other represents 1.0 Nm. In the latter case, one centimeter on the screen represents 5,000 centimeters or 50 meters. Check your owner's manual to find out how to switch from one type of scale indication to the other, then record the procedure in The Workbook. How you choose to display the scale is your own decision.

Once you have learned how to display the scale in use, read the instruction manual to find out how to change scale (zooming). Some models permit you to zoom with a single keystroke. Others may force you to access a menu and select a scale. Record this procedure in The Workbook as well.

The Dockside Test

With a plotter you can perform a dockside test any time your vessel is stationary. The plotter automatically plots the positions on the display; as the apparent position changes, the track history develops into the classic pattern. To view the pattern, select the maximum scale available. The pattern of positions should be roughly 0.02 Nm in diameter. You can verify this by checking the maximum width of the pattern against the latitude grid. (0.02 Nm is equal to 0.02' of latitude.)

In previous chapters, you saw diagrams representing plots derived from various Dockside Tests, so we won't duplicate any of those here, especially since your plotter can show the same images in a clear and graphic manner. This graphic display can help you understand how GPS error affects the positioning of your vessel when it is stationary and how its position is affected by the same errors at sea.

Sea Trials

To learn how to use the plotter, you must observe it in action, so cast off your lines and head away from the dock. The important part of this exercise is to familiarize yourself with the plotter display and its limitations. Don't despair if it seems to take a long time to develop familiarity. You will soon develop an intuitive understanding of the display, which will make traditional and perspective steering diagrams seem positively Neanderthal.

As soon as your vessel moves away from the dock, you will see the boat icon or flashing dot move across the display, depositing the track history behind the present position like a trail of bread crumbs. When the icon reaches the edge of the screen, the plotter re-draws the display and returns the icon to the center. The faster your vessel moves, the sooner the icon reaches the edge of the screen, but if this occurs too often, you have set the plotter scale too high.

Once a section of track history is laid down in the display, increase the scale to the maximum and observe the track itself. Is the track a series of dots or a continuous line? If it appears to be a series of unconnected dots, each dot represents a plotted position. If you can find a selection or menu choice for selecting a plotting interval, you can increase or decrease the time interval between plotted positions. A short plotting interval is useful since it allows the plotter to respond immediately to the GPS input, but too short a plotting interval will fill the plotter memory rapidly, since each dot represents a given number of bytes of memory. The plotter can store a limited number of positions before it starts to erase the oldest ones, so the track history has a limited length. If you select a longer plotting interval, the plotter will retain older portions of the track for a longer period of time, but it will be sluggish in responding to changes in course and speed. *Try varying the plotting interval and observe the resulting changes in response time.*

If the plotted track shows as a continuous line, the plotter is connecting the dots. A continuous line track is easier to read and has many other advantages as well, but it is essentially no different from a dotted track.

Once you find an appropriate scale for the display, you can have some fun. Proceed for a while on a steady heading and wait until the COG and SOG stabilize. Then, *if there are no other vessels in the area*, make a sudden, sharp turn. Note that the turn does not show instantly on the plot. It takes a few seconds, perhaps longer, for the COG and SOG to reflect the new heading and speed—due to the chosen plotter interval, the update delay inherent in your GPS receiver, and the amount of smoothing you have applied.

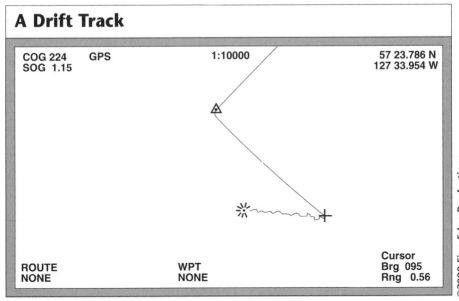

Figure 10.3

At the cursor position the engines were stopped and the vessel allowed to drift with the current.

Some skippers like to see if they can write their names on the plotter, using the twists and turns of the vessel's track as if it were a very slow pen. But try this "trick" yourself *only* if there is sea room and no other traffic around.

Next, bring your vessel to a dead stop, let the engine idle, and brew yourself a cup of tea. After a few minutes, the display will show the drift track of the boat. You can actually see the point at which you stopped the vessel [Figure 10.3]. If the display shows a dotted line track, in the track laid down while the vessel was drifting, you can see that the dots are close together because the vessel was moving very slowly. Where the boat was running at cruising speed, the dots are much farther apart [Figure 10.4].

If your plotter indicates the present position with a vessel icon, you will notice that the icon rotates randomly through all the points of the compass as you drift. This is because the vessel icon's indicated heading is based on the COG, which is completely unreliable at low speeds. When drifting, the only way to get the icon to show the correct heading is to incorporate input from a flux-gate or gyrocompass into the plotter interface. Most plotters do not have this capability, even though you may have the correct type of compass connected to your autopilot. Because of its unreliability, most users find the vessel icon dis-

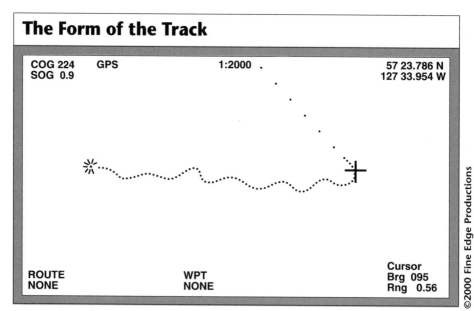

Figure 10.4

This display is shown at a scale of 1:2000. The track in this case is a series of dots, each indicating a plotted position. Note that where the vessel was up to cruising speed, the dots are farther apart than during the drift phase when the SOG was very low. For clarity, lat/long lines are not shown.

tracting and prefer the vessel position to be indicated by a flashing spot of light. Also, the vessel icon often obscures parts of the track.

Should you wish to return to the point at which you stopped the boat, just estimate the heading required and steer in that direction; the plotter will indicate when you have arrived at your destination.

Working With Waypoints and Event Marks

If your plotter is integral with the GPS Navigator, you can probably see all the local waypoints displayed. If it is a separate unit, you may have to activate a route in the GPS Navigator before any waypoints appear on the plotter display. In either case, once you activate a route, the Course Lines and waypoints comprising that route will appear and you will be able to use the plotter display as a steering diagram. Zoom in (increase the scale) to see how well your track follows the Course Line. Zoom out (decrease the scale) to see how your vessel is progressing in relation to other features such as waypoints in the route, avoidance waypoints, etc.

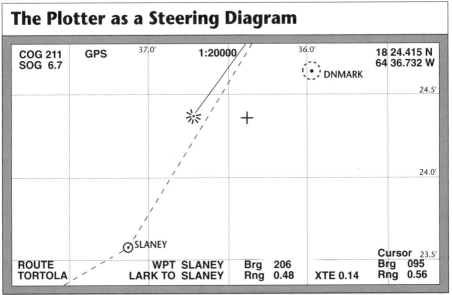

Figure 10.5

The leg from LARK to SLANEY appears on the plotter display as a dashed line. It is clear that the vessel is off the Intended Track by a small amount and should turn a few degrees to port to come back onto the Course Line. The present position of the vessel is shown in the upper right-hand corner. Bearing and range to waypoint SLANEY are shown at the bottom of the display. In addition, avoidance waypoint DNMARK is shown. The small + is the cursor; its position, range and bearing <u>from the present position</u> appear in the lower right-hand corner. The next leg is the dashed line extending southwest from waypoint SLANEY. You can easily see the direction to the next waypoint from waypoint SLANEY.

As you approach a destination waypoint, you can instantly determine the approximate next course to steer, and where that waypoint lies in the route. That information, and much more, is available in graphic form, which makes the plotter useful because, as a visual species, we humans react well to pictures. Anything that relieves us from the tyranny of numbers makes our work safer and more enjoyable [Figure 10.5].

Cursors

The presence of a **cursor** of some sort makes it possible to manipulate the plot. Without a cursor, a plotter is just a glorified steering diagram; waypoints, routes and other instructions must be input either numerically or electronically from another GPS Navigator or a computer. Once you begin to work with a cursor, you can interact with the plot graphically and enter waypoints and event marks without resorting to the use of numbers at all.

A cursor normally takes the form of a small X that is moved across the display by a trackball or a series of arrow keys. (How you manipulate a cursor is unimportant, but it should respond quickly and positively to your control.) As you move it across the screen, many plotters will display the co-ordinates of the cursor in latitude and longitude or its range and bearing from the present position. Some plotters display both types of information simultaneously.

Once you place a cursor in a specific location, it should remain there until you move it again. Thus, if the cursor is set to display its lat/long co-ordinates, the co-ordinates remain the same as the vessel icon moves across the screen. If you wish to find the lat/long co-ordinates of the position where you brought your vessel to a stop and allowed it to drift, simply move the cursor to that point on the display [Figure 10.4]. Not only will the lat/long co-ordinates be immediately apparent but so will range and bearing from your present position. If you wish to designate the cursor position as a waypoint, you can do so easily without resorting to any form of numerical data entry. Be sure you know how to enter a waypoint by cursor position and record this information in The Workbook.

If the cursor is configured to display range and bearing *from the vessel to the cursor* then—as the vessel moves across the display—the range and bearing to the stationary cursor should continuously change. Of course, all bets are off when the vessel icon moves off the edge of the display. Each time the display is re-drawn, the lat/long grid is shifted in order to center the vessel icon and although the cursor maintains its same position relative to the display, it no longer marks the same geographic position.

The same is true when changing the display scale. If the cursor is at the lower right corner of the display when the scale is switched from 1:2000 to 1:50000, it will remain there, but it will mark a significantly different geographic position! You will notice that the cursor range and bearing or latitude and longitude shift abruptly when either of these events occurs.

Scrolling

Using the cursor to move the display "window" to another portion of the lat/long grid is a process known as **scrolling**.

If your display is set to a relatively large scale (1:10000 or more), you will notice that the vessel icon rapidly marches off the edges of the screen and causes the plotter to regularly re-draw the display. It may be a simple matter to reduce the scale so you can view the entire track history, but if you do, the track will lose detail. Instead, you may wish to look at a large-scale representation of the track in an area that is no longer present on the display. Without some sort of cursor control, this is simply not possible. With the cursor included in all but the most rudimentary plotters, you will be able to scroll back along the vessel's track to find the feature you are looking for.

You may need to choose from a menu in order to do so, or you may have to select the scrolling function of the cursor in some other way. *Be sure you know how to turn the cursor scroll control on and off.* Then enter that information in The Workbook.

Once you have scroll control, just bump the cursor at an edge of the screen, and the plot display should move in the opposite direction, allowing you to inspect any portion of the track. It should be possible to scroll vertically, horizontally, and diagonally. To return to your vessel's present position, you can scroll back again or, to save time, simply instruct the plotter to re-center the vessel icon on the display.

Avoidance Waypoint

With the introduction of a common electronic navigation language, certain fundamental data—such as course and speed, position, waypoint, route, and most functions of route navigation—is universally understood by electronic navigation software. However, avoidance waypoint is one function that may not be included in the electronic language your plotter understands, even though your GPS Navigator uses avoidance waypoints and sends proper data to your plotter. Consequently, avoidance waypoints may not show on the plotter or they may be displayed as if they were any other waypoint. If this is the case, be sure that you know which are navigation waypoints and which are avoidance waypoints.

Event Marks

As your vessel's track progresses across the display, you may wish to insert a mark when you see something of interest such as a likely fishing spot or a position where two points are in line. Most decent plotters allow you to insert a mark rapidly and without fuss using the cursor.

You can record the position of any kind of event with an **event mark**, and the event will remain in the plotter's memory until you delete it. The mark on the display will outlast the track line, so it is often an advantage to use event marks liberally. Many plotters provide a selection of different types of event mark shapes; you might use one shape to record schools of fish, another to mark course alterations, another to record important navigational information, and yet another to mark positions you can later convert into waypoints.

Some plotters allow you to place an event mark by present position only. If your plotter lacks the ability to place an event mark or waypoint with the cursor, it is really just an advanced type of steering diagram—useful, but not a true plotter.

The procedure for placing an event mark should be so simple that you can place accurate marks while your vessel is bouncing around at sea.

You may be able to enter a line of text at an event mark then call up this text at any time by placing the cursor over the mark and activating the function. This allows the operator to record such information as "large school of herring" or "uncharted rock-dries 7 feet" or "dangerous overfalls at spring tides." [Refer to Figure 10.6.] It should be possible to enter the event mark immediately and then add the text later.

Many of the techniques demonstrated in Chapter 7 that require the operator to use waypoints other than those on the route being navigated can use event marks instead. For instance, to find the approximate set and drift of the current,

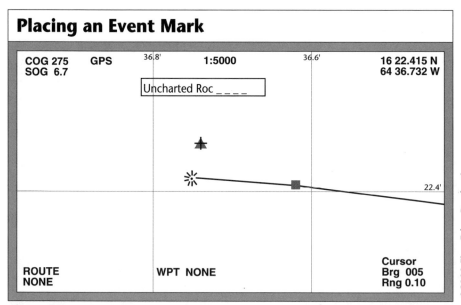

Figure 10.6

The vessel passes south of an uncharted rock, estimated distance 0.1 Nm. Scroll the cursor to the north of the vessel's position until the bearing and range of the cursor match the bearing and range of the rock observed on radar. Then enter an event mark and a text message that reads "Uncharted Rock 5 feet."

CMG, and SMG [Chapter 7, Figure 7.5], simply place an event mark at your present position at the beginning of the run. Then project the cursor along the course steered to establish a DR position. The use of a plotter in such situations allows the GPS Navigator to track the destination waypoint without interruption, and lets you perform more tasks in a paperless environment. [Refer to Chapter 7, Figure 7.10 for other techniques that could be worked with event marks.]

Horizontal Datum

When using a plotter to display positioning and navigation data, chart datum issues still apply. You must understand that the plotter display is just a graphic representation of the information stored in the GPS Navigator's "brain." If a GPS Navigator is supplying the plotter with navigation data, the correct datum must be set in that GPS. Then, when you enter waypoints in the GPS Navigator from a position taken from the chart, the chart will agree with the plotter.

On the other hand, the cursor position is always measured *relative to the present position of the vessel.* As a result, waypoints and event marks entered with a cursor have the same advantage as saved waypoints. As long as you don't attempt to refer these waypoints and event marks to a paper chart or the plotter's lat/long grid, they are *independent* of chart datum since they are referenced to the position of your vessel itself.

To illustrate this, consider an event mark entered when your vessel is stationary. When you change the horizontal datum of the plotter's controlling GPS unit, the vessel icon appears to jump across the screen a distance equal to the shift between the two datums (a graphic representation of datum shift). However, since the co-ordinates of all waypoints and event marks in memory are usually shifted by the same amount, they will maintain the same range and bearing from your vessel. If the waypoints and marks were originally entered by range and bearing from your vessel, or by present position, there should be no resulting datum conflict for these cursor-entered events. The difficulty is that once cursor-entered waypoints are entered into memory, you don't know whether they were entered by cursor or lat/long co-ordinates. So you must scrupulously match the plotter's datum to your paper chart and keep an accurate waypoint log.

Using Event Marks to Identify Danger Areas

You can use the event mark capability of your GPS plotter to mark danger areas such as the margins of a submerged reef. However, to do this you must first bring your vessel close to the edges of the reef without using your GPS Navigator/plotter for positioning. This requires good visibility and decent weather. Once you are as close to the reef as is safe, enter an event mark by present position, then proceed along its edges, placing more event marks until you literally have it surrounded. Figure 10.7 illustrates how your plotter display should look when you finish. *Remember to allow a margin for error.* Even if you generally operate in DGPS mode, allow the same margin for errors in case the differential reference station goes out of action. If your plotter lets you enter text at an event mark, include a comment such as "Edges of Sudden Reef" to remind yourself of the

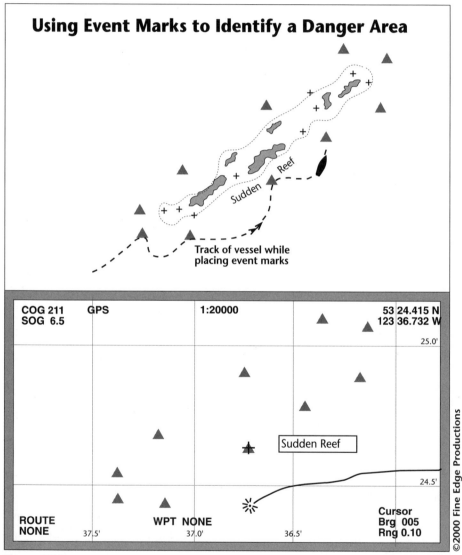

Figure 10.7

Sudden Reef, exposed only at low water, is a significant hazard to navigation. To make a semi-permanent record of the danger area, place event marks on all sides of the reef. In the future, you can use these event marks to stay well clear of the reef. The cursor has been placed on one of the event marks to reveal the text.

purpose of the marks.

Don't bother creating this type of guard zone unless you regularly navigate in a specific area. However, once you set up the event marks, you will always have the advantage of knowing the position of the reef, even at night or in heavy weather.

Anchor Watches

The graphic nature of the plotter display will be especially helpful when you first use it for **anchor watches**. The following guidelines will help you interpret the plotter display:

- After dropping anchor, set the plotter to the largest scale possible (commonly 1:2000) and leave it alone for a while. A classic pattern soon forms: a combination of the virtual track induced by the GPS error and the true swing of the vessel around its anchor. If the anchorage is shallow and your vessel swings just a short distance, the pattern will be much smaller than in deep water.

- If the wind or current changes direction while you are anchored, your vessel will swing to the other side of the anchor and begin to describe a track in a previously blank portion of the display.

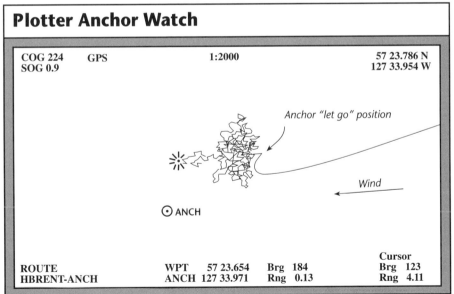

Figure 10.8

In this plotter display of a vessel at anchor during a storm, the pattern is caused by a combination of the vessel's swinging at anchor and GPS error. For a while, the anchor held and the pattern remained stable; then the anchor began to drag, and the vessel emerged to the west of the pattern. For clarity, lat/long lines are not shown.

Plotter Anchor Watch with DGPS

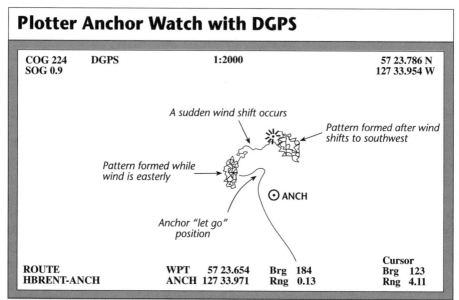

COG 224 SOG 0.9	DGPS	1:2000	57 23.786 N 127 33.954 W

A sudden wind shift occurs

Pattern formed after wind shifts to southwest

Pattern formed while wind is easterly

⊙ ANCH

Anchor "let go" position

©2000 Fine Edge Productions

			Cursor
ROUTE HBRENT-ANCH	WPT 57 23.654 ANCH 127 33.971	Brg 184 Rng 0.13	Brg 123 Rng 4.11

Figure 10.9

This pattern, caused almost entirely by the vessel's swinging at anchor, is far smaller than that with unassisted GPS; the direction of displacement is opposite to that of the wind. For clarity, lat/long lines are not shown.

- If your anchor drags more than a few tens of meters during the night, the vessel icon will move away from the anchor position and out of the original pattern [Figure 10.8]. Turn on your spotlight or radar to see where you are. If your vessel is dragging anchor, you must take immediate steps to avoid further dragging.

- You will even be able to tell on which side of the anchor your vessel is riding and, consequently, the direction of the operating current or wind [Figure 10.9].

Using these guidelines, even a novice boater should be able to tell if a vessel moves significantly during the night. If you anchor in a roadstead where your boat is likely to drag anchor, take a quick glance at the plotter every couple of hours to see if the pattern has changed.

Retracing a Course Line

Boating never goes exactly as planned. You may find yourself in places where you do not wish to be—in a patch of rocks and shoals, or in a channel you discover blocked by rocks or wrecks. In such cases, a plotter can be extremely valuable. You know that your track history describes a safe channel, so if you turn your boat around and retrace the track, it will guide you to safety.

Make sure the plotter scale is set high enough to show the best detail of the twists and turns of the track history, then simply follow the track to safety. If you place the cursor on the old track line at a bend ahead of your present position, the displayed bearing of the cursor is the heading to follow. Once you reach the cursor position, reposition the cursor at the next bend in the track. In this way, you are guided by your own previous movements.

Working with Limiting Lines

Using a GPS plotter, you can utilize Limiting LOPs of Latitude and Longitude. [See the discussion in "Limiting Lines of Latitude and Longitude" in Chapter 6.] However, if you chose a small scale in order to view the entire area on the display, you may find that the longitude (or latitude) you chose as a limiting LOP is not shown as a longitude line on the display. If you decide to use longitude 5°36.07' W, for example, you may find only 5°36.05' and 5°36.10' shown on the plotter screen. Increase the scale and you may see the desired longitude, but in all likelihood, it will appear only when the vessel icon closely approaches it. At all other times, it will lie far off-screen.

As a result, you must rely on the latitude/longitude readout to determine when you are approaching the limiting line of longitude, then increase the scale to view the controlling longitude as you draw near. After turning away from the limiting LOP, decrease the plotter scale again. If you are operating in heavy seas, this may not be easy. You may be forced to use whole or half-minutes or tenth-minute LOPs to avoid switching scale during critical maneuvers. In the example shown in Chapter 6, Figure 6.4, we chose the specific limiting longitudes and latitudes partly because of the difficulties imposed by heavy weather.

If you are able to plan ahead, you can establish waypoints so that the Course Lines between them are coincident with the limiting latitudes and longitudes. For a demonstration of this problem and its solution, see Figure 10.10.

Boundaries

In Chapter 7, we discussed using waypoints to define artificial boundaries such as military area, international, and fishing zone boundaries. You can use the same techniques with a GPS plotter. If you assign waypoints at specific locations along the boundary by lifting the co-ordinates off a chart, when you create a route from the waypoints, your plotter will display the route as a close approximation of the boundary. This is similar to using limiting lines of latitude and longitude, except that the **boundary** lines do not need to be oriented true north-south or east-west.

To define the boundary more precisely, it is always best to use saved waypoints. If the boundary extends in a straight line from one well-marked position on the shoreline to another, you can take your vessel close in to the boundary marks and save waypoints at those places. However, if all the waypoints that

Using a Plotted Route to Define Limiting Lines of Latitude and Longitude

WP2   Latitude 52°10.0'N   WP1

Cheeseman Rock

Milbanke Sound

Providence Rock

Cape Mark

Longitude 128°33.75'W

Hope Rocks

Godfrey Rock

Latitude 52°07.95'N

WP3   WP4

Latitude 52°07.40'N

WP6   WP5

Wind and waves from southeast

Rempstone Rocks

Limit I.

N

QUEEN'S SOUND

COG 032   GPS   33.5'   1:20000   32.5'   53 07.57 N
SOG 8.4   123 33.22 W
                                                         08.0'
WP3

+

                                                         07.5'

ROUTE   WPT   WP4   Cursor
CPMARK   WP3 - WP4   Brg 005
                                           Rng 0.10

©2000 Fine Edge Productions

define the boundary are located *away* from land or other geographic references, it may not be possible to use saved waypoints. Once you enter the waypoints in memory, they will always be available in the future.

Chart Plotters

Consumer electronic charting in its most rudimentary form arrived in the early 1990s in the form of sophisticated plotters. These units were good quality plotters with a socket for inserting a variety of digital electronic chart cards. Each manufacturer digitized its own charts—charts which would dismay anyone presently using electronic charts. The charts, which were extremely crude, consisted of straight-line segments and only generally followed the shorelines of existing features. When viewed at large scale these charts were disappointingly inaccurate; no depths or other navigational data were available. These plotters were driven by Loran C and extreme offsets were often encountered in coastal areas, so the relative accuracy of the chart was not important. The cost of each chart card was unbelievable!

Many manufacturers recognized a good thing when they saw it; despite the limitations, for the first time an electronic navigation device had been integrated with a chart system for small vessels. Approximate positions could instantly be assessed in relation to nearby land masses without having to copy lat/long coordinates and plot them on a paper chart. The tyranny of numbers had been overthrown; for that reason alone, many of these systems were sold. To differentiate plotters that displayed these rudimentary charts from those which did not, the terms "**Chart Plotter**" and "**Track Plotter**" were coined.

Fortunately, it did not take long before more sophisticated charts became available; with the introduction of GPS and then DGPS, the modern chart plotter emerged. (The GPS plotter shown in Figure 10.11 is one of these new generation chart plotters, which use chart cartridges with a storage capacity of megabytes instead of kilobytes.) They show shorelines, shoals, drying flats, traffic lanes, and lights and buoys, to name a few of the many features. Generally they do not show the wealth of detail available in the true PC-driven Electronic Charts (ECs). The charts themselves come in read-only cartridges, often manufactured by third party producers such as C-Map and Navionics but also available in a proprietary format from the equipment manufacturers themselves.

Figure 10.10 (opposite)
Limiting lines of latitude and longitude can be established by setting up a route that follows the limiting LOPs exactly. Once completed, the plotter will display all the legs of the route. You can then follow these legs visually as if they were controlling LOPs. Because none of the waypoints is treated as a destination, waypoint realization is irrelevant. Once the vessel passes to the north of Limit Island, deactivate the route because it is no longer useful. Note that the leg drawn between WP4 and WP5 doesn't represent any portion of the boundary. However, you must include this leg if you are to include both sides of the corridor of controlling latitudes in one route.

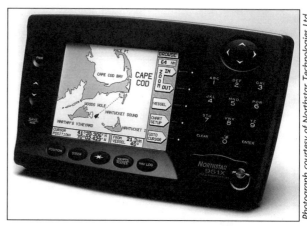

Photograph courtesy of Northstar Technologies Ltd.

Figure 10.11
Northstar 951XD

This model combines menus, soft keys, and special function keys with an alphanumeric keyboard and a large display. The result is a DGPS Navigator that is simple to operate.

Chart Plotters have been on the market for several years now, and their capability and utility have increased enormously since the early days. Chart plotters that were capable of just a very few functions have been replaced by equipment that is far more useful and user-friendly. As the capabilities of the equipment have increased, basic plotter functions have been added to the more inexpensive units, and now, virtually all new GPS equipment—even the simplest hand-held—contains some sort of basic plotting capability. (See Chapter 1, Figure 1.4) Some hand-held units support chart plotter capability that is just as sophisticated as many of the fixed units. [See Figure 10.12.]

The great advantage of these modern chart plotters is that they allow the operator to interface with navigation electronics using images instead of numbers. This greatly simplifies navigational tasks and encourages the operator to use the equipment as often as possible. While they are not nearly as sophisticated as the Electronic Charting Systems described in the next chapter, they are also not nearly as expensive, and consequently are very popular in the recreational boating market.

Courtesy of Magellan Systems Corporation

Figure 10.12
Magellan 6000
Hand-held Chart Plotter.

This small unit uses C-Map NT chart cartridges, and has all the features of a larger stand-alone plotter.

Although chart plotters are usually stand-alone units, they can be combined with other video equipment such as radar and depth sounder and normally they contain all the features of the best track plotters.

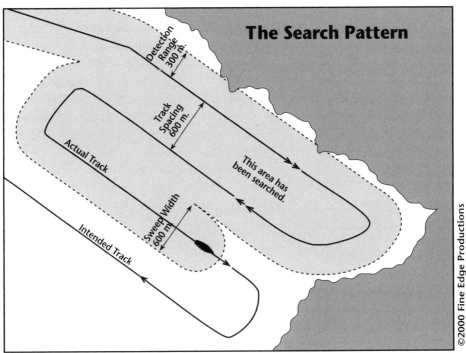

Figure 10.13

Using a GPS plotter interface, track spacing is easily maintained and the search effectively covers the entire area. [Details in sidebar.]

Search Patterns

One of the most important functions of a GPS plotter display is to show you the position of your vessel relative to where it has been in the past. A single glance at the display lets you know if your vessel is north or east of a previous position where some specific event occurred. Furthermore, the plotter actually assists you in following a course parallel to your previous track, thus making it easier to follow search patterns.

When you search for something, whether for a man overboard or for schools of fish, you need to know that you are covering the area in an effec-

tive manner for maximum probability of detection. For instance, in my work I commonly use search patterns to look for people or vessels in trouble and for locating schools of fish. In each case, I must thoroughly cover a specific area and try not to duplicate my search of one area at the expense of another.

When searching for schools of fish, I use a fishfinding sonar set to a 300-meter range to effectively search a strip 600 meters wide (the sweep width) by running a search pattern with legs 600 meters apart (track spacing) [Figure 10.13].

The Effects of Smoothing

With the smoothing function active, a GPS plotter tends to average the errors in position, COG, and SOG. You can see this effect on your plotter screen as the various kinks and bumps in the track history are smoothed out. An additional effect of smoothing is to increase the delay in plotting changes of course and speed; the delay is also affected by the update rate of the GPS itself, the update rate of the plotter, and the selected plot interval. Consequently, you should attempt to reduce to a minimum those factors contributing to the plotting delay.

Select a short plotting interval and turn off or reduce smoothing to a minimum. Don't worry if the COG, SOG, and position inputs are a little more erratic. The primary advantage of a plotter is that it allows an intuitive visual assessment of navigation information. Smoothing is used to allow the GPS Navigator to get a closer approximation of CMG and SMG, which you should be able to determine visually simply by glancing at the display; so smoothing will not help you interpret the display. *Introducing a delay in the response of the plotter is actually counter-productive, so leave the smoothing control off.*

Perils Associated with DGPS Update Delay

As discussed in the previous chapter, DGPS displays can actually be out of date by two or even three seconds, thus introducing a position uncertainty when a vessel is operating at high speed—the displayed position will always trail behind the true position. Thus you must assume that the true position lies ahead of the displayed position on the plotter. But by how much?

For each DGPS Navigator, the displayed position will lag behind the true position by a different amount and, when combined with a chart plotter (each of which has a different update rate depending on the speed of the central processor, the speed of the raster or LCD display, and the extra processing required to display a position on a chart), the update delay may be different for each installation. In some chart plotters, this processing delay can amount to another four or five seconds. Fortunately, modern computer-based electronic chart systems utilize much higher speed central processors and video cards and consequently the update delay rarely exceeds three seconds.

When travelling at 25 knots, the displayed position on a chart plotter can be in error by as much as 100 meters. Add to this the two or three second delay inherent in the helmsman's reaction time, and he might not have time to react to a charted obstacle that lies 150 meters ahead. This problem is also compounded by the lack of a distance scale on most chart plotters and electronic navigation systems which forces the operator to guess distances to charted obstacles.

High-speed inflatable rescue craft that attain speeds of 40 to 50 knots may be especially susceptible to the effects of update delays in chart plotter systems. In these vessels the update error could actually reach 0.1 Nm (200 meters). Crews of these craft are taught to follow exacting procedures to ensure that the

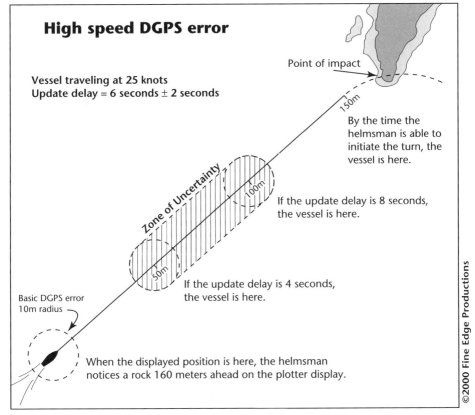

Figure 10.14

operator continually anticipates the position of the vessel, and to ensure that his orders are followed swiftly and surely.

If you operate a high-speed vessel of any type equipped with a chart plotter, you must learn to estimate distances on the plotter and you must take early action to avoid obstacles ahead. If necessary, slow down to provide yourself with more time to assess a situation.

You can get an estimate of the extent of this update delay, by using a stopwatch as you run past a clearly identifiable mark at high speed. Get a friend to help you and attempt this only when the weather is clear and calm and there are no other vessels in the vicinity. As you approach the marker bring your boat to its maximum cruising speed and maintain the engine RPM for the duration of the test. When the marker comes abeam, your friend starts the stopwatch, and when the plotter display indicates the mark is directly abeam the vessel icon, stop the watch. The amount of time elapsed will be a rough approximation of the update delay.

If you don't have charts for your plotter, you can do the same by saving a waypoint directly beside the marker and then running the experiment. Your friend will then need to stop the watch when the plotter indicates the waypoint is directly abeam.

It is impossible to determine the exact update delay of your plotter, so the best you can do is come up with a minimum and maximum amount. This introduces a further degree of uncertainty into the equation and stretches the basic DGPS error circle into an imaginary sausage, or oblong shape we describe as the **zone of uncertainty (ZOU)** [Figure 10.14]. In reality, there are other errors that effect the zone of uncertainty, such as errors caused by COG instability, which tend to widen the ZOU, but these errors are small in relation to the basic oblong shape and, consequently, are irrelevant.

This zone of uncertainty projects—forward of the vessel icon—a distance that is directly proportional to the vessel's speed. Though the width of the ZOU is not affected by speed, its length is. As you speed up the ZOU moves forward and grows in length. As you slow down, it shrinks and retreats toward the vessel icon until it takes on the familiar circular shape when the vessel comes to a complete stop.

At high speeds, much of navigation becomes a series of responses to rapidly changing situations; it is impossible to perform quick calculations, and so the operator must learn to operate by rules of thumb. We offer the following suggestions to help you when navigating at high speed.

- Make sure the smoothing control of your chart plotter is turned off.

- Set the scale low enough that you will not run the risk of running into an obstacle that is still off screen.

- At large scales, by the time an obstacle is visible on the display, it may already be too late to miss it.

- Obtain an approximate idea of the update error of your chart plotter (using the procedure outlined above), and calculate how far ahead the leading edge of the zone of uncertainty may be.

- Respond early, or slow down, when an obstacle becomes visible on the display.

- If one person is observing the plotter display and the other is operating the boat, make sure you can transmit a few simple commands instantly, by tapping on a shoulder or sign language (high-speed boats can be very noisy).

- Don't operate at high speed in confined waters at night or when visibility is poor.

CHAPTER 11

Electronic Charting Systems

Introduction to Electronic Charting Systems (ECS)

An Electronic Charting System (ECS) is composed of a GPS receiver, a personal computer (PC), an Electronic Chart (EC), and special navigation software that allows you to display the chart as well as engage in waypoint navigation. [See Figure 11.1.]

If a GPS Navigator in the pilothouse is worth an extra pair of hands, an Electronic Charting System is worth two—*and* an extra brain! It is this combination of GPS and electronic charts that makes navigation truly instant and allows you to base your responses on an image of the situation as it actually unfolds.

Imagine cruising the Inside Passage to Alaska while your computer screen provides a graphic display of what you can see out the pilothouse window. As you zoom in, you can see every rock, stream, and indentation on the shoreline (as the chart detail allows). New charts are automatically and continuously brought up on the screen as needed, and old charts neatly "folded" and stored away ready for instant re-use.

When a digitized copy of a navigational chart is generated as a background to an instantaneous, real-time plotter display, and a powerful navigation software program incorporated to manipulate the resulting images, the result is far greater than the sum of its parts. ECS is revolutionizing modern navigation. [See Chapter 10 for a discussion of plotter functions.]

This does not mean, however, that paper charts and dead reckoning are a thing of the past—far from it. Now, you simply have a very smart tool that can do much of your minute-to-minute detail work.

If you have learned to use a GPS Navigator, you can handle the far more powerful Electronic Charting System. The ECS is easy to understand and operate and literally takes the frustration out of GPS navigation. While your boat icon moves across the chart, the GPS receiver and ECS are at work in the background deriving en-route functions, all of which are readily available on custom

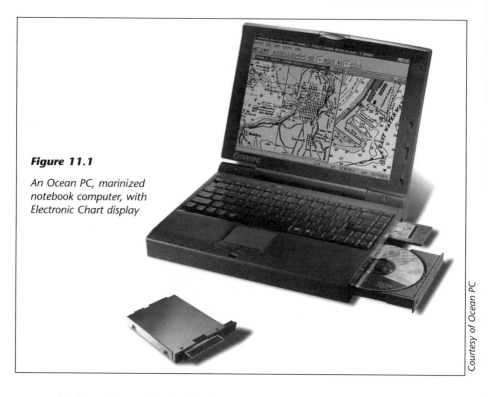

Figure 11.1

An Ocean PC, marinized notebook computer, with Electronic Chart display

Courtesy of Ocean PC

screen displays. As you look ahead on the Electronic Chart (EC) and identify hazards, you can energize a boundary or guard zone with the click of a mouse button without transferring lat/longs to your GPS Navigator from a paper chart. These programs can even predict your future position and log your track for later analysis.

The principles of classical navigation apply equally to electronic charting and conventional paper charting, but the advantage of an Electronic Chart System (ECS) lies in its instant, visual, and intuitive presentation of navigation information.

Don't be afraid to try two or more navigation programs. You will find that each program operates differently, yet they all share many common features. The trick is to learn how to activate those features. After developing your skills on one program, you will find that learning another comes easily.

PC Cards

As miniaturization reduces the size of everything electronic, the only reason most GPS receivers are larger than a small coin is that they must be large enough for (relatively) monstrous human fingers. Rockwell International Limited advertises a PC-card GPS that slips into a notebook computer's PC-card slot and has a small unobtrusive antenna attached. After loading the special Rockwell software, this PC-card GPS converts any notebook computer into a fully functional GPS Navigator.

The system runs on the computer's batteries though, and the antenna still has to "see" the sky in order to compute a position, so it does have some limitations. This type of technology represents one of the more innovative approaches to consumer GPS technology. The small size of the PC-card receiver makes it an extremely attractive option, if you need a truly portable GPS/computer.

Self-Contained Systems

At the high end of the chart plotter market, manufacturers are now offering self-contained systems that may not be PC based but, with CD and floppy-disk drives, and internal hard drives, are capable of competing with fully-fledged Electronic Charting Systems [Figure 11.2].

The self-contained system is DGPS ready, uses government-authorized electronic chart CDs, has a full-colour screen, and can perform nearly all the functions of any of the major electronic navigation programs. In addition, since the equipment comes in a single self-contained and weather-resistant box, it is often more useful to the skipper who has an open, or semi-enclosed navigation station. Also, since it is dedicated to a single purpose, the self-contained system is not subject to the software incompatibilities that are endemic to personal computers—especially when your children load their latest video game in your navigation computer.

To classify this type of equipment as a chart plotter is something like comparing a Jaguar sports car to a Volkswagen Beetle; it doesn't do credit to the highly sophisticated capabilities of the self-contained unit. Yet they have certain limitations when compared to the true EC system. For instance, they have a large,

Figure 11.2
A Northstar 961DX

This self-contained system has a full colour screen, a CD drive and a hard disk. It uses standard Maptech/BSB and NDI electronic chart CDs. A floppy disk drive is provided so you can save routes and waypoints to a backup. In addition it boasts a sophisticated tide and current software program which overlays current arrows on the display. With this unit you can do almost everything you can do with a full PC based charting system.

Photograph courtesy of Northstar Technologies Ltd.

but limited capability for storing waypoints and routes, and they require specific software—you cannot decide to try out a different brand of navigation program.

All this capability does not come cheaply. You can expect to pay as much for one of these systems as you would pay for the computer, GPS receiver, and navigation software in a standard EC system. When compared to a modern PC-based ECS, their capabilities are more limited, but they deserve serious attention; they are extremely useful in hostile environments and they provide a high-quality electronic navigation experience.

Electronic Charts (ECs)

Many of the world's hydrographic offices are now working with private interests (known as Value-Added Resellers) which convert authorized hydrographic data into value-added products (such as Electronic Charts on CD-ROM). These ECs are manufactured to a government-approved standard of accuracy that is equivalent to or better than the original paper charts on which they are based. These are the so-called "approved" electronic charts. They look just like the government charts in use for decades and can be read by powerful PCs equipped with Electronic Charting software.

Some manufacturers, however, have developed charts to their own standards and retain the rights to those formats. These proprietary (non-approved) electronic charts approximate nautical charts with varying degrees of quality and success and may not be manufactured to a government-approved standard.

If you own and use ECs, by law you are still required to carry the appropriate paper charts. In the next few years, certain government-approved EC formats are expected to meet the legal requirements for carrying charts on board.

There are two types of ECs available—**Raster Charts** and **Vector Charts**.

Raster Charts

A raster chart is an image of a paper chart that has been scanned into a computer and stored in digital form. As anyone who has worked with computer graphics knows, these images take up a lot of disk space—some raster charts occupy 6 megabytes or more of your hard drive—so in order to work with a selection of raster charts you must have either CD-ROM capability or a mountain of floppy disks. (British Admiralty Raster Charts are now produced using compression techniques that have reduced chart file sizes to 0.5 to 1.5 megabytes—similar in size to some vector charts.) Because they are exact copies of nautical charts, the appearance of raster charts is familiar to all mariners.

EC software allows you to zoom in to certain portions of the chart to increase the scale. But when you zoom in to a raster chart, you come to a point where the chart loses its usefulness because the amount of detail included in the original chart is not appropriate to the scale of display [Figure 11.3]. Beyond that point, it is actually dangerous to increase the scale.

Raster charts are drawn to a specific scale and supplied with detail proportional to their scale. If the entire world were drawn on an extremely small scale on a page of this book, many familiar features would not show up on the map. For example, the River Thames would not be visible at all. If you could zoom in on the map until it filled the room, the Thames would still not be visible because the map was not originally drawn to the increased scale. To view greater detail, you must actually choose a new chart that is drawn to a larger scale.

To avoid this problem, many EC manufacturers limit the zooming possible on any raster chart—usually when the scale of the chart on your display is identical to that of the original paper chart (the natural scale). Since the program knows only that it has been instructed to display a picture of the chart, when asked to expand the image, it does so without recognizing that the various data on the chart have any meaning. Be careful if you use a program that allows unlimited zooming.

Raster charts are normally oriented North-up. Should you wish to display the chart in a Course-up mode (to match the image you may see on your radar), the soundings and names on the chart will be displayed at an angle, or even worse—upside down. This is an inherent property of raster charts, since they are merely images of a paper chart.

Don't assume that raster charts are necessarily superior to paper charts—as you will see throughout this chapter, there are drawbacks. A raster chart presents the same information in a

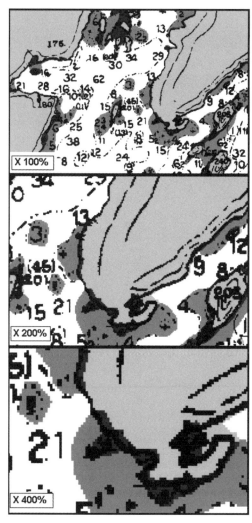

Figure 11.3

Even though the scale increases by 400% from the upper to the lower image, no additional detail has emerged. The detail is out of proportion to the displayed chart and the soundings cover a far larger area than they are valid for.

©2000 Fine Edge Productions

convenient electronic format, but reproduces the flaws of the original paper charts as well. In the same way you would be cautious when attempting precise navigation using paper charts that are based on surveys almost a century old, you should be cautious about the electronic versions of questionable charts.

Vector Charts

A **vector chart** is a completely different beast from a raster chart; it is not a scanned image at all but a highly complex collection of information stored in a database format. This format requires far less storage space than a raster image format (and less processing power). Vector charts are derived from the same authorized hydrographic data as their raster cousins.

Since a vector chart is actually a collection of information, it cannot just be scanned into electronic format. Instead, the data that forms the original paper chart must be extracted and separated into separate groupings or "layers." These "layers" are then stored separately in the database. This painstaking process required thousands of man-hours for each chart, because the entire chart had to be re-drawn several times. The result was that vector charts were significantly more expensive than raster charts. However, modern technology has made the data extraction process much simpler, and vector charts are now available for consumer EC programs.

Each time you call up a vector chart, the computer extracts data from the database and then draws the chart anew. When you increase the scale, the computer not only recognizes that certain features—such as landmasses—should be enlarged, but also that certain features (such as depth soundings and navigation marks) require different treatment. As you zoom in on a portion of the chart, additional depth soundings and other data appear, and geographic features appear in greater detail, though the depth soundings and navigation marks are not enlarged. You do not need to switch to a larger scale chart; the computer just draws a larger scale image based on the information in the database. Obviously there is a limit to the scale enlargement. This limit is based on the scale of the original government charts themselves. Consequently, where large-scale charts are available, the limit for that portion of the vector chart is consistent with the natural scale of the original government chart.

When creating a vector chart, a producer may group all soundings into one layer, or separate the soundings into two or more sub-layers, each representing a different depth range. Depth contours too may be grouped into one or more layers. Once the layers have been defined, and the chart data separated into the appropriate layers, the electronic charting program can lay one layer on top of another until the whole chart is re-created. Once the computer has drawn the chart, the operator takes over and may show or hide layers as he or she sees fit.

For example, all soundings and depth contours below a certain depth can be turned off, or you can hide navigation marks, thus giving you a clean uncluttered display [Figure 11.5]. You may even be able to click on a light or buoy and obtain data relating to that light, such as the light's characteristics or range of visibility. Vector charting systems also allow the operator to alter the chart colours to suit individual tastes.

In a vector chart, the soundings and names retain their proper orientation even when you choose to rotate the display to a course-up mode. In a raster chart, all the features of the chart rotate in course-up mode. [Figure 11.4]

Nobeltec Visual Navigation Suite version 5.0 is now compatible with a sophisticated brand of vector charts—**Passport World Charts**. These vector format charts are licensed by Transas and are based on authorized hydrographic data.

Passport World Charts display the usual groupings of data to be expected of vector charts, such as depth soundings, contours, Traffic Separation Schemes, and lights and buoys; but they also break navigation light data into several sub-layers. Consequently, you can turn on and off such features as light characteristics, light flashes, and arcs of visibility of sector lights. You may also enable a feature that displays only those lights that are within the range of visibility of your vessel. As you approach an area, more and more lights become visible, based on the nominal range of the lights as published in the official List of Lights.

Obviously not all vector systems are created equal. Whether or not a vector chart is superior to a raster chart depends partly on the power of your EC software and partly on the complexity of the chart database. Vector chart producers are free to collect the chart data

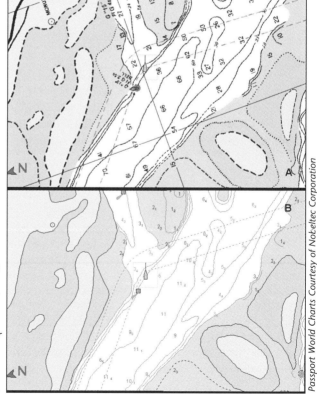

Passport World Charts Courtesy of Nobeltec Corporation

Figure 11.4   Raster Display vs Vector Chart

Two presentations of the same location in Wilapa Bay in Course-Up mode; NOAA raster display above (A), "Passport World Chart" vector display below (B). Note that the vector chart is clean and uncluttered. Also note that the soundings in the raster display are tilted and the text is difficult to read.

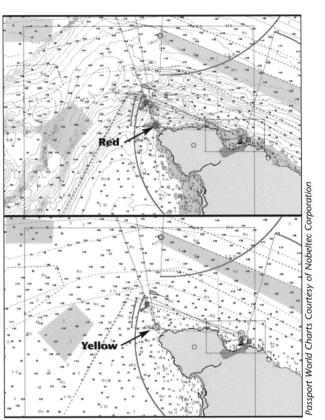

Figure 11.5
Two Vector Views

Two vector views of the same location at Cape Flattery. In both views the sectors of visibility of various lights are shown. In the lower view, the depth contours have been turned off. Similarly the Traffic Separation Zones and other features could be turned off as well.

Also note that in the lower view, as the vessel icon passed out of the red sector of the light on the small rock near Cape Flattery, the colour of the light has changed from red to yellow.

Passport World Charts Courtesy of Nobeltec Corporation

Passport World Charts

When you purchase Nobeltec Visual Navigation Suite, the install disk contains not only the install files for the navigation software, it also contains the entire folio of Passport World Charts! If you compare the size of this folio to a raster chart CD that can hold only the charts for one small region of the United States, it is clear that when vector chart databases are compressed, they take up very little space.

Once you have purchased the Nobeltec installation disk, you will be unable to access the Passport World Charts unless you also purchase the unlocking codes for the charts on the CD. An interesting security feature of the CD is that these codes are matched to the particular installation

of Nobeltec Visual Navigation Suite, so you won't be able to share the charts with other Nobeltec users. Each chart region costs about 25 per cent more than the equivalent raster chart region but, since the utility of the vector charts is so much greater, this is not a high price to pay—and you can purchase the charts over the telephone with your credit card. Since the charts are already in your possession, all you need is the codes, which means you can buy new regions while you are at sea. The initial purchase of the disk is the only time you must transport a physical object. After that, purchasing a new region is achieved by the transfer of pure information!

into whatever groupings they believe will attract the most customers (except in S-57 ECDIS charts—see Chapter 13). Consequently, vector chart programs with increasing flexibility and sub-divisions have appeared recently, and the promise is that there is more chart development to come. Using a rough analogy, a vector chart is like an onion. The utility and flexibility of the chart itself depends on how many "layers" are in the "onion."

Chart Formats and Sources

Like word-processing documents, Electronic Charts come in a range of formats and may be compatible only with certain programs. In the last couple of years, however, the various navigation software producers have made great strides in incorporating as many formats as possible into their software. Chart View Pro—produced by Nobeltec Corporation—is now able to utilize all the popular North American formats as well as British Admiralty ARCS.

ECs are available directly from private companies (Value Added Resellers or VARs) that work directly with Hydrographic agencies, such as NDI or Maptech/BSB or directly from Hydrographic Agencies themselves, such as the British Admiralty. In addition, proprietary formats are available from developers such as Transas, which are based on authorized hydrographic data. Hydrographic offices around the world have been working closely with chart developers over recent years to make government-approved formats available to the boating public.

In the early days of electronic charting, each developer was forced to produce its own charts, sometimes at great expense. However, as governments recognized the immense popularity of these charts, national agencies began to produce electronic charts to ensure that standards were maintained.

In Canada and the U.S., the manufacture, distribution and sale of electronic charts has been turned over to Value-Added Resellers who, working closely with the respective hydrographic agencies, have established standards of accuracy and presentation equivalent to or better than the original paper charts.

In the UK, the British Admiralty has retained sole authority to publish raster charts. In November 1993, the Admiralty began to release digitized hydrographic data for all areas covered by its charts worldwide.

Approved charts from the various Value-Added Resellers or the British Admiralty are updated prior to the time of sale with new information from *Sailing Directions, Notices to Mariners* and in many cases, additional data drawn from the original chart surveys. Consequently, you can be assured of a professional-quality chart package drawn from the latest available data.

Non-approved does not mean that a proprietary chart system is less accurate than an approved version available from a Value-Added Reseller; but it does mean there is no government guarantee of quality. If you use non-approved charts, you cannot expect support or backing from national hydrographic offices or their private sector partners such as Maptech/BSB or NDI.

The following list includes some of the chart formats available:

ARCS (British Admiralty Raster Chart Service)

NDI (Canadian Hydrographic Service)

Maptech/BSB (United States National Oceanic and Atmospheric Administration)

Norwegian Hydrographic

RNZN (Royal New Zealand Navy)

Maptech (U.S. and International proprietary charts)

Navionics (cartridge based proprietary vector charts)

Seafarer (Australian Hydrographic Office ARCS format ECs)

Transas (proprietary vector charts)

Passport World Charts (Nobeltec Corporation's proprietary vector charts)

C-Map (cartridge based proprietary vector charts)

Although some EC programs are able to work with charts of virtually any format, others are limited to just one or two. Check your program to see whether it can use the approved charts for your area. If you have an older system that uses non-approved charts, the software may not work with new government-authorized ECs. You should be able to purchase your electronic charts from the same supplier that provides the EC program.

Vector charts are normally proprietary charts, manufactured to standards set by the issuing hydrographic agencies or IMO.

Electronic Chart Datums

Government-approved charts are adjusted to WGS84 chart datum. This means you no longer have to keep track of different horizontal datums and constantly reset your GPS Navigator to compensate for differing datums you may require during a single trip. As long as you use government-approved charts and your GPS is set to WGS84, you should never have to reset it again.

If the underlying chart (the paper chart the EC is based on) was drawn to a datum other than WGS84, you may find that—even though your cursor gives positions in WGS84 datum—the latitude and longitude scales at the chart edges are still given in the original datum. This is the case with some government-approved charts. In addition, if you query the electronic chart for its properties, the program will indicate the properties of the *original paper chart*, not its electronic version (WGS84).

Both Canadian- and U.S.-approved charts ship on a CD that includes a free chart viewer. If you don't wish to use the navigation features of an EC program, you can simply use the free viewer to study the charts on the CD. Several software producers also provide free or inexpensive viewers for studying electronic charts.

To observe the datum shift of a particular chart, you can perform a simple test:

- Set the EC to the largest scale possible.
- Place the cursor exactly on a meridian of longitude at its intersection with the longitude scale at the top or bottom of the chart [Figure 11.6].
- If the displayed position is not exactly the same as the longitude you can read on the latitude and longitude scales at the edges of the chart, your EC and the underlying chart are demonstrating different datums.
- Only government-approved charts from Value-Added Resellers can guarantee that the cursor-indicated position will be given in WGS84. Where there is a discrepancy, as shown in Figure 11.6, use your cursor only to determine a precise position and not the lat/long lines on the chart.

If the datum of the original chart is unknown, it may not be possible to adjust the chart to WGS84. In this case, some hydrographic agencies, including

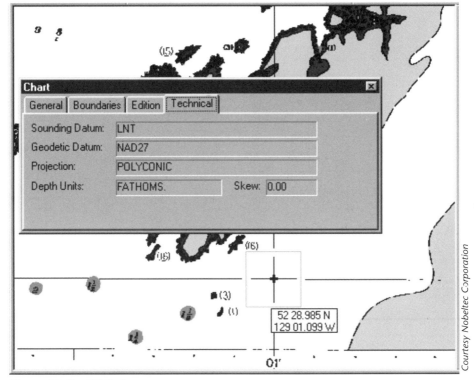

Figure 11.6   EC Datums

The cursor is located at the intersection of the 52°29' latitude and 129°01' longitude lines on the electronic chart. Since the original paper chart was drawn to NAD27 datum (note the chart properties box), the lat/long grid is inconsistent with the position indicated by the cursor in WGS84 datum. The difference between the two is almost 0.1 Nm (180 meters).

British Admiralty, insist that the software developer provide a warning that positioning cannot be determined on the electronic chart and that mariners should navigate with caution.

EC programs are still being sold with proprietary charts that *have not been adjusted to WGS84* datum. Often these programs are just scanned onto floppy disks or cartridges. *Caution:* In this case, take note that the charts are probably not updated to the latest *Notice to Mariners*; be sure that you regularly check the datum of the chart and that you set your GPS to the proper datum, as if you were working with a paper chart.

If you have just purchased an EC that uses electronic charts drawn exclusively to WGS84 or an equivalent datum and wish to use waypoints that you have collected over the years, you must convert the waypoints to WGS84 before you can use them accurately in the new program. For detailed instructions on converting local datum co-ordinates to WGS84, refer to Chapter 3.

Chart Scale Issues

When you zoom in to an electronic chart, you come to a point where the chart loses its usefulness because the amount of detail included in the original chart is not appropriate to the scale of display. Beyond that point, it is actually dangerous to increase the scale.

To avoid this problem, many EC manufacturers limit the zooming possible on any particular chart—usually when the scale of the chart on your display is identical to that of the original paper chart (the natural scale). *Be careful if you use a program that allows unlimited zooming.*

When you view a chart that was not originally drawn to WGS84 (or NAD83), positions referenced to the latitude and longitude lines on the chart will not agree with positions referenced to the overlying lat/long grid. Since the overlying grid is invisible, this discrepancy may not be immediately apparent. Do not attempt to plot cursor-indicated positions or waypoint co-ordinates directly onto the paper version of the chart. It won't work. This is because the electronically derived co-ordinates are in WGS84 (or equivalent) and need to be adjusted by the amount of the datum shift for that chart before they will agree with the paper chart.

One fellow we know tried to do this. He studiously checked the properties of the electronic chart itself and found that the datum was NAD27. Since he was plotting on the paper version of the same chart—which was drawn to NAD27—he felt he had investigated the situation adequately. So he was frustrated when the electronically derived positions couldn't be reconciled with the paper chart. What he didn't know was that he was attempting to plot NAD83 positions on a NAD27 chart. Once we explained it to him, he adjusted the positions by following the instructions printed in the Horizontal Datum note on the chart, and resolved the problem.

Our friend's problem arose because he was trying to make the navigation program do something it was not designed to do. So be careful when you plot electronically derived positions on paper charts.

If a larger scale chart covers the area in question, turn on automatic chart switching to access the larger scale chart. Far more detail will emerge, and you will be able to work with the larger scale chart with a higher degree of confidence.

In addition to the problems of increasing scale, there are problems with reducing scale *too much*. The raster chart has a natural scale; on that scale, all lettering is perfectly legible. However, when you engage in long-range planning, you may find that you have to reduce the scale to such a degree that you have difficulty seeing any detail at all. The chart may have been drawn on a sheet of paper a meter by a meter and a half, yet you are trying to display the entire chart on a 14-inch monitor. To avoid this problem, choose the smallest-scale chart of the area in question. Some programs allow you to open separate windows simultaneously. Thus, one window can display a smaller-scale version of the chart than the one you are using for navigation, which is a valuable feature.

The Dockside Test (Again)

If the dockside test was instructive when you worked with a simple GPS Navigator or plotter, performed with EC software it becomes positively illuminating. However, unlike the plotter dockside test, you must perform the test only when the dock appears on a *large-scale* harbour chart.

To begin, remain secured to your dock and leave your EC software running. Instruct the program to display the plotted track so you can see the apparent movement of your vessel when it is motionless. Select the largest scale possible, so that you can clearly see your position on the chart. Then activate a **range circle** centered on the vessel icon. Set the range circle at 0.01 Nm and watch the vessel icon move around the display.

During the test you can make the following observations:

- The position of the vessel icon moves around on the chart, but the range circle should almost always contain the true position of your vessel (the center of the pattern). If it doesn't, the GPS error at that time is greater than 20 meters. This error could be due to different factors, such as multipath error caused by the presence of numerous masts in the vicinity or by solar flare activity. [Refer to Chapter 8 for a description of possible GPS errors.]

- You will be able to determine the speed with which the error varies. If the icon jumps rapidly from one side to the other of true position, it means GPS errors are fluctuating rapidly.

- Change the datum of your GPS (not the ECS) from WGS84 to the local datum. The vessel icon will jump to a new location. The length of the jump will equal the shift between the two datums. This exercise should give you an intuitive understanding of the effect of different chart datums. (Don't forget to switch the datum back to WGS84 when you have finished!)

- If the pattern of the apparent track of the vessel is not centered on or not close to the true position of your vessel at dock, some influence may be giving a bias to your GPS positions. Your GPS could be set to the wrong datum (verify that you set it to WGS 84) or you may be using a system with its own proprietary charts which were not adjusted to WGS 84. Select the appropriate datum for the chart you are using and verify that the new pattern of apparent positions is centered on the true position.

- Note that the pattern is extremely small and is probably offset to some degree from the true position. (After all, the chart is probably not accurate enough to match the precision of GPS.)

Once you have completed this test, GPS errors should make more sense to you.

COG and Heading Vectors

Most EC programs allow you to activate a **COG vector** that projects from the vessel icon in the direction you are travelling. You can set the vector to any length of time and see where you will be in a given number of minutes. This feature is known as a **heading vector, predictor, look-ahead,** or **course extension arrow**—to name a few of the terms.

The important thing to remember is that the EC program determines the heading of the vessel icon (the direction the bow is pointing) from the COG information provided by your GPS. It has no way of knowing your vessel's compass heading. Thus, the COG vector will indicate your vessel's predicted track over the ground, and the termination of the COG vector will show the predicted position after a given number of minutes.

However, if your vessel is under the influence of a cross-current, the COG may not be the same as your vessel's true heading. In the EC display as well, the vessel icon may not appear to be heading in the same direction as that indicated by your compass. [See Figure 11.7.] In addition, at low speed, the COG supplied by your GPS will be excessively unstable. The result is that the COG vector will also become unstable and yaw back and forth, even though your vessel continues to head in the same compass direction.

For a more intuitive assessment of the effect of a cross-current, you must supply the EC program with true heading data; the only way you can do this is to enter the heading manually or provide heading input from a flux-gate or gyro compass. Some EC programs can make use of this data.

The Vessel Icon

Most ECs use a **vessel icon** shaped like a small ship. The icon is superimposed on the electronic chart and its position determined by your GPS receiver; its size may or may not change as chart scale changes. Some programs let you select the size of the vessel icon to match the length of your vessel, so that it represents the relative size of your vessel at any chart scale.

Although setting the icon to true ship size can be a valuable feature, at smaller scales it is too small to be seen on the display. (We don't feel this presents a problem, however.) Other methods can be used to indicate the direction of the vessel's heading, such as the COG vector, and the termination of the track line will indicate your vessel's position. The advantage to accurate vessel icon size is that, at larger scales, the vessel is displayed at its correct size in relation to surrounding land. An accurate representation of vessel size can assist you in maneuvering in tight quarters; it is reassuring to see your vessel represented almost as it is in real life when you navigate through narrow channels or come alongside a dock.

However, this feature is used best in conjunction with accurate heading information. *Remember:* At anchor or very low speeds, GPS-derived COG will be

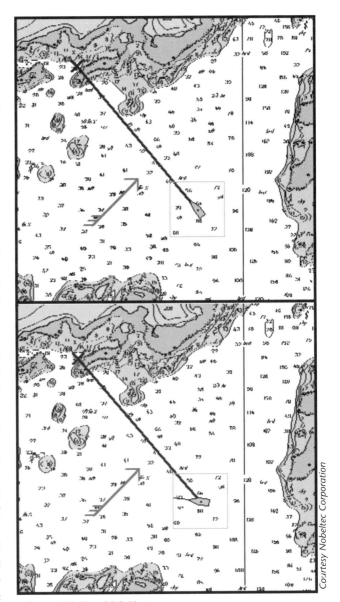

Courtesy Nobeltec Corporation

Figure 11.7   COG Vector

In the upper diagram, the vessel is shown proceeding on a heading of 320° T. However, since there is a cross-current setting 045° T, the true situation is shown in the lower diagram. In both cases, the COG vector (predictor) shows the vessel's predicted track over the ground.

The difference is that in the lower diagram, a compass input is provided which allows the true heading of the vessel to be displayed. This provides a more intuitive assessment of the effect of current.

completely erroneous because your vessel's SOG is almost zero, and the COG vector will be too short to be visible. You will notice that the vessel icon seems to rotate throughout 360°, randomly swinging back and forth. If you want to make the vessel icon act realistically, then you must resolve these COG instabilities by interfacing the ECS with a flux-gate or gyro-compass in order to provide accurate heading information at slow speed.

When an ECS is located on a large ship, it is necessary to instruct the software about the location of the GPS antenna relative to the center of the ship. (Your GPS calculates the position of the *antenna*, not the position of the pilot-house or the center of the ship.) Failure to do so will result in the vessel icon's being placed incorrectly on the display. Be sure that the GPS antenna is located near the position from which the vessel is normally steered.

The Vessel Track

Most navigation software allows you to display the vessel's actual track—a valuable feature. Not only can you see the path the vessel has taken, and thus infer the forces that are acting on the vessel to deflect it from the Course Line, but you can also save the track as a route.

The program will present you with a series of choices. You can create a track by saving the vessel's position at chosen time intervals, by course alterations of any number of degrees, or by positions taken at chosen distances. In any case, each time the program saves a position, a certain amount of computer memory is used. And if the intervals are short—and numerous positions saved—you can overload the computer's memory. If you then proceed to convert the track into a route, you may create a route of hundreds (even thousands) of waypoints.

A route like this is a veritable monster, making navigation a frightful chore for the skipper. Distances between waypoints are too short to be useful, and the computer may choke on the huge number of positions in active memory. Also, the skipper will be so busy dealing with the computer, that he may not be able to pay proper attention to the routine tasks of navigation. *If you use this feature, make sure that you select track interval criteria that will result in a manageable route.*

Automatic Chart Selection

An Electronic Chart System offers you the option of **Automatic Chart Selection** —a feature that always selects the correct new chart at the appropriate scale whenever the vessel icon moves off the edge of the previous chart.

Some programs automatically load the new chart and display it in a separate window, while others replace the chart containing the present position and center the new chart on your vessel's position.

Other programs may use a slightly different technique. As you move off the edge of the chart, the program automatically switches to the next smaller scale chart that contains both the present position and the cursor. All the charts of larger scale are outlined on this smaller scale chart and when you click on one of these outlines, the view switches to the larger scale chart containing your vessel's position. This makes the process of chart selection almost (but not quite) automatic.

However, if you want to look ahead by scrolling the cursor forward (panning) to the next chart, your program may not automatically open that chart—the process of chart selection is often triggered by your vessel's position, not the position of the cursor. If so, you must select the next smaller scale chart of the area, scroll ahead to the area you want to examine and select the large-scale chart for that area.

You may find it necessary to activate automatic chart selection; otherwise you will have to open all the charts you need manually. However, if your computer has limited memory, the automatic option may not be practical.

Although ECS producers have developed automatic chart selection to eliminate filing tasks, the process can be so smooth you may overlook important information. For example, when passing from a chart drawn in fathoms to one drawn in meters or feet, some programs fail to inform you that a change has occurred. If you believe you are still operating in fathoms—when in fact the new soundings are in meters—you could find yourself in a dangerous situation in shallow waters!

Similar problems can occur when you move between areas charted by different hydrographic agencies, such as Canada and the United States. Each country uses different tidal datums and, in some cases, different symbols for navigation features which doesn't create a problem if you are aware that a change has taken place. But when the change is automatic and silent, you might make incorrect assumptions about a chart.

For example, Dixon Entrance (on the border between Alaska and British Columbia) covers an area claimed by both Canada and the United States. When travelling south, your vessel could still be in U.S. waters according to the U.S. chart. But when the chart is automatically replaced by a Canadian chart, your vessel may be in Canadian waters according to the new chart. A passage from one country to another could take place without your knowing that you had crossed an international boundary. We hope that, in the future, ECS producers provide a warning alarm or a display indication that an international boundary has been crossed or that a newly opened chart is drawn to different measurements.

Despite the minor problems associated with automatic chart selection, as long as you are alert to chart switching and check to see whether important changes have taken place, you should have no trouble. One of the authors uses electronic charts between Alaska, British Columbia, and Washington State; with all three collections of CD-ROM charts loaded into memory and automatic chart selection engaged, the process is virtually seamless.

Chart Insets (Plans)

We have noticed that on some chart insets, the cursor position may be significantly in error. This is because a single lat/long grid has been superimposed on the entire chart, including the inset charts (plans). Since there is just a single lat/long grid for the chart, a cursor position read from any inset of the chart will reflect the cursor's position relative to the features on the larger chart and not relative to the inset.

Where the inset is drawn to a different scale than the main chart, all distances calculated on that inset may be incorrect, and it may not be possible to continue a route into an inset because the cursor or vessel icon may not automatically jump to the inset.

We even found one inset chart in a British Columbia EC where the cursor indicated position was almost 11 Nm in error. Maptech/BSB, authorized distributor of NOAA charts has solved this problem by blanking out all chart insets on the parent chart and re-issuing the inset as a separate chart with its own lat/long grid corrected to WGS 84. In response to our query about this problem, Nautical Data International, producer of Canadian raster ECs issued the following statement for the first edition of *GPS—Instant Navigation* in 1998:

> *NDI is in the process of upgrading its BSB raster production process to Version 2.0.3 All future releases of CDs will be in that format. Certain difficulties now being experienced with NDI charts, particularly those containing 'Plans,' will be eliminated in the upgrade. Users who experience difficulties in the meantime should call NDI Technical Support toll free at 1-800-563-0634.*

Version 3 NDI charts are now available. However, when using inset charts on earlier version CDs that appear against the background of the parent chart, do not use the cursor to obtain latitude and longitude.

Another problem arises with these earlier version chart CDs when **Automatic Chart Selection** (Scrolling) is enabled. When the program selects the next chart to be displayed, it looks for a chart at the appropriate scale. If the chart it selects contains insets, you may find that your vessel icon is now displayed on the inset, *in a totally inappropriate location* [Figure 11.8]. When this happens, select the next higher or lower scale chart for that location as appropriate. *(Note—this is a problem with the electronic chart, itself, and does not indicate any fault in the navigation program.)*

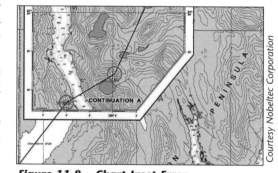

Figure 11.8   Chart Inset Error

Courtesy Nobeltec Corporation

Quilting

Quilting is a feature available in the latest releases of many navigation programs. With the quilting control turned on, you are able to view not only the active chart but also any charts adjacent, at the correct scale, so that the charted area fills the whole display. Where several charts come together, quilting instructs the computer to display them all.

Not only does quilting display adjacent charts, but it also permits the outlines of any other installed charts to be viewed against the background of the currently active chart. Since quilting selects the chart for you, the "select larger scale chart" and "select smaller scale chart" functions of the program are disabled, and you can select different scale charts only by using the zooming function.

No doubt about it—quilting is a useful feature. When coming to the edge of a chart, you can view areas beyond the chart margin and plan routes with greater ease than before. However, the utility of quilting comes at a price. Since numerous charts are open at the same time, your computer memory may stall. At minimum, it will take longer for the computer to do its ordinary work. You may also see discrepancies at or near the chart margins, especially if the two charts are not perfectly synchronized with each other.

With quilting active, when you view an area that is served by two overlapping charts, the program chooses which chart it will display. Sometimes the chart selected is not appropriate for the area. For instance, when plans are included in the chart, they may not be edited out and, consequently, if the program chooses to display that chart, you will have an inappropriate plan directly over the area you are navigating. To view the area at the same scale, you will need to turn off quilting, and select the proper chart for the area.

Some experienced users of navigation software feel that quilting takes control of the program away from the operator and makes the program less useful. We recommend that you should feel free to use quilting while setting up a route and performing other maintenance functions—but use the function only when it makes sense to do so, especially if your computer slows significantly with quilting turned on.

Dynamically Linked Notes

As you scroll across a chart you may see notations that state "See Caution A" or "See Note C." These are notations placed on the chart to draw your attention to information that is printed on the chart. These notes may refer to Precautionary Areas, Military Areas, or other information that is of interest to the mariner. With earlier versions of electronic charts, you had to scroll around the chart to find the notes, which were normally printed on land areas of the chart. (Remember, the electronic Raster Chart is merely a scan of a paper chart.) However, Maptech/BSB version 3 electronic charts come with a feature called

Dynamically Linked Notes. At a simple command, the latest EC programs can link to these chart notes and display them in a separate window without requiring that you scroll away from the area of the chart that is holding your interest.

Tools

Electronic Chart Systems generally provide toolbar buttons as in any Windows-based program. These buttons allow quick access to various functions such as zooming, panning and scrolling, chart selection, event marks, ranges and bearings, and waypoints and routes. Some toolbars can be made to "float" or "dock" in places on the screen minimizing interference with the chart. Other programs allow the toolbar buttons to be re-sized for use in a touch-screen environment.

If your program does not have toolbar buttons, you have to access the functions through choices on the menu bar at the top or sides of your display.

Some programs allow quick access to various functions through the right-mouse button. Generally the right-mouse button provides you with context-sensitive menus. (The choices vary according to the displayed item you select with the mouse.)

Since most small boat EC systems work with standard operating systems such as DOS, Windows or Windows 95 (and a few with Mac), the programs themselves use many of the features of the operating system itself. To be able to use an ECS successfully you need to understand simple computer terminology and be able to accomplish basic DOS or Windows functions.

Drawing on an Electronic Chart

A skipper can "draw" on an electronic chart with a number of different tools by clicking on the appropriate toolbar. When you indicate the start and ending points of a new route with these tools, a straight line snaps instantly into position. If you wish to move one of the waypoints in a route or create a new one and drag it to a new position, the previous line stretches like a rubber band until you finish setting the waypoint.

MOB

Some EC programs supply an easy-to-use MOB (Man OverBoard) function, while others do not. As you recall, MOB is a feature of most GPS Navigators that saves your present position as a waypoint with one keystroke, facilitating the recovery of the man overboard at the place you activated MOB.

When an EC program includes this feature, an MOB button appears in the toolbar. All you need to do is click the button; the software places an MOB icon on your display and begins displaying navigation information to the MOB position. The MOB waypoint remains active until you delete it. (Consult your EC owner's manual, or on-screen help, to see if this feature is included in your software, as well as to learn how to activate and delete an MOB waypoint.)

Entering Waypoints

EC systems have eliminated the need to work with long strings of numbers when inputting waypoints. Just make the appropriate menu or toolbar selection then move the cursor to the position on the chart where you wish to place the waypoint. Click the mouse once, and the waypoint is stored in memory. That's all there is to it.

Since a mouse click so easily creates a waypoint, many EC systems offer only this method of creating waypoints, unlike the better GPS Navigators which may offer three or four different methods. Consequently, if you want to enter a waypoint by present position, you must use the cursor and click it directly over the vessel icon itself. Once the icon moves past that position, you will see your waypoint revealed. This procedure substitutes for saved waypoints and waypoints entered by present position.

However, at least one program offers the option of converting your track history to a route by automatically assigning waypoints at significant changes in course then assembling them into a route. Since the computer lacks the judgement necessary to create a completely safe route, we suggest that you thoroughly check your route for errors and proximity of waypoints to navigational dangers.

Although the EC program is impressive in its ability to interact with the user in a visual graphic interface, there may still be times when you need to enter a waypoint by latitude/longitude co-ordinates. For instance, you might hear a MAYDAY call in which the caller gives his position in latitude and longitude, accurate to two decimals of a minute. First, create a waypoint at any position on the display with a click of the cursor and the proper menu commands. Then call up the properties of the waypoint, and edit its co-ordinates. As soon as the edits are properly entered, the waypoint will snap to its new position. It's as simple as that.

If your EC program does not permit you to numerically enter the waypoint or edit its properties, how can you do so using the cursor alone?

First, select the tool or menu choice that allows you to place a waypoint. While watching the cursor latitude and longitude display, move the cursor north or south until the indicated cursor position matches the desired latitude. Repeat the process for longitude, then fine-tune the position by trial and error until you are satisfied that the cursor is exactly where you want to enter the waypoint. Keeping the cursor still, click the mouse to position the waypoint. Once the waypoint is in place, activate navigation and you are on your way. *Caution:* Do not attempt to read lat/long co-ordinates by cursor in an inset chart unless you have verified that the indicated co-ordinates match the printed latitude and longitude at the edge of the inset. See Caution in "Electronic Chart Datums" above.

GOTO

The GOTO function is available in every EC program, but often under a different name—"Instant Waypoint" or "Steer to" for example. For the sake of consistency, we continue to use "GOTO" when referring to this function.

To activate GOTO, first select the appropriate menu choice or toolbar button; then create the GOTO waypoint by clicking the desired location on the chart. The program instantly creates the waypoint and starts navigation. That's all there is to it. You can modify your destination waypoint by selecting it and dragging it to a different position. When you move a waypoint, a new Course Line snaps to the new destination and the navigation information is updated. As with many EC features, all the hard work is done by your computer, leaving you free to pay attention to what counts—keeping a good lookout and enjoying your trip.

You can follow a complex route by creating a new GOTO waypoint as you reach each destination waypoint in sequence. This is helpful when you lack the time to plan your entire route in advance, or when conditions change and you want to "play" each route-leg by sight.

Working with Routes

The numerous options for working with routes vary according to the particular EC software. In fact, the variations in ECS software are probably greater than in GPS Navigators. In the following sections we deal with these features in a generic sense to give you an idea of what is possible. If your ECS lacks some of these features, it does not mean that you are doing something wrong or that your software is faulty.

A New Method for Creating Routes

Not only does EC make it easy to set individual waypoints, but the process of route-making is simplified as well. This feature, more than any other, is electronic charting's greatest strength. The process of reading lat/long co-ordinates, laying out legs with parallel rules, and entering long strings of numbers is a thing of the past. Navigation becomes a visual process, intuitive and simple, just as it should be. The entire process can be handled with simple mouse clicks and menu or toolbar selections as follows.

- First activate the route-making function. (In some programs, you must select a menu choice; in others, a toolbar button.)
- Once you know how to engage the route-making feature, place a series of mouse clicks on the chart where you want to create waypoints; the program does the rest for you. Notice that your software automatically numbers each waypoint.
- Next, zoom in on the initial waypoint and verify that you have placed it appropriately.
- If so, scroll along the route, examining each leg to be sure the route is clear of dangers and that you placed the leg appropriately.
- If you notice a leg that needs to be moved (i.e., away from a danger or

toward the side of a channel), simply activate the function that allows you to insert a waypoint. You can do this by menu or toolbar selection—or if you have Windows 95 or 98 compatible software, by clicking the right-mouse button over the route in that area.

• Once you have inserted a new waypoint, your software renumbers all the waypoints in the route.

• Now you can click and drag the new waypoint to its proper position. (Any waypoint can be dragged to a new position.) The route legs stretch like a rubber band, so
you will have no problem.

• Continue this process along the route until you have inserted as many waypoints as you need to set your entire route clear of dangers.

We often prefer to create a route by establishing the initial and final way-points first. In this case, it doesn't matter if the route crosses land or water because intermediate waypoints can easily be assigned by inserting, then click-ing and dragging them to the proper location. [The process is illustrated in Figure 11.9.]

One problem, however, is that most skippers want to navigate with the largest scale chart opened which means, in many cases, that a projected route leg continues over onto the next chart so you can't see the other end of the leg. In addition, your program may not automatically open the adjoining chart when

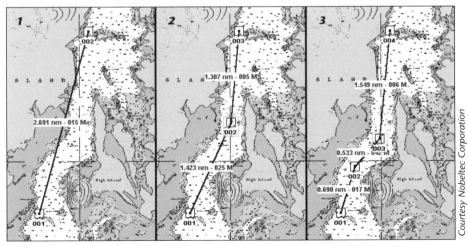

Figure 11.9   Creating a Route

First assign the initial and final waypoints; it doesn't matter if the route leg thus formed crosses land (left). Next insert an intermediate waypoint (center). Finally, insert as many other interme-diate waypoints as necessary to keep each leg a safe distance from the shore (right).

the cursor reaches the edge of the chart. In this case you have to manually select the large-scale chart containing that portion of the route. Once on the large-scale chart, you can scroll the cursor to the approximate position of the final waypoint then place that waypoint where you want it.

We prefer to assign all our waypoints on the smaller scale chart, then select the larger scale charts to optimize the positions of the waypoints and insert the intermediate waypoints. Don't worry too much about the initial placement of waypoints since you will drag them to their proper positions later.

To check that the waypoints are a sufficient distance from obstructions (*remember:* it is difficult to read distances on an EC!), activate the range and bearing tool. Use this tool to measure the distance and bearing between two points, specifically the waypoint itself and any danger. After a final check along the route to see if it is safe, you can consider the route finalized. At this point, your program should allow you to lock the route in place to prevent you from inadvertently dragging it to a new position.

Now sit back and look at your handiwork. Notice that each route leg is labeled with its length and direction. Also notice that each waypoint is numbered sequentially and that when you insert new waypoints, the software automatically updates the route leg data.

This method of route creation is unbelievably simple—twenty waypoints assigned in just a few minutes, all without having to measure lat/long co-ordinates or write down any numbers! To add to the convenience of EC, you can create a route when there is no active GPS input, whether you are at home or at sea. If you choose to plan and create routes at home, you can download the finished routes to a floppy disk and transfer them to your seagoing computer.

On short, complex routes where the waypoints are close together, some of the displayed information may mask geographic detail, especially on a small-scale chart. Since the route information is not part of the chart image, it remains the same size and may obscure important chart detail. However, most chart software allows you to hide route and other data; you can even change the colour of the Course Lines for better visibility.

Editing a Route

A route can be edited at any time (in the unlocked mode) by simply selecting and dragging its constituent waypoints to new positions.

Some programs allow you to add a new waypoint at the beginning or end of a route, a process called **appending** a route. To append a waypoint to the end of a route, right-click on the route leg adjacent to the final waypoint and choose the appropriate command or tool. The cursor then becomes a route tool again, allowing you to add waypoints to the end of your route.

If you wish to append a new waypoint at the beginning of a route, you may have to reverse the route, thus making the initial waypoint the final waypoint and vice versa. *When complete, be sure to select Reverse Route to return to the correct numbering*, with 001 being the initial waypoint.

When creating a route, you can also choose to use existing event marks as waypoints. In this way, an existing mark can be shared by more than one route. Be careful, however, that you don't accidentally move a shared waypoint; if you do, you will alter the layout of the other route as well.

You may likewise split a route into two separate routes, assemble two shorter routes into a longer one, or generate alternate routes that lead to the same eventual destination.

Joining a Route

In most cases, joining a route consists of first activating the entire route then selecting a specific waypoint in the route and activating or otherwise engaging navigation to that point. This creates a GOTO leg from the present position to the selected destination waypoint. (This is the same as joining a route from the present position [Chapter 5, Figure 5.7, Method 4].)

However, some programs may allow you to join the route along a designated leg, as in Chapter 5, Figure 5.6, Method 3, by activating the leg instead of the destination waypoint. To determine whether your program allows joining the route in this manner, just observe the XTE. When joining a route along a leg, your XTE will initially be large but will reduce as you approach the Course Line.

Reversing a Route

The process of Reversing a Route reverses the numbering of the waypoints and legs that comprise the route. Bearings and Course Lines are reversed as well, allowing you to navigate in the opposite direction (i.e. to return to the initial waypoint—now your final waypoint). To reverse the route, deactivate Navigation, then use your menu or toolbar to Reverse the Route. After this, you can join the reversed route at any point, as described in the previous section.

Automatic Waypoint Switching

When your vessel icon enters the arrival circle, or passes abeam of the destination (active) waypoint, the software should automatically select the next waypoint in your route as the active (destination) waypoint. At this time, the navigation information on your screen changes to reflect the new en-route data and the lat/long co-ordinates of the destination waypoint.

You can choose to have a waypoint arrival message displayed and manually choose when you want to turn to the next waypoint. One helpful method for increasing your awareness of switching waypoints is to set a waypoint arrival alarm. Your program may offer several choices, i.e. distance from waypoint, type of sound and frequency of the alarm.

If you miss the arrival circle and the software fails to realize the waypoint, you must follow the rules for switching waypoints demonstrated in Chapter 7.

Navigating Along an EC Route

Once you have selected a destination waypoint and engaged navigation, various en-route data will appear on some form of console or window associated with the chart. [See Figure 11.10.] Most EC software provides only this console of en-route data and the chart display itself to assist you in steering toward the destination waypoint.

The two items of greatest interest on the console are the Bearing to the Waypoint (Brg to Wpt) and the Cross Track Error (XTE).

Remember: The indicated bearing is the straight-line direction from your position to the destination waypoint. If a strong cross-current is setting you off the Course Line, or if you have to take action to avoid a navigation danger, the chart display will show your new position in relation to the Course Line, as well as the geographic features in the vicinity. As a result of straying off course, the Brg to Wpt and XTE will change in value. From the XTE, you can determine whether to turn left or right to regain the Course Line; from the Brg to Wpt, you can determine the new bearing to steer directly toward the destination waypoint.

You will also note that the COG vector indicates the direction you are actually travelling. So, if you bring your vessel icon close to the Course Line and alter course to ensure that the COG vector points directly toward the destination waypoint, you will proceed along the Course Line with very little deviation.

While this may appear to be more difficult than following a perspective steering diagram, with practice, you will find that you prefer this mode of navigation to all others. All the information you need is presented on the console and chart display in a graphic and intuitive manner.

The console also displays other information such as range or distance to the destination waypoint, Time to Go, and Estimated Time of Arrival. It may even be possible to customize the console to display the en-route data of your choice.

Using Range Circles

A Range Circle is a circle you can place on the chart, centered on the object of your choice—the vessel icon, a waypoint, event mark, or even a point of land or a reef. You can also select the range circle radius and colour.

Try placing a range circle with 0.10 Nm radius (200 meters) centered on the vessel icon. Since most EC programs fail to provide a scale of distances on the chart display, this will allow you to have an instant visual appreciation of the scale of the chart in relation to your own safety zone. If you have established a 200-meter range circle around the vessel icon when you navigate in tight quarters, you can instantly determine if you are approaching dangerously close to a charted feature [Figure 11.11].

You can also place multiple range circles around the vessel icon with ranges equal to the range rings on your radar [Figure 11.10]. Compare the image on the EC display with that of your radar and get a feel for the distances involved. This comparison can be quite helpful in the absence of a distance scale on your EC. Even though you must reset the range circles on the EC each time you change radar ranges, the benefits in this case far outweigh the inconvenience. And if you navigate without radar, the range circles can still be a great help

Many programs allow you to center a range circle on a hazard and use the circle as an avoidance boundary. Find out if your EC program allows you to do

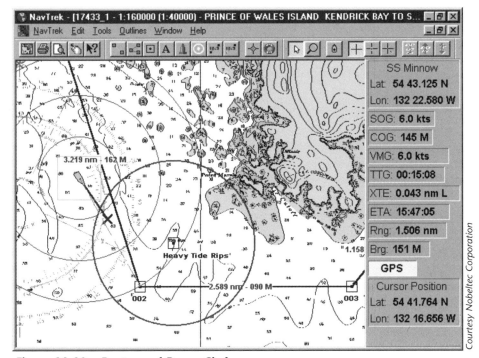

Figure 11.10   Routes and Range Circles

Each leg in the route is identified with the range and bearing from departure to destination waypoint. Each waypoint is identified by number and the present destination waypoint (active waypoint) is connected to the vessel icon by a bearing line. En route information appears in the display area to the right.

An event mark lies to the northeast of waypoint 002. Associated text provides a description—in this case a warning about heavy tide rips in the area. Also, a range circle placed around the event mark defines an area in which these tide rips may be expected.

Range rings around the vessel icon have been set to match the range rings on the vessel's radar. This allows the skipper to visually compare the image shown on the EC display with that shown by the radar. This is the next best thing to radar overlay.

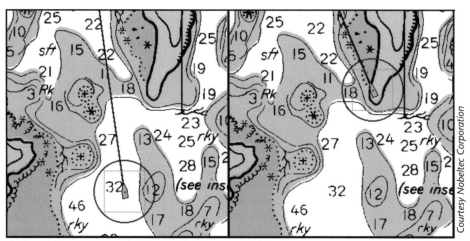

Courtesy Nobeltec Corporation

Figure 11.11   The Range Circle

The range circle centered on the vessel icon is set at 0.02 Nm (40 meters—twice the expected GPS error.

In the left-hand diagram, the vessel is clear of all dangers; in the right-hand diagram, the vessel icon is shown on land—unexpectedly high GPS errors have placed the vessel icon too far to the east.

so. If you can set an alarm to sound when you enter the range circle, the feature will be invaluable.

Using Ship-Centered Bearings

Most EC software provides the capability of laying out bearing lines from one object to another or from the vessel icon to an object. Ranges and bearings are displayed along the bearing line; in the case of the ship-centered bearing (from vessel icon to object), these ranges and bearings will be continuously updated as the vessel changes position.

To create a ship-centered bearing line, just select the appropriate tool or menu choice, move the cursor to the object, and click the mouse once. The bearing line will spring into view.

Most readers are familiar with the classical dictum, "If the bearing of another object as seen from one's own vessel does not change, then that object is on a collision course." Thus while navigating, if you place a bearing line from your own vessel to an object, you can tell when you are on a collision course with that object. This feature is especially useful when your SOG is low and consequently the COG vector is unstable; the ship-centered bearing line will indicate if you are headed for an object or not.

These simple guidelines will assist you in interpreting the ship-centered bearing:

1. If you are proceeding such that you will miss a rockpile by a small margin, the bearing should gradually *draw away* from your vessel's COG vector.

2. If the bearing remains *constant*, you will surely strike the rock.

3. If the bearing draws *toward the COG vector*, you will probably pass on the wrong side of the rock. [See Figure 11.12.]

To practice using ship-centered bearings, while proceeding at cruising speed observe the bearing of a point to one side of the vessel. The bearing should begin to draw aft; in other words, bearings to objects on the starboard side should increase, and those to objects on the port side should decrease. However, bearings to objects close to your heading will draw across the bow if there is a strong cross-current influencing your vessel. By observing the behaviour of the bearing, you can infer something about the cross-currents affecting your vessel.

This technique is especially valuable if your EC software does not allow the display of a COG or heading vector.

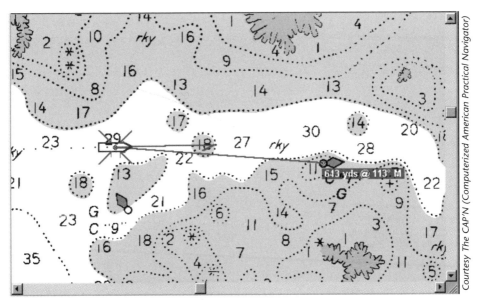

Figure 11.12   Ship-Centered Bearings

A ship-centered bearing line has been drawn to the light just a few degrees to starboard of the vessel's heading. If the bearing to this light decreases (draws toward the bow) as the vessel approaches it is a sure indication that the vessel is being set to the south by a current. If the bearing remains constant, the vessel is being set directly toward the light and will probably collide with it. If the bearing increases as the vessel approaches, then it will pass safely to the north of the light.

Update Delay Issues with DGPS

Generally the problems associated with update delay and DGPS are far less worrisome than with chart plotters. This is due to the high update rates of video monitors and central processors in modern computer hardware. Update delay in a modern EC system that is properly set up and configured should rarely exceed two to three seconds. However there are still some circumstances when you will encounter problems with the update delay of your computer based electronic chart system.

Modern navigation software—with its expanded functionality—takes up more hard disk space and requires a higher speed processor and more RAM than older versions of the same software. If you have updated your program several times, but are still operating with a 486 PC or even with an older Pentium computer, you may find the program operates slowly. Make sure you use only software that is designed for the computer and operating system you currently use. Read the specifications on the software box and ensure that your computer meets the minimum requirements.

Many new navigation programs require a minimum 32 Mbytes of RAM. If you attempt to run the program on a computer with 16 or even 24 Mbytes, you will encounter problems. We have attempted to do so—and believe us—the

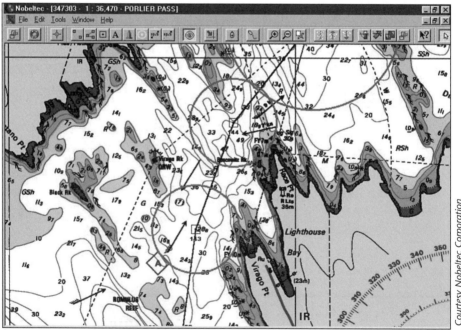

Figure 11.13   Porlier Passage

Range circles are set at 0.20 Nm. (400 meters).

results are simply not worth it. If you have an older computer, and are satisfied with the functionality of the older version of the program, do not attempt to install an update that exceeds the capacity of your hardware. If you decide to buy a new computer—that is the time to get the latest version of the program.

Memory Overload

In March 1999, I approached Porlier Passage in British Columbia in a 20-meter Coast Guard Cutter. At the time, I was not navigating an active route; instead, I was just following the legs as shown on the display (in non-active mode). However, as I approached Porlier Passage from the north I plotted out my course on the chart and began to enter the waypoints into the computer.

Rocks and shoals abound in Porlier Passage, and wicked turbulent currents are set up as the Strait of Georgia waters roar through the passage under the influence of the tides. Porlier Pass is unforgiving to poor navigation, so it is essential to stay on the ranges as one makes the approach and follows the course line between Race Point and Romulus Reef. [Figure 11.13)

As soon as I input the waypoints at Race Point and Virago Point, the computer began to flash warning messages at me. And since they were written in a form of the English language that is known only to computer programmers, I could not understand a single message. All I knew was that I should shut down the program and re-start it. But I couldn't do that because each of the warning messages required an acknowledgement that would not allow anything else to be done until I had clicked the hateful little "Okay" box. Each time, before I could exit the program, more warning messages appeared. I found I couldn't close the program, and I didn't want to crash the computer just then.

Finally I was quick enough to close the program. I then restarted it, activated the route and began to navigate. Everything seemed to be working fine.

I always plot routes through tricky passages, even on a small vessel, so I began working my way through the pass against a five- or six-knot cur-

rent, confirming my position with radar ranges and visual transits as the current and chop pushed the vessel first one way then another. After having trouble inputting the waypoints, I was reluctant to place any faith in the computer until I had an opportunity to verify its behavior, so I abandoned it and reverted to the tried-and-true methods.

As I passed Virago Point, I glanced at the computer display. At first, I thought it was behaving properly, but when I looked closer (the next time I had the opportunity), I realized that the computer displayed my position alongside Race Point, approximately 0.25 Nm astern of my actual position! That quarter-mile represented one and a half minutes—quite an update delay! Had I not plotted my courses on the paper chart and worked out transits, radar ranges and bearings to prominent points, I could have been in serious trouble.

It didn't take me long to figure out the problem. I had been running for over 200 miles with the navigation program recording the vessel track history all the way. I had forgotten to erase the track daily, so I thought I had only a few hours of track history in memory. I had also forgotten that the program was set to record position every 10 seconds and had been doing so for over two days. That represents a lot of information. It was this huge amount of track history data that had jammed up the RAM in the ship's computer and caused it to slow to a crawl. In the end, all I had to do was delete the vessel track history, and the computer leaped back into life again and operated beautifully.

The most important lesson I learned from this was not just that computers can fail—this is nothing new—but that the system can fail and yet appear to be operating normally. (See Chapter 12.)   —K.M.

Even when you have a computer that meets or exceeds the minimum requirements, you may have problems. This is partly due to the amazing versatility of modern computers. When numerous programs are running at the same time, they may interact with each other, or overload the RAM, so that the computer seems to operate with bursts of activity separated by moments when the display seems almost frozen. If this happens to you, immediately close all the other programs on the computer. If that doesn't help, then you may have to shut down the navigation program itself, or even re-boot the computer. Whatever you do, make sure the navigation software is operating properly before you begin using it again for navigation.

You may also find that some aspects of the program itself, such as a very long active route, or vessel track history require more RAM than is available. As a result, the display may become minutes instead of seconds out of date. (See Sidebar.) Be alert for these problems. *Although Electronic Charting software can take much of the work out of navigation, it needs to be monitored constantly to ensure that the information provided is accurate and timely.*

Event Marks and Text Storage

In the ECS environment, event marks possess a high degree of flexibility and storage capability. [Event marks were discussed in Chapter 10 in relation to plotters.]

To establish a mark, simply select the appropriate tool or menu choice, move the cursor to the desired position, and click once with the mouse. In most EC systems, event marks can be created only with the cursor, so to create an event mark at the present position, place the cursor over the vessel icon and click the mouse.

Simple plotters may allow the use of just a few symbols for event marks, while a powerful EC program may provide an extensive choice of different symbols. You will find that you have access to symbols representing anchors, wrecks, fish—many more shapes than you had ever dreamed possible. You may also be able to place marks representing lights, buoys and fog signals. In fact, it is somewhat like being able to recreate many chart symbols yourself. There may even be a symbol to represent *Notices to Mariners*.

The event mark in its various forms may become the primary way in which you can update the chart itself from *Notices to Mariners* and other official sources. Some programs may allow 100 or more characters of text to be associated with any event mark. By entering an appropriate symbol at a certain point and associating a text description with the event mark, a powerful method of adding additional information to a chart may be just a mouse click away [Figure 11.14].

The information associated with event marks is stored in a separate file from the chart itself. If your ECS permits you to download the event mark data to a floppy disk, you can then share your local knowledge with friends who use the same system.

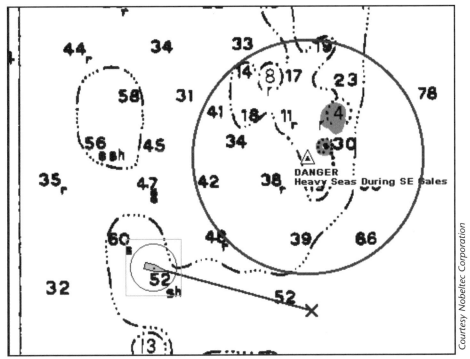

Courtesy Nobeltec Corporation

Figure 11.14   ECS Event Marks

A triangular mark has been placed on the chart to indicate a navigation warning. In addition, the skipper has placed a range circle around the mark to indicate the area in which heavy seas are to be expected. By placing the cursor on the mark and calling up the associated text, up to 100 characters of additional text can become available.

Other Types of Marks

In addition to simple event marks, EC programs allow you to assign boundary marks, text boxes independent of event marks and other types of marks. Any mark can become the destination of the GOTO command or be converted to a waypoint. You may also be able to manipulate these marks in other ways determined by your particular software. Figures 11.10 and 11.14 show marks in the center of range circles.

Boundaries and Guard Zones

You can create **Boundaries** or **Guard Zones** around any charted hazard simply by selecting the appropriate tool or menu choice then surrounding the obstruction with a series of mouse clicks. Each mouse click places a mark that forms a vertex—an intersection—of the boundary. If your vessel strays across such a boundary, an alarm goes off, giving you time to take avoiding action. You may even be able to set the alarm so that it sounds when the end of your COG vector strays across the boundary, thus giving you ample warning of entering the guard zone.

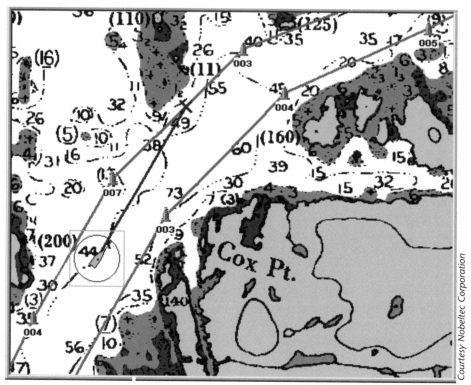

Courtesy Nobeltec Corporation

Figure 11.15   ECS Boundaries

In this figure, boundaries have been placed on either side of the safe channel. The COG vector has just crossed the boundary. This triggers an alarm indicating the vessel will cross the boundary in 6 minutes (the length of the COG vector). Another alarm will sound if the vessel actually crosses the boundary.

Once you have set up a boundary or guard zone, each time you make the same trip you will have an extra margin of safety working for you in hazardous areas. You may also have the option of establishing boundaries to either side of a safe channel as shown in Figure 11.15.

The boundary option is a powerful feature of ECS and its uses are endless.

North-up and Course-up Modes

With ECS you can orient the chart in a couple of different ways. The classical method is to display the chart with north at the top, the way most charts are drawn (**North-up mode**). However, you can also choose to have *the direction of the active leg* oriented toward the top of the display, an option called **Course-up mode**.

While most navigators find North-up the most comfortable option, there are times when Course-up is a useful choice. One such example is in limited visibility when you are using ECS to navigate, and using radar to detect any obstructions ahead and verify that the ECS is operating correctly. It is easier, in this case, to compare the two separate displays if they both face the same direction (Course-up).

However, Course-up mode does have its disadvantages:

- On a raster chart the names and depths are difficult to read and confusing when tilted.

- With a strong cross-current running, the direction of the vessel's heading will not match the direction of the active leg and the top of the chart will be skewed in respect to the radar by the amount of drift. In that case, it may be difficult to reconcile the radar and ECS displays.

Head-Up Mode

Head-up mode is potentially the most powerful feature of any EC system because the picture on the chart matches the picture ahead! It is the mode your radar supplies, so you will have no problem reconciling the two displays.

But Head-up mode also has a disadvantage. Unless you can supply input from a flux-gate or gyro-compass, the ECS will use COG information provided by your GPS to determine the orientation of the chart display—at low speeds, the chart orientation will become unstable due to the instability of the COG.

Radar Overlay

Radar Overlay is a feature that superimposes a radar image onto your EC screen. Although most modern radar sets are capable of passing radar data to an ECS, not all ECS hardware and software can process and display radar information. Once properly installed, however, a radar overlay significantly increases the usefulness of the ECS itself.

In order to interface with ECS, the radar must be capable of North-Up stabilized mode of operation, requiring that compass heading data from a flux-gate or gyro-compass be input into the radar. [For a further discussion of radar-stabilized mode, see Chapter 13.] Once the overlay is achieved, however, a transparent radar image is overlaid on the chart at the same scale as the chart without obscuring any of the chart data [Figure 11.16].

This blending of ECS with real-world data allows you to view on one screen charted features, as well as transients such as other vessels or rain and snow squalls. Where a difference between the position of a permanent charted feature and its radar image occurs, it might indicate an error in positioning input.

If a buoy appears as a radar image elsewhere than at its charted position, the buoy is probably out of position and you can take that fact into consideration when approaching the buoy. Individual targets such as isolated rocks or buoys can instantly be recognized as charted features. For instance, if another radar target appears in the vicinity of a buoy—which is also detected by radar—

the overlay allows instant recognition of which target is the buoy and which is another vessel.

The great advantage of the radar overlay is that it adds one more type of graphic information in one place, thus allowing you to get on with the most important aspect of navigation—safely guiding your vessel along its route. [See sidebar]

DR Simulation Mode

Most good EC programs allow you to turn off or disconnect GPS input and enter DR mode. (Or, in the event of a failure of GPS input, the program itself may default to DR mode.) In DR mode, the program does not assign a position to the vessel icon from its GPS input. Instead, it uses the last values for COG and SOG that were available from the GPS and applies these values to the last position fix to show where your vessel should be as time progresses and you maintain course and speed. Without this feature, your vessel icon would freeze in the last position provided by GPS.

With this feature, the EC program can survive temporary disruptions to its GPS input. However, as documented in Appendix D ["Incidents"], the program should give a clear and unequivocal indication

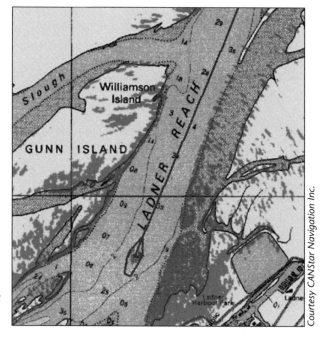

Courtesy CANStar Navigation Inc.

Figure 11.16
Radar Overlay

A view of a CANStar Integrated Navigation Display. The radar image is clearly seen superimposed on the raster chart background.

When you think of it, the use of radar during piloting and navigation operations in confined waters requires that the navigator commit the chart to memory in order to determine his or her position in relationship to shoals and other hazards below the surface. Looking at an unfamiliar radar image of a harbour approach is almost meaningless, unless you can match it up with the same features on the chart. Until now, the mariner had to constantly combine the radar image with the chart in his head—while looking at the radar—in order to determine his risk of grounding.

—Helmut Lanziner,
Chairman CANStar Navigation Inc.

that it is operating in DR mode and that the GPS input is missing. In time, the COG and SOG data the program uses will deviate from the true values; consequently, the displacement between the EC display and the true position will increase the longer the EC operates without GPS input. *Caution:* If you notice that your program has defaulted to DR mode, immediately determine the cause of the problem and, if you are in constricted waters, revert to some other form of navigation. Try also to determine how long GPS input has been interrupted.

You should be able to initiate DR mode yourself. In many EC programs you can manually enter values for SOG and COG which gives you the ability to simulate various navigation problems on any computer. (The diagrams in this chapter were created using DR simulation.) Some programs even allow you to enter values for set and rate of the current. The COG vector then emanates at an angle to the heading of the vessel icon; the icon itself will travel crab-wise across the display in the direction of the COG vector. This is an excellent technique for demonstrating the effects of current on a vessel [Figure 11.7].

Recording Local Knowledge

Most EC programs have an option that allows you to record, in a text box, notes associated with event marks. Some have tide and current programs with a similar feature. You can activate these text boxes (and sometimes, tide and current text boxes) simply by moving the cursor to the appropriate event mark, then clicking the mouse to gain access to the text. The information you record may be as simple as "fast current" or as complex as a description of events.

For example, you could record the fact that, at a certain wharf in a drying area, you had a depth of 3 feet under your keel at zero tide. On returning to the same wharf at a future date, you can pull up this information immediately.

Scientists use this function to record certain data regarding oceanographic or biological conditions. Fishermen record the fish they observe and catch. You can record whatever you want in these text boxes.

Packaged Programs

Some EC developers include packaged programs with their chart software which range from tide programs and vessel management to electronic sight reduction.

At least one developer has included an associated tide program which you can activate by a right mouse click on any part of the chart window, bringing up a tide graph or information box with the day's predicted tides for the closest secondary station.

Nobeltec Corporation's Visual Series shows, on request, arrows that represent strength and direction of the current for a certain location at the present time, as well as predicted future currents. These arrows appear as an integral part of the chart—the larger the arrow, the stronger the current. [See

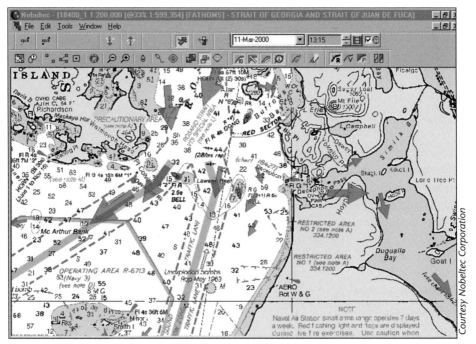

Courtesy Nobeltec Corporation

Figure 11.17   Packaged Programs—Currents

Nobeltec Visual Series display showing current arrows. The strength of the current is revealed by the relative size of the arrow.

Figure 11.17.] Tide station data may also be displayed as a bar, showing the height of the tide at the present time.

Another feature you may find in an electronic charting program is the vessel management feature. Packaged vessel management software will allow you to track engine maintenance, fuel consumption, parts inventories, etc.

Many EC programs offer the option of automatic log-keeping which is useful for keeping a record of your actual route over the ground including **CMG** and **SMG**. All you need to do is choose the intervals at which you want to record the information; the rest is automatic. Your lat/long will be recorded with time, date, course and speed, and any other information you want to include.

When navigating complex routes, you may want to record at intervals of 5 to 10 minutes; otherwise once an hour or more should suffice. In case you lose your GPS signals and are forced to use dead reckoning, automatic log-keeping is a help in providing a picture of your past actual progress.

Some manufacturers are working on a system of "embedding" information into the electronic chart itself, by incorporating visible "tags" that are linked to special files containing various types of data. This data could take the form of photographs [see Figure 11.18], sketches of a tricky passage, or even quotations from *Sailing Directions* or the List of Lights.

These and other extra packaged features add texture and depth to our navigation experience. As the programs become more sophisticated, these features are sure to become more numerous and seamlessly integrated into chart displays.

Uploading Routes to a GPS Navigator

At one time, the only way to program any form of GPS equipment was to enter all waypoints and routes manually by pressing the appropriate keys. For instance, if you wanted to enter 500 waypoints from a waypoint guide into a hand-held GPS Navigator, this might become a daunting process, requiring as many as 4000 keystrokes. It is now possible, using electronic charting software, to generate complex routes without entering data in the form of lat/long co-ordinates at all. Once you have created your own personalized routes, most of the more sophisticated navigation programs will permit you to transfer these routes into a compatible GPS Navigator. This process is known as **uploading a route** into a GPS.

This feature is a real time saver if you have a hand-held GPS without an alphanumeric keyboard. Entering the same 500 waypoints might require 12,000 keystrokes! (See the section titled **Data Input** in Chapter 4.)

The electronic charting program need not be connected to a GPS receiver to generate these waypoints; your navigation software is independent of any GPS input while you create your masterpiece. The software will create all the latitude and longitude references for waypoints and routes and then, with a few simple mouse-clicks the routes can be uploaded into your GPS. Check first to make sure that your software is compatible with the GPS equipment—the process only works between compatible software and equipment. But if you do have the appropriate hardware and software, you are in business.

You can then use these waypoints and routes as if you had entered them directly into the GPS itself. For instance, you could generate routes on a computer on board your cruiser or at home, and transfer the data into a small hand-held GPS for use at sea. With the difficulties of manual data entry out of the way, a hand-held GPS Navigator with a basic keyboard suddenly makes a lot of sense.

Planners

Many of the more popular navigation software producers offer inexpensive versions of their charting programs called **Planners**. These programs lack the ability to plot the movements of a vessel and many of the other more advanced features of the full versions, but they all have one thing in common. You can use them to lay out waypoints and routes on an electronic chart. These **Planners** are specifically intended for creating routes and then uploading them into a GPS.

Importing and Exporting Routes

Not only can you upload routes from your EC computer to a hand-held GPS, but you can also export the routes to a file on your hard drive. Whereas a route you upload to your GPS must be in a form of the NMEA marine electronic language (see Chapter 13), routes that you export to a file may be in any of a number of different formats, depending on the brand of navigation program you use. Some of these programs will export the route to a text file, which you can open and read with a simple word processor, such as Windows Notepad.

Not only can you export your routes to a file, but you can also import a set of routes from a file to your EC program. The routes will then appear on your chart display, just as if you had entered them yourself. This ability to export and import routes allows you to save your valuable data in case of a program or system crash. You can even copy the file to floppy disk and keep a backup, in case the worst occurs and your hard drive dies completely. Your waypoints represent hours of careful decision-making and should be treated as old friends. Keep them with you, take care of them, and they will take care of you in return.

But this is just the beginning of the possibilities. You can trade waypoints and routes between friends, or even keep a backup at home while another skipper operates the boat (then it won't matter if the other skipper deletes or changes your routes in the GPS on board). You can e-mail them to friends across the street or around the world. There are even web-sites beginning to appear that allow skippers to post their routes for others to download. Nobeltec Corporation hosts a "Nobeltec Community" page at its site where these routes are available for free exchange. However, a note of caution—*be careful about using routes you receive from others; their information may not have been as carefully checked as yours. And be sure to scan for viruses on any files you download from the internet.*

Proven Cruising Routes Volume One

Proven Cruising Routes, Volume I—Seattle to Ketchikan, by Kevin Monahan and Don Douglass is the first in a new concept of Route Guides. The book provides detailed information on the routes you can take, including waypoint positions in NAD83 and NAD27, distance to next waypoint, course to make good (true and magnetic) and other vital information. The 34 routes in the book are laid out in tabular form and in detailed maps that show the waypoints in relation to geographic features and hazards in the vicinity.

In addition to the print version of the routes, a companion disk is available which allows importing of the 34 routes directly into an EC program. At the time of printing, Proven Cruising Routes on Disk, Volume 1 is only compatible with Nobeltec Visual Navigation Suite. Soon, the routes will be available in formats compatible with all major EC software distributed in North America.

Sample routes are available for viewing and download at www.FineEdge.com or www.shipwrite.bc.ca

This feature allows you to work on your routes at home, on a separate PC equipped with the same program, before transferring the information to your shipboard PC. However, before you begin transferring your entire library of routes and waypoints between PCs, it would be a good idea to practice the transfer first with just a few routes.

The biggest problem with the process of importing and exporting routes is that, at this time, there is no common format that is shared by electronic charting programs. It seems that each software developer has chosen to use a format that is incompatible with all the other major EC programs.

Open Navigation Format

With the introduction of **Visual Navigation Suite**, Nobeltec Corporation developed the **Open Navigation Format (ONF)**, a format the company proposes as a universal medium for sharing waypoint and route information and for linking EC programs to other digital documents.

Nobeltec has made this format available to any software developer that wishes to incorporate waypoint, route, and document sharing into their own software. This technology implies far more than just route and waypoint sharing—though the import/export features of Nobeltec Visual Navigation Suite are part of the ONF functionality. ONF also permits "tags" to be embedded in the electronic chart which, in response to a simple command or mouse click, can call up any digital document, such as notes, pictures, or even videos.

Imagine going to the internet and searching for an agency that maintains marine boundaries, such as a military exercise area, or a no-fishing area. Then imagine that with a few simple commands you can download a small file that installs those boundaries directly into your software program. You need no longer be unsure of where a particular boundary or installation lies—it will be clearly shown in your display, along with any notes or text relating to the boundary. The possibilities for creative use of ONF are endless.

You can open the ONF file using any word processor program, and though the file size is quite large, and most of the data is meaningless to the non-programmer, selected portions of the data, such as latitude and longitude, can be extracted and copied into word processing documents, e-mail, etc.

We cannot tell at this early stage whether Nobeltec's ONF will become the standard data sharing format (remember Beta and VHS videotapes). In the long run, software developers *must* develop a common format because the consumer will demand it. Information sharing is a primary characteristic of our information age—it is no different with navigation software. In 1999 the Nobeltec's web site stated:

There are many different navigation systems in use today each using proprietary data formats for storing their navigation data. We at Nobeltec believe

*this situation retards the overall growth of the marine navigation industry,
and that the best interests of customers, and by extension the entire industry,
would be served if these disparate systems could achieve a level of common
communication.*

   *In the computer industry this is referred to as the Open Systems
Approach. It is the embracing of this philosophy which has led to the rapid
expansion of the personal computer industry over the last decade.
(www.nobeltec.com)*

Unfortunately this page is no longer available at www.nobeltec.com and the initiative to develop a true universal data exchange format appears to be stalled. We echo Nobeltec's expressed sentiments and look forward to the day when we can share navigation data with anyone who operates computer based navigation software.

Updating Electronic Charts

Hydrographic services around the world are presently working with the International Hydrographic Organization (IHO) and the International Maritime Organization (IMO) to set standards for the Electronic Charting industry. Their primary concerns are that these charts be accurate and reliable, and that they be updated with new navigational information as it becomes available.

   Various services are in place for replacing chart CDs with updated versions, but the cost is generally high—roughly half that of the original chart. The British Admiralty now has over four years experience in updating their Admiralty Raster Charts (ARCS) with raster "tiles" which are "pasted" to the existing raster chart. The BA guarantees that the process is now proven, and that corrections are accurately applied to every chart. Correction disks are available from British Admiralty agents.

   On-line updating of raster charts presents a particular challenge, because it requires adding sections of updated information to an already existing electronic image. (To update an entire raster chart on-line would take a very long time due to its large file size.) In 1999, Maptech/BSB followed the lead of the British Admiralty and began a weekly *Notices to Mariners* update service for NIMA (formerly Defense Mapping Agency) and NOAA charts. The *Notices to Mariners* corrections are formatted into a compressed file that is suitable for on-line downloading or transferring to a floppy disk. The update files are small, because the only information that is transferred is the correction for the raster chart, and downloading takes just a few minutes. Once loaded into a system that contains electronic charts, the update files automatically modify the information in the electronic chart file, resulting in a seamlessly updated chart. This is not an ONF tag that is superimposed on the displayed chart image—it is a permanent feature of the chart itself.

Since vector charts are databases, not images, the update process is even simpler, because the update file doesn't need to modify an image—it merely corrects data within a database.

The objective of all hydrographic agencies is to create a trouble free system for transmitting chart update files over radio frequencies, and, in fact, several experiments are already underway. When this technology is finally proven, we hope that hydrographic agencies will adopt a common system. For the present, you must ensure that the navigation program you purchase can utilize all the EC formats relevant to the area you intend to cruise, and that you are familiar with the update process for those formats.

In the meantime, be sure that you obtain and read the print version of *Notices to Mariners* (NTMs) and that you record the appropriate chart corrections. [Please refer to Appendix C for a listing of internet sites where you can obtain NTMs for a variety of locations world-wide.]

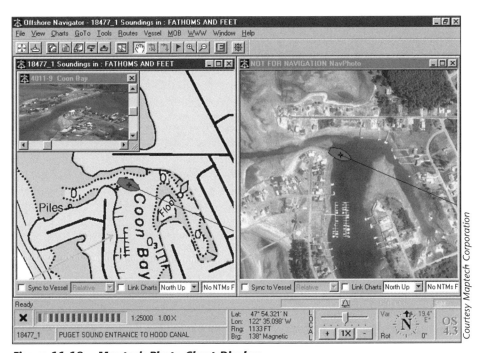

Figure 11.18   Maptech Photo Chart Display

A Maptech Navigator® series display with a Photo Chart window open. Note that the Photo Chart window provides far greater detail of the docks and shorelines in Coon Bay, and that shallow, and drying areas are clearly visible. In the upper left corner an oblique aerial view of the entrance to Coon Bay is shown.

Photo Charts

In 1999, Maptech®/BSB introduced a new concept to electronic charting—the **Photo Chartkit** (geo-referenced aerial photographs). Since raster chart technology consists of scanning a paper chart into electronic format, and then geo-referencing the electronic image to a specific horizontal datum, it was inevitable that someone would get the idea to do the same to aerial photographs. The result is a high resolution photographic "map" compatible with most major navigation software.

Photo Charts display just as if they were electronic charts in your navigation library. In fact, you can open a second window with the Photo Chart displayed, and view the chart and the aerial photograph side by side. The vessel icon proceeds across the Photo Chart just as it does across a raster chart. All the navigation marks, routes, boundaries and annotations are present. In shallow water, you can clearly see the shoals and other obstructions that appear on a raster chart merely as symbols cluttering up the display. [See Figure 11.18.]

With Photo Charts you can better relate the chart image to the real world and gain an enhanced situational awareness of the world around you. Be aware though, that these aerial photographs are not displayed in "real time". One

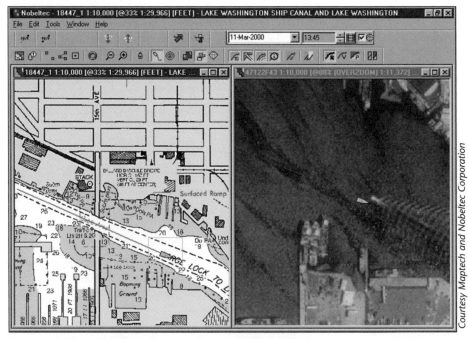

Figure 11.19   Transient Boats in Maptech Photo Charts

A Nobeltec Visual Series display showing the vessel icon crossing over a boat in the Photo Chart. This boat was present when the photograph was taken, but is no longer there.

Photo Chart we viewed showed several vessels exiting a busy harbour and another showed the current setting rapidly to the southwest. In Figure 11.18, the shallows and mudflats around Coon Bay are clearly visible, but it is not clear at what stage of the tide the photograph was taken. The Photo Chart snapshot is frozen in time, and unless you are careful, you may be deceived into believing that the present conditions are the same as shown in the Photo Chart. Go ahead, you can actually sail directly over the vessel in the display—it is no longer there (see Figure 11.19). For the most complete view of present conditions and the movements of other vessels, you must still look through the most amazing navigational device known to humanity—your own eyes.

Bathymetric Charts

A standard bathymetric chart focuses on the nature of the sea-floor and, using frequent contours and a minimum of depth soundings, presents a 3-D visualization of the underwater topography.

With the advent of more sophisticated personal computer technology, it is now possible to view the sea-floor in a 3-dimensional format in which the point

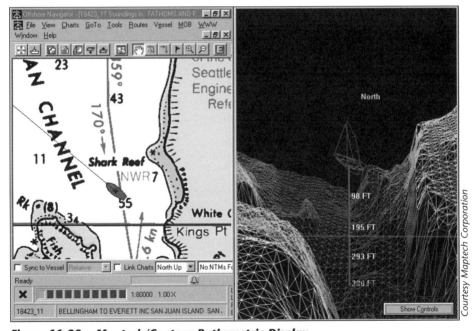

Figure 11.20   Maptech/Contour Bathymetric Display

A Maptech/Contour display. On the left is a standard electronic chart frame, but to the right of the screen, the Contour display shows the vessel in a three-dimensional bathymetric view. The seafloor display is continuously updated from the Maptech® Navigator Series positioning input and scrolls past in real time as the vessel moves through the water.

of view can be tilted and/or rotated to suit the operator's wishes. Maptech now offers "Contour," a powerful bottom tracking software that displays the sea-floor in a "wire-frame" format. The vessel icon moves as if floating above a ghostly submarine landscape. "Contour" is compatible with Maptech's Navigator® series of software. Routes and marks created in "Navigator" will show on the "Contour" display, and the vessel icon acts just as if it were in a normal EC environment. [See Figure 11.20.]

If the operator wishes, he can display the vessel track and any routes or marks. A database of underwater obstructions and wrecks can be purchased separately which may then be displayed on the "Contour" display as well. "Contour" can stand alone or be displayed as a side window in the Maptech environment.

This type of display is ideal for serious fishermen who wish to view the sea-floor in order to better visualize those places where fish are most likely to congregate. Data for the Contour charts is drawn from hydrographic surveys, and other public and private sources. At the present time, Contour charts are available only for the United States.

Beware—the Contour charts are referenced to tidal datum (in the United States tidal datum is the mean of the lowest tides). Therefore, passages that dry with the tide will show as land areas on Contour charts. *Bathymetric electronic charts are not designed to replace a keen watch on the depth sounder, nor are they intended for navigation.*

Another manufacturer, Electronic Charts Corporation, shows the sea-floor in a separate 3-D look-ahead view which simulates the view ahead as it might be seen underwater. Depth contours are shown in different shades of colour as depths increase. In addition, a depth sounder can be interfaced with the system, allowing you to read the data onscreen. Depths can be printed along the track line, or the track line itself can be colour-coded to match the colours of the bathymetric chart. In this way, a vessel captain can create a record of depths, sea temperatures, etc. for areas in which no bathymetric charts are published. This system, which is aimed primarily at serious commercial fishermen, is expensive; it is also used by oil companies, mining interests, and salvage ships.

Nobeltec Corporation is in the process of releasing its 3-D technology but, at the time we went to press, it was not yet available.

Bathymetric charts are powerful new tools, which permit fishermen, divers, and other interested boaters to view the seafloor as never before. These systems are sure to become more popular and sophisticated. It won't be long before these programs are interfaced with tidal prediction programs to provide a real-time view of tidal and drying passages. And it will surely be possible in the future for a boater to be able to construct his own bathymetric chart (or augment existing charts) with real time depth sounder readings.

RCDS

In June 1996, the Netherlands and UK proposed to the IMO (International Maritime Organization) that standards be established for **Raster Chart Display Systems (RCDS)** which would allow electronic charts to be legally considered equivalent to paper charts. Recently the IHO (International Hydrographic Organization) recommended limited implementation of RCDS to IMO. The IMO rejected the proposal but the issue remains.

Essentially, the proposal is that once standards for RCDS have been accepted, Electronic Chart Systems must comply with those standards before they are considered RCDS-compliant. Once accepted, electronic chart manufacturers will have to comply with these standards to be competitive in a rapidly-changing marketplace.

Since electronic chart CDs are far less expensive than paper chart folios, it stands to reason that hydrographic agencies will be pressured to adopt the RCDS standard and accept true electronic charting as the standard for navigation.

The objection to RCDS is that the technology is subject to failure, frequently when navigation is most critical. This is a valid objection, so until EC hardware and software can comply with the strict RCDS standards of reliability, RCDS is not likely to become a reality. *We suggest that since electronic equipment will always be subject to failure, prudent mariners should always retain their paper charts.*

Shipboard PC Specifications

Electronic Chart Systems are as variable in their demand for memory as the computers they run on. Some of the more rudimentary programs require a fairly simple computer, while others need a state-of-the-art Pentium processor.

Keep Those Paper Charts!

Eight hundred miles WNW of Cape Horn, Don and I were attempting to ride out one of the terrifying Southern Ocean storms. During the middle of the night, our 42-foot William Garden ketch pitchpoled and dropped vertically into the raging trough of a monumental wave. The impact sheered the booms, cracked the masts, forced the hatch open, and parted a doghouse seam. Icy saltwater poured in from all directions, inundating the cabin. The engine, chronometer, depth sounder, recording barometer, radios—all electronics—were ruined. For the next six weeks, in freezing weather and survival conditions, with just a small, damaged staysail to pull us along, we struggled to get to the Strait of Magellan. A sextant and soggy, discolored, paper charts were our only means of navigation, but we managed to save ourselves after a long ordeal.

Imagine the terror of trying to navigate one of the worst coasts of the world if we had not had those paper charts. In today's cruising world, total reliance on electronics is a grave mistake. Listen to the authors: Keep those paper charts!

—Réanne Hemingway-Douglass,
Author, Cape Horn: One Man's Dream,
One Woman's Nightmare

A modern system capable of running the better small vessel systems will require the following:

Computer:
- Pentium 133 MHz processor (only a few EC programs will run on Macintosh computers)
- 1.2 gigabyte hard drive
- 32 megabytes (minimum) of RAM
- Windows 95 Operating System (minimum)
- Two PS2 ports for external keyboard and mouse
- Trackball mouse which will not roll around in heavy weather and may be easier and quicker to operate than the standard variety.

Monitor:
- A 14-inch monitor works with EC programs, but a 17-inch monitor allows you to view more of any chart
- 800 x 600 pixel resolution (minimum); 1024 x 768 is better

In general, vessels that run a generator most of the time will find a desktop 110-volt system to be the least expensive. If you have inverter capacity or limited AC, you may want to use a notebook computer that runs on your vessel's DC voltage. The notebook model is convenient because you can easily carry it to your home or office; the disadvantage is that the display is much smaller than a standard desktop model.

Notebook computer:
- Same requirements as those listed under "Computer" above (notebook users can purchase a serial I/O card adapter to convert their PC card slots into one-to-four additional serial ports.)
- Active matrix colour display

An Electronic Charting System (ECS) is composed of five basic components: 1) a personal computer (laptop or desktop); 2) an operating system (i.e. OS2, Mac, or Windows); 3) electronic charting software; 4) electronic charts on disk or CD-ROM; 5) a compatible GPS or DGPS receiver.

It is the electronic charting software that provides the critical interface between you and the total system. The results you get, the screen display, and the ease of operation are largely dependent on the quality of your software. A hands-on demonstration is the recommended method to judge what is best for you. After that you need to be sure that all components in the system are compatible and reliable for your intended application.

Joe Kawaky, founder of *Captn. Jacks Software Source* says: "We always advise people to choose software first, then get the hardware to use it. This is true in any application! Software is what is critical—hardware is easy.

To guard against hard drive crashes, purchase a second hard drive with your new computer. Then copy the entire contents of your first hard drive to the back-up hard drive. In the event of a hard drive crash, you can operate from the back-up without losing your electronic chart capability. (See "ECS Caveat Emptor" below.)

Your computer should be mounted where it can be seen clearly from the navigation station. The keyboard should be placed within easy reach, and you should be able to secure both the monitor and keyboard in case of rough weather. As with any electronic equipment, protect all ports, keyboards, and screens from excessive moisture or from flying cups of coffee!

ECS Caveat Emptor (Let the Buyer Beware)

While we find ECS to be a fine navigation tool, the purchase, installation, and initial period of learning can be frustrating. One common thread in the numerous "horror" stories we've heard is that the individual components in the system were designed and developed as stand-alone units, with little thought as to how they should be connected. (The components are not easy to interconnect physically and they may have difficulty "talking" to one another.)

Be sure that you order the correct interconnecting cables, check the number of input and output ports, make all configurations (activation of specific ports, etc.) correctly, and select the common electronic language.

Sometimes the underlying operating system—such as Windows 95 or 98— is responsible for incompatibilities that will frustrate you. Be sure that you have technical service telephone numbers (and/or the internet address) for all your components in case you need assistance (as well as for ordering service packs and the latest software updates).

Computer "Crash" on the Sailing Vessel *Xephyr*

Lach and Becky McGuigan of S/V *Xephyr* out of Seattle, Washington regularly use their computer for e-mail, as well as for electronic navigation. They wrote from Mexico on a leisurely round-the-world cruise: "It was in California that we experienced our first Cruising Reality Check. We had a minor problem with our navigation computer (PC). All dealers in Ventura were closed for Christmas so we rented a car to take it to Los Angeles. The repair guys found a virus. The directory read "Ha, Ha, Ha"—nothing more. The only way to fix it before Christmas was to replace the motherboard and hard disk (which they didn't have). Not good news. In the few hours before they closed for the four-day weekend, Lach sweet-talked the service manager into gutting a new unit for parts. The hard drive now worked but was completely blank. It took me three days to reload everything and five hours of coaching by the technician over our cell phone. We swallowed hard when we got the $1,400 bill for the cellular phone call! Just another week in a cruiser's life. We were glad that it happened while we were still in the U.S."

It may be a good idea to purchase both the hardware and the software from a single reputable source and have the supplier's technician install your system so that it is guaranteed to be fully operational on completion. In any case, if you choose to install and set up the system yourself, be sure that it works well and that you are familiar with the software *before* you set out on a long cruise.

ECS is no longer a toy or novelty. Along with GPS, Electronic Charting Systems are becoming the new standard in marine navigation. Properly installed and operated, an ECS results in increased safety and efficiency of marine navigation. Don't let a horror story prevent you from getting involved with this revolutionary technology. Each year ECS component compatibility has become less of an issue, allowing more and more users to navigate with safety and confidence.

The Future of Electronic Charting

In the two years since the first edition of *GPS—Instant Navigation,* consumer EC systems have become more and more sophisticated and are now beginning to rival the "big ship" ECDIS systems. (See Chapter 13.)

As EC programs have become more powerful, their demands on the hardware have become greater, and now, a new software package may require 32 Mbytes of RAM or more—far more than was required a few years ago. Consequently the hardware to support these new software packages must be state of the art.

However, many software features do not necessarily provide greater navigational functionality. In this category you may find those features which are nice to have, and which may make your life easier—such as bathymetric and photo chart displays, tide and current features, guidebooks linked directly to the graphic chart display, and ship management sub-programs. These features are useful and can enhance your shipboard experience but they do not necessarily simplify the process of navigation.

Important new features such as radar overlay, "smart" vector charts, and integration with other navigation data sources are becoming commonplace. Soon these features will be standard issue with most new EC software.

Vector charts for consumer EC systems represent one of the most significant advances of the last couple of years because vector charts are "smart" charts. Data in a vector chart actually has meaning, whereas the data in a raster chart is

---

Frequently, I think about the difference between the recreational boater and the commercial user and I always feel that the former is mostly concerned with convenience and safety, while the latter usually has to justify the cost against some sort of financial gain. That may be the reason why we often see much more sophisticated and more expensive equipment on yachts than we do on forty million dollar ships.

Helmut Lanziner—CANStar Navigation Inc.
—past Chairman Offshore Systems Limited

just an image, which means nothing to the computer. As a result, vector navigation systems of the future may be able to identify a depth sounding, compare it to the height of the tide and the draft of your boat, and predict whether there will be enough depth of water when you attempt to cross that particular area. Shorelines have meaning and, consequently, automatic alarms may sound when you approach a shoreline, or a low water line. These charts are not here yet, but with consumer demand for more and more sophisticated products they cannot be too far off.

While the "big-ship" ECDIS systems are progressing slowly toward international acceptance as a replacement for paper charts, their cost is far greater than consumer systems. In the meantime, consumer EC technology advances in great leaps. While it will be years before consumer navigation systems can compete with the "big-ship" systems in terms of reliability and safety, they are already demanding to be taken seriously by professional mariners world-wide.

CHAPTER 12

When GPS Fails

GPS is a remarkable system—in our experience its accuracy and dependability are unsurpassed. You may work with the system for years and never experience any problems and consequently, you may become too dependent on it. If so, you are almost certain to be surprised when some portion of the system eventually does fail.

The fact that electronic equipment can fail is hardly news. You have probably experienced bank machines that refuse to pay out the cash you have requested, or VCRs that destroy your favorite movies. In our experience, computers crash and electronic equipment becomes demented just when it is most inconvenient.

Elsewhere in the book, we have examined many situations in which improper use of a GPS Navigator or ECS will lead you astray. At this point it is appropriate to examine just how GPS can fail and what you can do to help yourself when it does.

Types of Failure

Failures of GPS can be roughly classified into the following categories.

Total failure

The GPS receiver/Navigator display either dies completely or freezes up. This could be due to a power failure, corrupted software, faulty antenna connections, or failure of some component in the onboard equipment. It could also be due to the failure of one or more satellites.

Partial failure

The receiver/Navigator continues to operate but gives erroneous information. This could be due to an overloaded memory (see Chapter 11—Update delay issues with DGPS), corrupted software, faulty antenna connections, improper antenna placement, or external or onboard interference.

Human error

Usually due to improper data entry, the receiver/Navigator operates on the wrong instructions and provides information that is not appropriate for the situation.

A total failure of the equipment is easiest to detect, but when the display is out of sight and the unit is providing data to another navigation instrument, you must continuously verify that the data source (the GPS receiver) is functioning properly. See Appendix D for an example of a ship's crew that did not follow this basic rule.

Old Data

If your set is equipped with an "old data" alarm, stay alert for the alarm indication. An "old data" warning appears whenever the receiver loses contact with the satellite signals. This indication may not be audible, so be sure you can recognize it immediately, because the display will freeze at the moment the GPS signals were lost. An "old data" alarm is the surest way to determine if you have suffered a complete GPS failure.

The most likely cause of lost signals is a faulty antenna connection. So as soon as the indication appears, check the connection. Look for cracked insulation or pinched antenna wires. And finally, check the antenna itself. Small cracks in the covering can allow water to penetrate to the wire-wound core and corrode the fine wires inside.

An "old data" warning may appear when you carry a hand-held unit inside the cabin of a boat where it cannot sense any satellite signals. The warning may even appear when a large amount of rigging obstructs the satellite signals or when you are moored close alongside large steel buildings or a high cliff. Whatever the cause, the best solution is to place the GPS where it has an unobstructed view of the sky—hold it up in the air if you must. If you determine the cause is tall buildings or cliffs, there is not much you can do except wait a little and hope that, as the satellites move through the sky, enough satellites will become visible for the receiver to calculate a fix again.

Cues and Clues

Partial failures and human errors result in situations that are more difficult to diagnose because they are not always dramatic failures (though the consequences can be). These failures are probably more insidious than complete failure, because you have to examine the data itself to determine if it is faulty. If you depend on the GPS alone, you will have difficulty determining if the displayed information is accurate or not.

To determine the validity of displayed GPS information is really very simple. Regularly check your position/course/speed against other sources of information. We have stressed this throughout this book, but we feel obligated to repeat the caution here. However, there are several clues that will alert you to a possible GPS failure.

Even when a frozen GPS display is visible, it is not always immediately obvious. Remember that position data and course and speed will continue to change under the influence of GPS error even if the vessel is motionless. The position display is normally set to thousandths of a minute, so the last digit, which represents distances of 2 meters or less, varies constantly. However, other data such as distance to Go and Cross Track Error (XTE) may change more slowly because they display only tenths of a nautical mile.

Be sure your position display reads out in thousandths of a minute (three decimal places). If you do so, you will instantly notice if the last digit ceases to change (remember, this is impossible in an operating set, given the variable nature of GPS error). Many receivers will allow you to set up a "navigation page" with your most commonly used data. Be sure to include the position as part of your "favourite" data.

Any sudden change in a steady, or steadily changing value, such as COG, Distance to Go (DTG), or Cross Track Error (XTE) may indicate trouble. For instance, the COG may read anywhere from 8.2 to 9.0 knots, but it will oscillate around the mean value (8.7 kn). You would not expect to suddenly see the COG display read 0.8 kn unless something significant had changed.

The possible causes of this sort of change are:

1. You have actually stopped moving relative to the ground because of grounding, engine or propulsion failure, or a sudden contrary current.
2. A partial or complete GPS failure

If the GPS is acting up it should be fairly simple to rule out Number 1.

A sudden jump in position caused by a partial failure may cause the XTE to change rapidly; possibly the position shift will be large enough to trigger the XTE alarm. If you are at anchor, the sudden shift of position may trigger the anchor alarm, indicating that you have exceeded the established limits.

A plotter display with the vessel tracking option enabled is especially useful for recording these radical shifts in position. Many plotters retain only the most recent positions in order to keep most of the available memory free for navigation functions. If your plotter or ECS allows you to accumulate lengthy vessel tracks, you must delete the vessel track on a regular basis in order to avoid overloading the memory.

Causes of Failure

Antenna Connections

As demonstrated above, perhaps the most common cause of failure is a damaged antenna or faulty antenna connection—almost always due to corrosion or vibration. The only way to avoid this type of problem is to maintain the equipment properly. Use vaseline or some other type of sealant to seal the outside of any connection which is exposed to the weather; inspect the cables regularly for mechanical damage, and cracks and corrosion caused by weathering of the plastic coating.

Interference

Interference from shipboard and outside sources can also give you grief. External sources include microwave towers, television and radio transmitters and other industrial equipment that radiates energy in the microwave band. Shipboard sources include alternator surges, electronic equipment, fluorescent lights, microwave ovens, radios, video monitors or other equipment with CRT displays, radio antennas and amplifiers, radar scanners, and improper grounding of the vessel's electrical system.

A GPS receiver should be mounted at least 0.5 meter (1.5 feet) from a magnetic compass. Since the compass requires clearance from electronic equipment in order to operate properly, the requirements of compass and GPS are the same. GPS antennas should be mounted away from other radiating antennas on board. See Figure 8.8 and follow the manufacturer's recommendations. Keep the GPS away from any of the possible sources of onboard interference. In most cases, the receiver will perform flawlessly for many years if you follow the simple installation procedures in your owner's manual. But if problems persist, you will have to do some trouble shooting.

First turn off all the electronic and electronic equipment on board. Then find the display page on your receiver that shows signal quality or signal to noise ratio (SNR) to each satellite [Figure 12.1]. As you begin to switch the vessel's electric and electronic equipment back on again, you may see some small fluctuations in SNR. SNR normally varies by about 15%, but if a single piece of equipment causes a noticeable drop in signal quality, then you have found one culprit at least. Take a note of that equipment and then shut it down again.

Continue to switch on electronic equipment until the entire vessel is "alive," including navigation lights. When you have identified all the offending equipment, there are a number of possible solutions. Some equipment may radiate RF

A Difficult Wheelhouse

On one vessel I operated recently I found the following types of electronic interference:

• An HF radio that sent the wind speed gauge up to hurricane intensity, changed the course setting on the autopilot and, when transmitting for more than a few seconds, set off the engine-room fire alarms and sirens.
• Windshield wipers that created a 20-degree deviation in the magnetic compass.
• Power surges that turned the video sounder/fishfinder off then on again, causing it

to re-set to factory defaults.
• A Loran C plotter that for some mysterious reason would suddenly send the vessel icon on a trip around the world.

Fortunately, a helpful radio technician found that the problem was due to faulty grounding of the aluminum wheelhouse. Installing a length of 02 gauge copper wire from the wheelhouse to the vessel's ground reduced all these problems to manageable proportions.

interference, in which case you will have to relocate either it or the GPS. Video monitors, or CRT displays are the most likely equipment to cause this radiated interference. The interference may induce fluctuations in electrical power and data wires, or it may directly affect the GPS. Other interference may be in the form of noisy or erratic voltage in power cables (bilge pumps may be especially noisy). In either case, properly grounding all your electronics may help, but you may also have to consider shielding the affected wiring or the offending CRT itself.

You may notice a large drop in signal quality when you start your engine. If the signal quality picks up again once the engine is running, the problem is likely due to the sudden voltage drop when your starter motor kicks in. If the problem persists, it is probably due to a noisy alternator. It is probably a good idea to install a separate battery system for your electronics. That way, the starter motor will not cause line interference to the electronics, but if the alternator or generator itself is the cause of the problem you will have to take steps to reduce this noise.

It is beyond the scope of this book to get into great detail about how to reduce noise and interference. Perform the necessary tests, and relocate any equipment as appropriate; if the problem persists, you should contact a marine electronics technician for assistance.

Data Entry Errors
Often your problems will be due to data input errors such as entering the wrong hemisphere, or the wrong numeral in a waypoint entry. On some keyboards, it is especially easy to hit the wrong keys, and if you do not find your mistake, you may find yourself on a trip to Kalamazoo, Michigan instead of your favourite anchoring hole. This type of error is easy to spot if you always verify your routes. (See Chapter 5—Verifying Waypoints in a Route.) Data entry errors usually show up as large errors, so a quick reference to your chart will often make it possible for you to identify that something has gone wrong.

Whatever the cause, you should always double-check any instructions you enter into your GPS Navigator and train yourself to recognize when things are progressing in a manner you do not expect. Make sure you

Figure 12.1
A Northstar 961DX

A Northstar 951DX showing the SNR and Satellite health display. The horizontal bars on the left represent the SNR associated with the signals from each satellite that is being tracked.

Courtesy of Northstar Technologies Ltd.

always keep an accurate waypoint and route log—and record all waypoints on your chart. Lifting the wrong co-ordinates off a chart, or using the wrong datum may create additional problems, but if you have a waypoint log and chart to refer to, you will be able to quickly resolve most problems of this type.

If you are purchasing a GPS, find one with a keyboard you feel comfortable with and displays that make sense. There is no point in fighting with software logic that makes no sense to you.

Protect Yourself

Throughout this book we have repeatedly cautioned you to revert to some other form of navigation when necessary, or to compare your GPS display to other equipment to verify position. In the rest of this chapter we intend to discuss exactly how to go about this in order to protect yourself from a GPS failure.

Dead Reckoning

The most important thing you can do to protect yourself is to maintain backup information about your position on a regular basis. The simplest way to do this is to record your position on the chart with the time noted beside it. Draw a course line in the direction of your heading and project your position along this line a distance in proportion to your speed through the water. This will generate your Dead Reckoning position after a given amount of time. When you alter course, note your new position on the chart, and project your position along the course line to a new Dead Reckoning position. Should your GPS fail at a critical moment, you can revert to your Dead Reckoning and figure out approximately where you should be at that time.

While it is true that a current or wind acting on your vessel will cause it to deviate from the course line you have noted, you can project the effect of current as well. Make sure you have a good idea of the effect of current and wind on your vessel at any time. You can do this by solving the navigational triangle (Appendix F), or by informally observing the development of XTE as you progress along your route. Tide and current tables and current atlases will also help you determine the set and drift of current.

To obtain a fairly accurate Estimated Position, simply project your Dead Reckoning position in the direction of the set of the current for a distance proportional to the speed of the current. In most cases, the Estimated Position that results will be tolerably accurate.

If you are navigating along a twisted, narrow channel, you may not be able to record each change of course, but you can record your progress along the channel. When GPS fails at night, use your spotlight to keep you safely off the shore, and estimate your progress according to the speed you are making through the water. The effects of current in a narrow channel usually occur along, rather than across the fairway, so you can develop an Estimated Position with very little trouble, as long as you have a rough idea of the force of the current prior to the GPS failure.

Two conditions are essential for effective Dead Reckoning. First, you must maintain steady course and speed. If your speed varies, you will have no idea how far you can travel in 15 minutes and, if you do not steer as accurately as possible, you will not be able to predict the direction of future positions. Second, you must have an accurate compass. A compass with unknown deviation will not help you when you are forced to rely on it for heading information.

Make sure you regularly check the accuracy of your compass. Get it swung by a professional if you have to, and check it again whenever you reposition any large metal items on the vessel, or when you add new electrical or electronic equipment.

Other Navigational Aids

Regularly verify your position with other navigation devices, such as radar. When you plot your position, check it against a radar plot taken at the same time. Any discrepancies will show up on the chart. These discrepancies may indicate that your GPS is out by a certain amount. But remember that the precision of a GPS position is far greater than the precision of a radar-generated position, so do not be concerned with small discrepancies. Unless you have ideal conditions and a high-quality radar, you will probably not be able to obtain a radar position with more than 0.05 Nm accuracy.

When you operate in confined channels, keep your radar and depth sounder operating. It will do you no good when your GPS fails, to discover that it requires 5 minutes to warm up your radar and begin navigating again—especially if you are close to a lee shore with high winds and heavy seas running. *Navigation should*

Total Electrical Failure

In the spring of 1999 I was operating a 20-meter vessel at night in the Gulf Island area of British Columbia, when both the main and auxiliary generator failed. This vessel was equipped with a split 24-volt electrical system supplying the bridge electronics. When, after a few minutes, the battery voltage dropped below a certain value, the non-vital bus kicked out, leaving only the most vital 24-volt electronics connected—in this case, a single 24-volt VHF radio. Though the non-vital bus drop-off delay gave me time to switch off sensitive electronics, someone had forgotten to connect the GPS to the vital bus. Consequently, the sum total of my navigational aids on the bridge were a mag-netic compass and a VHF radio. Suddenly I was back to the basics and, when the engineer reported that the problem would take some time to fix, I was faced with navigating in confined waters with minimal assistance.

However, I had been maintaining a Dead Reckoning plot and was able, with the assistance of various lights and lighted buoys, to bring the vessel to a safe harbour, while we fixed the problem. Had I not maintained my log and plotted my position on the chart, I could have been in big trouble. Equipment failures can occur at any time and only the most credulous or apathetic navigator will fail to make some contingency plans. —KM

not only be a seamless blending of numerous sources of information; it should also be continuous.

You can verify your progress along a route by obtaining lines of position from a magnetic compass. If a certain point bears 045°T from your position, then your position must lie somewhere on the reversed line of bearing (225°T from the point). If the LOP crosses your route at a position that makes sense in terms of visual observations, then your GPS is probably acting properly. If your GPS is not working, and you are working your way along a route, a single LOP will give you a rough idea of your position. You can always obtain another LOP which, when crossed with your first LOP, will provide a good position.

Most small-boat compasses lack azimuth rings for taking bearings, so the bearings you obtain will be approximate at best. However, you can obtain excellent bearing lines with visual transits. You can get a visual transit by observing two objects in line. When you connect the selected objects with a straight line on your chart and extend that line toward your own position, you have an excellent LOP. These objects must be charted for you to plot the LOP, and at times it may be difficult to find two points in line. But when the opportunity presents itself, whether it be a chimney and a point of land, two points of land, or certain other charted features, the resulting LOP is probably the most accurate you can get. Be aware of any visual transits that may appear as you progress along your route, and once you see the objects in line, note the time beside the LOP on the chart. Does this make sense in relation to your GPS position? If not, you may be experiencing a GPS failure. If your GPS has already failed, a second, approximate bearing may resolve your position with a surprising degree of accuracy. *Caution—never base an LOP (bearing or transit) on a buoy. Buoys may swing on their anchors or may be completely out of position.*

Remember that a line of soundings is also a line of position, though it may not be a straight line. When lines of soundings are relatively straight, they provide good, approximate LOPs. If you combine a line of soundings with visual transits or bearings, you will have a fairly accurate position. Remember as well that your depth sounder indicates the distance from the bottom of the boat to the sea-floor, so you must compensate for the height of the tide and for the draft of your own vessel.

Above all, use logic to deal with the situation. If you don't know where you are, you cannot figure out how to go somewhere else. So, if your GPS fails, you must immediately find out your own position. If you have been maintaining your progress on a chart, and regularly checking your GPS against other sources of information, not only will you recognize a GPS failure as soon as it occurs, but you will also be able to continue navigating with very few problems.

This book is limited in scope to GPS, and consequently we are unable to present a complete navigation primer, but the few basic concepts we have outlined here will help you navigate with confidence.

CHAPTER 13

Advanced Systems

Almost all modern marine electronics are capable of interfacing with other devices which means that an individual boat owner has the ability to create a truly "integrated" instrumentation package for his vessel. The result is an almost bewildering number of possibilities for interconnecting navigational devices. Addressing all possible combinations of equipment is beyond the scope of this book so, in this chapter, we have limited the discussion to just a few of the ways GPS (or DGPS) information can work with other equipment to enhance navigation.

The cornerstone of these integrated systems is a universal marine electronic language that allows various electronic instruments to communicate with each other. It is now possible to interconnect virtually every instrument on the bridge of any vessel and display the resulting information on just one or two computer-type monitors that change the information displayed according to the skipper's requirements. The last section of the chapter describes ECDIS, a professional "big ship" integrated system that may well become the model for the small vessel systems of the future.

National Marine Electronics Association (NMEA) 0183 Standard

NMEA 0183 represents the standard set by the National Marine Electronics Association for interfacing marine electronics of different types.

Using the universal "language" of NMEA 0183, almost all modern marine electronics can now be interfaced, allowing GPS positioning information to be supplied to virtually any other electronic equipment. The various "dialects" of NMEA 0183 consist of a series of similar "sentences," each relating to one aspect of navigation. For instance, one sentence may refer to COG, the next to SOG, etc.

The navigational message output by a GPS Navigator (the "talker") is composed of numerous sentences that instruct the receiving equipment (the "listener") to display certain information on screen or to use the data generated from the talker's calculations. The NMEA 0183 standard requires that the listener know what sort of data is being spoken. A "talker ID" sentence tells the listener whether the message comes from a Loran C, GPS, or an Integrated Navigator.

Other "talker IDs" which utilize an entirely different set of sentences are available for sensor and communications equipment.

Although problems associated with differing dialects of NMEA 0183 will continue to arise, electronic language incompatibilities have become far less of a problem in recent years and no doubt will decline in the future. Some devices may not be able to utilize all the sentences your GPS Navigator outputs. In that case, you can turn off the unnecessary sentences using the controlling software in the "talking" set.

A new NMEA 2000 standard will soon be available that allows multiple "talkers" and "listeners" to share data bi-directionally—that is in both directions down a single wire. Using NMEA 2000, electronic navigation devices, engine monitors and even entertainment systems will be able to share the same signaling channel. At the time we go to press, the standard is still in the testing phase but it will be incorporated in marine electronics in the very near future.

Autopilot Interface

An autopilot is a device that steers a vessel along a pre-determined heading. It compares the heading it has been instructed to steer to the electronic output of a flux-gate or gyro-compass and steers the vessel left or right until the compass heading agrees with the heading instructions. The heading instructions can be input by simply turning a knob or pressing a button to enter a heading, or in electronic form from another device such as a GPS Navigator. That's all there is to it.

Let's look at what happens when you connect your GPS to an autopilot:

One of the NMEA 0183 sentences output by a GPS Navigator is the *bearing to destination waypoint (Brg to Wpt)* which your autopilot interprets as "Course to Steer." As soon as you activate navigation to a destination waypoint, the GPS Navigator begins to output a Brg to Wpt sentence and, as soon as you engage it, the autopilot begins to steer the vessel on that heading, performing an electronic "ballet" of sorts, which goes like this:

- Check the compass heading
- Compare the heading to the Brg to Wpt
- Send power to the motor that turns the rudder
- Monitor the changing heading
- Compare the heading to the Brg to Wpt, etc.

The vessel turns left, then right, then (perhaps) right again, continuing in this manner and remaining on course as long as the autopilot is active. Until you turn it off, except for various temporary override features for avoiding logs and debris, you retain very limited control of the vessel. You have "dropped out of the loop."

When the GPS Navigator realizes the first destination waypoint, it automatically switches over to the next and instantly outputs a different *Brg to Wpt* sentence. This instructs the autopilot to immediately begin following the new *Brg to Wpt* toward the next destination waypoint which means that your vessel will instantly turn to the new course, whether or not any obstacles or other vessels are in the way. Thus we strongly advise that if you use a GPS Navigator/autopilot interface, you very closely monitor your progress as you approach a destination waypoint and *turn off the autopilot if a large alteration of course is expected.*

In calm, open water, an autopilot can almost eliminate the drudgery of steering a vessel. However, in sloppy conditions, your autopilot may become confused and act erratically, causing you to assume manual steering control again. *And if there are numerous vessels around, or any particular maneuvering required, you should never navigate with your autopilot engaged.* In spite of these cautions, autopilots are generally rugged and durable devices which allow you to navigate safely and confidently.

The relentless pursuit of *Brg to Wpt* is both the greatest advantage of the GPS interfaced autopilot and its biggest flaw. Once set to follow the *Brg to Wpt*, an autopilot continues to perform its function even if that bearing changes by a large amount, as might occur if the vessel were swept off its Intended Track by a cross-current. [See Figure 7.6, Chapter 7.]

When the current pushes a vessel farther and farther off its Intended Track,

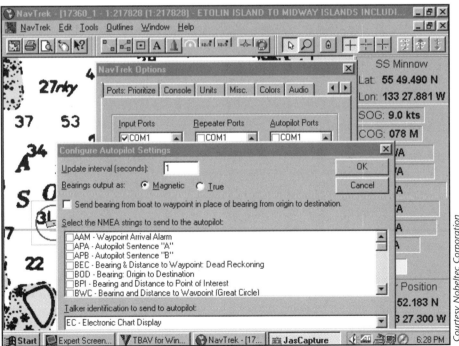

Figure 13.1   Configuring the Autopilot Interface

the *Brg to Wpt* "sentence" changes in value and the autopilot alters course. However, it does not oversteer to compensate for the current. Since the autopilot does not monitor XTE, the error can grow to extreme amounts without the autopilot's knowing something is amiss. The result is a Hooked Course Line (demonstrated in Figure 7.7) which may place the vessel in jeopardy in an area of rocks or shoals.

Recently a few small vessel autopilots have emerged that monitor XTE as well as Brg to Wpt. When a vessel with this type of autopilot drifts off its Intended Track, the autopilot detects that the XTE is growing and, at a predetermined value, over-steers to compensate for the drift until the XTE is reduced to zero. This is an ideal arrangement and is common on large ships. We are thankful that manufacturers of autopilots for small vessels are beginning to incorporate this technology.

ECS and Autopilot

Many of the more basic EC systems are passive systems which means that although they can display information fed to them by one or more sources—such as a GPS or a compass—they lack the ability to *pass* instructions to other equipment.

Your GPS Navigator may already be interfaced to an autopilot, but since the ECS draws only fundamental information from the GPS Navigator (position, COG, and SOG), its major features, such as waypoint and route functions, are left out of the loop. These navigation functions are handled by the ECS itself. Since it is the GPS Navigator which instructs the autopilot, and since it is the

---

GPS/Autopilot Interfaces in Small Vessels: The Devil's Work?

When autopilot interfaces first became available for smaller vessels, the reaction from the boating community was both euphoric and critical. Some mariners began to dream about setting up a route, sitting back, and idly sipping drinks while the electronics took over the job of navigating complex routes for hundreds of miles. Short-handed skippers saw this as a significant advance and rushed out to buy the equipment. However, the doomsayers among the boating community saw GPS Navigator-autopilot interfaces as the devil's work.

"Who will be watching the wheel while all this happens?" they asked. "Who will be guarding against collisions and wrecks?"

The truth is that both sides were partly right. GPS Navigator-autopilot interfaces can definitely relieve the burdens a short-handed skipper experiences in long-distance travelling. Just as the autopilot, itself, relieves a skipper from the drudgery of steering and allows him to spend time more usefully plotting courses on a chart and keeping a lookout, an autopilot *interfaced* to a GPS Navigator provides even more time for the tasks of navigation.

However, it is still vitally important for a skipper to keep a good lookout, and be ready to respond instantly to emergencies, or just take over manual steering to avoid floating debris or other vessels.

waypoint and route functions of the ECS that you use for navigation, you cannot interface one of these basic EC systems with an autopilot.

However, if your ECS does allow autopilot interface, you still have to determine how to achieve the interface. For example, you will need to run a cable between your computer and the autopilot—is this possible? Does your computer have enough ports? Most modern navigation software permits your computer to receive NMEA sentences from a GPS receiver and to transmit instructions to the autopilot through the same single serial port. Once you have made the decision to purchase an ECS, if you wish to interface it with an autopilot, or any other equipment, you will have to do some research about the types of hardware and software to buy.

Once installed, the interface passes information to the autopilot in a manner similar to that used with a GPS Navigator alone. [See Figure 13.1.] Just the method for selecting waypoints and routes actually changes.

Radar

Almost all new radars come equipped with an input port for NMEA 0183 data; thus most radars can be interfaced to GPS Navigators. This capability provides the radar's brain with the data needed to display a graphic representation of the destination waypoint, as well as other information such as vessel position, waypoint position, and waypoint range and bearing, all of which it displays in the margins of the radar image.

Radar plays a vital role in navigation and collision avoidance, and its performance should not be compromised by cluttering the display with data, so the amount of graphic navigation information displayed on the radar should be restricted to destination waypoints, avoidance waypoints, and event marks. This allows you to use the radar itself as a steering diagram.

Figure 13.2 shows a typical radar display accessing navigation data. The destination waypoint appears as a "lollipop"—a circle connected to the center of the display by a straight line representing the bearing to the destination waypoint. By ensuring that the heading marker of the radar crosses the waypoint circle, you can navigate toward the destination waypoint with ease.

If, due to rough weather or the presence of debris in the water, the vessel yaws away from its Intended Track, the waypoint acts just as if it were a geographic feature on the display and rotates away from the heading marker along with all other displayed targets.

When the vessel turns back toward the waypoint, the "lollipop" circle rotates back onto the heading marker. In other words, steering to the waypoint is as simple as steering toward any other destination shown by the radar.

The ease with which any helmsman can steer to a destination waypoint is the greatest advantage of this type of interface. However, there are a couple of difficulties, which will soon become apparent.

"Lollipop" Waypoint Display

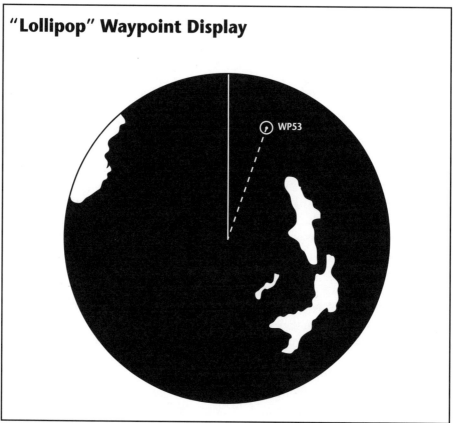

Figure 13.2

Shown here is a relative motion radar in "Course Up" mode. Radar range scale is 6.0 Nm. WP53 is shown on the screen bearing 018° Relative, range 4.5 Nm. The destination waypoint ID appears next to the "lollipop," but there is no other information inside the 6-mile range circle. The screen remains uncluttered, yet the waypoint is presented in a clearly defined manner that allows even a novice helmsman to steer towards it.

Guided by the COG, range to destination waypoint *(Rng to Wpt)*, and *Brg to Wpt* sentences spoken by the GPS Navigator, the radar's circuitry places the waypoint in the correct location on the radar display. The *Rng to Wpt* sentence is obviously needed to determine how far from the center of the radar screen the "lollipop" icon should be placed. The other sentences are required to calculate the angular displacement between the heading flash and the "lollipop." The radar uses COG to calculate where to display the waypoint in relation to the heading flash, yet we know that COG is totally unreliable at low speed. This unreliability causes the waypoint to wander back and forth in an arc around the center of the display whenever the vessel is proceeding at low speed. When the vessel is stopped, the waypoint rotates completely "around the clock." Only at cruising speed does the waypoint achieve any stability; even then, COG rolling error causes the displayed waypoint to be unstable in all but the calmest seas. The vessel's heading also wanders around under the influence of waves and minor steering alterations which adds to the waypoint's instability.

A stabilized radar display tends to give more satisfactory results, but it requires input from a gyro or a flux-gate compass. (If you use an autopilot, you already have one of these instruments.) Once accurate heading information is incorporated into the system, you can instruct the software to use compass heading, not COG, when placing the "lollipop" icon.

Caution: This method of navigating to a waypoint may also produce a Hooked Course Line. Since the radar does not monitor XTE, you will not be aware when you have drifted off the Intended Track unless you monitor your GPS Navigator at the same time.

In spite of its limitations, our experience has shown that radar waypoint displays can be extremely useful. Imagine yourself in a narrow channel or under restricted visibility when you can become confused about the correct direction to follow on the next leg of a route. When properly set up, your radar will display the direction to steer and automatically switch to the next waypoint at the same time the GPS Navigator does. Since many vessels are now equipped with flux-gate compasses, all it takes to set up the interface is a small amount of a technician's time and some wire!

Radar/ARPA Integration

Many users of modern radars have noticed a button marked "plot" or "echo trail" gracing the front panel of their equipment. Activating this function allows a vessel target to lay down a "ghost trail." This feature is provided to allow the operator to estimate the future course of other vessels. However, as your own vessel yaws, the trail laid down by the target moves around the display, greatly complicating the process of determining the other vessel's future course. In addition, the land masses, buoys and other vessels leave their own ghosts, which soon hopelessly clutter the screen.

The modern radar plotter was designed to allow the operator to select only specific targets and to plot their course and speed with a high degree of accuracy.

Ever since the early days of sail, it has been necessary to intercept other vessels or, in more extreme situations, to avoid them—perhaps to avoid a collision or a pirate attack. Thus it was necessary to know the other vessel's course and speed relative to the observer's vessel. The old-time sailors developed keen eyes and were able to intuitively assess another vessel's relative course and speed, but not very accurately. As soon as they wished to intercept the other vessel, they had to revert to mathematical methods, using a plotting board.

Using a plotting board, they could determine an interception point and alter course and or speed to suit. In an age of limited technology, this manual method was the best available and, if things were seen to change during the interception, the navigator could still resort to an intuitive assessment of the situation and change plans accordingly. The method worked very well if the target vessel had no need to change course, and it was the mainstay of naval gunnery until the development of electronic computers. But it took time to work out a solution, and during that time things could change—if, for instance the target vessel suspected that it might be the target of a torpedo fired from a submerged submarine.

When radar came into common use, mariners found it to be ideally suited to working with electronic plotting computers as a collision-avoidance tool for large ships. The radar/electronic plotter simply selects vessel targets and calculates the same type of information that once was obtained through tedious manual methods. When the international marine community established standards for these instruments, the term **ARPA** (Automatic Radar Plotting Aid) was coined.

The target's true or relative course is represented by a vector arrow drawn in the direction of its travel, its length in proportion to the vessel's speed. Course, speed and **CPA** (Closest Point of Approach)

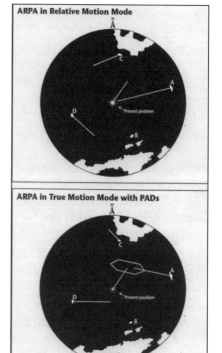

ARPA in Relative Motion Mode

ARPA in True Motion Mode with PADs

Figure 13.3   Three ARPA Displays

Upper
ARPA in Relative Motion Mode
In relative motion mode, the vector associated with a vessel on a collision course points directly at the center of the display. Target A is a probably a large ship and is definitely on a collision course.

Middle
ARPA in True Motion Mode
In True motion mode, the vectors point in the vessel's true direction of travel. A PAD (Potential Area of Danger) is projected on the other vessel's vector if there is risk of collision. In this case, the observing vessel's own vector enters the PAD, indicating a possible collision situation.

Lower
ARPA Trial Maneuver
An ARPA in relative motion mode allows the operator to simulate the results of a course change. Here, a projected 60° alteration to starboard will result in passing clear of target A.

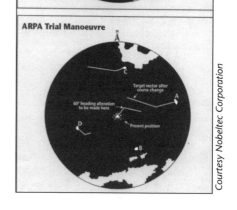

ARPA Trial Manoeuvre

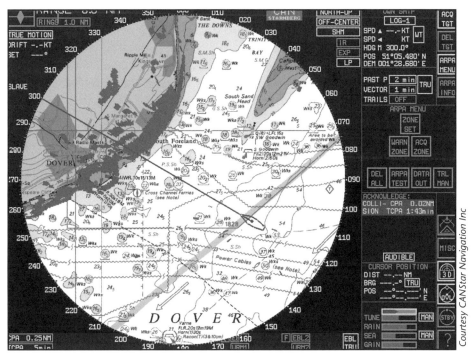

Figure 13.4   CANStar ARPA/ENC/Radar Overlay Display

The CANStar is a sophisticated ARPA/ENC/Radar display. Selected targets are shown (with their heading vectors in direct proportion to their course and speed relative to own ship) against a background ENC/Radar overlaid display.

CANStar

CANSTAR Navigation of North Vancouver, B.C., Canada produces a unique hybrid of electronic chart and **ARPA** displays. The CANSTAR unit requires only the raw input from a radar scanner (the radar display unit is not needed) and a compass sensor. Simply insert an electronic chart CD and, on its display, the CANSTAR provides a seamless integration of electronic navigation software and radar overlay. However, since this is an **ARPA** module as well, you can select vessel targets and display the true or relative vectors of each. [See Figure 13.4.] On command, the CANSTAR will show a perspective view of the active leg at the bottom of the display. Vessel targets and their heading vectors are shown in the perspective view, superimposed on the familiar

perspective (or road) display, in proper relation to the course line and your own vessel.

This system achieves an integration of not just two technologies, but three— **ARPA**, electronic charts/navigation software, and radar overlay. The system is still more expensive than a simple small-boat radar, but not by a great deal, and it provides a unique integration of several navigation technologies, all in one compact unit.

As we stated toward the end of Chapter 11, modern consumer navigation technology now has capabilities that were reserved for only the most sophisticated of the big-ship systems just a few years ago. This type of moderately-priced integrated system is demanding to be taken seriously. It will probably not remain "unique" for long.

information is provided in a window on the **ARPA** display. When a great many other vessels appear on the display, a vessel's safety in congested waters is significantly increased. [See Figure 13.3.]

At one time **ARPA** units were valued at over $100,000 and were available only to the budgets of wealthy ship owners or on ships that operated in waters congested by marine traffic. Now, small radar sets can be purchased for $5,000 to $10,000 which have many of the capabilities of **ARPAs** of the recent past. Clearly this is a great improvement over the echo trails laid down by simple small-boat radars.

To return to the original example of a sailing vessel skipper attempting to intercept another—it was necessary to factor his own vessel's course and speed into the calculation. In the distant past, this was obtained from a compass and a speed log—possibly a chip of wood tied to a string and tossed over the side; when a certain number of knots in the string were pulled out in a given time, the vessel was said to be making that many "knots."

In the modern world, we have instruments that can perform these functions. Input from a GPS source should be used to provide the speed data. In order to avoid the inevitable course error associated with GPS at low speeds we strongly recommend that you use a compass sensor or gyrocompass to provide heading data.

If you are contemplating purchasing this type of equipment, be aware that it must be interfaced with other equipment. If you do not already own an autopilot with a compass sensor, then the cost of installing the radar will be much greater than the cost of the plotting radar alone. Since plotting radars are so very new in the small-boat market, there are not very many installed sets to look at. Most new radars are fully capable of interfacing with navigation plotters and displaying waypoint and route information (though it has proved more difficult to show radar information on an electronic chart display) and all for a price very similar to the cost of a basic radar that just a few years ago lacked these functions.

Electronic Chart Display and Information Systems (ECDIS)

Electronic Charting Systems (ECS) are a perfect example of the trickle down of technology from "big ship" professional ECDIS systems. In the late 1980s, **Electronic Chart Display and Information Systems (ECDIS)** were first conceived and realized. From inauspicious beginnings as an initiative of private companies and hydrographic services, ECDIS has grown into a modern system with international standards, and national authorities are now committed to implementing it as a primary aid to navigation system for commercial shipping.

ECDIS is a professional system, yet the inevitable trickle-down of this technology is likely to propel the development of the small-vessel electronics of tomorrow. So here is a glimpse at the present and the future.

ECDIS utilizes Differential GPS positioning, a *powerful* processing capability, inputs from on-board sensors and instrumentation, and highly sophisticated vector electronic charts. The implementation of DGPS is a major feature of the new paperless approach to shipboard navigation. In fact, DGPS is considered an enabling technology which makes ECDIS systems possible. For a sample of an ECDIS display in action, see Figure 13.5.

Unlike the Electronic Charting Systems discussed in Chapter 11, ECDIS is primarily an information management tool. True, the main display has an un-canny resemblance to the EC systems available in small vessels, but ECDIS also provides an interface to a vast database of navigation information.

ECDIS electronic charts allow the operator to select the type of information to be displayed. In order to eliminate screen clutter, it may show only those sound-ings hazardous to deep-draft ships, or even none at all. The various symbols for buoys and other charted features may be accessed and, at the operator's request, characteristics of the charted feature read in a separate window at the side of the display. For instance, if a ship's officer wishes to view detailed information regard-

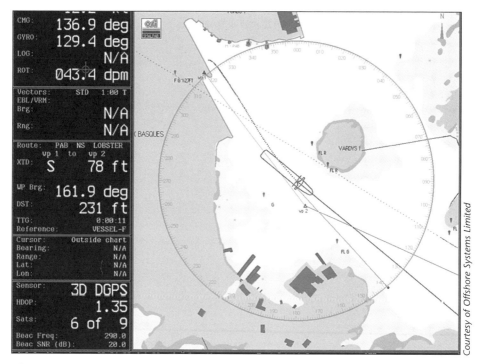

Figure 13.5   ECDIS Display

Track history, ownship vector, and a sized-to-scale ship icon are all clearly shown in this screen capture from an operating OSL ECDIS. [Original in colour.] Typical chart data and waypoints are also shown. This image is north-up, but it could be oriented in any other orientation. The combination of all these features, plus the navigation data window at the left side of the screen, allows an instant determination of the ship's actual behaviour in real time. Note that soundings have been deleted to aid in the interpretation of the display.

ing a dock or berth, at the touch of a cursor, he can access the depths alongside the dock, its type of structure, its age, etc. Any other information associated with a specific location can also be called up from the chart database.

Whenever a ship's officer wishes to view possible routes to a destination, an ECDIS can sweep the soundings ahead in relation to the ship's draft and identify the best course to avoid grounding.

If a large-scale chart of a specific wharf or structure is not available, ECDIS can insert engineering drawings or other large-scale maps to enhance the chart. In fact ECDIS has been so successful in supplying detailed information to navigators that there are stories of captains who con their ships to a dock in zero visibility using ECDIS alone. While operating the controls, the captain can easily see graphic information regarding the ship's sideways movement, the vessel's angle to the wharf, and the under-keel clearance. Another officer can monitor the radar to watch for transient phenomenon not stored in the chart database—such as other vessels. This handling in tight quarters is made possible by *very large-scale* (so-called super-scale) charts and, in some systems, by providing a choice between head-up and north-up displays.

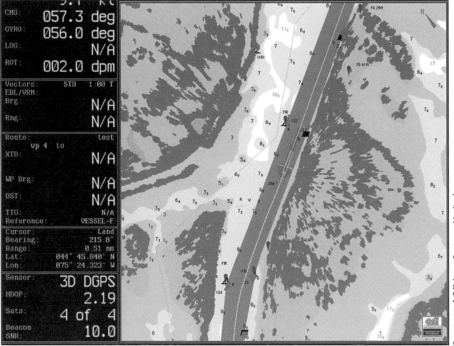

Courtesy of Offshore Systems Limited

Figure 13.6   ECDIS with Radar Overlay

A screen capture from an OSL ECDIS [original in colour] demonstrating radar overlay applied to the display. The radar images are shown in dark grey. In the image, there is a very close correlation between the radar image and the electronic chart. This creates confidence in the ECDIS itself.

As depicted by ECDIS, [Figure 13.5] the vessel icon (actually a scale drawing of the individual ship) increases in size as chart scale increases, and it rotates on the screen as the vessel turns.

Electronic bearing lines on the display originate from the actual position of the radar scanner on the ship icon. This helps to correlate the view on the display with what the captain actually sees through the bridge windows, and ensures consistency with data from the radar and other navigation sensors. The actual pivot point of the ship serves as the origin of the COG vector so that the ship behaves on the display exactly as it does in real life.

Obviously, in order to provide such a complete picture in one place, numerous sensors and instruments must supply the ECDIS with data, and the ECDIS data processing capability must be powerful enough to manipulate all the information and provide twice per second updates to the display.

With radar overlay [Figure 13.6], the radar image appears on the chart in proportion to the charted features. This blending of navigation chart and real-world data allows the operator to view not only all charted features but also transient features such as other shipping, racons, and rain and snow squalls. Where a difference exists between the position of a fixed charted feature and its radar image, it indicates that the DGPS or other positioning input may be in error, so the ECDIS allows the operator to apply an offset to compensate for the error.

However, when the charted position of a buoy does not agree with its radar image, the ECDIS display is probably correct and the buoy out of position. This must be considered when taking bearings or ranges on the buoy.

An Automatic Radar Plotting Aid may also provide target data to an ECDIS, providing the speed and course of other ships and allowing an operator to work with target displays in true-motion format, within a highly sophisticated electronic charting environment.

The implications of this technology on all mariners are profound. In light of the high accuracy and confidence levels associated with DGPS and ECDIS, national governments are proceeding to de-activate or remove certain lights, buoys and fog horns which they consider redundant now that precise electronic positioning is available. For small vessel operators, this is not as fearsome a prospect as it may seem, since the aids to be discontinued are those identified for the benefit of major shipping.

It is a totally new experience for a Master to issue a command to the rudder or bow-thruster, while witnessing an immediate response on the ECDIS display at large enough scales to see a detailed outline of own ship. Never before has a Captain had the opportunity to observe the entire operation from a bird's eye perspective in near real-time, while manoeuvring close to surrounding hazards. It is often at this point in the process that the mariner—through on-board experience—finally understands the fundamental difference between an ECDIS and the paper chart.

—Helmut Lanziner—Chairman
CANStar Navigation Inc.

The International Maritime Organization is deeply involved in the development of ECDIS technology, and it finally issued standards for ECDIS manufacturers in 1997. The new standard, known as DX-90 S57, will be the blueprint for all future ECDIS development.

ECDIS vector charts are fully compliant with the IHO S-57 standard, and are known as **Electronic Navigation Charts** (ENCs). They are produced from authorized data supplied by hydrographic agencies and are subject to rigorous testing before they may be known as ENCs. Since they are fully vectored databases, they can be updated on-line on a regular basis, making it possible to keep each chart completely current. In fact, national authorities have begun to experiment with radio transmission of these updates to ships at sea via Inmarsat C satellite communications.

Most professional mariners agree that ECDIS provides navigators with the ability to intuitively understand a wealth of information that, in a non-ECDIS environment, they must gather from a variety of sources. A mariner must make real-time decisions but, if he has to spend too much time collating information from different sources, his decisions are then based on old data, which reflect his vessel's past history. While history is important, the present moment contains all the forces he must take into account. For the first time, ECDIS makes possible complex navigation decisions based on real-time information—truly instant GPS Navigation!

ECDIS on the Saint Lawrence River

An early test of ECDIS came during the winter navigation season in the Saint Lawrence River in 1986. There, Canadian Coast Guard icebreakers are regularly used to break up ice jams and keep the river open. In the featureless winter environment—a uniform cover of ice and snow over both land and water—navigation can be time consuming and extremely difficult. In addition, weather and darkness often hamper ice operations. However, a Precise Integrated Navigation System (PINS)—an early form of ECDIS—had just been installed on Coast Guard icebreakers, immediately enabling captains to be sure of ship's positioning and to focus on the job of clearing ice. The result was that, for the first time ever throughout the winter, the Saint Lawrence River was open to shipping between Montreal and Quebec.

The Canadian Coast Guard now states that there have been no closures of the St. Lawrence due to conditions of poor visibility since 1986, when they first started using ECDIS. Prior to that year, closures ranged from three to eighteen days annually.

The St. Lawrence Seaway Authority now permits ships equipped with ECDIS/Radar Overlay to continue to operate during periods when they shut down other traffic in sections of the waterway. The same holds true for their U.S. counterpart, the St. Lawrence Seaway Development Corporation.

"Operating on the Seaway after daylight is permitted for vessels fitted with ECDIS systems with Radar Overlay. For example, a vessel transit from Cape Vin to Port of Montreal, which normally takes 36 hours via daylight-only navigation, with night-time navigation could be reduced to 24 hours, a savings of 12 hours."

(The St. Lawrence Seaway Authority)

Appendices

APPENDIX A
Decimal Minutes vs. Seconds

Decimals of a Minute to Seconds

1 degree	=	60 minutes
1 minute	=	60 seconds

Minutes	Seconds	Minutes	Seconds
0.01 =	0.60	0.51 =	30.60
0.02 =	1.20	0.52 =	31.20
0.03 =	1.80	0.53 =	31.80
0.04 =	2.40	0.54 =	32.40
0.05 =	3.00	0.55 =	33.00
0.06 =	3.60	0.56 =	33.60
0.07 =	4.20	0.57 =	34.20
0.08 =	4.80	0.58 =	34.80
0.09 =	5.40	0.59 =	35.40
0.10 =	6.00	0.60 =	36.00
0.11 =	6.60	0.61 =	36.60
0.12 =	7.20	0.62 =	37.20
0.13 =	7.80	0.63 =	37.80
0.14 =	8.40	0.64 =	38.40
0.15 =	9.00	0.65 =	39.00
0.16 =	9.60	0.66 =	39.60
0.17 =	10.20	0.67 =	40.20
0.18 =	10.80	0.68 =	40.80
0.19 =	11.40	0.69 =	41.40
0.20 =	12.00	0.70 =	42.00
0.21 =	12.60	0.71 =	42.60
0.22 =	13.20	0.72 =	43.20
0.23 =	13.80	0.73 =	43.80
0.24 =	14.40	0.74 =	44.40
0.25 =	15.00	0.75 =	45.00
0.26 =	15.60	0.76 =	45.60
0.27 =	16.20	0.77 =	46.20
0.28 =	16.80	0.78 =	46.80
0.29 =	17.40	0.79 =	47.40
0.30 =	18.00	0.80 =	48.00
0.31 =	18.60	0.81 =	48.60
0.32 =	19.20	0.82 =	49.20
0.33 =	19.80	0.83 =	49.80
0.34 =	20.40	0.84 =	50.40
0.35 =	21.00	0.85 =	51.00
0.36 =	21.60	0.86 =	51.60
0.37 =	22.20	0.87 =	52.20
0.38 =	22.80	0.88 =	52.80
0.39 =	23.40	0.89 =	53.40
0.40 =	24.00	0.90 =	54.00
0.41 =	24.60	0.91 =	54.60
0.42 =	25.20	0.92 =	55.20
0.43 =	25.80	0.93 =	55.80
0.44 =	26.40	0.94 =	56.40
0.45 =	27.00	0.95 =	57.00
0.46 =	27.60	0.96 =	57.60
0.47 =	28.20	0.97 =	58.20
0.48 =	28.80	0.98 =	58.80
0.49 =	29.40	0.99 =	59.40
0.50 =	30.00	1.00 =	60.00

Seconds to Decimals of a Minute

1 minute	=	1/60 degree
1 second	=	1/60 minute

Seconds	Minutes	Seconds	Minutes
1 =	0.017	51 =	0.850
2 =	0.033	52 =	0.867
3 =	0.050	53 =	0.883
4 =	0.067	54 =	0.900
5 =	0.083	55 =	0.917
6 =	0.100	56 =	0.933
7 =	0.117	57 =	0.950
8 =	0.133	58 =	0.967
9 =	0.150	59 =	0.983
10 =	0.167	60 =	1.000
11 =	0.183		
12 =	0.200		
13 =	0.217		
14 =	0.233		
15 =	0.250		
16 =	0.267		
17 =	0.283		
18 =	0.300		
19 =	0.317		
20 =	0.333		
21 =	0.350		
22 =	0.367		
23 =	0.383		
24 =	0.400		
25 =	0.417		
26 =	0.433		
27 =	0.450		
28 =	0.467		
29 =	0.483		
30 =	0.500		
31 =	0.517		
32 =	0.533		
33 =	0.550		
34 =	0.567		
35 =	0.583		
36 =	0.600		
37 =	0.617		
38 =	0.633		
39 =	0.650		
40 =	0.667		
41 =	0.683		
42 =	0.700		
43 =	0.717		
44 =	0.733		
45 =	0.750		
46 =	0.767		
47 =	0.783		
48 =	0.800		
49 =	0.817		
50 =	0.833		

Decimal Minutes vs. Seconds

Given the position of Longships light in degrees and decimal minutes as 50°03.95' N, 5°44.75' W, to convert the *latitude* of Longships light to degrees, minutes, and seconds, simply multiply the decimal portions of minutes by 60 to find the number of seconds:

0.95' X 60 = 57"

and add to the whole number of degrees and minutes:

50°03' N + 57" = 50°03'57" N

To convert the *longitude*, multiply the decimal portions of minutes by 60 to find the number of seconds:

0.80' X 60 = 48"

and add to the whole number of degrees and minutes

5°44' W + 48" = 5°44'48" W

The position in minutes and seconds is:

50°03'57" N   5°44'48" W

You can also find the correct number of seconds by referring to the tables.

To convert the position from degrees, minutes, and seconds to degrees and decimal minutes, divide the number of seconds by 60:

$$\frac{57"}{60} = 0.95' \qquad \frac{48"}{60} = 0.80'$$

then add these decimals to the whole number of minutes

50°03' N + .95' = 50°03.95' N

5°44' W + .80' = 5°44.80' W

APPENDIX B
GPS and DGPS Internet Sites

Due to the number of sites available and the limited space, the following listing of internet sites contains no comments—with a few notable exceptions. This list is by no means complete and may omit some important sites. Not all of these sites have been visited by the authors, and we make no guarantees for the material contained in any site; some sites may no longer be accessible through the listed URLs. (Many of these sites were used in gathering information for this book.) For a more exhaustive list of GPS web sites, go to www.shipwrite.bc.ca

Be aware when downloading demo programs from internet sites that some programs may carry viruses and/or be incompatible with programs already installed in your computer, such as an anti-virus program. Empty your web browser cache and the recycle bin *before* running anti-virus software.

Our Favourites:

www.fineedge.com
Home page of FineEdge.com; Nautical publishers; first to provide GPS corrections to published waypoint guides. View sample chapters from FineEdge publications. Download sample routes for use with Nobeltec Visual Navigation Suite.

www.shipwrite.bc.ca
Home of Shipwrite Productions: Nautical publications and consulting by Captain Kevin Monahan—specializing in the Pacific Northwest and books on electronic navigation. [Refer to this web-site for addenda to this and other FineEdge.com titles and for the latest news about the Global Navigation System.]

www.igeb.gov
Inter-agency GPS Executive Board. Read the press releases regarding the removal of Selective Availability on May 1, 2000.

http://bluegrass.net/~hal/index.html
GPS Novice Net—GPS for the non-Rocket Scientist

www.bst-tsb.gc.ca
Transportation Safety Board of Canada

http://www.cyber-dyne.com/~jkohnen/boatlink.html
The mother of all maritime links—a huge collection of links to nautical sites—(from soup to nuts)

www.dot.gov/affairs/cgind.htm
U.S. Coast Guard Public Affairs

www.gpsnuts.com
GPS Nuts—GPS information, tips and tricks, reviews of popular models of GPS equipment.

www.hydro.gov.uk/
United Kingdom Hydrographic Office home page—source of Notices to Mariners and the Admiralty Raster Chart Service

http://www.beta.ialahq.org/pages/english/p1.htm
International Association of Lighthouse Authorities—the governing body for international standards relating to lights, buoys, and DGPS reference stations

www.navcen.uscg.mil
U.S. Coast Guard Navigation Center, previously known as GPS Information Center (GPSIC). This is the official site for information about GPS and DGPS. This is the best place to get the NANUs, the navigation advisories that tell of GPS outages or other major changes to the GPS constellation that can affect the geometry and ultimately the accuracy of the constellation

http://www.nautinst.org/index.html
The Nautical Institute—The world's leading institute for professional mariners

www.starlinkdgps.com/index.htm
Starlink: Extensive information available on GPS,DGPS etc.

www.marinesoft.com
Links to numerous software producers

http://www.rin.org.uk/
The Royal Institute of Navigation—for those with an interest in navigation in its broadest terms

www.rssi.ru/SFCSIC/SFCSIC_main.html
GLONASS: site of the Russian Space Forces

http://satnav.atc.ll.mit.edu
MIT Lincoln Laboratory: GLONASS page

http://gps.faa.gov./Programs/WAAS/waas.htm
Federal Aviation Administration WAAS site—WAAS (Wide Area Augmentation System) is a satellite based differential GPS system

http://www.trinityhouse.co.uk/dgps.htm
Trinity House—UK lighthouse authority—DGPS page

http://vancouver-webpages.com/peter/index.html#gps
A site with numerous documents and other information related to GPS and boating in general

www.cruisingworld.com/joegps97/joegps97.htm
Cruising World magazine. A review of 10 popular handheld GPS receivers— complete with comparison tables

Notices to Mariners:

For a more complete listing of Notices to Mariners sites, go to your favourite search engine and type in "Notices to Mariners"

http://adam.enmb.ee/
Estonian Notices to Mariners

www.bsh.de/Surveying/Notices/Notices.htm
German Hydrographic Agency Notices to Mariners

www.chartco.com/
Commercial Notices to Mariners Service for US and British Admiralty Charts

www.cil.ie/
The Commisioners of Irish Lights—Notices to Mariners for the Republic of Ireland

www.chartpilot.ru/
Russian Federation Notices to Mariners and nautical charts

www.dhi.tel.hr/ozpweb/index.htm
Croatian Notices to Mariners

www.hydro.gov.uk/distributor.htm
Listing of agents of British Admiralty charts, Notices to Mariners, and other Hydrographic Office publications.

www.hydro.linz.govt.nz/ntm/index.html
New Zealand Notices to Mariners

www.hydro.navy.gov.au/prodserv/n2m/notices.htm
Australian Notices to Mariners

http://www.hydro.nl/nl/baz_main_nl_pdf.htm
Netherlands Hydrographic Office Notices to Mariners

www.info.gov.hk/mardep/ntm/ntm.htm
Hong Kong Notices to Mariners

www.jhd.go.jp/cue/TUHO/nme.html
Japan Maritime Safety Agency

www.navcen.uscg.mil
US Coast Guard Notices to Mariners

www.nima.mil/Navigation/index.cfm
National Imagery and Mapping Agency, Marine navigation Department—online versions of Sailing Directions, Notices to Mariners and the American Practical Navigator (Bowditch). Formerly DMA.

www.notmar.com
Canadian Notices to Mariners

www.notmar.com/eng/services/notmar/notice.html
Report DGPS anomalies in Canadian waters on this site.

www.shom.fr/index_e.html
French Naval Hydrographic and Oceanographic Service—Notices to Mariners

www.statkart.no/efs/gbindex.html
Norwegian Notices to Mariners

Commercial Sites:

www.dgps.com
DCI: Land-based DGPS technology

www.geoline.com
Geoline Inc.: GPS Surveying technology

www.gpsgis.com
Honkus and Associates: GPS technology and links

www.iimorrow.com
Apollo: Motorola GPS technology

www.lambdatech.com
GPS technology

www.omnistar.com
Omnistar: land-based DGPS systems

www.topcon.com
GPS surveying instrumentation

Equipment Manufacturers and Sites:

www.boatservices.com
Information on products from various manufacturers including Si-Tex, Northstar, Furuno, Magellan, Icom, B&G, Trimble, Shakespeare, Garmin, Raytheon, KVH, Navionics, Micrologic, C-MAP, Cetrek

www.conexant.com/home.asp
Conexant—formerly Rockwell Semiconductor Systems: GPS technology including PC card GPS receiver

www.furuno.com
Furuno Electric Ltd. USA—manufacturer of a complete line of marine electronics

www.garmin.com
Garmin—manufacturer of GPS hardware

www.gps4fun.com
Adventure GPS Products

www.magellangps.com
Magellan Systems Corporation marine and auto-motive products

www.northstarcmc.com
Northstar Technologies

www.raymarine.com
Raytheon

www.raymarine.com
Raytheon Marine Electronics

www.shakespeare-ef.com
Shakespeare Electronics

www.simrad.com
Simrad Marine Electronics

www.teletype.com
Teletype: GPS manufacturer

www.trimble.com
Trimble Navigation—GPS hardware

www.vitinc.com/nn/manf/
Information on products of various marine electronics manufacturers

Electronic Charting:

www.advmarine.com
Instar Navigation Systems—Seaplot navigation software

www.bsbcharts.com
Maptech—Chart Navigator software and source of authorized U.S. government NOAA electronic charts

www.c-map.com
C-Map: electronic charts

www.clark.net/pub/thubin/aocs
AO Chart Service—Navigation Made Easy—Tides and Currents software

www.euronav.co.uk
seaPro2000: navigation software and vector charts—demo download available.

www.fix.net/radarcomm
P-Sea Windplot for Windows: Chart software—free demo available.

www.fugawi.com
Fugawi navigation software

www.jeppesen.com
Jeppesen Marine—Marine navigation software

www.jjmsystems.com
JJM Systems—Mariner's Eye navigation software—integrated radar charting software

www.laserplot.com
Chartnav: chart software—demo download available

www.maincourse.com
Nav Master II and III: navigation software—demo download available

www.maptech.com
Maptech—Chart Navigator software and source of authorized U.S. government NOAA electronic charts

www.maxsea.com
Net Sea Inc: Home of MaxSea Yacht navigation software for the Power MacIntosh—weather forecasts overlaid on chart software—demo available

www.microplot.co.uk
Microplot: navigation software— home of Sea Information Systems—free demo download available

www.navionics.com
Navionics: electronic charts

www.ndi.nf.ca
Nautical Data International: source for authorized Canadian Hydrographic Service electronic charts

www.nobeltec.com
Home of Nobeltec Visual Navigation Suite and Passport World Charts—free demo download available

www.quintessencedesigns.com
Navima Q navigation software and Weatherma Q weather fax software—for MacIntosh

www.sevencs.com
Seven Cs GmbH—ECDIS software

www.tides.com
Nautical Software Inc.: producers of Chartview navigation software and Tides and Currents software for North America (Said to be the only software that correctly predicts tides in South America)

www.transas.com
Transas—World-wide vector charts based primarily on NOAA, British Admiralty and Russian Hydrographic Service charts

www.capjack.com
Captain Jack's Software Source: electronic chart software, including NavimaQ for Macintosh

Other Sites of Interest:

www.asf.alaska.edu
*University of Alaska synthetic aperture radar
satellite imaging project*

www.erin.gov.au
*Australian Environment On-line: list and links to
world wide marine environment resources.*

www.geo.ed.ac.uk/home/giswww.html
Links to geodetic sites of interest

www.geod.emr.ca
*Energy, Mines and Resources Canada: producers of
Canadian Topographic Survey maps*

www.ghgcorp.com/wagenx/gps.htm
Jenny's GPS links

www.grdl.noaa.gov
NOAA Geosciences Laboratory

www.gpsworld.com
*GPS World Magazine—including a GPS buyer's
guide*

www.ion.org
Institute of Navigation

www.joe.mehaffey.com
*GPS information—including numerous links and
GPS hardware reviews*

www.lasertech.com
Laser surveying technology

www.larc.nasa.gov
NASA Langley Research Center

www.ngs.noaa.gov
United States National Geodetic Survey

www.noaa.gov
*United States National Oceanic and Atmospheric
Administration: producer of official US navigation
charts—among numerous other functions*

www.nhc.noaa.gov/
National Hurricane Center

www.ocens.com
*Oceans and Coast Environmental Sensing Inc.—
Satellite weather imagery*

www.sgo.fomi.hu
Hungarian Satellite Geodetic Observatory

www.spatial.maine.edu/~leick/gpshome.htm
*University of Maine Spatial Information Science
and Engineering: GPS and GLONASS information
—including links to other GPS sites*

http://www.rdc.uscg.mil/rdcpages/software.html
*From the United States Coast Guard Research and
Development Center; a DOS based program for
converting Loran C time differences to Latitude
and Longitude*

www.usno.navy.mil
United States Naval Observatory

APPENDIX C
Units in Use and Conversion Factors

Conversions from Nautical Miles to Statute Miles to Kilometers

Nautical Miles	Statute Miles	Kilometers	Nautical Miles	Statute Miles	Kilometers
0.10	0.12	0.19	5.10	5.87	9.45
0.20	0.23	0.37	5.20	5.98	9.63
0.30	0.35	0.56	5.30	6.10	9.82
0.40	0.46	0.74	5.40	6.21	10.00
0.50	0.58	0.93	5.50	6.33	10.19
0.60	0.69	1.11	5.60	6.44	10.37
0.70	0.81	1.30	5.70	6.56	10.56
0.80	0.92	1.48	5.80	6.67	10.74
0.90	1.04	1.67	5.90	6.79	10.93
1.00	1.15	1.85	6.00	6.90	11.11
1.10	1.27	2.04	6.10	7.02	11.30
1.20	1.38	2.22	6.20	7.13	11.48
1.30	1.50	2.41	6.30	7.24	11.67
1.40	1.61	2.59	6.40	7.36	11.85
1.50	1.73	2.78	6.50	7.47	12.04
1.60	1.84	2.96	6.60	7.59	12.22
1.70	1.96	3.15	6.70	7.70	12.41
1.80	2.07	3.33	6.80	7.82	12.59
1.90	2.19	3.52	6.90	7.93	12.78
2.00	2.30	3.70	7.00	8.05	12.96
2.10	2.42	3.89	7.10	8.16	13.15
2.20	2.53	4.07	7.20	8.28	13.33
2.30	2.65	4.26	7.30	8.39	13.52
2.40	2.76	4.44	7.40	8.51	13.70
2.50	2.88	4.63	7.50	8.62	13.89
2.60	2.99	4.82	7.60	8.74	14.08
2.70	3.11	5.00	7.70	8.85	14.26
2.80	3.22	5.19	7.80	8.97	14.45
2.90	3.34	5.37	7.90	9.08	14.63
3.00	3.45	5.56	8.00	9.20	14.82
3.10	3.57	5.74	8.10	9.31	15.00
3.20	3.68	5.93	8.20	9.43	15.19
3.30	3.80	6.11	8.30	9.54	15.37
3.40	3.91	6.30	8.40	9.66	15.56
3.50	4.03	6.48	8.50	9.77	15.74
3.60	4.14	6.67	8.60	9.89	15.93
3.70	4.26	6.85	8.70	10.01	16.11
3.80	4.37	7.04	8.80	10.12	16.30
3.90	4.49	7.22	8.90	10.24	16.48
4.00	4.60	7.41	9.00	10.35	16.67
4.10	4.72	7.59	9.10	10.47	16.85
4.20	4.83	7.78	9.20	10.58	17.04
4.30	4.95	7.96	9.30	10.70	17.22
4.40	5.06	8.15	9.40	10.81	17.41
4.50	5.18	8.33	9.50	10.93	17.59
4.60	5.29	8.52	9.60	11.04	17.78
4.70	5.41	8.70	9.70	11.16	17.96
4.80	5.52	8.89	9.80	11.27	18.15
4.90	5.64	9.07	9.90	11.39	18.33
5.00	5.75	9.26	10.00	11.50	18.52

APPENDIX C *(continued)*

Conversions from Knots to Miles per Hour to Kilometers per Hour

Knots	Miles per Hour	Km per Hour	Knots	Miles per Hour	Km per Hour
0.10	0.12	0.19	5.10	5.87	9.45
0.20	0.23	0.37	5.20	5.98	9.63
0.30	0.35	0.56	5.30	6.10	9.82
0.40	0.46	0.74	5.40	6.21	10.00
0.50	0.58	0.93	5.50	6.33	10.19
0.60	0.69	1.11	5.60	6.44	10.37
0.70	0.81	1.30	5.70	6.56	10.56
0.80	0.92	1.48	5.80	6.67	10.74
0.90	1.04	1.67	5.90	6.79	10.93
1.00	1.15	1.85	6.00	6.90	11.11
1.10	1.27	2.04	6.10	7.02	11.30
1.20	1.38	2.22	6.20	7.13	11.48
1.30	1.50	2.41	6.30	7.24	11.67
1.40	1.61	2.59	6.40	7.36	11.85
1.50	1.73	2.78	6.50	7.47	12.04
1.60	1.84	2.96	6.60	7.59	12.22
1.70	1.96	3.15	6.70	7.70	12.41
1.80	2.07	3.33	6.80	7.82	12.59
1.90	2.19	3.52	6.90	7.93	12.78
2.00	2.30	3.70	7.00	8.05	12.96
2.10	2.42	3.89	7.10	8.16	13.15
2.20	2.53	4.07	7.20	8.28	13.33
2.30	2.65	4.26	7.30	8.39	13.52
2.40	2.76	4.44	7.40	8.51	13.70
2.50	2.88	4.63	7.50	8.62	13.89
2.60	2.99	4.82	7.60	8.74	14.08
2.70	3.11	5.00	7.70	8.85	14.26
2.80	3.22	5.19	7.80	8.97	14.45
2.90	3.34	5.37	7.90	9.08	14.63
3.00	3.45	5.56	8.00	9.20	14.82
3.10	3.57	5.74	8.10	9.31	15.00
3.20	3.68	5.93	8.20	9.43	15.19
3.30	3.80	6.11	8.30	9.54	15.37
3.40	3.91	6.30	8.40	9.66	15.56
3.50	4.03	6.48	8.50	9.77	15.74
3.60	4.14	6.67	8.60	9.89	15.93
3.70	4.26	6.85	8.70	10.01	16.11
3.80	4.37	7.04	8.80	10.12	16.30
3.90	4.49	7.22	8.90	10.24	16.48
4.00	4.60	7.41	9.00	10.35	16.67
4.10	4.72	7.59	9.10	10.47	16.85
4.20	4.83	7.78	9.20	10.58	17.04
4.30	4.95	7.96	9.30	10.70	17.22
4.40	5.06	8.15	9.40	10.81	17.41
4.50	5.18	8.33	9.50	10.93	17.59
4.60	5.29	8.52	9.60	11.04	17.78
4.70	5.41	8.70	9.70	11.16	17.96
4.80	5.52	8.89	9.80	11.27	18.15
4.90	5.64	9.07	9.90	11.39	18.33
5.00	5.75	9.26	10.00	11.50	18.52

APPENDIX C *(continued)*

Conversions—Nautical Miles to Meters—Meters to Nautical Miles

Nm.		Meters	Nm.		Meters	Meters		Nm.	Meters		Nm.
0.01	=	19	0.51	=	945	10	=	0.005	510	=	0.275
0.02	=	37	0.52	=	963	20	=	0.011	520	=	0.281
0.03	=	56	0.53	=	982	30	=	0.016	530	=	0.286
0.04	=	74	0.54	=	1000	40	=	0.022	540	=	0.292
0.05	=	93	0.55	=	1019	50	=	0.027	550	=	0.297
0.06	=	111	0.56	=	1037	60	=	0.032	560	=	0.302
0.07	=	130	0.57	=	1056	70	=	0.038	570	=	0.308
0.08	=	148	0.58	=	1074	80	=	0.043	580	=	0.313
0.09	=	167	0.59	=	1093	90	=	0.049	590	=	0.319
0.10	=	185	0.60	=	1111	100	=	0.054	600	=	0.324
0.11	=	204	0.61	=	1130	110	=	0.059	610	=	0.329
0.12	=	222	0.62	=	1148	120	=	0.065	620	=	0.335
0.13	=	241	0.63	=	1167	130	=	0.070	630	=	0.340
0.14	=	259	0.64	=	1185	140	=	0.076	640	=	0.346
0.15	=	278	0.65	=	1204	150	=	0.081	650	=	0.351
0.16	=	296	0.66	=	1222	160	=	0.086	660	=	0.356
0.17	=	315	0.67	=	1241	170	=	0.092	670	=	0.362
0.18	=	333	0.68	=	1259	180	=	0.097	680	=	0.367
0.19	=	352	0.69	=	1278	190	=	0.103	690	=	0.373
0.20	=	370	0.70	=	1296	200	=	0.108	700	=	0.378
0.21	=	389	0.71	=	1315	210	=	0.113	710	=	0.383
0.22	=	407	0.72	=	1333	220	=	0.119	720	=	0.389
0.23	=	426	0.73	=	1352	230	=	0.124	730	=	0.394
0.24	=	444	0.74	=	1370	240	=	0.130	740	=	0.400
0.25	=	463	0.75	=	1389	250	=	0.135	750	=	0.405
0.26	=	482	0.76	=	1408	260	=	0.140	760	=	0.410
0.27	=	500	0.77	=	1426	270	=	0.146	770	=	0.416
0.28	=	519	0.78	=	1445	280	=	0.151	780	=	0.421
0.29	=	537	0.79	=	1463	290	=	0.157	790	=	0.427
0.30	=	556	0.80	=	1482	300	=	0.162	800	=	0.432
0.31	=	574	0.81	=	1500	310	=	0.167	810	=	0.437
0.32	=	593	0.82	=	1519	320	=	0.173	820	=	0.443
0.33	=	611	0.83	=	1537	330	=	0.178	830	=	0.448
0.34	=	630	0.84	=	1556	340	=	0.184	840	=	0.454
0.35	=	648	0.85	=	1574	350	=	0.189	850	=	0.459
0.36	=	667	0.86	=	1593	360	=	0.194	860	=	0.464
0.37	=	685	0.87	=	1611	370	=	0.200	870	=	0.470
0.38	=	704	0.88	=	1630	380	=	0.205	880	=	0.475
0.39	=	722	0.89	=	1648	390	=	0.211	890	=	0.481
0.40	=	741	0.90	=	1667	400	=	0.216	900	=	0.486
0.41	=	759	0.91	=	1685	410	=	0.221	910	=	0.491
0.42	=	778	0.92	=	1704	420	=	0.227	920	=	0.497
0.43	=	796	0.93	=	1722	430	=	0.232	930	=	0.502
0.44	=	815	0.94	=	1741	440	=	0.238	940	=	0.508
0.45	=	833	0.95	=	1759	450	=	0.243	950	=	0.513
0.46	=	852	0.96	=	1778	460	=	0.248	960	=	0.518
0.47	=	870	0.97	=	1796	470	=	0.254	970	=	0.524
0.48	=	889	0.98	=	1815	480	=	0.259	980	=	0.529
0.49	=	907	0.99	=	1833	490	=	0.265	990	=	0.535
0.50	=	926	1.00	=	1852	500	=	0.270	1000	=	0.540

APPENDIX C *(continued)*

Conversions—Meters to Feet—Feet to Meters

Meters		Feet	Meters		Feet	Feet		Meters	Feet		Meters
0.1	=	0.33	5.1	=	16.73	1	=	0.30	51	=	15.55
0.2	=	0.66	5.2	=	17.06	2	=	0.61	52	=	15.85
0.3	=	0.98	5.3	=	17.39	4	=	1.22	54	=	16.46
0.4	=	1.31	5.4	=	17.72	6	=	1.83	56	=	17.07
0.5	=	1.64	5.5	=	18.04	8	=	2.44	58	=	17.68
0.6	=	1.97	5.6	=	18.37	10	=	3.05	60	=	18.29
0.7	=	2.30	5.7	=	18.70	12	=	3.66	62	=	18.90
0.8	=	2.62	5.8	=	19.03	14	=	4.27	64	=	19.51
0.9	=	2.95	5.9	=	19.36	16	=	4.88	66	=	20.12
1.0	=	3.28	6.0	=	19.68	18	=	5.49	68	=	20.73
1.1	=	3.61	6.1	=	20.01	20	=	6.10	70	=	21.34
1.2	=	3.94	6.2	=	20.34	22	=	6.71	72	=	21.95
1.3	=	4.27	6.3	=	20.67	24	=	7.32	74	=	22.56
1.4	=	4.59	6.4	=	21.00	26	=	7.92	76	=	23.17
1.5	=	4.92	6.5	=	21.33	28	=	8.53	78	=	23.77
1.6	=	5.25	6.6	=	21.65	30	=	9.14	80	=	24.38
1.7	=	5.58	6.7	=	21.98	32	=	9.75	82	=	24.99
1.8	=	5.91	6.8	=	22.31	34	=	10.36	84	=	25.60
1.9	=	6.23	6.9	=	22.64	36	=	10.97	86	=	26.21
2.0	=	6.56	7.0	=	22.97	38	=	11.58	88	=	26.82
2.1	=	6.89	7.1	=	23.29	40	=	12.19	90	=	27.43
2.2	=	7.22	7.2	=	23.62	42	=	12.80	92	=	28.04
2.3	=	7.55	7.3	=	23.95	44	=	13.41	94	=	28.65
2.4	=	7.87	7.4	=	24.28	46	=	14.02	96	=	29.26
2.5	=	8.20	7.5	=	24.61	48	=	14.63	98	=	29.87
2.6	=	8.53	7.6	=	24.93	50	=	15.24	100	=	30.48
2.7	=	8.86	7.7	=	25.26	52	=	15.85	102	=	31.09
2.8	=	9.19	7.8	=	25.59	54	=	16.46	104	=	31.70
2.9	=	9.51	7.9	=	25.92	56	=	17.07	106	=	32.31
3.0	=	9.84	8.0	=	26.25	58	=	17.68	108	=	32.92
3.1	=	10.17	8.1	=	26.57	60	=	18.29	110	=	33.53
3.2	=	10.50	8.2	=	26.90	62	=	18.90	112	=	34.14
3.3	=	10.83	8.3	=	27.23	64	=	19.51	114	=	34.75
3.4	=	11.15	8.4	=	27.56	66	=	20.12	116	=	35.36
3.5	=	11.48	8.5	=	27.89	68	=	20.73	118	=	35.97
3.6	=	11.81	8.6	=	28.21	70	=	21.34	120	=	36.58
3.7	=	12.14	8.7	=	28.54	72	=	21.95	122	=	37.19
3.8	=	12.47	8.8	=	28.87	74	=	22.56	124	=	37.80
3.9	=	12.80	8.9	=	29.20	76	=	23.17	126	=	38.41
4.0	=	13.12	9.0	=	29.53	78	=	23.77	128	=	39.02
4.1	=	13.45	9.1	=	29.86	80	=	24.38	130	=	39.62
4.2	=	13.78	9.2	=	30.18	82	=	24.99	132	=	40.23
4.3	=	14.11	9.3	=	30.51	84	=	25.60	134	=	40.84
4.4	=	14.44	9.4	=	30.84	86	=	26.21	136	=	41.45
4.5	=	14.76	9.5	=	31.17	88	=	26.82	138	=	42.06
4.6	=	15.09	9.6	=	31.50	90	=	27.43	140	=	42.67
4.7	=	15.42	9.7	=	31.82	92	=	28.04	142	=	43.28
4.8	=	15.75	9.8	=	32.15	94	=	28.65	144	=	43.89
4.9	=	16.08	9.9	=	32.48	96	=	29.26	146	=	44.50
5.0	=	16.40	10.0	=	32.81	98	=	29.87	148	=	45.11

©2000 Shipwrite Productions

APPENDIX D
Incidents

Inevitably, being human, some of us have accidents. This is as true in the practice of navigation as in any other field of human endeavour. In the vast majority of cases, the use of the GPS technology results in safer, more confident, and more exact navigation than was ever possible before. Electronic chart systems and other derivative GPS technology further enhance the safety and pleasure of boating for professional and recreational boaters alike.

Even though new systems and technologies are developed, we will still have accidents. The Global Positioning System, just like anything manmade, has limitations that we often ignore at our peril. Following are two incidents which illustrate these limitations, and the dramatic consequences that could follow.

Royal Majesty

On June 10, 1995, at about 2230, while transiting from Bermuda to Boston, the Panamanian cruise ship *Royal Majesty* ran aground on the Rose and Crown Shoals near Nantucket Island, Massachusetts. On board were over 1500 people, including crew. Luckily, the weather was fine at the time and no injuries or deaths resulted from the grounding. However, weather conditions worsened. The passengers, who were forced to remain on board while the ship was refloated, were not able to disembark in Boston until 48 hours later. The incident resulted in a nasty repair bill and a great deal of embarrassment on the part of the navigation officers. The *Royal Majesty* had deviated 17 Nm off course at the time of the grounding!

The ship was fitted with an Integrated Navigation system, with positioning information provided by GPS and Loran C receivers. This type of equipment bears the same relationship to the average consumer GPS Navigator as the space shuttle does to a bicycle. The Integrated Navigation system was of the type that takes inputs not only from positioning devices, but also from a gyro-compass and a Doppler speed log; it is programmed with waypoints and the maneuvering characteristics of the individual vessel. It was capable of being connected to an autopilot and steering the ship in reference to a predetermined track, automatically compensating for gyro-compass error, wind, and current.

The Integrated Navigation system was capable of calculating a dead reckoning position based on course steered and speed through the water. It was programmed to sound an alarm if it detected a difference of more than 200 meters between its DR position and the GPS or Loran C position.

At the time of the grounding, the Integrated Navigation system was in operation, but for some reason it failed to keep the ship on course. Afterward, many people wondered how this happened. An investigation by the United States National Transportation Safety Board revealed the cause: a frayed wire and a duplicated function in the GPS that provided position data to the Integrated Navigation system.

As is common with many older satellite-based positioning systems, the GPS unit on board the *Royal Majesty* was programmed to default to a DR position when satellite signals became unavailable. Rather than freezing up and displaying the last satellite-based position available, it applied data from the gyro-compass and speed log to project the position along its course steered. (When the unit was manufactured this was an intelligent choice, because in the early days of GPS there were frequently not enough satellites available to provide an adequate fix.) When the GPS itself reverted to DR mode, it sounded an alarm, but this alarm was not very loud.

At some time prior to the grounding, the shielding on the GPS antenna wire came loose from the antenna itself. The GPS could not derive a position, so it defaulted to DR mode. Because the GPS was mounted behind a bulkhead, both its alarm and visual fault-indication display went unnoticed. Since it continued to supply position data to the Integrated Navigation system, the system did not automatically switch to Loran C positioning, but the GPS Navigator was supplying *DR positioning* based on the courses steered and the speed logged since the last valid position fix.

The Integrated Navigator was using the same gyro-compass and speed inputs as the GPS to derive a DR position, so the two positions never differed by more than 200 meters; consequently, the Integrated Navigator never sounded an alarm. It "assumed" that the position data it was receiving was a GPS-derived position, not a DR position, since the data came from the GPS Navigator itself.

Meanwhile, current and winds forces were slowly pushing the *Royal Majesty* off her Intended Track until the time of the grounding when the vessel was 17 Nm off course. For this amount of Cross Track Error to have accumulated, the antenna shielding must have separated several hours before. The NTSB report noted that at no time were the bridge officers aware that the ship had strayed from her course, even though they had numerous other means at their disposal to determine their position, or at least to realize they were no longer following their Intended Track.

Complacency seems to be the main cause of many accidents; navigators must constantly guard against placing their trust where it might not be due. Though there were valid reasons for the failure of the Integrated Navigation system, the report indicates that the officers neglected to monitor the ship's progress by other means at regular intervals.

In this case, the marvelous accuracy and ease of use of GPS and its derivative systems may have lulled the navigators of the *Royal Majesty* into the habit of using the GPS/Integrated Navigation system as their sole means of establishing position. Although not categorically affirmed, this is implied by the NTSB report. At some point, according to Murphy's Law, if you depend on it, it will fail, and it will fail at the most inconvenient time. Hopefully we can all learn a lesson from this incident.

The Salty Isle

(The following incident took place prior to the removal of Selective Availability on May 1, 2000. It is reproduced here to show the dangers inherent in making assumptions about GPS positioning in the absence of any other navigational information. What would have happened if this incident had taken place after the removal of SA? We will never know, but it is possible the vessel would still have run aground in the narrow channel.)

The *Royal Majesty* incident may seem rather mundane. After all, there was no loss of life and probably the greatest consequence was that numerous passengers missed airline connections. Under different circumstances—for instance, if the grounding had taken place during a storm on a rocky coast—the story might have been very different.

The next incident is full of drama: a small fishing vessel runs onto an iron-bound coast during a major gale; a dramatic rescue ensues; fortunately, once again no lives are lost.

The *Salty Isle* was a 73-foot wooden fishing vessel built in Peterhead, Scotland in 1954. On the night of February 18, 1995 the *Salty Isle* was attempting to enter Grant Anchorage in British Columbia during a gale. She was carrying supplies for a fleet of sea urchin harvesting skiffs sheltering inside the anchorage. Winds were estimated to be gusting to SE 40 knots, southwest swells three to four meters high were running, and an opposing tidal current created chaotic seas. The skipper attempted to navigate by radar and GPS plotter through torrential rains.

Grant Anchorage, which lies at the western entrance to Higgins Passage, is surrounded by numerous rocks and reefs. Compounding the difficulty of navigation that night was the fact that the only charts available for the area are small scale. Consequently, the islands and passages in the reef-strewn approaches are difficult to identify. There are several possible entrances to Grant Anchorage, and the skipper wisely chose the widest entrance that night, but even that passage is only approximately 200 meters in width.

Unfortunately for the *Salty Isle*, the heavy rain obscured visibility so that the skipper was unable to use the flashing red light on the buoy at Jaffrey Rock to assist in lining up the approach to the channel, though the rock did show on his radar. Once the vessel came close to the entrance, it became clear that the radar display was not going to be much more help. The rain and sea clutter controls had to be turned so high to eliminate interference from the rain and breaking seas that it became difficult to identify Kipp Islet at the entrance to the anchorage. According to the GPS plotter, the *Salty Isle* was on her Intended Track, so the skipper proceeded to negotiate the passage at slow speed. The deckhand was shining a searchlight when, suddenly, he saw breakers directly ahead. Immediately afterward, the vessel struck. The propeller and rudder were immediately disabled and the vessel began to pound heavily on the rocks. The skipper was able to make a distress call on VHF channel 16 and a local working frequency. The three crew then climbed into their survival suits, sure they were headed for death.

However, some of the boats in the anchorage heard the distress call and proceeded to effect a rescue. It soon became clear that they would not be able to approach the wreck from seaward, so several divers landed on the lee side of the island in breaking seas. In darkness, they walked 200 meters over slippery rocks to a position near the *Salty Isle*. The skipper of the *Salty Isle* then attempted to float a life line to shore, but his attempts were frustrated by the violent pounding the vessel was taking in the breakers. The once proud *Salty Isle* was rapidly becoming a wreck. During this process, one large wave tore the wheelhouse off, but the backwash of the wave deposited all three crew into the now gaping cavity of the vessel's engine room. The divers on shore were engulfed by the wave, but they managed to hang onto the rocks. Finally, after several more minutes, the divers managed to grab the end of the life line, and the crew of the *Salty Isle* were able to drag themselves to safety. It was estimated that it took almost an hour from the time the rescue began to the time the survivors finally made it to shore.

The next day all that remained of the *Salty Isle* was a mass of debris stretched along the west side of several small islands, and the insulated foam cube of her fish hold, thrown intact far above high water on an island about 500 meters to the north of the grounding site.

It seems incredible that the vessel remained intact for the length of time needed to rescue her crew, but she was obviously well built and lasted as long as she could; long enough, it turns out. One of the survivors was quoted in a local magazine, "We really felt that the boat didn't want to hurt us. She really was a live person . . . She was going and she didn't want us."

The *Salty Isle* was equipped with radar, GPS plotter, and a properly compensated compass. The radar performance, however, was degraded by heavy interference from breaking seas and rain, rendering it difficult to identify landmarks. When the skipper attempted to reduce the clutter by turning up the sea and rain clutter controls, there was no improvement in the image. In this situation, the GPS plotter would have been of limited additional value because the error circle of the unassisted GPS was approximately equal to the width of the entrance channel itself. Even if the Intended Track had been plotted down the middle of the passage, the GPS plotter may have indicated that *Salty Isle* was right on course when, due to GPS errors, she was up to 100 meters off course. Wind and seas would have compounded the problem, making navigation even more difficult. The result was a dramatic, though not tragic, grounding.

As we have stated repeatedly, although GPS is wonderful, it is not a magical system. It has limitations, and we must understand and accept these limitations.

In the discussions above relating to the Royal Majesty *and the* Salty Isle, *the author (KM), has come to certain conclusions. These conclusions are opinions, based on publicly available information including official reports, and on my own personal experience at sea. Some of the people involved in these incidents may not agree with my conclusions.*

APPENDIX E—Sample Waypoint Log

Waypoint Log	Area	or Route	Waypoint Name	Location	Latitude Longitude	Chart #	Datum	Notes and drawings

©2000 Shipwrite Productions

APPENDIX E

Sample Route Log

Route Log		Route Name				
			When working along the route		When reversing the route	
Waypoint Name	#	Location	Bearing	Distance	Bearing	Distance

APPENDIX F
Compensating for Current

Though the following diagrams and descriptions may seem frightening, they merely represent the forces in play as you proceed under the influence of a crosscurrent. Using these procedures, not only can you find the set and drift of the current, you can also calculate the course to steer to counteract the effect of the current.

Finding the Set and Drift of the Current

In the diagram (Figure F.1), a vessel departs position A at 1200 Noon, steering 030° T at a speed of 8.0 kn, for a destination at position B. However, a current of unknown strength and direction carries the vessel away from the Course Steered; after six minutes of travel, the GPS shows the vessel at position C.

Had there been no current acting to carry the vessel away from the Course Steered, the vessel would have arrived at the DR position after six minutes. However, the current carried the vessel bodily to the west such that after six minutes, the vessel arrived at the observed position C. By plotting the various positions

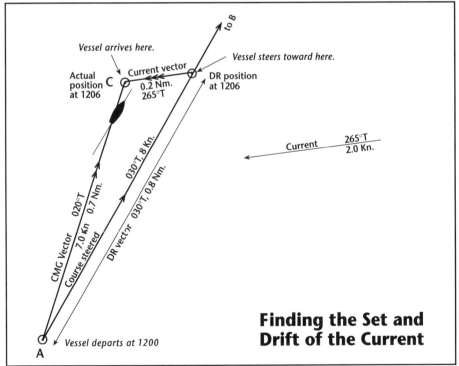

Figure F.1

Finding the Set and Drift of the Current

on the chart, the magnitude and direction of the current becomes apparent. Here the current sets 265° T at 2 kn.

To Counteract the Effect of Current

To counteract the effect of any given strength or direction of current (Figure F.2), you must determine the correct Course to Steer that will keep the vessel on its Desired or Intended Track.

In order to ensure that the vessel arrives at position G, first you must find where the vessel will be after six minutes drifting with the current. From this point, position F, you must find the Course to Steer to get back on the Intended Track after six minutes. Here the correct course to steer is 042° T.

1. Imagine what would happen to your boat if it drifted with the current for six minutes, without any power applied. (Because the six-minute time interval is so convenient to use, we will continue to do so.)

2. From position F, you must find a course to steer to get back on your Intended Track in six minutes. To do this, assume that no current is acting

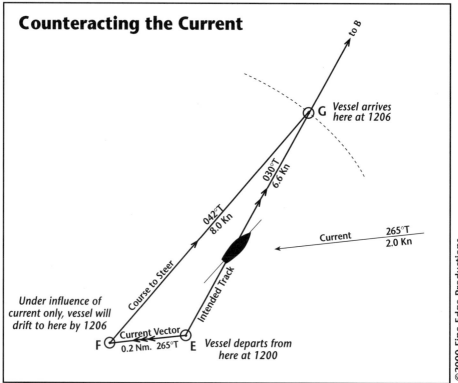

Figure F.2

Counteracting the Current

on the vessel. (This is essentially true, because you have already accounted for the effect of the current by starting from position F.)

3. If you wish to get back on the Desired or Intended Track in six minutes, you must find a point on the Desired or Intended Track that is exactly 0.8 Nm from position F. To find this point is simple: Just set a compass to 0.8 Nm and, placing the point of the compass on position F, swing the arc of the compass until it crosses the Desired or Intended Track; label this point of intersection position G.

4. Draw a line from F to G and measure its direction on the compass rose; this is your Course to Steer. In this case, if you steer 042° T, you will exactly negate, or counteract, the effect of the current, and continue along your Desired or Intended Track toward the destination.

APPENDIX G
List of Horizontal Datums

Adindan—*(Africa)*
Afgooye—*(Somalia)*
Ain El Abd 1970—*(Bahrain Island)*
Anna I Astro—*(Cocos Islands)*
ARC 1950 Mean Value—*(Southern Africa)*
ARC 1960—*(Kenya, Tanzania)*
Ascension Island 1958
Astro Beacon "E"—*(Pacific Islands)*
Astro B4 Sorol Atoll—*(Hawaiian Islands)*
Astro DOS 71/4—*(Atlantic Islands)*
Astronomic Station 1952
Astronomic Station Tern Island
Australian Geodetic 1966
Australian Geodetic 1984
Ayabelle
Bathurst Base East End—*(Gambia)*
Belleview (IGN)
Bermuda 1957
Bissau
Bogota Observatory—*(Colombia)*
Bukit Rimpah
Campo Inchauspe
Camp Area AS
Canton Astro 1966
Cape—*(South Africa)*
Cape Canaveral
Carthage
Castania
Chatham 1971—*(SW Pacific Islands)*
Chua- Astro
Corrego—Allegre
Cyprus
Dabola
Djarkarta—*(Batavia)*
DOS 1968—*(SW Pacific Islands)*
Easter Island 1967
Egypt
European 1950-(ED50)

European 1979
F. Thomas 1955
Falkland Islands 1943
Finnish
Fiji 1956
Fiji 1986
Gandajika Base—*(Indian Ocean)*
Geodetic Datum 1949
Graciosa Base
Guam 1963
Gunung Segara
Gunung Serindung
Gux 1 Astro
Herat North
Hermanskogel—*(Vienna)*
Hjorsey 1955—*(Iceland)*
Hong Kong 1963
Hu-Tsu-Shan
IGN 1954
IGN 1947
IGN 47-51
IGN 1972
ISTS AS 1968
ISTS 073 Astro 1969
Indian—*(India/Thailand/Vietnam)*
Iran
Ireland 1965
Itarare N Base, Itajuba-Santa Catarina
Johnston Island 1961
Kandawala—*(Sri Lanka)*
Kerguelen Island—*(Indian Ocean)*
Kertau 1948—*(Malaysia)*
Kusaie AS 51
KKJ—*(Finland)*
LC. 5 Astro—*(Caribbean)*
La Reunion
Le Pouce
Liberia 1964

Lisboa
Luzon—*(Philippines)*
M. Mercury 68
Mahe 1971—*(Indian Ocean)*
Marco Astro—*(Salvage Islands)*
Massawa—*(Africa)*
Merchich—*(Africa)*
Mindanao
Midway Astro 1961
Minna—*(Africa)*
Monte mario 1940
Montjoy
Montserrat 58
M'Poraloko
Nahrwan—*(Arabia)*
Nanking
Napartma BWI—*(Trinidad and Tobago)*
New Porto Santo
New Zealand
North American Datum 27
North American Datum 83
Noumea, Nouvelle Caledonie IGN 1972
Norwegian
Observatorio 1966—*(Atlantic Islands)*
Old Egyptian
Old Hawaiian
Oman
Ordin. Survey of Gr. Britain 1936
Ordin. Survey of Ireland
Panama Colon
Phare d'Ayabelle
Pico De Las Nieves—*(Canary Islands)*
Pitcairn Astrological - 1967
Pte. Noire
Porto Santo
Point 58
Polish
Potsdam

Provisional S Chilean 1963
Provisional S. American 1956
Puerto Rico
Pulkovo 1942
Quatar National
Qornoq—*(Greenland)*
Reunion—*(Indian Ocean)*
Rev. Kertau
Rev. Nahrwan
Reykjavik
Rome 1940
Santo (DOS)—*S.W. Pacific Islands*
Santa Braz—*(Atlantic Islands)*
Sapper Hill 1943
Schwarzeck—*(Namibia)*
Selvagem
Sicily
Sierra Leone 1960
South American 1969
South Asia
Southeast Base
Southwest Base
Swedish
Swiss CH 1903
Tananarive
Tete
Timbalai 1948—*(Malaysia)*
Tokyo—*(Japan, Korea, Okinawa)*
Tristan Astrological 1968—*(Atlantic Islands)*
Viti Levu 1916—*(SW Pacific Islands)*
Voirol
Wake Island 1952
Wake-Eniwetok 1960
WGS 72
WGS 84—*(GPS World Standard)*
Yacare
Zanderji—*(South America)*

APPENDIX H
GPS Time and Clock Bias

The position fixing ability of GPS is intimately related to the accuracy of measured time. That much is abundantly clear. But the question remains, "Whose time?" The answer to that question is not simple.

The official U.S. Department of Defense accuracy specification for GPS time on the civilian Standard Positioning Service, prior to May 1, 2000 was 340 nanoseconds (0.000340 seconds). When converted to a range measurement, this infinitesimal amount of time equals 55 Nm. Since we know that a GPS receiver can resolve a position with far greater accuracy than that, there must be something we do not know.

Return, for a moment to Chapter 8, Figure 8.3. In the diagram, the distance to three charted objects is measured by radar. Where the three circles cross is the position of the vessel. To determine the distance traveled by the radar pulses, it is necessary only to measure the elapsed time between the emission and reception of the radar pulse. The same is not true of GPS, for the signal travels one direction only. The receiver is passive and consequently depends on the satellite to tell it exactly when the signal is broadcast. By comparing this time to the time *determined by the receiver clock,* the elapsed time can be calculated and the distance established. These distances are drawn as circles on an imaginary globe in the receiver's brain, and the point where three or more circles intersect is taken to be the position.

The satellite clock standard is a cesium oscillator that may deviate by only 1 millisecond in seven days. These clocks are adjusted continually by a ground-control network, so their accuracy is orders of magnitude higher than the published accuracy. In order to measure the distance of the signal path, the clock in your receiver must be highly accurate as well. It seems impossible that for a few hundred dollars, you could buy a clock that would equal the accuracy of the cesium satellite clocks, and in fact, your receiver uses a clock that is probably no more sophisticated than a Timex. Even though the satellite data message contains a correction for the receiver clock which is applied as required, the measured distances are sure to be far more than 20 meters in error. (Even 100 nanoseconds error represents a distance error of 162 Nm Thus the three curves (or more, if more satellites are visible) will certainly not intersect in a point, and this is why the measured ranges to the satellites are known as **pseudoranges**.

Now comes the clever part. The GPS receiver knows that the same clock error has been applied to each of the pseudoranges; thus each pseudorange can be cor-

The formal accuracy specification for the military Precise Positioning Service is 100 nanoseconds (0.000100 seconds). Following the removal of Selective Availability, the time accuracy of the system is expected to increase, but until further testing is performed, it is unclear by how much.

rected by applying a bias, or correction, to the clock and re-computing the range until enough of a correction has been applied to the clock that the pseudoranges do, in fact, meet at a point. That point is then assumed to be the correct position. It doesn't matter what amount of error is present in the GPS receiver's clock, since the same amount of error is removed from each pseudorange in establishing the position fix [Figure H.1].

It is also clear now that the inherent time/position accuracy of a receiver has

GPS Receiver Clock Bias

©2000 Fine Edge Productions

Figure H.1

Each dashed circle represents the pseudorange to a particular satellite. Since the receiver clock has an unknown error, the three Circles of Position do not meet at a point—a large triangular area of possible positions is created. As the GPS receiver adjusts the time of its own internal clock, the pseudorange to each satellite shortens and thus the three Circles of Position shrink by an equal amount. As the time is retarded more, the three Circles of Position will eventually meet at a point—the intersection of the solid lines. The receiver has fooled itself into believing that the true time is whatever is necessary to establish a single-point position.

very little to do with its own clock; it is almost totally dependent on the quality of its software and the GPS satellite clocks. It is the software which is the receiver's brain and resolves the position, and it is the same software that reads the time embedded in the satellite message, and corrects the internal clock to arrive at the displayed time. The advertised accuracy of GPS, then, is the accuracy of the receiver clock, once it has been corrected by the satellite data signal. In this way the system is able to meet the specification for time accuracy.

However, there are reports of observers comparing their GPS to national time signals (i.e. the United States WWV signals on 5, 10, and 15 megahertz), and finding their GPS to be in error by up to 1.5 seconds. Part of the problem lies in the GPS satellites themselves. The Global Positioning System uses its own time standard instead of Universal Coordinated Time (UTC) or Greenwich Mean Time (GMT), which is the time standard on which all mariners depend for the accuracy of celestial navigation. On earth, UTC and GMT drift apart at a steadily predictable rate, and are kept in step by the introduction of leap seconds into UTC—just like the leap day introduced into calendars each four years on February 29th. When the drift reaches a value of about one-half second, the introduced leap second corrects UTC to within one-half second again.

The time standard for GPS was established by the U.S. Naval Observatory on January 6, 1980 using a standard that was known to differ from UTC; so, at this date, after the incorporation of several leap seconds into UTC, GPS time is advanced on UTC by 14 seconds and is departing from UTC by an ever-increasing amount. At the same time, drift between UTC and GMT introduces fractions of a second into the equation.

How is it then that the time displayed by GPS receivers agrees much more closely with UTC as broadcast by WWV broadcasts and other national standard time signals? The GPS satellite signal includes in its coded message a phrase, which says "I am fast on UTC by 14 seconds." As this amount increases, the message is changed to reflect the new time difference. Thus the software corrects the receiver clock a second time, to convert GPS time to UTC.

This accounts for only a portion of some observed errors in displayed GPS time. It turns out that the remaining GPS time errors are caused by software. In the most extreme case we have observed, a 25-second error in one receiver was eliminated by the installation of new software. The problem was that it updated its time only when it was turned on. Given that the unit had been continuously active for over three months, the clock had drifted by 25 seconds. *In fact, this degree of drift was expected by the manufacturer.* An accumulating error of up to 2 seconds per week was well within the specifications of the receiver's clock. The new software solved this problem by updating the time on a regular basis.

Modern GPS receivers update the time regularly enough that there is rarely a noticeable time error, but if you own an older GPS receiver, and if accurate time is important to you, it may be possible to update the software in your set.

APPENDIX I
GPS Features—Good and Bad

If you intend to purchase GPS equipment but are perplexed by the incredible diversity of functions and manufacturers, rest assured that you are not alone. The best advice we can offer is that you buy the best equipment you can afford to meet both your navigational needs and the available space in your wheelhouse.

We do feel, however, that we can help you make an appropriate decision by listing many of the features and functions found in various types of GPS equipment. No equipment will contain all of these features, but for any type of GPS, the more features it contains, the more flexible and suitable it will be.

Though it is doubtful that any marine GPS manufactured in 2000 will be a multiplexing (sequencing) type, you may come across such older sets when looking for second-hand equipment. Be aware of the limitations of multiplexing GPS sets. [Refer to Chapter 8.] (The Magellan Pioneer and the Garmin 38 are both sequencing receivers—the Magellan tracks with one channel and sequences with the other; the Garmin sequences up to eight satellites on its single channel.)

A *Basic* GPS Navigator Should Contain:

- As many channels as possible. Most sets manufactured in 2000 now have 12-channel capability, far more channels than you need.
- A good selection of horizontal datums.
- Clear indication of the active datum on position display and steering diagrams
- GOTO
- MOB
- Frequent time updates
- Clear and easily understood steering diagrams
- Allows re-setting of default hemisphere
- Old data alarm
- Visual indication of alarm condition
- Will restart navigating a route from present position
- Will allow joining a route at any waypoint or along any leg
- Will allow saving a waypoint with just one or two keystrokes
- Will allow the operator to reverse a route
- Clear display of signal strength

A *Good* GPS Navigator Should Contain:

- A large, easy to read display that is clearly visible in bright sunlight
- Adjustable brightness so that it will not interfere with your night vision
- Numerous routes and large number of waypoints per route
- Will store up to 1000 waypoints

- Simulator mode—makes it possible to learn procedures in the comfort of your own home
- An alphanumeric keyboard
- A comprehensive selection of horizontal datums
- Allows waypoint entry by present position
- Allows waypoint entry by range and bearing from present position
- Shows all waypoints on steering diagram
- Avoidance waypoints with separate avoidance limits
- Shows avoidance waypoint on the steering diagram
- Waypoint realization by the bisector of the angle
- Allows the operator to customize the steering diagram with a selection of enroute functions
- Will display one or more of ETA, ETE, DTG, VTD, or TTG to the destination waypoint or the final waypoint
- Identifies the route, leg, and destination waypoint on the steering diagram
- Shows the next leg, and the bearing and range to the next waypoint on the steering diagram
- Allows updating/editing of a waypoint
- Allows skipping a waypoint
- Adjustable limits on boundary, anchor watch, and arrival alarms
- Easily audible alarms with visual indication
- Allows insertion of a waypoint into a route
- Simple activation of GOTO function
- Simple method to stop navigation
- Smoothing control (COG, SOG averaging)
- A choice of manual or automatic waypoint switching

An *Excellent* GPS Navigator Should Also Contain:

- Accuracy prediction display
- Satellite health display
- Will allow the operator to set a lower limit on satellite elevation (mask angle)
- Separate XTE boundary limits for each leg of a route
- Will allow insertion of a waypoint into an active route
- A trip log function which shows total miles travelled
- Waypoints are visible on the steering diagram after they have been realized
- Allows its software to be updated
- Will upload/download waypoints and routes from/to a PC
- Allows updating a waypoint with the present position
- Lists local waypoints separately from the main waypoint list
- Shows range and bearing of any waypoint

- Boundary alarm limits, anchor watch limits, waypoint arrival circle, and avoidance limits are all clearly visible on the steering diagram.
- Arrival radius can be set for individual waypoints
- Allows navigation to be suspended without clearing a route
- Four choices for starting/joining a route.
- Selection of waypoint realization methods including realization by the bisector of the internal angle and the perpendicular of the exterior angle.
- Route display, showing ranges and bearings between all waypoints
- Displays lat/long for any position entered by range and bearing

A *Basic* DGPS Must Contain:

- GPS/DGPS mode indication on all position and navigation screens
- Displays position, name, and characteristics of the reference station

An *Excellent* DGPS Should Contain:

- Choice of manual/automatic selection of reference station
- Allows updating of reference station information

Remember: The best GPS equipment should be user-friendly!

GLOSSARY

2drms—Two times the drms (distance rms). A statistical measure indicating 95% to 98% probability.

50th percentile—A statistical measure indicating that 50% of the measurements will fall below that level. For GPS the 50th percentile level of accuracy is 40 meters.

Abeam—Directly to one side of a vessel, perpendicular to the vessel's heading.

AC—Alternating current. Usually supplied by a generator or alternator at 110 or 220 volts; also available from DC to AC inverters.

Accuracy—A measure of the difference between the position indicated by measurement and the true position.

Almanac—The general "bus schedule" broadcast by GPS satellites to inform the GPS receiver where to look for satellites. All satellites transmit an almanac.

Appending—Adding a waypoint to either the beginning or end of a route.

ARCS—Admiralty Raster Chart Service. The acronym is also used for the British Admiralty ENC format.

ARPA—Automatic Radar Plotting Aid

Arrival radius—The distance from a waypoint to the perimeter of its arrival circle.

Arrival circle—An imaginary circle drawn around a destination waypoint in the GPS memory. When the GPS detects that it is inside the arrival circle, it will realize the waypoint.

Autopilot—A device used for automatically steering a vessel.

Avoidance radius—The radius of the danger zone around an avoidance waypoint.

Avoidance waypoint—A waypoint that designates a navigational danger.

BA—British Admiralty.

Bathymetric chart—A detailed chart of the seabed. Bathymetric charts show far more seafloor detail than normal nautical charts.

Bearing—The direction of a line joining any two points on the surface of the Earth. May be expressed in degrees True or Magnetic, the same as for any measurement of direction.

Bias—If a device gives a position that is always in error in the same direction, it is said to have bias. Loran C bias is known as offset.

BSB—The initials of the Value-Added Reseller which distributes NOAA (U.S.) electronic charts. Also taken as the name of the U.S. chart format.

Cartographer—A person who practices cartography.

Cartography—The science of map-making.

CCG—Canadian Coast Guard.

CDI—Course Deviation Indicator—a type of steering diagram.

CD ROM—A system of data storage on compact disks. The data is read using lasers. A CD can hold numerous charts.

CEP—Circular error of probability—the radius of the circle containing 50% of the measurements being made.

CHA—Channel of High Accuracy—the GLONASS frequency reserved for the Russian military.

Chart datum—Horizontal datum—the basis for calculations of positioning in surveying. Charts drawn to one datum may not be consistent with those drawn to another.

Chart plotter—A plotter which has the capability of displaying rudimentary charts.

CHS—Canadian Hydrographic Service

CLL—Curvilinear Leg—A leg in a route that must not be followed too closely due to the fact that it will take the vessel into danger. Instead the helmsman must navigate the leg visually or by radar.

CMG—Course Made Good or Track Made Good (TMG)—The direction of a line from the point of departure to the position of the vessel (sometimes confused with COG); in the navigational triangle, designated by a double arrowhead.

COA—Course of Advance. (See Course to Make Good.) The intended direction over the ground to make good from the present position of the vessel to the destination.(Sometimes confused with COG and CMG.) In the navigational triangle, designated by a double arrowhead.

COG—Course Over the Ground. The direction of travel along the Actual Track at any moment. Sometimes it is confused with CMG. The difference is subtle. CMG is calculated over a period of time. *COG is an instantaneous value.*

COG vector—A vector representing the direction of a vessel's COG and the vessel speed.

Cold Start—(As opposed to a "warm start.") Powering up the GPS receiver when it needs to be initialized. For instance, the first time the receiver is powered up or after it has been moved more than 300 Nm while in a non-powered state. The GPS will need to acquire a new almanac and ephemeris. This may take from just a few minutes to more than twenty minutes.

Compass rose—A circle marked off in degrees found on all nautical charts.

Co-ordinates—A set of measurements that define the position of a point. Co-ordinates may be in latitude and longitude, Loran C TDs, or UTM northings and eastings.

COP—Circle Of Position—A circle drawn on a chart. If the vessel is known to lie somewhere on the circle, it is known as a Circle of Position.

Cosine—In a right triangle, the ratio of the side adjacent to an angle and the hypotenuse.

Course—The direction in which a vessel is intended to travel along the Course Line. Some electronic navigators confuse this with COG.

Course Line—The line laid down on the chart to represent the course on the chart. It is this Course Line that the GPS sets up as the ideal path to follow between two way-points.

Course Steered—See Course.

Course to Make Good—A direction over the ground to be followed by counteracting the effect of current so that a vessel is able to follow the Intended Track

Course to Steer—The specific Course or Heading to steer to ensure that the vessel will counteract the current and follow a particular Course to Make Good.

Course up   When the direction of travel is represented at the top of a radar or EC display, the display is said to be Course-up.

Crash—When a computer fails, it is said to crash.

CSA—Channel of Standard Accuracy—the GLONASS frequency available for civilian use.

Cursor—In a chart plotter or Electronic Charting System, the arrow, or other indicator that the operator moves around the screen with a mouse, trackball, or arrow keys.

Datum shift—The difference between co-ordinates of the same point made according to two separate horizontal datums.

DC—Direct current. Usually supplied by batteries at 12, 24, or 32 volts.

Degree—An angular measure equal to 1/360 of a circle.

Depth Sounder—An electronic device which emits sound waves to determine the depth of water beneath a vessel.

Deviation—The difference in degrees between a magnetic direction and the direction indicated by a magnetic compass.

DGPS—Differential GPS.

Diameter   The distance from one side of a circle to the other across the circle's center. Diameter is equal to twice the radius.

Displayed position—Where the GPS thinks it is.

Dithering—The intentional introduction of errors into the GPS satellite clock in order to reduce accuracy to civilian users of GPS.

DMA—United States Defense Mapping Agency (now called NIMA—National Imagery amd Mapping Agency).

DOS—A computer operating system. DOS uses text to communicate with the user.

Download—When a computer retrieves data from another computer or stores data to a passive device, it is said to download data.

DR—Dead Reckoning—Projecting a course and speed ahead in time to estimate the position of a vessel at the end of that time period.

DR Position—The point at which the vessel would have arrived had there been no current or wind. Projected by advancing the vessel's position along the Course Line a distance equivalent to the distance which would be travelled by the vessel at its Speed over a specific time period.

Drift—The distance, parallel to the direction or Set of the current, that the vessel has been carried from its DR (Dead Reckoning) position. Also in U.S. usage, the speed of the current. May also refer to the total movement caused by current and wind.

Drift angle (deflection)—The angular difference between the heading and the CMG, caused by current and/or wind.

drms—A statistical measure indicating 63% probability.

DTG—Distance To Go. The distance between the present position and the destination, measured along a straight line connecting those two points. DTG may refer to the destination waypoint or to the eventual destination, the final waypoint of the route.

Dynamically Linked Notes—Printed notes on BSB version 3 electronic raster charts that are available by clicking on an icon or by querying chart properties.

EC—Electronic Chart

ECDIS—Electronic Chart Display and Information System.

ECPINS—An earlier version of ECDIS.

ECS—Electronic Charting System—a combination of GPS, computer, navigation software and Electronic Charts, which permits the operator to view the position of the vessel in real time against a background chart.

ENC—Electronic Navigation Chart—electronic (vector) charts that are fully compliant with the IHO S-57 standard for ECDIS. An electronic chart that does not meet the standard in every detail may not be known as an ENC.

EPE—Estimated Position Error. A value calculated by modern GPS Navigators instead of GQ (Geometric Quality) and HDOP (Horizontal Dilution of Position). It is the product of the HDOP and an assumed value for ionospheric and tropospheric refraction.

Ephemeris—Detailed orbital information broadcast by a GPS satellite which allows a GPS receiver to determine pseudoranges to satellites.

EPIRB—Emergency Position Indicating Radio Beacon

Equator—A great circle which is at all points the same distance from the north and south poles.

ETA—Estimated Time of Arrival—The time at which it is calculated, based on present speed and Distance to Go, that the vessel will arrive at the destination.

ETE—Estimated Time En-route, also known as Time To Go (TTG). The number of hours to complete the trip to the destination (usually the final destination of the route).

Event Mark—An icon which may be entered at a particular position on an ECS or a plotter which may be used to store information, or to present a visual indication of a particular function.

Fix—A position determined by a human or an electronic navigator.

Floppy disk—A system of data storage that uses magnetically charged plastic disks. At most, one or two charts may be stored on a floppy disk.

Frequency—When referring to radio or microwave radiation, the number of cycles of the radio energy per second. Measured in kilohertz or megahertz.

Fringe reception area—An area in which DGPS correction signals are faint or intermittent. Also applies to any area which is so far from a reference station that the accuracy of the correction signal is affected.

Geodetic—Pertaining to the size and shape of the earth.

Geometric Quality—A scale of geometric quality used in some brands of GPS equipment rather than HDOP. High geometric quality values represent a high potential for accuracy.

GLONASS—GLObal NAvigation Satellite System—The Russian Federation satellite positioning system.

GMT—Greenwich Mean Time—A time standard located at the meridian of longitude that passes through Greenwich, England, on which celestial navigation is based.

GOTO—A GPS Navigator feature that allows quick selection of a single destination waypoint.

GPS—Global Positioning System—Also used to refer to GPS receiving and navigation equipment.

GPS Navigator—GPS *Waypoint* Navigator—A GPS receiver that is also able to calculate and display solutions to waypoint navigation problems.

GPS receiver—An electronic receiver which decodes GPS satellite broadcasts and displays solutions for position, course and speed. Also the portion of a GPS Navigator that receives the satellite signals.

GPS Sensor—A GPS receiver that has no display capability or controls. A GPS sensor is designed to output raw GPS data in NMEA 0183 format to another unit such as a PC or plotter.

Great Circle—The shortest distance between two points on the surface of the earth. When laid out on a standard Mercator projection chart, a great circle appears as a curved line. Meridians of longitude and the equator are great circles.

Greenwich meridian—The meridian of longitude which passes through Greenwich, England. The prime meridian, designated as longitude 0°.

HDOP—Horizontal Dilution of Position—A measure of the degradation of accuracy caused by the geometric arrangement of the GPS satellites used to calculate a fix.

Heading—The direction a vessel's bow is pointing as indicated by a compass. Not necessarily the direction of travel.

Heading flash—The illuminated line visible on a radar screen which indicates the direction the vessel is heading.

Head-up—When the vessel's heading is represented at the top of a radar or EC display, the display is said to be Head-up.

Horizontal datum—See Chart Datum.

Hydrography—The science of measurement and description of the oceans, particularly for navigation purposes.

Hypotenuse—In a right angle triangle, the side opposite the right angle.

IALA—International Association of Lighthouse Authorities.

Icon—A symbol on the computer display that represents something. A vessel icon's position on the chart display represents the actual position of the vessel.

IHO—International Hydrographic Organization.

IMO—International Maritime Organization (the keeper of the ECDIS standards).

Initialization—The process of setting up a GPS receiver to enable it to calculate fixes.

Intended Track—See Course. Sometimes may also refer to the Course to Make Good when counteracting the current.

Ionosphere—A shell of charged particles surrounding the earth above the atmosphere.

kHz—(kilohertz)—1000 cycles per second.

kn—(knot)—A speed measure of one nautical mile per hour.

Kilometer—1000 meters.

Latitude—An angular measurement indicating how far a position lies north or south of the equator.

Lat/long—A position given in latitude and longitude is given in lat/long co-ordinates.

Lead angle—The amount of opposite helm to apply to counteract the drift angle (deflection) caused by a current or wind.

Leeway—A measure of how far a vessel is pushed off its heading by wind only.

Leg—The portion of a route defined by a line between two waypoints.

Lollipop—A visual indication of the position of a waypoint on a radar display.

Longitude—An angular measurement indicating how far a position lies to the east or west of the prime meridian. Lines of longitude are all great circles and include both the north and south poles of the earth.

LOP—Line of Position—A line on a chart. If the vessel is known to lie somewhere on the line, it is known as a Line of Position.

Loran A—An obsolete electronic navigation system, based on low frequency radio transmitters.

Loran C—Long Range Navigation and Ranging, an electronic navigation system based on low frequency radio transmitters (100 kHz).

MOB—Man Over Board—A feature of many GPS Navigators that tracks the position at which MOB was engaged.

Magnetic direction—Directions in 360-degree notation referenced to the magnetic pole rather than the true pole.

Menu—A word or icon visible on the display which, when selected, gives the user a choice of many different functions. These menu items may each provide further choices.

Meridian—A line of longitude.

Meter—A unit of distance equal to 3.28 feet.

MHz—megahertz—one million cycles per second.

Microwave—Electromagnetic frequencies which are at higher frequencies than radio bands. Microwaves are employed by radar and GPS satellites.

Mile—Refers to either the Statute Mile of 5280 feet or the Nautical Mile of 6076 feet.

Minute—One sixtieth of a degree (also one sixtieth of an hour).

Mouse—A device which is used to move a cursor on the computer screen.

Navcen—The U.S. Coast Guard Navigation Center.

Navigational triangle—A triangle laid out on a chart to solve navigational problems.

Navstar—The proper name for GPS is the Navstar Global Positioning System to differentiate it from the now obsolete U.S. Navy Transit Global Positioning System (SatNav)

Navtex—A radio communication system for broadcasting navigational information to vessels at sea. The information is printed out without requiring an operator.

NDI—Nautical Data Incorporated. The initials of the Value-Added Reseller that distributes CHS (Canadian) electronic charts. Also taken as the name of the Canadian chart format.

Nm—Nautical mile—A nautical mile is equal to one minute of latitude (1852 meters or 6076 feet).

NIMA—National Imagery and Mapping Agency (formerly known as Defense Mapping Agency).

NMEA—National Marine Electronics Association.

NMEA 0183—An electronic language used between navigation electronics to allow various equipment to be interfaced. (Current version is 2.5.)

NOAA—The United States National Oceanic and Atmospheric Administration.

North-up—When north is represented at the top of a radar or EC display, the display is said to be North-up.

Notices to Mariners—Printed notices of interest to mariners including chart and publication amendments.

Notices to Shipping—Notices broadcast by coastal stations and then issued in print regarding navigational information of interest to mariners.

NTM—Notices to Mariners.

Offset—The distance between the true position and an electronically-derived position.

Omega—A world-wide radio navigation system provided by eight transmitters strategically located around the world (no longer operational).

Operating system—The basic software which instructs a computer how to handle programs.

Parallel rule—A tool for transferring a line across a chart in such a way that it will remain parallel to the original line.

Parallel (of Latitude)—A line of latitude.

PC—Personal computer.

Perspective display—A type of steering diagram.

Perpendicular—When two lines meet at a 90-degree angle to each other they are perpendicular. When referring to a perpendicular distance from a line, the distance has been measured at 90º to the line.

Plotter—An electronic display which presents a plan view of the movements of a vessel by displaying a continuous series of position fixes.

Pole—North Pole or South Pole—Either the true pole or the magnetic pole. The true pole is the point at which the earth's axis of rotation meets the surface of the earth. Lines of latitude and longitude are referenced to the true poles. The magnetic poles are the places at which the axis of the earth's magnetic field meet the surface of the earth. The magnetic poles are not clearly defined and lie over a thousand miles from the true poles.

Port (data port)—A socket in the casing of an electronic device where a cable can be connected to provide either input or output of data.

Port side—The left side of a vessel when facing forward toward the bow.

PPS—Precise Positioning Service—The military GPS system, which uses coded signals and a second satellite frequency, neither of which are available to civilian users.

Predictable accuracy—The degree to which a position-fixing system can calculate lat/long co-ordinates that closely match the true position.

Precision—A position given to several decimals of a minute is said to have a high degree of precision; not to be confused with accuracy. A position given to a high degree of precision may not be accurate at all.

Program—The instructions which tell a computer to perform certain actions. An Electronic Chart Program is the software which allows the computer to manage navigational data.

Prime meridian—The Greenwich meridian. Designated 0º longitude.

Proprietary charts—Electronic charts which are manufactured by independent organizations. Proprietary charts carry no government guarantee.

Pseudorange—The initial distance measurement to a satellite made by a GPS receiver. Pseudoranges are not true ranges due to errors in both satellite and receiver clocks.

RLS—Royal Lifeboat Society.

rms—root mean square—The square root of the mean of the squares of a group of numbers. A statistical measurement.

Radar—RAdio Detection And Ranging—Equipment that uses microwaves to determine range and bearing to various objects.

Radius—The distance from the center of a circle to its outer edge.

Range—A distance to a pre-selected target.

Raster chart—A chart that is stored as an image. Raster charts cannot be manipulated and form a passive background to an electronic charting system.

Rate—The speed of the current. (See **Drift**.)

RCDS—Raster Chart Display System. A proposed standard that would allow EC systems to be considered the equivalent of paper charts.

Realization—When a GPS Navigator determines that it has arrived at a waypoint, the waypoint is said to be "realized."

Real-time—Implies that information is made available without appreciable processing delays.

Reference station—In DGPS networks, reference stations measure the error in GPS satellite signals and broadcast an error correction.

Refraction—The deflection of a propagating radio wave as it passes through a medium of non-uniform density.

Repeatable accuracy—The accuracy with which an electronic Navigator can return you to a position. Repeatable accuracy is high if the errors change little over time, even though the error may be quite large.

Right angle—In trigonometry, a 90° angle.

Route—A series of waypoints between a starting point (initial waypoint) and a destination (final waypoint).

SA—Selective Availability. The term used by the U.S. military for the intentional errors introduced into GPS satellite clocks to degrade the accuracy of the civilian frequency prior to May 1, 2000.

SARSAT—Search and Rescue Satellite System—A joint Russian, Canadian, U.S. and French satellite system that listens for signals from Emergency Position Indicating Radio Beacons and can pinpoint the location of an automatic distress message to within two miles.

SatNav—The U.S. Navy SATtelite NAVigation system. (No longer operational.)

Seamless—Transitions that occur without notice are said to be seamless.

Second—One sixtieth of a minute of arc or of time.

Set—The direction toward which the current is moving.

Sine—A trigonometric function representing the ratio of the side opposite an angle to the hypotenuse.

SLL—Straight Line Leg.

SMG—Speed Made Good. The speed of the vessel along the Course Made Good; i.e. along the straight line joining the point of departure and the point of arrival or the present position.

SOA—See SMG. (Sometimes confused with SOG or VTD.)

Software—Programs or operating systems which instruct a computer to perform certain tasks.

SOG—Speed Over the Ground. The speed of the vessel at any instant along its Actual Track over the ground. The SOG may differ significantly from the Speed through the water. Sometimes SOG is confused with SMG. The difference is subtle. SMG is calculated over a period of time. *SOG is an instantaneous value.*

Soundings—Measurements of depth of water. On a chart the soundings are corrected to lowest low water (U.K.) or Mean Low Water (U.S.).

Speed—The speed of the vessel through the water as measured by a speed log.

SPS—Standard Positioning Service—The GPS service available to civilian users.

Starboard side—The right side of a vessel when looking ahead.

Statute mile—Land mile—5280 feet (1610 meters).

STD—Speed Toward Destination. Also known as VTD, Velocity Towards Destination: the speed at which the vessel closes on the destination waypoint.

Steering diagram—A GPS Navigator display which instructs the operator what direction to steer to arrive at a designated waypoint.

Tangent—A trigonometric function representing the ratio of the side opposite an angle to the side adjacent to the angle.

Target—An object detected by radar.

TD—Time Difference. Loran C calculates distances based on the different amounts of time it takes for a signal to be received from two separate radio transmitters.

Tidal datum—In the U.S., the height of the lowest normal tide. In Canada and the UK, the height of Lower Low Water.

Toolbar—An area on the EC display which

contains tool buttons. These buttons may be clicked with a mouse to activate certain functions.

Traditional display—A type of steering diagram.

Transit—When two landmarks are in line visually, they are said to form a transit.

TRANSIT—See SatNav.

True direction—Directions in 360-degree notation referenced to the true north pole.

True position—Where the GPS is actually located.

TTFF—Time To First Fix. The time required to obtain a fix after a cold start.

Turning Point—A waypoint that is used as a guide in narrow twisting channels.

Upload—When a computer retrieves data from a passive device, it is said to be uploading data.

USCG—United States Coast Guard.

UTC—Universal Co-ordinated Time—An international time standard based on the atomic time standard UTC is kept synchronized with the Sun by the use of the leap second. (There is a leap second, January or June, when the Sun differs from UTC by more than 0.7 sec.)

UTM—Universal Transverse Mercator projection—a map projection and co-ordinate system used in topographic maps.

Value-Added Reseller—An organization that manufactures Electronic Charts for sale from authorized hydrographic data.

Variation—The difference in degrees between Magnetic north and True north at any particular location.

Vector—A line that possesses direction and quantity, i.e. length or speed.

Vector chart—A vector chart is stored as data in a database. This data can be manipulated to a surprising degree.

Velocity—A measure of direction and speed.

VHF—Very High Frequency radio waves. The VHF band is used by line of sight marine radios.

VMG—Velocity Made Good; another version of STD.

VTD—Velocity Toward Destination. See STD.

WGS 84—A universal chart datum used by all modern navigation systems and referenced to the earth's true shape rather than to a local datum. WGS 84 and NAD 83 are virtually the same for marine applications.

Waypoint—A position recorded in the memory of an electronic Navigator that represents a position on the surface of the earth.

> **active**—A destination waypoint.
>
> **avoidance waypoint**—A waypoint that must be avoided. It represents a navigational hazard.
>
> **destination waypoint**—The waypoint at the end of the current leg. A waypoint toward which a vessel is navigating at any particular time.
>
> **departure waypoint**—The waypoint which begins the current leg.
>
> **final waypoint**—The waypoint which terminates the route. It is the eventual destination.
>
> **intermediate waypoint**—Any waypoint located between the initial and final waypoints.
>
> **initial waypoint**—The waypoint at the beginning of a route.
>
> **saved waypoint**—When the present position is stored in memory as a waypoint, the waypoint is known as a saved waypoint.
>
> **shared**—(hub) A waypoint that is part of two separate routes.

Waypoint realization—When the GPS Navigator determines that it has arrived at a destination waypoint, the waypoint is said to have been realized.

Windows, Windows 95—Operating systems which use images instead of text to communicate with the operator.

Windward Ability (of a sailboat)—the angle which describes the degree to which a sailing vessel can make good a course into the wind. The boat may be able to point closer to the wind than the windward ability would indicate. The difference is the effect of leeway.

XTE—Cross Track Error. The perpendicular distance of the vessel at any time from the Course Line. This value is displayed on the steering diagram.

ZOU—Zone of Uncertainty. On a high-speed vessel, the displayed position will lag behind the actual position of the vessel. A Zone of Uncertainty (in which the true position of the vessel must lie) projects forward of the displayed position by an unknown amount.

Zooming—Magnifying a chart image on the display.

BIBLIOGRAPHY & REFERENCES

Admiralty List of Radio Signals, Vol. 2, 1996.

Admiralty Notices to Mariners, 2649(P)/96. The United Kingdom Hydrographic Office.

Alexander, Lee, Ph.D. Electronic Charts: What, How, and Why? Groton, Connecticut: U.S. Coast Guard Research and Development Center.

Alsip, D. H., Butler, J. M., and Radice, J. T. *The Coast Guard's Differential GPS Program,* USCG Headquarters, Office of Navigation Safety and Waterway Services, Radionavigation Division, June 1992.

American Practical Navigator—Bowditch, Publication No. 9. U.S. Defense Mapping Agency Hydrographic/Topographic Center, 1995.

Arnot, Alison. "The Wreck of the Salty Isle." *Westcoast Fisherman Magazine,* April 1995

Bole, A. G., and Jones, K. D. *Automatic Radar Plotting Aids Manual, A Mariner's Guide to the Use of ARPA.* Cornell Maritime Press.

Chinery, Mik. *Simple GPS Navigation.* West Sussex: Fernhurst Books, 1994.

CHS Notices to Mariners. Ottawa: Canadian Hydrographic Service, Department of Fisheries and Oceans.
  "Geodetic Problems in Higgins Passage, B.C." No. 70, 1996.
  "Horizontal Datum Unknown—Chart 7193." No. 546, 1996.
  "Important Notice to Mariners." January, 1997.
  "Horizontal Datum of Chart." Annual Notices to Mariners, No 45, 1996.

Cockroft, A. N., and Lameijer. *A Guide to the Collision Avoidance Rules.* Heinemann Professional Publishing, 1990.

Contour Magazine, Canadian Hydrographic Service, Department of Fisheries and Oceans, Ottawa:
  _____. "The Digital Chart: Raster or Vector." Spring 1993.
  Casey, M. J. "Hey! Why is My Ship Showing up on the Dock." Number 8, Fall 1996.
  Grant, S., and Casey, M. "Updating Charts: High Priority for all HOs." CHS, Winter 1994.
  Holroyd, Paul N. "S-57 Implementation." Number 6, Summer 1995.
  Kraikiwsky, Dr. Edward, and Casey, Michael J. "Intelligent Ship Navigation Systems: What's Available and What Do They Do?" Number 6, Summer 1995.
  Pace, Captain John D. "ECDIS at Sea: Come On In—The Water's Fine." Winter 1993.

Dahl, Bonnie. *The User's Guide to GPS—The Global Positioning System.* Richardson's Marine Publishing, 1993.

Dixon, Conrad. *Using GPS.* Dobbs Ferry: Sheridan House, 1994.

Endres, Dan. "GPS-Derived Time Baffles NOAA Researcher." *Ocean Navigator Magazine,* March/April 1995.

Fact Sheet : "U.S. Global Positioning System Policy." The White House Office of Science and Technology Policy, National Security Council, March 29, 1996.

Ferguson, Michael. *GPS Land Navigation*. Boise: Glassford Publishing, 1997.

Furuno GP-70. GPS Navigator Instruction Manual, Furuno Electric Co., 1992.

Gooding, Nigel R. L. "The Navigational Chart and Marine Positioning in the 1990s." *Marine Geodesy*, Vol. 14, pp. 197-203.

GPS Navstar User's Overview. Prepared by ARINC Research Corporation for the Program Director, Navstar Global Positioning System, Joint Program Office, March 1991, available from USCG NAVCEN.

GPS World Magazine, May 1996.

"Grounding and Sinking of the Fishing Vessel *Salty Isle* off a Small Unnamed Island near Kipp Islet, British Columbia, 18 February 1995." *Marine Occurrence Report*, Report Number M95W0007, Transportation Safety Board of Canada.

Heathcote, Captain Peter, with Williams, D. R., and Taylor, Captain John M. "The Use of Precise Integrated Navigation System (PINS) in Marine Atlantic." *Marine Atlantic*.

Higgins Passage and Approaches (map), catalogue number MTS01-95, Victoria: Shipwrite Productions, e-mail: kmonahan@shipwrite.bc.ca.

Horst Hecht and Dr. Lee Alexander, *"What is an ENC?—Revisited,"* Hydro INTERNATIONAL *Magazine* published by GITC, Netherlands (May/June 1999).

Hurn, Jeff. *Differential GPS Explained*. Trimble Navigation Ltd.

_____. *GPS—A Guide to the Next Utility*. Trimble Navigation Ltd.

Hydro International Magazine. Vol. 1, Number 4, GITC bv. The Netherlands, August 1997.

Jones, Colin. *Yachtsman's GPS Handbook: A Guide to the Global Positioning System of Satellite Navigation*. Waterline Books, 1995.

Lanziner, Helmut and Alexander, Lee. *ECDIS-Radar Integration: Why, What and How*. Records of the 1995 RTCM Annual Assembly, St. Petersburg, Florida, May 1995

Lanziner, Helmut, *The Manufacturer's Difficult Path to ECDIS*. CANStar Navigation Inc., 1996.

Letham, Lawrence. *GPS Made Easy: Using Global Positioning Systems in the Outdoors*. Seattle: The Mountaineers, 1995.

List of Radionavigation Services, DGNSS Reference and Transmitting Stations in the Maritime Radionavigation (Radiobeacons) Band. International Association of Lighthouse Authorities, Issue 4, April 1996.

Magellan NAV 6500 User Manual. Magellan Systems Corporation, 1996.

Magellan NAV DLX10 User Manual. Magellan Systems Corporation, 1995.

Merchant Ship Search and Rescue Manual. IMO (International Maritime Organization).

Mils, Dennis, and Sexton, Jim. *The Cap'n Computerized American Practical Navigator User's Guide*. Nautical Technologies Ltd., 1996.

Monahan, Kevin. "Electronic Charting Systems." *Westcoast Fisherman Magazine*, Vancouver: Westcoast Publishing, April 1994; reprinted in *The Fisherman's News*, Seattle, June 1994.

Monahan, Kevin. "GPS; Errors and Insights." *Westcoast Fisherman Magazine*, Vancouver: Westcoast Publishing, January 1994.

Monahan, Kevin. "Loran C: Getting the Most Out of Your Unit." *Westcoast Fisherman Magazine*, Vancouver: Westcoast Publishing, April 1993.

Navigating with GPS. Scarborough, Ontario: Canadian Power and Sail Squadrons, 1998.

Nobeltec Visual Navigation Suite User's Guide. Nobeltec Corporation, 1996–2000.

Northstar 941 X Reference Manual. Northstar Technologies, a division of CMC Electronics Inc., 1994, 1995.

The Power of ECPINS. Offshore Systems Limited.

Queeney, Tim. "Marine Technology Notes." *Ocean Navigator Magazine*, March/April 1997.

Radar Navigation Manual. Publication 1310, U.S. Defense Mapping Agency Hydrographic/Topographic Center, Fourth Edition 1985.

Radio Aids to Marine Navigation (Pacific). Ottawa: Canadian Coast Guard, Department of Fisheries and Oceans, April 1996.

Radio Navigational Aids. Number 117, U.S. Defense Mapping Agency (DMA), 1996.

Raytheon R40XX Users Manual. Raytheon Inc. 1995.

Sharpe, Richard T. "GPS Receiver Configurations—How Many Channels Do You Need?" *The Official Journal of the NMEA*, Marine Electronics.

Tetley, L., and Calcutt, D. *Electronic Aids to Navigation: Position Fixing*. Edward Arnold, a division of Hodder and Stoughton, 1991.

U.S. Coast Guard Differential GPS—A Service for Users of the Global Positioning System. U.S. Department of Transportation U.S. Coast Guard, revised January 1993.

United States National Transportation Safety Board Safety Recommendation re: M-95-26 and -27, Washington, D.C. 20594, August 9, 1995.

THE WORKBOOK

As you become familiar with your GPS set, we suggest you keep this workbook with you. When you discover how to set up a route, or some other function, enter the keystrokes necessary to achieve that end **in pencil!!!** You will inevitably discover shortcuts in activating some of the many functions available to you, so you will want to amend the workbook from time to time. If you buy a new GPS, you will need to amend the workbook to enter the new procedures.

Once you have completed the workbook, all the critical instructions for operating your GPS Navigator/plotter will be in one place in an easily accessible form that you have written yourself. Once you have become familiar with the functions identified in The Workbook, you will have confidence in your work.

This confidence is especially important if you decide to change routes or waypoints in mid-route because there could be quite a bit of work required to set up a new route quickly. In addition, if you are entering lots of lat/long coordinates, that means lots of key strokes and the possibility of finger-poking errors. We are convinced that Murphy's second law is, "If you are in a rush or under pressure, **everything** is sure to go wrong." We hope that faithful use of this workbook will eliminate some of the pressure.

THE WORKBOOK
Basic Functions

Function	Key Strokes Required
To activate MOB	
To view Lat/Long of MOB	
To deactivate MOB	
To activate GOTO	
To deactivate GOTO	
To display position, course and speed	
To display the steering diagram	
To select an alternate steering diagram	
To display the time	
To change to a new chart datum	
To change the default hemisphere	

THE WORKBOOK (continued)
Handling Waypoints

Function	Key Strokes Required
To display the waypoint list	
To "save" a waypoint	
To convert a "saved" waypoint to permanent memory	
To create a waypoint by present position	
To create a waypoint by entering latitude and longitude	
To create a waypoint by entering range and bearing	
To create a waypoint by entering Loran C TDs	
To create an avoidance waypoint	
To delete a waypoint	
To update (edit) a waypoint	
To begin navigating to a single waypoint	
To deactivate navigation to a single waypoint	
To restart navigation to a single waypoint	
To view the range and bearing to any waypoint.	

THE WORKBOOK (continued)
Handling Waypoints

Function	Key Strokes Required
To start route navigation from present position	
To start route navigation from the first waypoint	
To join a route from any waypoint	
To join a route from present position	
To exit a route	
To suspend a route	
To reverse a route	
To verify the direction of a route	
To enable/disable automatic switching	
To set waypoint realization mode	

THE WORKBOOK *(continued)*
Creating and Modifying Routes

Function	Key Strokes Required
To create a route	
To delete a route	
To display the contents of a route	
To read the range and bearing between waypoints in a route	
To "save" a route	
To skip a waypoint in a route	
To insert a waypoint in a route you are setting up	
To insert a waypoint in a route you are following	
To remove a waypoint from a route	

THE WORKBOOK *(continued)*
Other Functions

Function	Key Strokes Required
To apply an offset to the GPS position	
To display the DGPS reference station	
To update information about any DGPS station	
To display HDOP/geometric quality	
To view satellite geometry	
To display satellite health	
To set magnetic variation	
To set the time zone	
To customize the navigation display	
To set the update rate	
To display predicted accuracy	
To adjust smoothing	
To download waypoints/routes to disk	
To upload waypoints/routes from disks	

THE WORKBOOK *(continued)*
Plotter Functions

Function	Key Strokes Required
To switch from Nm to scale ratio	
To change scale	
To enter a waypoint by cursor position	
To place an event mark by present position	
To place an event mark by cursor position	
To delete an event mark	
To delete all event marks symbol	
To change event mark symbol	
To convert an event mark to a waypoint	
To enter text associated with an event mark	
To read text associated with an event marker	
To switch cursor between latitude/longitude to range and bearing	
To switch on/off cursor scroll control	
To download/upload the track history	

THE WORKBOOK (continued)
Alarms and Boundaries

Function	Key Strokes Required
To set the arrival radius	
To switch on/off arrival alarm	
To set the XTE boundary limit	
To switch on/off boundary alarm	
To set the avoidance waypoint radius	
To switch on/off the avoidance waypoint alarm	
To set the anchor alarm radius	
To switch on/off the anchor watch alarm	

INDEX

Enjoy these other publications from FineEdge.com

Proven Cruising Routes, Vol. 1—Seattle to Ketchikan
Kevin Monahan and Don Douglass
With our 34 routes you have the best 100 ways to Alaska! We've done the charting! This route guide contains precise courses to steer, diagrams and GPS waypoints from Seattle to Ketchikan. Check www.FineEdge.com to view or sample downloadable routes. ISBN 0-938665-49-9 (book) *Optional:* Companion 3.5" IBM diskette to directly download routes into electronic charts. ISBN 0-938665-74-X (diskette)

Exploring Southeast Alaska
Dixon Entrance to Skagway: Details of Every Harbor and Cove
Don Douglass and Réanne Hemingway-Douglass
Completely all-new revision of the best-selling classic guidebook, *Exploring the Inside Passage to Alaska*, with an increased focus on virtually all places to anchor in Southeast Alaska. ISBN 0-938665-58-8 View entire 576-page book for free at www.AlaskaOnLine at www.FineEdge.com

Exploring the San Juan and Gulf Islands
Cruising Paradise of the Pacific Northwest
Don Douglass and Réanne Hemingway-Douglass
The first publication to document all the anchor sites in the paradise of islands that straddles the U.S.-Canadian border, an area bounded by Deception Pass and Anacortes on the south, Nanaimo on the north, Victoria on the west, and Bellingham on the east. ISBN 0-938665-51-0

Exploring Vancouver Island's West Coast—2nd Ed.
Don Douglass and Réanne Hemingway-Douglass
With five great sounds, sixteen major inlets, and an abundance of spectacular wildlife, the largest island on the west coast of North America is a cruising paradise. ISBN 0-938665-57-X

Exploring the South Coast of British Columbia—2nd Ed.
Gulf Islands and Desolation Sound to Port Hardy and Blunden Harbour
Don Douglass and Réanne Hemingway-Douglass
"Clearly the most thorough, best produced and most useful [guides] available . . . particularly well thought out and painstakingly researched." — *NW Yachting* ISBN 0-938665-62-6

Exploring the North Coast of British Columbia
Blunden Harbour to Dixon Entrance—Including the Queen Charlotte Islands
Don Douglass and Réanne Hemingway-Douglass
Describes previously uncharted Spiller Channel and Griffin Passage, the stunning scenery of Nakwakto Rapids and Seymour Inlet, Fish Egg Inlet, Queens Sound, and Hakai Recreation Area. It helps you plot a course for the beautiful South Moresby Island of the Queen Charlottes, with its rare flora and fauna and historical sites of native Haida culture. ISBN 0-938665-45-6

Exploring the Marquesas Islands
Joe Russell
Russell, who has lived and sailed in the Marquesas, documents these beautiful islands—the first guide dedicated entirely to this little-known paradise. "A must reference for those wanting to thoroughly enjoy their first landfall on the famous Coconut Milk Run."—Earl Hinz, author, *Landfalls of Paradise—Cruising Guide to the Pacific Islands* ISBN 0-938665-64-2

Exploring the Pacific Coast—San Diego to Seattle
Don Douglass and Réanne Hemingway-Douglass
A user-friendly pilothouse guide documenting every harbor and cove from the Mexican to the British Columbian border. Contains local knowledge with specific entrance, mooring and anchoring waypoints. Detailed diagrams and aerial photos document entrances. Check www.FineEdge.com for release date and to view sample chapters. ISBN 0-938665-71-5

Cape Horn *One Man's Dream, One Woman's Nightmare*
Réanne Hemingway-Douglass
His dream: To round Cape Horn and circumnavigate the Southern Hemisphere.
Her nightmare: Coping with a driven captain and the frightening seas of the Great Southern Ocean.
"This is the sea story to read if you read only one."—McGraw Hill, *International Marine Catalog*
"Easily the hairy-chested adventure yarn of the decade, if not the half-century."
—Peter H. Spectre, *Wooden Boat*   ISBN 0-938665-29-4

Trekka Round the World
John Guzzwell
This international classic is the story of Guzzwell's circumnavigation on his 20-foot yawl, *Trekka.*
Includes previously unpublished photos and a foreword by renowned bluewater sailor-author Hal Roth.
"The stuff of dreams . . . John Guzzwell is an inspiration to all blue-water sailors."—Matthew P.
Murphy, editor, *Wooden Boat* ISBN 0-938665-56-1

Sea Stories of the Inside Passage
Iain Lawrence
A collection of first-person experiences about cruising the North Coast; entertaining and
insightful writing by the author of *Far-Away Places.* ISBN 0-938665-47-2

The Arctic to Antarctica
Cigra Circumnavigates the Americas
Mladen Sutej
The dramatic account of the first circumnavigation of the North and South American
continents, continuing around Cape Horn via Easter Island and then to Antarctica before
returning to Europe. Told through the words of a notable circumnavigator with
beautiful photographs throughout. ISBN 0-938665-65-0

Arctic Odyssey
Dove III Masters the Northwest Passage
Len Sherman
Len Sherman was the third crew member on the epic Northwest Passage voyage of the *Dove III,*
one of the first west-to-east single-year passages on record. ISBN 0-938665-63-4

Sailboat Buyer's Guide
Conducting Your Own Survey
Karel Doruyter
This book guides you and provides you with an essential checklist of what to know
and look for *before* you buy a sailboat! ISBN 0-038665-72-3

Destination Cortez Island
A sailor's life along the BC Coast
June Cameron
A nostalgic memoir of the lives of coastal pioneers—the old timers and their boats,
that were essential in the days when the ocean was the only highway. ISBN 0-938665-61-8

The Final Voyage of the *Princess Sophia*
Did they all have to die?
Betty O'Keefe and Ian Macdonald
This story explores the heroic efforts of those who answered the SOS at first to save,
then later to recover, the bodies of those lost. ISBN 0-938665-60-X

FineEdge.com
13589 Clayton Lane
Anacortes, WA 98221
www.FineEdge.com

ABOUT THE AUTHORS

CAPTAIN KEVIN MONAHAN *(right)*, is a Canadian coast guard Officer with over 20 years experience navigating the British Columbia coast. Born in London in 1951, Monahan—now a resident of Vancouver Island—emigrated to Vancouver, B.C., where he later attended the University of British Columbia. His articles and short stories have appeared in various magazines, including *Monday Magazine*, *Fine Homebuilding*, and *Westcoast Fisherman* which published a series of his articles on electronic navigation. Captain Monahan has testified in court as an expert witness in the navigational uses of GPS. He is the principal author of *Proven Cruising Routes Volume One, Seattle to Ketchikan*.

DON DOUGLASS *(left)* has over 150,000 miles of cruising experience, from 60°N to 56°S. His intensive practice with GPS has been gained in the Inside Passage to Alaska, around Cape Horn, and in the Strait of Magellan. He is an honorary member of the Cape Horner Society, and his wife's book, *Cape Horn: One Man's Dream, One Woman's Nightmare*, has become a cruising classic. A Californian by birth, Douglass holds a Bachelor of Science Degree in Electronic Engineering from California Polytechnic University and a Masters in Business Economics from Claremont Graduate University. He has authored and co-authored ten outdoor guidebooks, including five nautical cruising guidebooks.